50 FABULOUS PLACES TO RAISE YOUR FAMILY

THIRD EDITION

By

KATHLEEN SHAPUTIS

CAREER
PRESS
Franklin Lakes, NJ

50 Fabulous Places to Raise Your Family
Edited by Astrid deRidder
Typeset by Eileen Munson
Cover design by Johnson Design
Printed in the U.S.A. by Book-mart Press

To order this title, please call toll-free 1-800-CAREER-1 (NJ and Canada: 201-848-0310) to order using VISA or MasterCard, or for further information on books from Career Press.

CAREER
PRESS

The Career Press, Inc., 3 Tice Road, PO Box 687,
Franklin Lakes, NJ 07417
www.careerpress.com
www.newpagebooks.com

Library of Congress Cataloging-in-Publication Data

Shaputis, Kathleen.
    50 Fabulous places to raise your family / Kathleen Shaputis. –3rd ed.
        p.cm.
    Rev. ed. Of: Lee and Saralee Rosenberg's 50 fabulous places to raise your family / by Melissa Giovagnoli. 2nd ed. 1993.
    ISBN 1-56414-826-2 (paper)
        1. Quality of life—United States. 2. Family life surveys—United States. 3. Metropolitan areas—United States. 4. Social indicators—United States. I. Title: Fifty fabulous places to raise your family. II. Giovagnoli, Melissa. Lee and Saralee Rosenberg's 50 fabulous places to raise your family. III. Title.

    HN60.G56 2005
    306'.0973—dc22

                                                                                    2005050172

Acknowledgments

I want to thank my incredible support team for their continued energy during the process of this book: the Bobbsey Twins Jean and Tana, Bob, Kurt and Norma Gorham, and the infamous Eva Shaw. Also sincere appreciation goes to my agent, Margot Maley at Waterside Productions, a woman of strength and heart, plus the indelible staff at Career Press. Thank you for letting me share in the adventure.

CONTENTS

The Mobile Generation

Families in the 21st century come in a variety of sizes, values, and priorities. Like snowflakes, no two have the same dimensions or facets, and are each unique in their properties. Whether the adult portion equals two parents, a single parent, or multi-generations living under one roof, a family's needs and preferences are its own. One thing most families have in common though is that they're part of a changing society.

Why do people move? Are they striking out on their own for the first time, seeking better job opportunities, upgrading to bigger homes, or buying their first home? What makes us such an itinerant society?

According to the latest Geographical Mobility report from the Census Bureau, more than 40 million Americans relocated during 2002 and 2003. That number is a little less than the previous year's 41 million, but still, an impressive 14 percent of the country packed their belongings in cardboard boxes and changed locations. Over half of those moves were within the same county, 20 percent moved to different counties in the same state, and 19 percent moved to a different state altogether. That's a lot of packing and unpacking! Compared to the total population, though, the percentage of movers in our country has declined over the last few decades. Back in 1948 when the Census Bureau first started recording such numbers, only 20 percent of the country moved.

In 2002, those who took the mobility plunge had four main reasons for moving: (1) Family-related reasons: getting married, afflicted with empty-nest syndrome, or crowded nest syndrome. (2) Job-related reasons: transferred to the company's west coast office, or position was eliminated from down-sizing. (3) Accommodation-related reasons: they needed cheaper square footage. (4) Miscellaneous reasons: they wanted weekends on the ski slope instead of at the beach. Of these four, the largest percentage fell in the accommodation-related category, which included renters and people upgrading to a larger home, or buying a first home.

What's interesting is the majority of people picking up stakes are of Generation Next, or X, or whatever *Time* magazine calls the after-Baby-Boomer generations these days. More than a third of 20-something's in 2003 moved—almost double the number of all other age groups. This mobile generation encompasses the new foundation for families. Which poses the question: does a disposable society concept include living locations as well?

Technology has played an enormous part in the last five years. The popularity of the Internet, a proliferation of digital cameras, and lower long-distance telephone rates have allowed relocated families the enjoyment of staying in touch easier, faster, and cheaper than ever before. Moving to a new location is not the dramatic "we'll never see each other again" plight it used to be.

Flexibility in maintaining or making new friendships through technology may have lessened the impact of moving for children. Today's youth knows as much about surfing the Internet as their parents did about television. From clicking on a picture of Elmo to Instant Messaging friends about homework, most kids have improved their fine motor skills and hand-eye coordination on keyboards, mice, and game consoles.

Some families on the move want the hustle and bustle of throngs of people around them, finding safety in numbers. Others want a more rural, slower-paced environment, easing the stress and concerns when raising their family. But the majority of people exist somewhere in between.

All parents are in search of communities where the priority of important aspects in their heart matters. Such things as public schools that are not only safe but capable of turning out well-prepared students for college or vocations, and where the price for that quality education is not sky-high.

The 50 Fabulous Places

When you consider the thousands of desirable communities across the country, winnowing the list down to 50 is a tremendous challenge. An almost universal agreement on what the ideal community should offer is a strong local economy with growing job and business opportunities, quality schools, a diversified real estate market, low taxes, great recreation and culture, minimal crime, and an aggressive plan to preserve the environment.

Tourism is a strong indicator when investigating a new location and determining if an area is family friendly. According to Roger Brooks, CEO of Destination Development, Inc., "Most of the more popular tourist destinations typically top the list of places to live. Why? Because visitors are naturally drawn to places with beautiful streetscapes and strong curb appeal, an intimate and pedestrian-friendly downtown, an abundance of activities and entertainment, all wrapped by a spectacular natural setting including hills, mountains, or water." Have you ever traveled to a new town and said, "Wow, what a beautiful place!"? Those first impressions are lasting impressions, and are often followed by the comment, "This would be a great place to live." Most important, the best places to raise a family were ones passionate about kids! Parents gave their hometowns rave reviews when evidence showed there were child-centered ongoing events, programs, and activities.

No area was given consideration unless it offered a majority of 15 important criteria. Here are the criteria all 50 cities had to pass:

Criteria for evaluating communities

(Not necessarily in order of importance).

1. **Strong economic outlook**. Low unemployment, projected job growth and expansion, growth in new business, and easy access to major employment centers.

2. **Exceptional education facilities and access to nearby colleges.** High student-achievement levels, well-rounded curriculum, abundant programs and activities, and a broad range of programs for gifted and special education students.

3. **Diversified housing market.** A good mix of single-family houses and multiple dwellings, and a wide range of housing prices.

4. **Ample recreation, culture, and family fun.** Plenty of quality activities and entertainment indoors and out, year-round.

5. **Abundance of community services and programs.** Progressive, local government in tune with the needs of residents, and a strong mix of programs, services, and events, creating a positive community spirit.

6. **Affordable living costs.** Access to affordable housing with reasonable utilities and services.

7. **Low taxes.** Fair balance of sales, property, and state income taxes.

8. **Low crime.** Statistics on major crime is less than the national average and local law enforcement agencies are proactive and community minded.

9. **Quality medical care.** Access to Joint Commission Accredited hospitals and specialized care, excellent ratio of physicians to patients, and well-received community outreach programs.

10. **Environmentally aware attitudes.** High standards for air/water quality. Communities have been recognized for aggressive environmental efforts.

11. **Religious/ethnic diversity.** Where no one race, religion, or ethnic background is so dominate as to the exclusion of others.

12. **Fast-growing area/welcoming attitude toward newcomers.** Areas experiencing rapid growth and are happy about it.

13. **Scenic beauty.** Either from natural assets or manmade aesthetic improvements.

14. **Access to airports/highways.** Proximity to major roads, good transportation, relatively easy commutes, and within a reasonable distance to major airports.

15. **Hospitable climate.** An area was permitted one miserable (hot or cold) season, but that's all.

If you peeked ahead and read the list of 50 places, you may be stomping your foot saying, "Hey, I've been to Chino, California, and I know the rush hour on the freeway is nasty." And it's true! *50 Fabulous Places to Raise Your Family, Third Edition* does allow for some exceptions. Central location and other amenities help make up for rush-hour drawbacks in Chino. Another example, some of the cities listed in this book are the wrong place for anyone whose blood pressure rises with the temperature. However, they have much to offer in many other respects, including fabulous culture, recreation, booming economies, excellent schools, and more.

Putting a price tag or priority points on these intangibles is not a simple calculation, but if you're looking to relocate to a new area, *50 Fabulous Places to Raise a Family, Third Edition* will help you juggle variables by providing the latest information about key areas. The assessment of facts in this book, blended with characteristics of your family, will help enquiring parental minds know where the best places are.

Once you've combed through the pages of this book, looking up additional details on a city is as easy as searching the information highway. Are you torn between the historical beauty of Providence, Rhode Island and the incredible forests of Olympia, Washington? This book will help you Google through various sites and find out if there's a city with both. Check out Websites such as *www.FindYourSpot.com* or *www.BestPlaces.net* for more information on municipalities everywhere. Forget cracking the DaVinci code, try using area codes and zip codes to find more information about your ideal location chosen from this book.

But which is the *best* city? Because they each have their own special virtues, it hardly seems fair to designate just one. The area profiles in this book are laid out in such a way you can read them in their entirety or "cherry-pick" by subjects of interest (for example, jobs, schools, recreation). You can be your own judge of how much or how little information you need at a time.

Before you start your expedition, however, read the first few chapters, which show you how to discover the locations right for your family, while offering hundreds of great ideas to save you headaches and money. Perhaps the most important chapter of all is Chapter 2, with its expert guidance on managing your assets so you can build a "relocation nest egg."

If you are thinking of moving, you are about to embark on one of life's most fascinating journeys. May *50 Fabulous Places to Raise Your Family, Third Edition* be the vessel that takes you to your greatest destination ever!

Home Is Where the Heart Is: Beginning the search for a fabulous hometown

Millions of Americans like you live in a place they didn't choose. It chose them. Perhaps they were born and raised in an area and never questioned whether they liked it—it was home. Or maybe they accepted a job in another city and moved the family more for the opportunity than the locale. In many cases, people followed a friend or family member to a new city.

The problem with decisions made for us, particularly the important ones such as where we live, is they can leave us feeling guilty and frustrated. "Why didn't we realize the high cost of living would make things difficult?" "How could we have been so lax about checking out employment possibilities and the schools?" Round and round the questions go until one day you might say, "Let's get away from here." But what then? Some will ponder the question for years before taking action (if at all). Others will get right on the project and start "Operation: Move Out." Either way, the burning question is: "Where?" Where are the real opportunities in this country today? Where can a family enjoy a great quality of life?

The "where" question is undoubtedly the single biggest hurdle in getting started. This country holds literally tens of thousands of cities, suburbs, and towns. How do you narrow down the prospects? Just as important, with your job, carpools, volunteer work, the house, the kids, doctor appointments, and soccer games, who has time to do the research?

Similar to online dating services, you can go to *www.findyourspot.com* and click on a variety of most-important and least-important attributes. Then *voila!* A list of 24 choices appears. Find Your Spot provides facts, figures and photos about each city from the list. Their reports are easy to follow and cover the basics of climate, culture, recreation, and education.

Is there a magic formula for finding the perfect hometown? No. No book or Website can tell you how you'll actually *feel* about a place. You have to see the community and talk with its people. This book can't tell you the best place to live for you, but it will show you how to conduct the most effective search possible, providing the important questions to answer and the best way in narrowing down the prospects. Then it will guide you through 50 fabulous places found to be well worth consideration. However, you first have to apply a list of your own personal priorities to determine if they're worthy of consideration.

Two things you should know

Before you get started, keep two very important things in mind. The first is no place on earth is perfect and doesn't have its share of drawbacks. Not even the 50 selected for this book. (In fact, the drawbacks of each place are listed along with the good stuff.) As great as it would be to find Ideal Hometown, USA, it is not a realistic expectation.

Instead of perfection, look for a community that offers you dramatic improvements in your lifestyle—greater opportunities, an easier pace, a shorter commute, better schools, a nicer home, or safer neighborhoods.

The second important consideration is beginning your search with an open mind. If you eliminate locations based on preconceived notions, you could end up overlooking some excellent possibilities. It's like when you're coaxing your kids to try a new food and they refuse, what's the universal parental response? All together now: "How do you know you won't like it unless you try it?" The same can be true of places you've heard about, but have never seen.

Also remember places are as apt to change and improve over the years as people are. In an early press review for the first edition of this book, a reporter reviewed the list of 50 cities and was baffled. "You picked Eugene, Oregon? When I was there, everything was practically boarded up. The town was dying," he said. But when asked when he was there, he replied, "I guess about 1979." When you evaluate prospective hometowns, it is only fair to base your decisions on what the city or community has to offer in the present or future, not the past.

Happily ever after?

When Dorothy Gale found herself in Technicolor Oz, all she could think about was going home. She missed some wonderful opportunities to enjoy a new life by worrying about Kansas. And once she woke up in her own bed, surrounded by family and friends, she admitted there were parts of her adventure that were beautiful, and others that were frightening. Welcome to Anywhere, USA.

How do you find a fabulous hometown? It may sound basic and sensible, but the only chance you have of living happily ever after in your new community is by selecting an area that meets your family's unique needs. You may be thinking, "Who would be crazy enough to move to a new city that didn't have what they needed?" Believe it or not, many parents—otherwise intelligent people—overlook the important stuff when choosing a new hometown and they simply pick a place that fulfills their fantasies of ideal living.

Born and raised in an orange-grove area of southern California, known now as the Inland Empire, I thought I'd enjoy the fast life and bright lights of living in Los Angeles back in the early 1970s. Lured by boundless job opportunities and modern living, I settled in the town of Glendale and found a job before I finished unpacking.

Fast-forward one year later. Deep furrows had etched into my forehead from the strain of gripping the steering wheel during my daily commute. Even back then, what took 20 minutes to drive during non-rush hours, took an hour and a half with stop-and-go motions. Literally on the surface streets, a section of cars moved ahead in blocks one signal at a time. Brown air and police sirens as background noise pushed the nightmare over the edge. Did I want to waste the early years of my child's life sitting in traffic, explaining why the sky wasn't blue like in her storybook?

The point of this story is not to scare you (all right, perhaps you should feel a little unnerved), but to enlighten you as to the risks of relocating when you don't look at the big picture.

How to start your search

Anyone who's ever gone camping knows to take a survival kit with food, a flashlight, first-aid equipment, and other necessities. Similarly, people who move to a new city need a survival kit of sorts. Not aspirin and Band-Aids, but the essentials your family needs to survive—the right environmental conditions and medical care, probability of finding a decent job, affordable living costs, and the best possible educational opportunities. These are foundations on which to build a future.

Naturally, every family will have its own personal list of needs and priorities, but, at a minimum, it is important to start your search by checking out the following:

Dusting the Chalk off Education. Younger generations have more choices today about education than ever before—traditional, charter schools, private, parochial. One size does not have to fit all where reading and writing are concerned. Parents want to know what their options are, and what a new residence has to offer. You can't underestimate the value of accessing the best possible education for your family. If you are happy with your current schools, at a minimum you'll want a guarantee of comparable quality in a new city.

Are your children homeschooled? Every state now has homeschool groups and information available on additional support and recreational activities. Public schools detail the average number of students per class and the number of institutions in the area. Academic awards, school report cards, and statistics represent one quotient of the quality of education in an area, but a lot can be said of the staffing and atmosphere of the institutions. A dedicated principal who has collected a treasure of teachers may mean more to you than the last three years' math decathlon scores.

Are you interested in private or parochial schools? Are you looking for year-round schedules versus traditional? Do you need after-school care for your student until you get home from work?

Mayberry PD or Miami Vice? Parents are the stronghold to change in protecting their children. Bicycle helmet laws and Amber Alerts are only two examples of the power of parents when their young are threatened. Parents and grandparents both view public safety as a top priority in raising a family. Homeland Security is now a common theme in life. What lowers crime statistics in a city is a strong public safety core with local citizens for support and encouragement. Whether state troopers or county sheriffs patrol the area, it's the commitment of the people looking out for each other and supporting their municipality's uniformed servants that lower crime stats. Organized groups such as Neighborhood Watch programs and Anti-Graffiti add to a safe environment. Total number of uniformed personnel is not the key as much as the ratio to the population in predicting a city's or town's effectiveness against crime. Local reservists or senior citizen patrols also add to the quality of public safety.

In checking out a new location, parents need to know about fire protection. Is a full-staff available, or do they have a volunteer fire department with two or three permanent positions? Unless you move into a metropolitan area, check for fire hydrants in the neighborhood you're thinking about. Some smaller areas rely on tanker trucks for water during an emergency.

What are the response times to an emergency call? Cozy cottages in the forest may seem fine for raising children, but be aware should anything happen, emergency vehicles may take a longer time to appear.

Salary or Hourly? Over the last five years, economic development has caused major shifts in business and industry. Outsourcing and downsizing are common occurrences, not just "headline news." Corporations are moving jobs overseas and trimming middle management layers. And the dot-com crash was not that long ago. New and small businesses have sprung up, filling needs, and creating jobs. Whether you are looking for a new career or to move ahead in the same market, check out the leading employers of a city. What good is tremendous growth in medical services and high-tech products in an area when these aren't your fields? Other considerations are the diversity of companies (areas dependent on a single industry are at greater risk for economic downturns) and a range of different-sized companies.

Fun, Frolic, and Festivals. Finding a new residence for you may hinge on the availability of sports, music, or literary treasures. Rock climbing or Disneyland, opera or Oprah, families everywhere have different viewpoints on fun and relaxation. Does the area support Little League or the American Youth Soccer Organization? Are the number of playing fields or the location of fields important to your family? Are you linked to your golf clubs or tied to your fishing lures? Family traditions of attending annual events are important to little ones. County fairs, art walks, parades, and major events may be the keys to your family's happiness. Making memories with the children may start by marking the calendar.

If the rock is wet, it's raining. Smog-colored haze, blue skies, or liquid sunshine, locations come with good news and bad news in the weather department. You can't enjoy a brilliant azure blue sky in the country if you're busy sneezing from pollen or grass allergies. If you own more sweaters than bathing suits or don't own a bumper shoot (umbrella), you'll want to know what local forecasters say about an area. Check out the annual rainfall and average temperatures of a new community.

Airplanes, buses, and trains, oh my. As much as you love any new area, someday you or your loved ones are going to use the local or nearest transportation system. Decide now whether you want to make it easy or difficult for relatives and friends to find you. Where is the nearest airport? Will Grandma Jean extend her visitation days because the train only goes through once a week? Does Greyhound make a stop downtown or do they leave the driving up to you? Check out the major highways and public transportation available to a new locality.

What does your family need?

It's time to identify your family's particular needs. You can list them in the box on page 18, in order of importance. Be as specific as possible. The key is not to confuse this list with that of desires (that's next). For example, do you need to be in an area where there's a military base, or a major university or college, or a specific business opportunity? Does your profession require you be within a short distance of an airport or major highways? Or is your priority to live in a community offering first-rate parochial schools?

What does your family want?

Fantasizing about a different lifestyle is most often the engine driving the relocation train. Do you dream of living in a mountainous area where the views are breathtaking and the opportunities for outdoor adventure start with the word *snow*? Or crave a life on the ocean with warm breezes and year-round recreation? Others may long to live in a 100-year-old Victorian-style home or a gorgeous contemporary showplace. Maybe you want out of middle suburbia for the chance of living in a small town or a bustling city of highrises.

Whatever your fantasy, let's figure out what's really important to you so when you are intrigued by an area, you can look at what you identified as your priorities and determine if there's a match. Remember, many cities are great, but if they don't have enough of the attributes you're looking for, who cares?

For instance, Bangor, Maine is absolutely terrific for families. Job opportunities abound, public education is excellent, crime is low, and the culture and recreation are wonderful. However, if you simply can't function when temperatures dip below the freezing mark or you had your heart set on living near mountain peaks, it's not likely you'll consider this area.

Our family's survival checklist
(in order of importance)

1. _____

2. _____

3. _____

4. _____

5. _____

6. _____

7. _____

8. _____

9. _____

10. _____

In addition, should you discover you can't agree on lifestyle choices, now is the time to discuss it. Imagine the problems when one of you goes along for the ride and then later announces, "I can't stand humidity! How did I ever let you talk me into moving to a place where the bugs are bigger than the cars?"

Use the handy charts on pages 18 and 19 and identify your greatest desires. Let's see how you feel about different climates, scenery, recreation, and cultures. The idea behind these charts is creating a family profile readily identifying your priorities and desires. You can fill these out as a family or make copies for everyone and compare notes. This is not about scores and rankings. It is about being conscious of your personal "hot buttons" so you know what to consider when weighing the merits of a new community.

Will we fit in?

Now that you are aware of your family's basic needs and wants, there is one other very important consideration before you can decide on a new hometown. It has to do with something less obvious. Something you can't read about in a chamber of commerce brochure. It's called compatibility, or the sense you fit in.

Research for the first edition of this book revealed the single biggest reason families left a new area, aside from a lack of employment opportunities, was they felt like outsiders. Maybe local politics (whether red states or blue states) were completely at odds with their orientation and beliefs. Maybe being a single parent in a sea of couples, or the community was cliquish and not particularly interested in newcomers. Or perhaps a deeper problem existed—bigotry or other forms of prejudice. In any case, nothing is more disconcerting than feeling ostracized; particularly in a place everyone told you was so "nice."

No guarantees are assured when relocating, but there are several things you can do in advance to learn about a community's true colors:

1. Look at the growth of the area. Fast-growing and/or transient communities are accustomed to newcomers and are more likely to be open to diversity of backgrounds. Small towns and suburbs with only marginal growth in the last 20 years may be totally homogenous and more difficult to acclimate to if you're not one of the crowd.

2. Contact the county or local Board of Elections. Find out how the area voted in the last few presidential and congressional elections. If you're a staunch Republican whose blood pressure would go up living among liberal Democrats, let the buyer beware.

3. Contact a minister or rabbi (or two or three). Ask pointed questions about the size of the religious community with which you are affiliated. Does it have a strong presence?

4. Subscribe to the local newspaper. Read up on the local issues and controversies. Over a period of time, you'll recognize news items that seem to be pervasive and those that are isolated events. This is an excellent way to scope out schools, crime, the environment, local government, and business development of a new area.

5. Contact a community center, a service club, or any place you would expect to spend time if you actually lived there. Inquire about the cost and benefits of membership and ask yourself if the person sounded not only friendly, but interested in you. Was he or she helpful, anxious to "sell" you on the city and happy with your interest in the community? Were you able to engage him or her in conversation about its merits and possible drawbacks? These are all good signs. Caution: Don't make a judgment on an area based on one or two negative conversations. Some people are just unpleasant or snobbish by nature. Or you may have approached them at a bad time. Try to form an opinion based on your overall encounters.

Criteria: Scenery				
How would you feel about living in a place:	**Love it**	**Hate it**	**Flexible**	**Not sure**
On or near the Atlantic Ocean?				
On or near the Pacific Ocean?				
On or near the Gulf of Mexico?				
On or near lakes, rivers, and beaches?				
Landlocked (not surrounded by any water)?				
In the Southwest desert region?				
In a mountainous region?				
On a flat terrain (no rolling hills)?				
A skyline with skyscrapers and modern architecture?				
Mostly historic buildings/architecture?				
A combination of old/new architecture?				
Other scenic preferences:				
Other scenic aversions:				

Criteria: Climate				
How would you feel about living in a place:	**Love it**	**Hate it**	**Flexible**	**Not sure**
12 months of sunshine—sub-tropical?				
High humidity for months on end?				
Frequent thunderstorms?				
Four mild seasons (never above 75° F)?				
Desert weather—intense heat, but dry?				
Cloudy skies, intermittent rain for weeks?				
Four diverse seasons—cold winter, hot summer, mild spring, and mild fall?				
30 inches or more of rain each year?				
20 inches or more of snow each year?				
Prone to some type of natural disaster?				
Other climate preferences:				
Other climate aversions:				

Criteria: Recreation and Culture				
How would you feel about a community with access to:	**Love it**	**Hate it**	**Flexible**	**Not sure**
Professional sports teams?				
Collegiate sports teams?				
Extensive art museums and galleries?				
Opera, ballet, and theater companies?				
Extensive live entertainment?				
Historic sites and tourist attractions?				
Ongoing local annual events?				
State and regional parks?				
Community centers, YMCAs?				
Year-round outdoor activities?				
Community parks and playgrounds?				
Other cultural/recreation preferences:				
Other cultural/recreation aversions:				

Criteria: Recreation and Culture

After filling in these lists, consider these other essentials. Check off all those important to you.

Type of community
- ☐ Small town
- ☐ Rural community
- ☐ College town
- ☐ New suburb
- ☐ Older, established suburb
- ☐ Medium-sized city
- ☐ Large city

Population preference
- ☐ Under 10,000
- ☐ 10,000–50,000
- ☐ 50,000–250,000
- ☐ 250,000 or more

Type of commute
- ☐ Length (no more than _____ minutes)
- ☐ Preferred method of transportation (walk, car, train, bus)

Background and beliefs
- ☐ Prefer racial/ethnic diversity within community
- ☐ Prefer large Jewish/Black/Indian/Asian/Other population

Environment
- ☐ Landfills, nuclear power plants, military bases, have to be ___ miles away
- ☐ Water and air pollution have to be within EPA standards

What to do with all this input

Now that you understand the most important criteria for your family, how will this knowledge help you find the best place to live? Good question. For one thing, the thought process you went through did as much in helping you decide which types of places you would want to live as not. Secondly, by being so conscious of your family's needs and desires, you can read or inquire about a place and eliminate it without the usual hemming and hawing. No more, "I don't know. Sounds nice, but I can't tell." You will definitely know both the places worth considering and those that aren't.

5-step plan to finding a fabulous hometown
Step #1: Round up suspects

Begin collecting the names of cities, suburbs and towns that have always intrigued you. Places you visited on vacation or business trips, what made you remember them? Places friends moved to and love. Read the 50 area profiles featured in this book and select places that capture your imagination. Look through an atlas and pick out cities or regions whose locations appeal to you because of the climate, scenic beauty, and/or lifestyle options. Ask friends and family about places they've never forgotten and why. Look through books, magazines, or online for information on fast-growing cities. Whether you come up with one name or 100 names, this is your official list of "suspect" cities.

Step #2: Put on your detective hat

It's time to gather the facts. Pick up to five cities from your list and get to work. *Note:* every area profile in this book contains the information you need to get in touch with the following offices or organizations.

Contact the chambers of commerce. If you need an address and phone number, ask your reference librarian to show you the current *World Chamber of Commerce Directory*. Or Google online with the name of your city and the words "chamber of commerce." Example: Olympia Chamber of Commerce. Write, call, or request online a newcomer's package. (Ask specifically about background information on major employers.) Some chambers send this free of charge, others ask for a nominal fee. *Note:* Once you're on a chamber's mailing list, you may receive literature from the area's real estate agents, insurance companies, movers, and other firms wanting your business. As with all contacts, some may be valuable to you, some may not.

Contact the convention and visitors bureaus located either directly in the city you're interested in or in the nearest major metropolitan area. The bureaus are also listed in the *Chamber of Commerce Directory* as well as online. They will gladly send you material on recreation, culture, and things to do in the entire area/region.

Contact a relocation specialist at a local realty office. Relocation experts are full-time professionals who have been trained to work exclusively with out-of-town buyers. Unlike part-time salespeople, they are the most qualified to advise you about all aspects of your relocation. Naturally, they would like to be your only real estate contact, but if you feel it would be in your best interest to get several different perspectives, this is your right. Get the names of local agents and/or managing brokers (licensed to manage real estate agents) from the chamber of commerce, local newspaper ads, the area realty board, and personal contacts in the area.

Contact the school district office. Any local real estate company can provide the address and phone number. Go online and most municipal Websites will have a link to the area's school district. Most school Websites, since the inception of the No Child Left Behind Act, include report card or grading information. Request literature describing programs, facilities, curriculum, special education, and gifted programs. If available, there is generally no charge for this information.

Subscribe to the Sunday edition of the local newspaper for one month. Check with the chamber of commerce for the publication's name and address. This should be the biggest paper of the week, and packed with information on job and business opportunities, real estate, upcoming community events, local issues, and more. The subscription should average $15 to $20 a month.

Let your fingers do the walking. If you plan to start a business and want to scope out the competition, or if you are curious about the churches or synagogues, the physicians and dentists, contact your local telephone company and order a copy of the Yellow Pages for that area. Again, there will be a charge, but it is a terrific way to size up a place without having to first move there. *Caution*: Do not investigate more than five cities at a time, or you may overload.

Search the Net. If you don't have online services with your computer, check with your local library for access. You'll find a wealth of information about lots of cities at your fingertips. Start with general sites such as *www.city.net* or *www.bestplaces.net,* then look up specifics about the area in which you are interested.

Step #3: Take inventory

Organization is the key to a successful search. Set up a folder or box for your list of "suspect" cities and create files as the information comes in. If you're using your computer, create separate folders for each city. Depending on the amount of materials you receive, either set up the files by specific location or create state/regional files. When time permits, sit down in a quiet place and start your comparison shopping. You are about to turn your "suspects" into "prospects." Here's how to keep track of what you learn:

1. Create a master family profile. On the top of a page, leave a line to write in the name of the location you're considering and the date. Then put three numbered lists down the left side of the page: 10 Needs, 10 Desires, and 5 Things We'd Feel Comfortable With—in that order. Remember these are the issues you've already established as your priorities. On the right side of the page, make three columns titled "Yes, they have it," "No, they don't," and "Not sure." Make enough copies of this master profile for every place you are investigating.

2. For each location under consideration, fill in your needs, desires, and compatibility issues. As you learn about various aspects of the community, check off the corresponding Yes, No, or Not Sure box.

3. If you find you are checking off lots of No's for a particular city, take the city off your "suspects" list and start the inquiry process for a new one.

4. If you find you are checking off lots of Yes's for a particular city, add the name to your "prospect" list—the list of cities you plan to learn much more about. Should there be several "Not Sure's" checked off, at least you know the criteria needing further investigation.

Step #4: Search and destroy

Now that you've inquired and received sufficient information about all the cities on your "suspect" list, it's time to narrow down the possibilities. Naturally, some places will have already eliminated themselves. The others will be your "prospects."

The best way to proceed is to select any two "prospects" and compare them on their merits as well as downsides. Ask yourselves, "Which one comes closest to what we're looking for?" If they are of equal interest, compare each of them to another city and ask the question again: "Which one comes closest to what we're looking for?"

Go online to Sperling's Best Places at *www.bestplaces.net* and use their Compare Cities process. Click on the specific states and cities from two of your "prospects" list. If they are included in the site's 3,000 cities, you can compare more than 100 categories, such as housing, population, and education.

The idea is to eliminate those communities that don't hold up to scrutiny when compared with another location. Ultimately, you want to create a list of semifinalists where you can prepare for the final step and pick the winner.

Step #5: The on-site inspection

You can talk to people for endless hours, read volumes about a place, you can even watch videotapes or DVDs of a location. All this will be helpful, but is by no means a substitute for a visit. You must experience the community with your own eyes and ears.

The wonderful thing about on-site inspections is nobody can influence your feelings. You're on your own in the opinion department. You'll either be thrilled about an area or turned off. Here are two examples of comments people typically make after their initial visits. They give new meaning to the saying "Seeing is believing."

"We knew from the videos that this was a beautiful town, but we weren't prepared for just *how* magnificent the views were. It's what really sold us."

"We were all set to buy in this development. But when we went down to see it, we were shocked. It was much smaller than we expected, and situated next to an old landfill. It smelled awful. The Realtor kept telling us it was unusual for the wind to be blowing this way and it was almost never like this. We said, 'Even if it only smells like this once in a blue moon, we would still never live here!'"

Here are suggestions on how to prepare for your visit:

1. Plan the visit around a business trip and/or vacation and take in as many "prospect" cities as possible.

2. Notify the real estate agent(s) you feel most comfortable with of your visit and schedule blocks of time when they can show you around. Don't devote an entire day to house-hunting. After a few hours, take a break to reflect on what you've seen.

3. If the children are traveling with you, schedule a fun activity for them in the middle of the day.

4. Put one family member in charge of the "journal"—the copious notes you take describing observations, facts, questions, and comments. There will be too much going on to commit your impressions to memory.

5. Assign the best photographer in the family to take pictures, and preferably, videos. Nothing will be more valuable upon your return than the visual reminders of what you saw.

6. Keep careful track of your travel expenses because if they are related to a job search, they may be tax deductible (more details in Chapter 2).

This is gonna be hard

During the writing of the book's first edition, a friend, interested in relocating, asked to read the manuscript in progress to get a head start on her search. When she reached this point of the chapter, she said, "I hate to say this, but I'm disappointed. The steps you outlined are really logical, but I was hoping this was going to be a lot easier. I can't believe how much time and money I'm going to have to spend to do this right."

No debate here. But whatever amount of time and money goes toward long-distance phone calls, postage, material costs, and travel will hopefully come back to you in many years of happiness. Yes, the carpel tunnel from online searches is worth it. Take it from people who have relocated and been miserable. You will have to work at this as though your family's lives depend on it. Quite frankly, they do.

And the winner is...

If you've really done your homework, the answers to if and where to move will come easier than you think. One of two things will occur: you'll either discover there's no place like home and run back with open arms, or you'll be so incredibly excited about the place you've discovered that wild horses couldn't keep you from moving there.

Whatever the decision, take solace in the fact that neither choice is irreversible. If you did not find a suitable place, you can always try again. Perhaps the underlying reasons that held you back, such as financial pressures, children experiencing difficult transitions, and lack of job opportunities, will be less problematic in the future. Conversely, should you relocate and realize it was a mistake, there is no law preventing you from moving again.

In the end, one simple truth stands out: the real key to finding the best place to raise your family is listen to what is in your head *and* in your heart.

Can You Afford to Relocate?
Financial strategies
to make it happen

One of the greatest rewards of relocating is the promise of a clean slate, mentally as well as physically. Details of financial problems, broken marriages, dead-end jobs, or other "old business" can be left behind. In fact, the prospect of starting over can be so exhilarating, many people let their impulses be their guides. And they discover fabulous new hometowns—places offering gainful employment, a nice home, good schools, and a higher quality of life than they ever imagined.

But happy endings have less to do with luck than with proper planning. Many families also encounter: (1) trouble with finding jobs; (2) difficulty in earning decent wages (a common pitfall in many cities); (3) the feeling of being outsiders no matter how hard they try; and, (4) the inability to shake off longstanding problems (for example, runaway credit card debt and emotional difficulties).

Nothing is more devastating than moving a family cross-country only to be no better or, perish the thought, worse off than before. In fact, from a financial perspective, a wrong move can be debilitating because the costs involved are so high.

Based on the Employee Relocation Council survey in 2001, it costs corporations an average of $57,279 to relocate current home-owning employees and $45,948 for relocating new hire employees. Average cost of relocating for a non-home-owning employee was $16,701 for current employees and $13,456 for new hires.

Even if you're paying for your own move, it can be helpful to understand how companies budget an out-of-state move because relocation costs vary widely based on numerous circumstances (distance, size of the home, number of people)—*not* on who picks up the tab. In addition to the costs of the actual move, other significant, yet forgotten, expenses can enter into the picture, including:

▶ Loss of one or two incomes if family relocates without firm job offers.

▶ Capital gains taxes if buying a home for less than the one sold (and under age 55).

▶ Cost of new furniture, furnishings, appliances, paint, and wallpaper.

▶ Costs of first-time consultation fees charged by doctors and dentists.

▶ Cost of medical insurance if unemployed/without benefits.

▶ Cost of deductibles on new insurance policies (medical, automotive, homeowners).

▶ Possible private school tuition.

▶ Cost of joining recreation centers or health clubs plus loss of money if previous membership costs were nonrefundable before expiration.

▶ Possible purchase of a second or even third car (occurs when families move from big cities with extensive public transportation to suburbs with limited facilities).

▶ If changing climates, need for additional clothes for all members of the family.

▶ New registration fees (motor vehicles, day-care centers, colleges).

Now you're probably thinking: "Moving is so expensive, we're never going to pull this off." But wait. The intent of this chapter is not to discourage you, but help you see that relocation stakes are simply too high to "wing it." Give yourself time to build an adequate relocation nest egg. Specifically, if you have a job in place in your new city, you'll want to have enough cash resources to cover three months of added expenses after the relocation. If you'll be job hunting after you move, you'll need at least six month's worth of cash resources.

How much will you need exactly? The best way to gauge estimated monthly expenses is to ask a realty relocation specialist for help in identifying your average costs—rent, mortgage payments, utilities, and taxes. Sperling's Best Places Website has a Cost of Living comparison process where you type in your annual salary and your current location as well as the city you're hoping to relocate to, if they are of the 3,000 cities in their database. In seconds the data will show you how much more or less you would need to live in the new community, with breakdowns in cost of housing and more.

Financial planning basics

Now that you understand the reasons for building an adequate nest egg in advance of the move, you may be wondering how to go about accumulating cash when the task has eluded you under normal circumstances. The most important step you can take is putting your "financial house" in order by taking a look at your investments, savings, assets, and liabilities. This balance is the backbone of your family's existence and the best indicator of your "fiscal fitness."

Step #1: What is your net worth?

The first step in assessing your financial health is looking at what you've accumulated over the years. Itemizing your personal savings, home equity, pensions, and investments, as well as your debts—a mortgage, installment loans, and so on—gives you a personal balance sheet, or net worth statement. In effect, when you subtract what you owe from what you own, you have a like-it-or-not snapshot of your personal wealth. Here's how to prepare your personal net worth statement:

Cash reserve assets. Add up your cash or near-cash resources such as checking accounts, savings accounts, and money market funds. These are your liquid assets because they can be liquidated quickly without penalties.

It's also possible to include the cash value of a life insurance policy as well as a bank certificate of deposit (CD). These vehicles are liquid to the extent that it's possible to tap into them in an emergency. However, doing so may result in penalties for early withdrawal, or in the case of borrowing from the cash value of a life insurance policy, trigger interest charges on the value of the loan. Under normal circumstances, between 15 percent and 20 percent of your total assets should be liquid.

Equity/retirement assets. Generally, the most valuable asset in your portfolio is the equity in your home. But hopefully you will also have a combination of other investment assets including stocks and options, mutual funds, taxable and tax-free bonds, annuities, investment property (not your residence), and/or equity in a business.

Retirement assets include IRAs/Keogh Plans, 401(k)s, vested pension plans, employee savings, and stock option programs. In tandem, these should represent 50 to 60 percent of your total assets. Keep in mind that if you do sell off investment assets, it will more than likely trigger tax liabilities and penalties for early withdrawal.

To establish the values of these assets, ask your insurance agent, accountant, stockbroker, real estate agent, and certified financial planner for assistance. You can also refer to recent price quotes in the newspaper. Although establishing values for real estate limited partnerships is complex, it may be helpful to contact the general partner to assess current value. As for vacation time shares, for the purpose of this exercise, place the value at the price you paid.

Finally, to determine the value of your 401(k) or other company benefit programs, ask your employee benefits department to provide the calculations.

If you intend to liquidate personal property—clothing, furs and jewels, cars, furniture—appraise the value by estimating how much money they would generate if they were sold today.

Liabilities. This represents the outstanding balances on your mortgage(s), cars, installment loans, credit cards, and so on. It also includes your projected state and federal tax bill. Ideally, your liabilities should represent no more than 30 to 50 percent of your total assets. In preparing for a relocation, however, it is important to carry as light a load as possible with respect to debts. They add significantly to monthly living expenses while reducing the amounts you can be saving or investing.

Assets

Cash Reserve Assets

Checking accounts/cash $_____

Savings accounts $_____

Money market funds $_____

Certificates of deposit (CD) $_____

Life insurance (cash value) $_____

Equity/Retirement Assets

Time deposits (T-bills) $_____

Stocks and options $_____

Retirement savings (IRAs/Keoghs) $_____

Annuities (surrender value) $_____

Pensions (vested interest) $_____

Profit-sharing plans $_____

Collectibles $_____

House (market value) $_____

Other real estate/limited partnerships $_____

Business interests $_____

Personal property (auto, jewels, and so on) $_____

Loans owed to you $_____

Other assets $_____

Total assets $_____

Liabilities

Mortgage or rent (balance due) $_____

Auto loan (balance due) $_____

Credit cards $_____

Installment loans $_____

Annual tax bill $_____

Business debts $_____

Student loans $_____

Brokerage margin loans $_____

Home equity loans/mortgages $_____

Total liabilities $_____

Total net worth $_____

In addition, the interest on car loans, credit cards, and installment loans is no longer deductible. Furthermore, with banks charging anywhere from 18 to 26 percent interest on credit card debt, but only paying 2 to 4 percent on savings, it doesn't take an accountant to tell you that this is a raw deal. If you do not have a current net worth statement, please fill out the chart on page 30.

Calling all assets. Now it is crucial to review your list of assets to determine if any can be converted into liquid and/or income-producing investments. As mentioned before, you'll need access to enough cash resources to cover the unusually high level of expenses that mark the first three to six months following a move.

One possibility is to look at any nonperforming stocks that don't pay dividends. It can be highly advantageous to sell them off and purchase income-bearing government security mutual funds. These pay a predictable monthly income. Other strategies involve selling off investment property (long-term assets) to buy bonds or dividend paying stocks. Or when a CD paying 4 percent or less comes due, it can be rolled over into bonds or income mutual funds paying 6 percent or more.

Step #2: Check current cash flow

The next step in putting your financial house in order is examining your income versus your "outgo"—what you earn compared to what you spend. It's called a cash flow analysis—an exercise that generates about as much enthusiasm as stepping on the scale in January. Still, combined with your net worth statement, the cash flow analysis will be the tool you use to create a realistic family budget.

To collect the data for your analysis, you need go no further than wherever you stash your checkbook register, monthly bank statements, tax returns, and credit card receipts. It's also important to dig a little deeper for the more invisible expenditures—cash purchases, which are often the true culprits of cash flow problems. The proof of the purchase disappears into thin air—as though it never existed.

To figure out where the money goes, add up all your cash withdrawals for a three-month period, multiply by four, and then write down the types of things you usually pay for with cash—lunches, dry cleaning, hair and nail care, movies and videos, health and beauty aids. Provided on pages 30 and 31 are charts for recording the details. In the ideal scenario, when you add your estimated living expenses for the year and subtract that number from your after-tax income, there should be enough left over for savings and investments. Even better is if the balance represents 7 to 10 percent of your net income. If it doesn't, the likely culprit is credit card debt or overspending on nonessentials.

Step #3: Establish priorities

Cash flow analyses are ready-or-not reminders of how innocent and unimportant small purchases seem—until they're added up. We don't deliberate about most of these purchases; we buy now and ask questions later.

The result is that most people are very disappointed that their money never seems to buy the important things. College educations. Vacations. Investments. They attribute it

Cash Flow Analysis

Income

Husband's salary/bonus/commissions	$_____
Wife's salary/bonus/commissions	$_____
Dividends and interest	$_____
Child support/alimony	$_____
Annuities/pensions/Social Security	$_____
Rent, royalties, fees	$_____
Moonlighting/freelance work	$_____
Loans being paid back to you	$_____
Total income	$_____

Taxes

Combined income taxes	$_____
Social Security contributions	$_____
Property taxes	$_____
Total taxes	$_____

Living Expenses

Rent or mortgage payments	$_____
Food	$_____
Clothing and uniforms	$_____
Utilities	$_____
Dining out	$_____
Furniture/electronics	$_____
Vacations/recreation	$_____
Entertainment	$_____
Gasoline	$_____
Car payments	$_____

Cash Flow Analysis

Living Expenses (continued)

Auto repair and maintenance	$_____
Financial and legal services	$_____
Medical care/medications	$_____
School tuition/day care	$_____
Life and disability insurance	$_____
Car insurance	$_____
Health insurance	$_____
Property and casualty insurance	$_____
Pet care	$_____
Birthday and holiday gifts	$_____
Babysitting/housekeeping	$_____
Commutation (tolls, trains, and so on)	$_____
Cable TV	$_____
Household maintenance	$_____
Telephone bills	$_____
Religious institutions	$_____
Books, magazines, and papers	$_____
Clubs, sports, and hobbies	$_____
Dues—union and other	$_____
Alimony/child support	$_____
Parental support/nursing home	$_____
Personal allowances (kids, lottery, and so on)	$_____
Other:	$_____
Other:	$_____

Total annual living expenses _____ $

to not earning enough and paying high taxes. While this is true in part, the real reason money fails to perform is that when priorities aren't established, there is a tendency for it to be spent on impulse items.

It's time to find out what your financial goals are. You already know you are serious about relocating to another part of the country, so put that at the top of the list. What else is important to you and your family? Just fill in the chart on page 33.

Step #4: The dreaded "B" word

Now you know how much you are worth and what it buys you—which is not enough! But you are going to change that now that you also have financial goals. As a way to make sure those goals become realities, it's time to take the most important step of all: establishing a budget with which you can live.

Some people may define a balanced budget as the month and the money running out at the same time. But consider this: when you strip the word "budgeting" of all the negative associations, the truth is, a budget is a plan for spending your money. It doesn't mean you can't spend money, it means you're going to decide in advance of spending it where it's going to go. And with a major relocation in your plans, there is never a more critical time to take control of the money reins.

You've already started getting into the budgeting process by taking a good hard look at what you've got coming in and what's going out. The next step is to forecast your income and return on investments for the year so you lay the groundwork for that budget. You'll be amazed at what a big number that probably is.

In addition, don't make the mistake of waiting to see what's left over at the end of the month for savings. The secret to saving money is to pay yourself every month (pretend you're paying a utility bill). As long as you earmark a certain amount of your paycheck savings, the nest egg will grow.

Budget systems

The first step in creating a working budget is deciding what it will look like.

One individual set up an elaborate budget-tracking system on his personal computer. He had spreadsheets and forecasting tools and year-to-date figures and analyses…and you guessed it: he never entered a single piece of information. "Takes too much time," he said.

That's an important lesson. Here are some less complicated ideas for keeping a budget that might work for you.

Monthly reviews. Every month, add up what you spend in each category versus what you were budgeted to spend. Compare the numbers to see where you're overdoing it, or not spending what you anticipated. After three months, look for trends and readjust the budget accordingly. While this system may not keep you from splurging, you'll be able to count on having a good sense of where the money is going…12 times a year. If things start getting out of control, just apply the brakes.

Establishing Your Goals

Goal	Not Important	Important	Very Important	Absolutely Necessary
Move to _____				
Chop debts				
Build savings				
Increase insurance protection				
Buy a first house				
Buy a bigger house				
Buy a new/second car				
Start a family				
Save for children's education				
Have a better lifestyle				
Take a great vacation				
Open your own business				
Retire early				
Retire comfortably				
Other:				
Other:				
Other:				
Other:				

Accountant's spreadsheets. This is an extended version of the monthly review, but in this case, all the information is confined to ledger sheets, which can be found at any office-supply store. The advantage of using this format is that you can put an entire year on one sheet, or "spread it out" on a quarterly basis. The other difference is that there is room on the spreadsheet to record your banking transactions, paychecks, and investment income—giving you a complete bird's-eye view of your finances at a moment's glance. If you are computer literate, you can set the system up on your PC and let the software do your year-to-date totals and projections. By the way, projections are made by comparing "actual" expenditures in a category thus far to the amount that is budgeted for the remainder of the year. Such projections will immediately indicate an overspending situation.

"The envelope, please." Borrowed from cash businesses, this system is simple yet effective. It involves cashing your paychecks or other income, dividing the cash into envelopes labeled by expense categories, and paying the bills from that cash. When the envelope is empty, you stop spending in that category. Of course, you can always rob Peter to pay Paul, but you get the idea. This idea is probably best for those on a fixed income whose financial needs are uncomplicated and predictable.

The bank account method. This is a more sophisticated version of the envelope method, but similar. It involves setting up three different bank accounts: a savings account for long-term goals (investments), an interest-bearing checking account or money market, funds for short-term goals (tuition payments), and a checking account for bills and cash withdrawals. Budget how much is to go into each account on a monthly basis, and withdraw a certain allotment for bills. If your withdrawals exceed the budget for the month, stop taking the money out.

Truthfully, the final execution is the least relevant. What's important is that the tracking system is simple to use *on a continuing basis*.

Budget tips

Once you and your budget are comfortable with each other, here are some suggestions to keep the ball rolling!

As in Monopoly, pick the banker first. Decide which family member is the most organized, has the better memory for dates and obligations, likes working with numbers, has free time to handle the recordkeeping and bill-paying, and is preferably the saver, not the spender.

Build in a reward system. Give both small and large payoffs for good behavior as often as possible. Perhaps a family membership at a health club is a way to say thanks, or a nice vacation, dinner out…you get the idea.

Charge yourself a "check" fee. Some people find they can save small amounts of money if they deduct $10 or $20 every time they write a check. They call it a check fee, and after a month of bill-paying, they've accumulated a few hundred dollars that can be thrown into an interest-bearing account.

Leave home without it. You can leave your American Express card home, along with your other credit cards, and you will survive. You'll also cut back on credit card spending in a big way. If you use your cards, let them be for planned purchases. Also, if you're not always carrying your cards, you'll be less likely to ever report them lost or stolen.

A certified financial planner can help

Admittedly, the strategies outlined here are general in nature. And yet, each of us has our own set of circumstances, financial philosophies, and goals, all of which can impede our ability to do what is "textbook" simple. All the more reason to seek the advice of a certified financial planner (CFP). CFPs are the only experts who have gone through rigorous educational training to manage all aspects of a client's financial affairs. A certified planner will meet with you, discuss your needs and goals, and then develop a highly customized, detailed, financial plan that will factor in all of your personal goals and circumstances. The cost of a plan will vary with the extent of the work that needs to be done, but ultimately it won't cost you, it will pay you. Check the yellow pages or call the Institute of Certified Financial Planners for a referral (800-282-7526).

In the meantime...

To help you address possible concerns, here is a list of the most frequently asked financial questions as they pertain to a major relocation.

Q. *We're concerned that in a soft real estate market, we won't be able to sell our home at the big profit on which we originally counted. That would probably prevent us from buying our dream home in the city we're moving to. What are our options?*

A. If you trade up to a bigger house before you're financially able, you'll be house rich and cash poor. That will trigger a chain of events such as running up credit cards to compensate for the income that isn't there. That, in turn, will prevent you from having enough money at the end of the month to save or invest. However, if you buy a home within your means and use some of the profits from your old home to pay off debts, you'll get your financial affairs back on track.

Q. *We've heard it is smarter to rent a place when you move to a new city, just in case you don't like it. But with such low interest rates, wouldn't it be better to buy?*

A. If you immediately buy in the new area, you lose your flexibility. What if you can't find a job, or you discover you like another community better? What if you decide you made a big mistake and want to head home? Whatever you saved on the interest will be wiped out by closing costs, real estate commissions, and other major expenses. Rent first and buy later. It's the best insurance policy you can buy.

Q. *Can we deduct our moving expenses on our tax return and, if so, what is deductible?*

A. Even if you are self-employed, you can deduct moving expenses if your new job location is at least 50 miles farther from your former home than your old job location. For example, if your old job was 7 miles from your home, your new job must be at least 57 miles from that former home. Moving expenses are no longer an itemized deduction, but you can deduct them when figuring your adjusted gross income. You must also remain a full-time employee in the new locale for 39 weeks in a year (they don't have to be consecutive or with the same employer). Moving expenses that are fully deductible include you and your family's expenses for traveling to your new home (such as lodging, tolls, gas, and oil, but not meals), the total cost you paid to the moving company, storage fees, and other reasonable moving-related expenses (except for pre-move house-hunting costs, temporary living expenses, or expenses related to buying and selling a home). Tax laws change often, such as the standard mileage rate for moving expenses was raised from 12 cents to 14 cents a mile in 2004. Obtain a free copy of Publication 521, Moving Expenses, from the Internal Revenue Service (800-TAX-FORM; *www.irs.gov*).

Q. *Can we also deduct our job-search expenses?*

A. Whether or not you relocate, job-search expenses may be tax deductible, with several qualifications. According to the IRS, you can deduct the cost of lodging, meals, and other travel-related expenses for interviews and job hunting if you are looking for a job in the same line of work in which you are currently employed. These expenses are allowed in the miscellaneous deduction category, which is subject to the 2 percent AGI (adjusted gross income) limit. For example, if your adjusted gross income is $30,000, the 2 percent floor is $600. That means the first $600 of expenses are not deductible, but the balance of your expenses would be. Unfortunately, if this is your first job out of college, your first job in a new field, or your first job after a long period of unemployment, your job-search costs are not deductible.

Q. *Will I still be eligible for unemployment benefits if I relocate?*

A. Yes. If you are unemployed and still receiving benefits in your present location, your eligibility status will not be changed due to a move. Notify your local unemployment office so they can arrange to transfer your records. You'll have to reregister in the new city and wait until payments resume. The waiting time will vary significantly by state and city.

The bottom line

Unfortunately, most people live in fear of their money. They worry endlessly about not having enough, and when they do accumulate assets they worry that the people managing it will make bad decisions. And as they get closer to retirement, they panic that they'll outlive their money.

All of this angst is understandable, but unnecessary. At any point in the game, you can take charge of your financial affairs and look forward to a decent night's sleep. All it takes is the willingness and commitment to plan ahead, budget, save, and make prudent investment decisions with the help of a trained professional.

Dusting the Chalk off Education: How to evaluate schools

No matter how excited a family is about moving to a new part of the country, the one thing that makes parents and kids pause is looking for a new school. Without a doubt, it is very frustrating to take a tour of a school and not have a clue about what to look for or what to ask. If you are told that test scores in the district are well above the national average, should you be completely satisfied? If you see new computer labs and cases full of trophies, does that suggest the school is a "winner"? If you hear that spending per student is high or the ratio of teachers to students is low, is that a guarantee of a quality education? Not necessarily.

How, then, *does* a parent judge the merits of a school? The answer, according to today's leading educators, is to act as a consumer and comparison-shop, much as you would for any major purchase. Although there is considerably more at stake when it comes to your child's education, there are similarities. You have the right to demand information before you buy, check out the merchandise, and to speak up if you are not satisfied with the product.

Before you can objectively evaluate a school, however, there are four important considerations to keep front and center.

1. **Perfect schools do not exist.** No one has yet discovered a Shangri-La Middle School or Garden of Eden High. It is unrealistic to expect any school to be all things to all people. Every school has its share of attributes and drawbacks. The key is to find one with the most attributes important to you and your child.

2. **To thine own child be true.** What does your child need in order to thrive? A small school setting? How would he or she handle a highly competitive academic curriculum? Does he or she show more of an inclination toward music and the arts, or

do you foresee a pursuit of vocational skills? Take this opportunity to assess your child's goals, needs, and capabilities to find the best possible educational arena.

3. **Think positively.** Understandably, parents feel overwhelmed comparing new schools. But relocating gives you the perfect opportunity to match your child's needs and abilities to the best possible environment.

4. **Keep an open mind.** If you feel strongly that only a brand-new school will do, consider that many older facilities are impeccably maintained and offer the latest technology. Some parents prefer the traditional elementary, junior, and high schools, but may have to consider districts that segment schools; in that case, at least the children will be in the most age-appropriate environment. Is the new school district on a traditional or year-round schedule?

How to evaluate a school

On January 8, 2002, President George W. Bush signed the No Child Left Behind Act. This program has stretched school district finances even further. For more information on the aspects and details of NCLB, go online at *www.ed.gov*. Be open in your discussions with the school district or principal of a potential school regarding changes and accountability. Keep this in mind with the following list of important things you should ask and know when evaluating a new school.

School building

What you should ask: How old is the building? If not new, was asbestos identified as a health hazard and removed? Have any safety violations been found in the past two years, and what was done to correct them? Is there an overcrowding problem, and if so, what is being done to accommodate the growth? Are there portable classrooms on the site, and if so, is there adequate ventilation and heating with the units? Are there adequate funds for maintenance and repairs? Regarding facilities and support resources, what is lacking (lockers, restrooms, computers, or audio/visual equipment, and so on)?

What you should know: The ideal school is in a safe neighborhood, clean and well maintained, completely up to code, and has an excellent safety record (minimal student injuries) as well as adequate financing to meet the needs of operations.

School budget

What you should ask: How is the school financed and the budget determined? What have voters done lately? Is there money from a state lottery? How does the latest budget compare to prior years? If there have been substantial cuts, what is being done to deal with the shortfall? What programs or materials have been affected? What is the class size policy and have class ratios been altered? How many students must there be before an aide is brought into the classroom?

What you should know: It's not the amount allocated per student, but how the school spends it. Monies should be earmarked for technology, textbooks, supplies, resource centers, and school specialists—not heavily skewed toward administration and fringe benefits. Incidentally, a good ratio for primary grades is 15:1 and no more than 20:1 for upper grades, although this is more often not financially realistic. Also, every district applies its own formula for calculating ratios, so you could be comparing apples to oranges.

Faculty and administration

What you should ask: What is the average number of years of teaching experience? What percentage of teachers have advanced degrees? How do teacher salaries compare to the area, and what is the turnover rate (sometimes a reflection of low salaries)? How long has the principal been in education? How accessible is he or she to parents and students? What are the most significant accomplishments of this administration and, conversely, what remain the biggest challenges? Also, what type of inservice and staff development is available?

What you should know: Ideally, teachers are well trained in their fields, working toward advanced degrees, and are also good managers. Effective administrators should be able to clearly state the goals and objectives of the school; show strong leadership abilities; and encourage staff, faculty, parents, and students to work together.

Curriculum and academic performance

What you should ask: How often is the curriculum revised, and who makes the decisions? What is the school's academic philosophy? What percentage of coursework is academics, and what percentage is music, art, and special interest? How are textbooks selected? At the high school level, what percentage of students take the SATs and ACTs, and what percentage enroll in college?

Parental involvement

What you should ask: What opportunities are there for parents to volunteer their time and expertise? To what extent do parents get involved in policy decisions? What functions are performed by the PTA or PTO, and how effective is the organization?

What you should know: Show us a school where volunteerism is the lifeblood of the operation, and we'll show you a school where attendance and test scores are excellent, where teachers give 110 percent, and student achievements run high at every level. A school's failure to foster community spirit will be reflected in student apathy.

Extracurricular activities

What you should ask: What types of clubs and organizations are available and who pays to run them? Is there a strong emphasis on athletics? Have school teams (from debate to track) earned any state or national honors recently? What type of cultural programs are offered and have they earned any honors?

What you should know: Busy, well-rounded students are the best overall performers. According to a study from the University of Colorado, high school students who participate in sports and other extracurricular activities have a low absentee rate and higher grades. The most effective schools don't just run clubs and sports, they are zealous in their efforts to recruit and reward participants.

Gut reactions

Some schools may meet your most important criteria and yet, as first impressions go, just won't "feel" right. Here are some common "turnoffs" not to be ignored:

▶ You and/or your child were not made to feel welcome.

▶ The classrooms looked sterile, not bursting with creativity.

▶ The school did not appear to be well maintained (classrooms and hallways were untidy, bathrooms needed repairs).

▶ Activity in the classrooms or hallways appeared chaotic.

▶ The manner in which students and teachers were addressed was disturbing.

Explore those concerns and ask probing questions. If you are ultimately convinced that the school is the wrong fit—go with your instincts. You do have a choice.

Homeschool arena

What are the organizations and state or district rules about homeschooling? What outside activities such as art classes, physical education, or computer labs are available on a regular basis (through YMCA or the city's parks and rec) for homeschooled children? Research the available resources through the Internet.

Wave of the future

As demands on both schools and students change to accommodate a growing global economy in the 21st century, the following qualities will prove to be vital:

School-based management. Historically, school districts were managed through a single office where decisions were unilateral. Today, the trend is for schools to operate autonomously from the district, giving them a strong sense of ownership. Where there is school-based management, administrators, faculty, parents, and students may have a say on hiring practices, curriculum, allocation of resources, and other decisions.

Magnet schools. When magnet schools first opened in the late 1960s and early 1970s, their goal was to identify at-risk students and place them in a special setting where they'd get greater attention. Today, an estimated 2,200 magnet schools and "niche" environments for the academically gifted, artistically talented, or vocational bound exist in the United States.

Computer-assisted learning. There are an estimated 6 million computers in use at schools across the country. In today's competitive world, ideally, you want your school to offer opportunities well beyond computer literacy and programming.

As you can see, evaluating a school is much more involved than comparing test scores or being razzle-dazzled by a high-tech appearance. The best way to survive the ordeal is to stay focused on the essentials, try to stay objective, and take time to focus on the many things that will change for the positive.

New Job, New City: Conducting an out-of-town job search

Job-hunting is a tough proposition for everyone—whether you're an entry-level worker fresh out of college or an experienced career veteran dumped unceremoniously into the job market from down-sizing. Add to this the opportunity of starting over in a new location and you've compounded the stress factors.

Deciding to take an out-of-state job offer within a large organization can weigh heavily on a family—though job transfers ensure one partner having a job when you arrive, more and more spouses are holding full-time jobs, which may decrease their readiness in making long-distance moves to advance their partner's career.

More than 42 percent of married couples in 2002 fell in a dual-earner or dual-career profile. (Dual-career couples are where both partners work full-time at managerial and professional jobs; dual-earner couples include at most one partner working in a managerial or professional job but both people working full-time). Families headed by couples in which both partners are employed full-time are roughly 40 percent less likely to migrate out of state than single parent families, for reasons of doubling the job-hunt within a family.

Age also factors into job-seeking mobility in our country. Young people—ages 18 to 29—are more likely to make a long-distance move as they establish their independence, and marry or start families. Clutching their resumes and business cards, young parents are seeking more flexibility in the job market. Single parents look hard at healthcare benefits and child-care possibilities when looking for employment. Young couples renting may have an easier time pulling up stakes for a new employment adventure without the hassle of selling property, but the difficulty of the job-hunt remains the same.

A happy ending in the trials and tribulations of long-distance job-hunting is possible if you take certain key steps to make your efforts more effective. To begin, master the basic skills, the foundations of good job-hunting: networking, resume preparation, locating job opportunities, conducting job-winning interviews, and negotiating salary and benefits. If you lack any of these skills, start by working on them.

Feeling ill-equipped to handle a job-search? Go online and research the information on career locations such as *www.Monster.com*. If you don't have a computer, get to the bookstore or library and read up on strategies and techniques you'll need, whatever job you're seeking and wherever the city you're moving to.

A resume is a synopsis of who you are as an employee. Where you've come from and what your goals are compacted on one or two pages. Resume attributes include an objective, experience, education, skills, and additional information. You want key words or power words to highlight in quick sound bites your best features. The challenge is finding the right key words to describe your experience or talents.

Once you've completed your resume, write a cover letter that will catch the employer's attention in a professional, efficient manner. Including a cover letter with every resume you send could make the difference in whether you get an interview. It's another opportunity to sell yourself. Don't cut and paste parts of your resume onto the cover letter, just stress the high points of yourself and your background. Be professional. You don't need personalized stationery, but don't use your child's notebook paper either.

Order business cards. With digital printing available online, there is no excuse for not having cards to pass out to any and all potential employment leads. Check out *www.VistaPrint.com* for their specials in ordering 250 cards. Be sure sufficient and current information is on the front of the card. Do you have a home phone and a cell phone? Put both numbers down. Make yourself available.

Once you've mastered the basics, here are 10 pointers identifying the trickiest problems—and their solutions—for long distance job hunters.

Top 10 job-hunting tips

1. Know what you're getting into first

Learn everything you can about the job market and economic climate of your prospective new home. Gorgeous ocean vistas, great air or water quality, terrific schools, and affordable homes are one thing, but if no jobs are available, how will you afford all this?

Wherever and whenever you are hoping to relocate, find answers to the following questions: What is the current job climate in your dream locale? Where are the majority of the jobs? Who are the key employers? Are there one or two major employers, or a crop of new upstart companies? Are businesses moving into the area or fleeing as fast as the moving companies can arrive? Which companies are planning to expand? Which are downsizing? Where—specifically—is job growth expected, and is it in your area of expertise? (Areas dependent on a single industry or a large employer are at greatest risk of economic downturns.)

The "Earning a living" sections of each area profile in this book give you an overview ("Economic outlook"), a detailed industry-by-industry discussion ("Where the jobs are"), and the particular outlook for new businesses ("Business opportunities"). In addition to this information per area, you may want to go online and access various job Websites such as *www.Monster.com* or *www.CareerBuilders.com*.

If you don't have online access, spend time at your local library with specific job-search reference books. A few good ones include: *Dun & Bradstreet Million Dollar Directory*; *Standard & Poor's Register of Corporations, Directors and Executives*; *The Career Guide: Dun's Employment Opportunities Directory*; and *Ward's Business Directory of U.S. Private and Public Companies*.

You can also research or contact the following for more information about earning a living in your new community:

1. Economic development organizations in the area.

2. Small business development centers.

3. Chamber of Commerce.

4. Local daily and business papers.

5. Local Yellow Pages.

6. Friends who live in the area.

7. Professional and civic organizations with chapters in the area.

8. Check the *HireVetsFirst* Website for possible opportunities. Be aware when a company's policy is to hire veterans.

2. Subscribe to the local paper

Once you have an overall idea of the job market in your chosen area(s), you can zero in on specific job opportunities. Subscribe to the local paper in the area to which you want to move. While its classified ads are an obvious source for job leads, the rest of the paper will continue to "fill in" the picture of your potential new home, giving you time to learn about it before you sink your roots.

Other national publications, such as the *Wall Street Journal's National Business Employment Weekly*, may well be helpful. And while you're at the library, don't forget to ask about the availability of databases and online services. Depending on your particular field, you may find a specific database listing nothing but opportunities in your profession (and giving you the opportunity to list your own credentials for potential employers).

3. Network—with a twist

Don't depend solely on the newspapers, directories, and online services. Most career counselors confirm that as many as 75 percent of all jobs are never advertised. So unless you want to restrict your search to only 25 percent of the jobs actually available in your area, you must look for "hidden" opportunities. Fine-tune your networking techniques and take advantage of any and every contact you know—and everyone they know. Doors may open in the most unlikely places.

Your biggest contact, of course, could be the very company for which you're currently working. If they have a division, office, or affiliate in or near the area you'd like to move, that's where you start your search (presuming you *like* the company you're working for).

Your neighbor knows someone at the biggest plant in your prospective city? Uncle Bob has a friend who has started his own new successful business there? What about your fellow Elks, colleagues, and church-goers? Or your dentist, doctor, banker, or lawyer? Once you start making a list of everyone you know—and everyone they know—you'll be amazed how quickly your network grows (and how much closer this brings you to the place to which you'd like to move).

Keep a fresh supply of business cards handy. Digitally printed cards are easily created, buying prepunched card stock at a local office supply store, or order small quantities online for passing out to potential leads. Your networking techniques start with a handful of cards in your pocket or briefcase at all times. Be sure sufficient and current information is on the front.

4. Let the professional help you look

Hook up with a search firm, preferably one specializing in your career area or profession—and one with an office in the city to which you're hoping to move. If you are at a middle-management level or above, contact a respected executive search firm. The good firms are in contact with businesses nationwide. Keep in mind that executive search firms are working for the employers—not you—so shop around, find one or several that seem to have a lot of contacts and make the most of them. If you're looking for an administrative position or a lower-level job, you'll have your best luck with a local employment agency in your new city.

5. Consider a pilot trip

Taking an initial trip to your dream city is a good idea for many reasons other than to job-hunt. Spend one to two weeks really tasting the local flavor and experiencing the life you're considering making yours. But do make the most of your trip: meet with employment agencies and go on as many interviews as possible during your stay.

6. Tailor your resume to your search

Be up-front: Put your current address on your resume but mention your intention to move to that city prominently in your cover letter. And don't be afraid to create two or three totally different resumes if your experience allows you to consider two or three different jobs. Each may accentuate something different, and downplay something else.

7. Prepare for tricky questions

"Why do you want to move?" Your interviewer leans back in his chair, squints his eyes, and glares. Message: your answer is crucial to landing this job.

You may not be able to decipher what he or she wants to hear from you, but the safest bet is to assume that prospective employers are looking for someone who is goal-oriented, directed, and clear on what he or she wants. So avoid such answers as: "I just hate Tampa; I'll do anything to get out of there!" or "Well, I haven't really decided whether I'm moving here or Seattle." The former is a negative response—and you should avoid negatives entirely during the interview process. The latter, even if true, reveals a complete lack of commitment to the interviewer's town. If you're that unsure, wait until you have made a decision before going on actual interviews.

Whatever your response, frame it in a positive light. For example:

> "It's a very important goal for me to live in a community that meets our needs and wants. We've carefully explored many locations, and this city, by far, is the best location we've found—not the least because of the opportunity to work in a company such as yours."

Will your prospective employer really buy that part about the possibility of working with his or her illustrious company? Well, he or she certainly doesn't want to hear the opposite.

Do you risk revealing something "personal" about yourself by implying your move is primarily a search for "family values"? As a rule, career experts do advise refraining from discussing issues that may bias an employer (Hmm…she's got kids. May not be willing to put in much overtime.) And it is illegal for the employer to ask about your marital status (or plans) or family (including plans). But in this situation, you may touch on it; just avoid unnecessary details such as: "The school's athletic program would be great for the twins, day care has an excellent reputation here, and our oldest likes the local university."

8. Negotiating salary with all the facts

Let's fantasize: You've been offered a terrific job with a $10,000 raise in salary. Should you break out the Dom Perignon? A lot of good that raise will do if you're moving to a place where living costs are twice as high. Again, take time to research everything about the location before you have to accept or decline a good job offer.

9. Consider "temping"

What if you can't find a job but want (or need) to move anyway? Or you've found a great new job but your spouse is still looking? While it's inherently risky to move without a job, if you're sufficiently committed to moving, there's no law that says you can't.

And while you're looking in your new city, why not consider working for a temporary agency? It allows you to get a feel for the workforce in the area and scout around for other opportunities while you're at least earning a paycheck. Who knows? By being in the right place at the right time, you may well end up with a job offer and a permanent place where you're currently temping.

10. Maintain a positive attitude

Job-hunting in your own city wouldn't be easy; doing it long-distance requires even greater patience and perseverance. Keep in mind that the process won't happen overnight, and don't take any rejections personally. Everything usually works out for the best in the end.

The Internet has largely leveled the playing field. Technology industries have wired the smaller towns and the need for employees is growing. The digital age is knocking down the fences between metropolitan areas and the scenic smaller cities. Remote doesn't mean stranded from civilization, it means having the opportunity where you want to live and being able to create a small business or sign on with a fast-growing company.

Moving 101:
Getting across the country with your possessions and your sanity

Why is it we can microwave dinner in a matter of minutes, fax documents from coast to coast in seconds, and access the world on the Internet, but we can't make moving a snap? Nothing is more miserable than packing up a household of goods and trucking them cross-country. The only way to get from here to there is the old-fashioned way, using back labor with upper body strength and large trucks.

In this chapter, you'll learn how long-distance movers arrive at their estimates (let alone their destinations), the lowdown on liability coverage and making claims, great ways to keep moving costs down, how to pick a mover and—most important—strategies for helping your kids make it through the move, too.

What does it cost to move?

If moving to the next town can run into the thousands, moving cross-county will certainly give one pause. Your first question, "What's this going to cost me?" When buying a house, you and the salesperson can bat questions and answers back and forth until the salesperson arrives at a figure—then negotiating begins. Moving can be the same way.

The best way to get a fix on moving costs is to be aware of all the charges that can be factored into an estimate. The three most important variables include:

1. **Distance.** Movers will first determine the approximate mileage between your new and old homes. This is accomplished by mapping out the shortest distance between points A and B on *highways that are suitable for truck travel.*

2. **Weight.** Prices are based on every 100 pounds moved, so it's best to ask at least three movers to guesstimate the size of your shipment.

Don't be surprised by wide variations as each mover refers to its own table of weights when working up an estimate.

3. **Time of year.** Movers' discounts will vary with the time of year. Reserving a carrier between May 15 and September 30 (when 50 percent of all moves take place) almost guarantees that discounts will not be as deep. In fact, you can count on paying a 10-percent premium for moving during busy season. What's more, service is often slower because of peak demand.

The following section will give you a brief overview of these services and introduce you to others that can be factored into your estimate. As you'll see, hiring a long-distance mover is much like dining at your local buffet restaurant, where you choose from a list of entrees and side dishes. Movers can make tempting, but costly, suggestions. The key to negotiating a fair price is being aware of the different ways they earn their living.

Basic transportation

Basic transportation includes use of the mover's truck, use of labor to move goods out of your house and load them on to the truck, driving to your destination, and reassembling everything in your new home. If your move originates and/or terminates in a high-density area, there will be additional transportation charges (ATCs). In congested locations, movers will face traffic jams, construction delays, inaccessible entrances, and more. To compensate for lost time, expect to pay up to a few dollars more per 100 pounds.

Liability insurance

By law, every interstate moving company must assume some liability against damage or loss when agreeing to move your household goods. Unfortunately, the liability they assume is at a minimum, compelling the shipper to purchase additional coverage. And even with that, the mover is protected from you almost as much as the other way around. In other words, the coverage actually limits the mover's liability if it loses or damages your shipment. The good news is that full replacement value insurance, the maximum protection you can buy, is relatively inexpensive and worth every penny. However, before you purchase any insurance from the mover, check your homeowner's policy. It's possible your belongings are already covered during a move, alleviating the need for additional coverage.

If you do buy liability insurance from the mover, know your rights. By law, the mover must provide you with a copy of your policy (or a formal receipt) at the time of purchase. Without proper documentation, the moving company can be held fully liable for any claim that is a result of its negligence.

Packing services

Movers offer two types of packing services. The first is *packing materials*—dishpacks, wardrobes, cartons, and so on. Say what you will about movers, they have sturdier boxes than the supermarket and liquor stores. For fragile and valuable items, the mover's boxes are worth the money. The second packing service is *labor*. You can opt to have the mover pack up your old residence and/or unpack your cartons at your new home.

There are two very important reasons for having the movers do your packing: time and money. You can avoid weeks and possibly months of standing, bending, folding, and rolling valuable breakables into newspaper when the movers are in charge. Secondly, if the movers do the packing and there is damage, they can't blame you. Otherwise, when the boxes are marked PBO (packed by owner), it allows the mover to argue that damages were the result of a bad packing job (and they may be right).

The cost for packing services will vary according to your home county's current labor rates. On average, packing should be 10 percent of your total costs. Again, it is well worth the money. *Note:* The mover will try to talk you into packing the house on moving day. Insist on starting a day or two before. Moving day is hectic enough. The rush can lead to unnecessary loss and damage.

More extras, additional costs

Numerous other factors can be included in your estimate. Here is a rundown:

From north to south. With more people moving south than north, some movers charge more per 100 pounds to compensate for an almost certain empty van on the return trip.

Apartment buildings. As many young families move into high-rise condos, it's important to know that movers get added compensation for dealing with elevators, stairs, and long carries.

Storage. Unfortunately, storage can be a necessary evil even with the most advance planning. When people are forced to move out before their new place is ready for occupancy or when unexpected delays (illness or travel arrangements) prevent people from meeting the van when it arrives, the mover has the right to place the entire shipment in storage. It happens more often than you think, so build storage costs, even for a few days, into your moving budget.

Expedited service. If you absolutely have to be at your new home by a certain date (such as school is starting), the mover can speed up the amount of time it takes to make the trip. Ordering expedited service is costly, but possible.

Exclusive use of a vehicle. If you do not want your shipment commingled with other shipments for fear of delays or problems with sharing space, you can request that your shipment be the only one on the van.

Guaranteed service on or between agreed dates. If you need to know the exact day the mover will show up on either end, you can arrange for guaranteed service, which ensures that your shipment be picked up, transported, and delivered on agreed-upon dates. If the mover fails to deliver as scheduled, you'll be entitled to compensation.

How to keep moving costs down

Here are some proven tips from the professionals:

Time of year: One of the biggest fallacies about relocating with school-age children is the assumption that the move must take place during summer vacation. The thinking is that it is too disruptive to yank a child from the clutches of a familiar classroom, only to throw him into a new lion's den in the middle of a school year. "Baloney," say the relocation experts who are responsible for hundreds of thousands of corporate transfers each year. Move during the year because:

▶ Teachers are more sensitive and aware of a new student's needs because they will already be familiar with the other classmates. At the beginning of a new school year, teachers are so busy, they may not have time to give special attention to anyone.

▶ Children who move during summer months lose out on the biggest outlet they have to meet others—school. The neighborhood kids might be away at camp or on vacation, delaying any chance of meeting new friends. It can be counterproductive when a child has the entire summer to build up anxiety about a new school.

▶ The new area may be on year-round scheduling. Check for school breaks and take advantage of moving between September and May. You may cut your moving costs by as much as 40 to 50 percent.

▶ **Weight:** The other major cost consideration is weight. Because you will pay for every 100 pounds shipped, use this proven method for moving only the minimum:

Sell it; donate it; toss it; give it away!

▶ **Furniture:** If it's old and you're tired of it, if it's not going to match your new décor, if it won't fit in the new rooms, it makes more sense to replace than to move.

▶ **Books:** Just hang on to your most treasured favorites. If you can't part with any of them, inquire about shipping them UPS or by Media Mail with USPS.

▶ **CDs, videos, DVDs, cassettes:** Purge your collections where possible.

▶ **Plants:** Without oxygen and water, how would you look after five days? Besides, they require a certificate of inspection from your county Department of Agriculture, and in some states, such as Florida, plants are subject to inspection upon arrival. Find them a good home and start over.

▶ **Clothes:** If you're moving to a warm-weather climate, hang on to a few cold-weather items for return visits. Anything that's not likely to be worn again should never see the inside of the van.

▶ **Toys and hobby equipment:** This is a wonderful time to teach your children the meaning of charity. Toys for Tots, area hospitals, and many other organizations are always looking for well-made unbroken toys.

▶ **Miscellaneous/junk:** Every home has its own special assortment. You know where it's hiding. Is it worth hundreds of dollars to have it follow you?

▶ **Rugs:** Unless they are valuable or match your new décor, leave them behind.

▶ **Artwork:** Take only what is an investment or has such sentimental value it won't feel like home without it.

▶ **Musical instruments:** Pianos and organs are very expensive to move and require special handling and tuning afterward.

▶ **Chandeliers, ceiling fans, and so on:** Movers have special handling charges for these, and electricians charge to disconnect and reconnect. It could be cheaper to buy new rather than haul the old ones.

▶ **Appliances:** Major appliances may not withstand the jostling and/or not fit in your new home, plus they are costly to ship.

Contemplate what goes and what stays before the moving estimates, otherwise they won't accurately reflect what is being moved.

Moving planner

Get a 2 or 3 inch three-ring binder (the kids probably have an old one you can use) and start keeping your lists and papers together for the move. One section should be for medical information: copies of child(ren)'s immunization records, and such. In another section, keep copies of your car insurance and registration papers.

Two months before: Get a floor plan of your new residence and decide what household items/furniture you plan to keep. Start an inventory of all household items. Get estimates from several moving companies (see page 58). Contact your insurance agent, and ask whether your possessions are covered when moving by your homeowners policy. Arrange to transfer child(ren)'s school records. Choose a moving company.

One month before: Search for good healthcare professionals in your new location. Fill out post-office change-of-address cards available at any location or go online. Clean out closets and cabinets, and sort all items not going with you into boxes marked yard sale or charity. Hold a moving/garage sale. Take donated items to charities' locations. Send furniture or drapes for repair or cleaning as needed. Put all valuable personal papers you may need at your new location, including medical and dental records, school records, and birth certificates in one accordion folder. Make any motel or other reservations or travel plans.

Three weeks before: Arrange for your utilities to be disconnected in your present location on a certain date, and connected at your new home on a specified date. Unless your children are old enough to help or entertain themselves, arrange for child care on moving day.

Two weeks before: Give your houseplants to their new owners. Properly dispose of all common household items the mover can not take in the van because they are considered hazardous materials. A few examples of these products include flammables such as paint, varnish, gasoline, aerosol cans, nail polish and remover, and cleaning fluids. If necessary, have your automobile(s) serviced and ready for the trip.

One week before: Cancel any local deliveries. Be sure you have two weeks' worth of any family member's medications with you. Though most places accept debit cards, buy a few traveler's checks just in case. Take your camera and go through the house snapping shots of furniture and household items, providing a visual inventory that may be useful in filing a claim should there be damage. Withdraw items from your safety deposit boxes and close the account.

We'll go into moving day itself a little later.

Getting estimates

Movers provide two types of estimates: binding and nonbinding. A nonbinding estimate allows the mover to give you a best guess as to the cost of your move, but does not bind him to that price. Ultimately, you could pay more, or in some cases, less. This is because the final cost will be based on actual, not estimated, weight.

You would think that the problem with nonbinding estimates is that movers might "lowball" a bid to get the job. Yet a recent ICC study found that movers overestimate prices as often as they underestimate them. With a binding estimate, the mover sizes up the job and commits to a final price based on the estimated weight of your shipment. Keep in mind that if the mover is going to have to live or die by this price, he's going to build enough profit into it to cover himself for certain contingences. That could mean you're paying more than necessary.

Another drawback of binding estimates is lack of flexibility. For example, if you told the mover not to include the cost of shipping your piano because you were certain you could sell it, you'll have to get another estimate if that plan fails. Without a second estimate, the mover is not obligated to take the piano because, according to your contract, he's not going to be paid to do so. In addition, there might not be room on the van because only a certain amount of space was allocated for you.

Most people opt for nonbinding estimates because they only want to pay for what they actually ship. Regardless of which type you settle on, the estimate must be put in writing in order for service (initial commitment) and the Bill of Lading (final contract).

Hiring a mover

Given the number of personal circumstances that can affect a move, coupled with the different services to opt for, it's vitally important to shop the competition. Prices will vary greatly, particularly off-season.

However, and this is a big however, the cheapest quote is by no means the best quote. Movers that "lowball" their estimates have to save money somewhere and often that somewhere is in their service. Hiring a mover is like making any other major purchase. Bargain hard, but make your final decision based on price as well as other important criteria, including:

▶ **Personal recommendations:** Do you know anyone who used the mover and was pleased with the service?

▶ **Overall treatment:** How were your questions and concerns addressed when you spoke with representatives of the moving company?

▶ **Overall appearances:** An industry spokesperson recommended making an on-site inspection of the mover's offices and warehouse to confirm they're a legitimate, seemingly well-run operation.

▶ **Better Business Bureau Reports:** It never hurts to check with your local BBB to see if there are complaints on file.

Independent versus national carriers

Most people prefer to buy brand names because a recognized company stands behind the product. It's no different with movers. When a truck is pulling off with your valuable possessions, there is a certain comfort level in choosing an Allied or United Van

Lines over Joe's Fast Moving. Also, if there are problems with an agent affiliated with a nationally known company, at least there's a home office to intervene. More importantly, "common carrier" agents are under contract to meet certain performance requirements. They are not intentionally going to make mistakes or jeopardize their standing. On the downside, common carriers may not have as much price flexibility, because they split their profits more ways than do independent movers.

As for the independents, many have excellent reputations and can provide very personalized service. They may also be more flexible on price. The trade-off is that resolving problems can be frustrating. Should you decide to hire a local independent mover, an on-site inspection is very important. In addition, ask for proof that the firm is authorized by the Surface Transportation Board to move goods out of state. If the mover isn't licensed, your liability coverage is null and void.

Keep in mind that neither the size of the moving company nor claims that it is "bonded," "certified," or "insured" are any guarantee of reliability. However, if you see that the mover has a CMC designation, for Certified Moving Consultant, you know that at least it passed arduous tests and complies with the highest standards set by the industry. For more information about CMC and other moving tips, contact the American Moving and Storage Association (703-683-7410; *www.moving.org*).

Tips for a smooth moving day

Here are some important suggestions for orchestrating a calm moving day:

Be prepared to stay until the movers are finished. You want to be there to answer questions and give directions.

Read the Bill of Lading (your contract) carefully before you sign it. Make sure it confirms the proper liability coverage you purchased when signing the order for service. Keep it in your possession until your shipment is delivered, charges are paid, and all claims are settled. It is your only proof that the mover is working for you.

Join the movers as they take inventory of each item being shipped. Watch to see which items they designate as damaged. If you disagree, argue your case right there. When the items are on the van is no time to discover the report is not accurate.

If you got a nonbinding estimate and are concerned that it may be off, you can observe the official weighing of the van by going to the scales immediately before and after the van has been loaded. This will confirm or deny your suspicions.

Make sure you have worked out payment arrangements with the mover in advance. Unloading day is the wrong time to find out that your certified check is unacceptable. You may be able to pay by credit card.

If your estimate was nonbinding, there's always a chance the final cost will be higher. *By law, you are only obligated to pay the estimate plus 10 percent of the remaining balance at the time of delivery.* You can usually request 15 to 30 days to pay off the balance.

Take one final look around the house before the van leaves to make certain nothing has been left behind.

Be sure the driver has explicit directions to your new home. Notify both the driver and the van line office where you can be reached during the move. Include your cell phone number as well as any motel or relative's home where you may be staying.

Before unloading gets into full swing, take your copy of the inventory sheets and check the condition of the items as they're pulled off the van. If you see damage, or notice something is missing, alert the mover and ask him to mark it on both your copy and the mover's copy of the inventory. This is called "taking exceptions."

Filing claims against the mover

1. It's not necessary to unpack and inspect all the cartons before signing the inventory sheet, but you should indicate any obvious damage to the cartons' exteriors.

2. Concealed damage discovered at a later time can be reported. Because you'll have to offer some proof of the mover's negligence, leave the damaged items in the carton until the claims adjustor inspects the damage, or else the claim can be denied.

3. Claims for loss and damage can legally be filed within nine months of delivery, but don't delay. The longer you wait, the easier it will be for the mover to claim the damage occurred after the move.

4. Movers must acknowledge claims within 30 days and settle them within 120 days.

5. Claim forms must be submitted with the Bill of Lading; keep it in a safe place.

6. All claims must be submitted in writing, but first find out if there is a special hotline number for instructions on filing claims.

7. Don't be afraid to be overly detailed in your claim report. Settlements are often delayed because more information was needed.

8. List lost and damaged items separately, along with estimates for repairs or replacement. You may be asked to justify a replacement cost. If you no longer have a receipt, check catalogs or store ads for similar values.

9. If you incurred any hotel or other living expenses caused by the mover's delays or losses, add those to the claim forms.

10. Finally, understand that the actual dollar amount you receive from the mover will be determined by the representative who does the claim inspection. You can take your case to arbitration (at no cost to you) if you are unhappy with a settlement.

Moving with children

Moving to a new location can be stressful for anyone, but especially for younger children. Preschoolers often become confused when their daily routine is disrupted, while adolescents dread the prospect of having to make new friends in a strange school and fear the loss of their old ones. You can help alleviate their fears, and help get them involved in the move.

Talk—Communicate—Listen

Provide your children with as much information as possible about the move. Allow them to participate in a few of the decision-making discussions. This gives children a sense of control and helps relieve anxiety. Talk about positive aspects of their new home and what they can look forward to (different climate, outdoor activities). Encourage children to talk about their worries. They may question you over and over about the same concern, especially the smaller ones. That's their job, they're kids. Listen to their feelings about the move and offer extra support.

Head to the library for some great books on the subject of moving, make sure they're age appropriate, and enjoy reading them together. Give your child a special box including a directory with the names and addresses of special friends to write to, envelopes, and postage stamps.

Pretend it's moving day. Make the move into an exciting adventure. Encourage your children to pack his or her own things in special boxes, but be sure they leave their favorite toys out until the very end. Act out the schedule for moving day ahead of time.

If at all possible, take the children with you to look at potential neighborhoods, homes/apartments, and schools. Though possibly more expensive and extra effort, it will improve the transition process, helping children begin to make adjustments. If taking them with you is not possible, use a camera during your trip. Your children will appreciate the photos and/or video you bring back, and it will help them begin the transition.

If your children are young, consider hiring a baby-sitter while you pack and on moving day. Otherwise, resist the temptation to send children away during the move. Participating will help them adjust more easily to their new surroundings. Don't be concerned if your child regresses in some behaviors such as bed-wetting or thumb-sucking, it's quite normal.

Leaving friends and sports teammates behind can be extremely difficult. Help your kids by hosting a good-bye party. Provide each of your children with his or her own address book and during the party, encourage friends to write their personal contact information. Emphasize how easily e-mail will keep them in touch.

Give older children a disposable camera and ask them to photograph your move. Once you arrive and are settled in, make time together to create a moving chapter of your family photo album. Have your kids draw a picture of how they will arrange their new rooms. Resume familiar routines as soon as possible in your new home. If it is a tradition in your family to watch cartoons on Saturday mornings, for example, get back in the practice as soon as possible.

Keep a box of Kleenex handy and let them know it's okay to cry. Grown-ups sometimes cry even though they look forward to the adventure of a new home. Don't take it personally if your children are upset or angry about moving. Allow them time to grieve. They will grow to love their new home just as much as the old one.

Wrapping it all up

You don't need an expert to tell you that relocating to another part of the country will be a stressful and highly emotional period for the family. It is a time of beginnings and endings, and intense feelings and infinite details. It's not necessarily a time to think clearly (in fact you can count on it). That's why you should be kind to yourselves by organizing a smooth, uneventful, and perfectly boring move. There *will* be plenty of excitement.

Alabama	1. Hoover
Arizona	2. Fountain Hills
Arkansas	3. Fayetteville
	4. Little Rock
California	5. Chino
	6. Pismo Beach
	7. Sacramento
	8. Vista
Colorado	9. Colorado Springs
	10. Loveland
Florida	11. Coral Springs
	12. Fort Myers
	13. Jacksonville
Idaho	14. Boise
Illinois	15. Naperville
Indiana	16. Bloomington
	17. Indianapolis
Iowa	18. Iowa City
Kansas	19. Overland Park
Kentucky	20. Bowling Green
Maine	21. Bangor
Minnesota	22. Eden Prairie
	23. Rochester
Missouri	24. Columbia
Montana	25. Billings
Nevada	26. Henderson
	27. Reno
New Hampshire	28. Portsmouth
New Jersey	29. Morristown
New Mexico	30. Albuquerque
North Carolina	31. Raleigh
Ohio	32. Cincinnati
Oregon	33. Bend
	34. Milwaukie
	35. Salem
Rhode Island	36. Providence
South Carolina	37. Charleston
	38. Greenville
Tennessee	39. Nashville
Texas	40. Austin
	41. Galveston
	42. Plano
Utah	43. Provo
Vermont	44. Burlington
Virginia	45. Chesapeake
Washington	46. Kent
	47. Olympia
	48. Spokane
Wisconsin	49. Green Bay
	50. Sheboygan

50 Fabulous Place

to Raise Your Family

How to Use the Area Profiles

Area profiles are presented in alphabetical order by state—from Alabama to Wisconsin—then city. ("Fast Facts," the handy cross-reference beginning on page 355, will help you locate them in alphabetical order by city.) You can read the entire summary in each profile or quickly refer to the topics of greatest interest, such as schools, jobs, recreation, or living costs. The terms and associations most frequently mentioned within these topics are briefly explained here.

Median Housing Price: A median price indicates half the houses in the market are selling for less than the median, half are selling for more. Average prices, however, are a more accurate reflection of what people are paying and generally run higher.

ACCRA: Using the latest American Chamber of Commerce Researchers Association report (third quarter 2004), comparisons of living-cost differences in nearly 300 urban areas were made. The figures reflect expenses for a household with two adults (one a salaried executive) and two children, but what's most relevant is how much more or less they spent to purchase the same products and services in that city versus another.

Utility costs: The average monthly bills for gas and electric service are an excellent way to compare costs between locations. Actual bills, however, will vary substantially based on square footage, number of people, number of appliances, personal habits, unusually hot or cold weather, and method of heating/cooling.

Climate: The Weather Channel, the 24-hour all-weather satellite network, or *www.weather.com*, was one source of climatological data as well as *www.city-data.com*. Everything in a community is subject to change except the weather, so be sure you're looking at areas where the climate suits you. Elevation: For every 1,000 feet of increased altitude, the temperature decreases by an average of 3.5° Fahrenheit. **Relative Humidity**, when combined with high temperatures, puts stress on the human body. If the temperature is 88° Fahrenheit and the relative humidity is 78 percent, it will feel like 106 ° Fahrenheit.

Public education overview: Only communities with excellent school districts for academics, extracurricular programs, special education and gifted programs were featured in the book. Since 2002 The No Child Left Behind Act means each district will work in limiting the number of students per classroom and the ratio of teachers and staff to students. The basis for these ratios differs widely across the country. Check the Websites of the city's district you're interested in for School Assessment Report Cards. Each school listed out it's score for the math, reading, and writing segments of their standardized testing results.

1 ▶ Hoover, Alabama

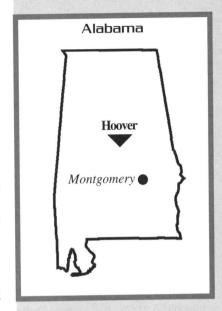

Fabulous features

The low cost of living is one of Alabama's greatest attributes for families, besides the southern charm and beautiful rolling hills. Alabamians pay less than most Americans for residential natural gas, water, and electrical power. Yet the city of Hoover is so much more than affordability. It's community spirit on a backdrop of old-growth forests and blue skies.

Just outside the bustle of Birmingham you'll find smaller communities such as Hoover, in a shady nook all clean, green, and a great place to raise a family. Growing economic development in the area provides stress-free access to business districts in a 20 minute commute by interstate. Though the population has grown 47 percent since 1990, there's still a sense of small-town pride and commitment among its residents.

For relaxation on the weekends, head for the Moss Rock Preserve, which has nearly 10 miles of hiking paths throughout 250 acres of natural wonder. Or head to the Alridge Gardens, a woodland retreat surrounding a lake right in the middle of Hoover. Step into splashes of color from the famous hydrangeas or delight at the native brush and trees.

Possible drawbacks: Sudden summer rains can hit hard with a curtain of water making driving treacherous. But what would you expect with all the natural green around? No one's leaving their sprinklers on.

▶ Local Population: 66,429

▶ County: Shelby/Jefferson

▶ Population of surrounding metropolitan area: 155,500

▶ Region: Central Alabama

▶ Closest metro area: Birmingham, 10 miles

▶ Median home price: $203,327

▶ Median household income: $71,964

▶ Best reasons to live here: Lush, green streetscapes, award-winning schools, a dynamic business environment, low crime and pollution, and tremendous community spirit.

Climate

Elevation 560'	Average high/low (°F)	Average precipitation		Average no. days precipitation	Average humidity (%)
		rain (")	snow (")		
January	54/31	5.5	0	11	64
April	75/48	4.5	0	9	57
July	92/69	4.6	0	12	62
October	76/50	3.2	0	6	58
Number days 32°F or below: 39			Number days 90°F or warmer: 60		

Earning a living

Economic outlook: A geographical center of the southeastern United States, and in one of the fastest growing corridors in the United States, Hoover is located within the Birmingham metropolitan area. The sixth largest city in Alabama, Hoover has all the amenable attributes a business owner looks for when opening or relocating a business. Situated at the crossroads of two major interstates, Interstate 65 and Interstate 459, Hoover has easy access and travel to and from downtown and the Birmingham International Airport. Businesses within the city limits range from light industry to services. Hoover's low cost of living is good news to corporations and small entrepreneurs alike, with affordable commercial real estate and utility costs. Hoover has no city occupational tax, and other taxes remain among the lowest in the metropolitan area. According to a 2003 Tax Foundation study, the state's tax system ranks 16th in the "business friendly" category.

Where the jobs are: Some of the major employers include Blue Cross-Blue Shield of Alabama, Raytheon Engineers and Constructors, the Hoover Board of Education, the city of Hoover, and AmSouth Bank. Hoover sits approximately halfway between the city of Vance (which has the Mercedes Benz M-class vehicle manufacturing facility), and the city of Lincoln (where Honda has a vehicle manufacturing facility).

Business opportunities: The local retail industry includes the Riverchase Galleria, the largest mixed-use shopping center in the southeast. How many malls can brag of a four-star hotel next door like The Wynfrey Hotel at the Galleria? The mall includes a branch of the U.S. Post Office and a 250,000 square foot office tower. The Galleria visitors have mass produced other retail and commercial growth in the Highway 31 and 150 corridors. The Inverness Corners development and other centers along Highway 280 offer options for people who live and work in the area.

Local real estate

Market overview: Older homes are mostly brick ranch-style with traditional layouts. New developments have larger two-story homes with open interiors and decks. Lakefront communities are still available.

Average rent for a two-bedroom apartment: $810 per month

Other areas to consider: Vestavia Hills, a smaller community in population but not in heart, sits north, sharing the Interstates and rolling hills with Hoover. Going south,

Pelham is a great choice, nestled at the foothills of Oak Mountain. Birmingham is the largest city in the state of Alabama and provides additional job opportunities, being a decent commute from Hoover. You just find more of everything in the "big city," including fine dining, cultural events, and traffic.

What things cost

ACCRA's national comparisons: Overall living costs are 1.3 percent below average, with housing at 7.4 percent below average, followed by utilities at 6.9 percent below. Above average are health care at 3.7 percent, followed by miscellaneous goods and services at 1.8 percent above and transportation at 1.1 percent above.

Utilities: Phone: $30 per month; electric and gas: $60 per month.

The tax ax

Sales tax: 9.5 percent

Property tax: $6.26

State income tax: 5.0 percent

Making the grade

Public education overview: The Hoover school system began the 2004 school year with a new superintendent and a record budget. The third largest city school system in Alabama, Hoover is ranked among the best in the state. The district includes 10 elementary schools, three middle schools (with another on its way), and two high schools. Hoover's only alternative school, Crossroads, is for students in grades 6 through 12 who don't fit the traditional curriculum mold. The Hoover Community School provides after-school and summer care for elementary school children, as well as adult education. The Hoover Board of Education approved a record $136 million budget for the 2005 fiscal year, representing a 14 percent increase over 2004. Construction projects have been allotted $29 million, including a new middle school at Spain Park and a proposed facility near Hoover High School, initially housing ninth graders, and eventually becoming a middle school.

Class size (student to teacher ratio): 13:1

Help for working parents: Extended care program providing before- and after-school supervision available, and all-day summer programs.

Boys & Girls Club info: There are no centers available.

School year: Runs from third week in August to the end of May. Children must be 5 years old by September 1 to enter kindergarten.

Special education/programs for gifted students: All children are kept together in the classroom as much as possible, because the community favors mainstreaming efforts. Under the Schoolwide Enrichment Model, students work on ability-appropriate materials within the same subjects.

Nearby colleges and universities: Though no colleges exist in Hoover proper, just a quick drive to Birmingham provides Samford University, the University of Alabama at Birmingham, and Jefferson State Community College.

Medical care

Hospitals/medical centers: An acute-care facility, serving the seven county Birmingham-Hoover area, St. Vincent's specializes in a variety of areas, including oncology care, cardiology services, women and children's services, orthopedics, neurology, and surgical services. Next door is St. Vincent's One Nineteen Health and Wellness facility, which has an integrated approach to healthy living, guided by the values of St. Vincent's Hospital. The facility offers state-of-the-art medical services along with lifestyle amenities such as an upscale day spa and full-service fitness facility.

Specialized care: Children's Hospital in Birmingham, a research and teaching hospital, has a diagnostic center, emergency department, and one of the largest pediatric outpatient centers in the United States.

Crime and safety

Police: The Hoover police department's commitment to a safe and peaceful community includes a "take the car home" program for officer's living in a specific radius of the city limits. This makes the patrol more visible when officers are coming or going to work and home. The department has a second operations center and sub-station in Hoover's Inverness Fire Station and in the Riverchase Galleria. The department's divisions include special teams such as bomb disposal, canine operations, school services, and mountain bike patrolling. Other officers focus on crime prevention through patrols, and also by working with schools and neighborhoods to foster crime awareness and drug prevention programs including the DARE program. Shelby County has the lowest crime rates in the state.

Fire: There are eight fire stations located throughout the city of Hoover, ensuring rapid response times to any emergency. The department maintains a Class 2 ISO rating, resulting in lower insurance rates for Hoover's businesses and residents. Of the 150 Fire Department employees, 107 have emergency medical training. All Hoover paramedics have completed Advanced Cardiac Life Support training, plus all eight engine companies and four rescue units are equipped with defibrillators. The fire department participates in Safeplace, the national program encouraging children to seek help at their neighborhood fire stations. Even Santa rides with the Hoover firefighters each year and greets children in their neighborhoods.

Let the good times roll

Family fun: Did you know the Cahaba, Alabama's longest free-flowing river, runs through Hoover? The area of the Upper Cahaba River provides a natural habitat for a variety of birds. Aldridge Gardens is a 30-acre oasis specializing in hydrangeas. Their trademark is the Snowflake hydrangea. Hoover's Folklore Center offers a look into the past including a smoke house, corn crib, spring house, and outhouse. Volunteers through the Historical Society dress up in period costumes and entertain with stories, crafts and music from the pioneer days. Or take the family to Moss Rock Preserve, 250 acres of trees and plants, streams, waterfalls, wildlife, and other unique natural features, creating perfect balance of nature and community. E.X.P.L.O.R.E. (Experience Programs, Leisure Opportunities, and Recreational Excitement) is the program name for therapeutic recreation activities offered through Hoover Parks and Recreation Department, designed to meet the needs of individuals with mental and physical disabilities.

Sports: The Birmingham Barons (basketball) play at the Hoover Met field, with the season running from April to September. Michael Jordan played on the Barons in 1994. Bruno's Memorial Classic, held in April, was rated the number one Senior PGA tour event by *Sports Illustrated* magazine. Don't forget to cheer on the University of Alabama teams. And for thrills and chills, you have Barbers Motorsports Park in Birmingham, the exclusive home of the Porsche Driving Experience. The Alabama Sports Hall of Fame, in Birmingham, tributes infamous sports figures such as Olympic Medalist Jesse Owens, the baseball legend Willie Mays, and football coach Paul "Bear" Bryant.

Arts and entertainment: Writers, editors, musicians, and artists come together every year at Southern Voices, a three-day conference of classes and presentations exploring the characteristics of southern culture through contemporary art forms. Join the Bluff Park Art Association, or the Hoover Art Association's events for local talent and enjoyment. Birmingham offers more cultural pleasures, such as the Museum of Art, the State of Alabama Ballet, the Alabama Symphony Orchestra, and the Birmingham Opera Theater.

Annual events: Birmingham Festival of Arts, Birmingham International Educational Film Festival, Alabama State Fair

Community life

The Hoover Memorial Trees Program was established for local residents and organizations interested in planting a tree in memory or honor of a loved one, and is run by the Urban Forestry Division, with approval from the Parks and Recreation Department. The department will plant and maintain native species of trees at designated city parks and facilities.

The environment

Keep Hoover Beautiful and the Hoover Beautification Board are volunteer organizations dedicated to improving the quality of life in Hoover. As Hoover grows, the efforts to strike a balance between what's good for the economy and what's good for the environment shows up in Hoover's programs of preserving and protecting the environment for current and future residents.

In and around town

Roads and highways: I-65, I-459, highways 31, 150

Closest airports: Birmingham International Airport and Shelby County Airport provide national and regional air service.

Public transportation: There is no public transportation currently available.

Average daily commute: 20 minutes

More Information

City of Hoover
100 Municipal Drive
Hoover, AL 35216
205-444-7500
www.hooveral.org

Hoover City Schools
2810 Metropolitan Way
Hoover, AL 35243
205-439-1000
www.hoover.k12.al.us

Hoover Chamber of Commerce
3659 Lorna Road Suite 165
Hoover, AL 35216
205-988-5672
www.hooverchamber.org

One Nineteen Health and Wellness
7191 Cahaba Valley Road
Hoover, AL 35242
205-408-6600
www.onenineteen.com

Alabama Power Company
600 North 18th Street
Birmingham, AL 35291
800-245-2244
www.southerncompany.com

Birmingham Water Works
3600 1st Avenue North
Birmingham, AL 35222
205-251-5634
www.bwwsb.com

ALAGASCO
605 Richard Arrington, Jr. Boulevard
Birmingham, AL 35203
205 326-8200
www.alagasco.com

Charter Communications
12405 Powerscourt Drive
St. Louis, MO 63131
205-773-8778
www.charter.com

2 ▶ Fountain Hills, Arizona

Arizona

Fountain Hills

Phoenix● ▼

Fabulous features

Have you wondered what it's like to live on the other side of the mountain? Residents of Fountain Hills have discovered the air is cleaner and the grass is greener. Separated by the spectacular McDowell Mountains, this master-planned community, only 15 years old, is a short commute from three booming metropolises: Phoenix, Scottsdale, and Mesa. But when you come home, it's to a mountain retreat nestled in the flora-covered Sonora Desert. Like its legendary Fountain in the Park, imported from Zurich, Switzerland, it's the world's tallest fountain, with a jet stream soaring 560 feet (higher than the Washington Monument, taller than Notre Dame Cathedral in Paris, and more than three times as high as Old Faithful in Yellowstone Park).

As for the environment, it too is vast, with sprawling homes resting atop canyons. In anticipation of growth, the town was incorporated in 1989 and today is a self-sufficient community. In nearby Scottsdale you'll find a regional cultural center, and more than 125 golf courses in the area. The job opportunities make all this leisure affordable. The unemployment rate in the area has fluctuated around 3 percent for more than three years, and the local business base in Fountain Hills is continually growing.

Possible drawbacks: Property taxes are some of the highest in Maricopa County, but still reasonable. Many summer days hit the triple digits, so keep moving, drink plenty of water, and be thankful there's no humidity and bugs!

▶ Local Population: 20,235

▶ County: Maricopa

▶ Population of surrounding metropolitan area: 3,072,149

▶ Region: Central Arizona

▶ Closest metro area: Scottsdale, 10 miles

▶ Median home price: $217,200

▶ Median household income: $61,619

▶ Best reasons to live here: There are strong job possibilities, affordable housing, no state income tax, endless outdoor recreation, good schools, and fabulous scenery.

Climate

Elevation 4,500'	Average temp. high/low (°F)	Average precipitation		Average no. days precipitation	Average humidity (%)
		rain (")	snow (")		
January	65/40	1.5	0	4	32
April	84/52	0.4	0	2	17
July	105/76	1.0	0	4	20
October	88/59	1.1	0	3	22
Number of days 32°F or below: 32			Number of days 90°F or warmer: 164		

Earning a living

Economic outlook: As more and more families discover the benefits of Fountain Hills, residents are creating jobs in town or commuting to the greater Phoenix area. The services industry is a large part (more than 30 percent) of the local business economy. More than 500 small private-sector companies including real estate, construction, and specialty shops, help keep the unemployment rate well below the national average. Fountain Hills has so far managed to avoid growing pains such as congestion and pollution.

Where the jobs are: The Fountain Hills Unified School District is the community's largest employer. In the surrounding metro area Charles Schwab moved here, as well as the credit card divisions of Chase Manhattan and the Bank of America. The reason? Living and operating costs are low and the availability of an educated labor force is high.

Business opportunities: Fountain Hills has a new 30,000 square foot convention facility for hosting events for the community. With the new facility, several upscale hotel and resort accommodations have opened in Fountain Hills, and the town officials hope this will attract small- to medium-sized conventions and conferences. The Avenue of the Fountains will undergo a major face-lift in 2006, revitalizing the downtown area. Projects include a hotel and condominiums. The south side of the Avenue of the Fountains remains undeveloped and a potential for business possibilities.

Local real estate

Market overview: Home building is at a frantic pace—75 percent of the real estate industry is single family homes, 15 percent is patio homes (duplexes) and 10 percent is condos.

Average rent for a two-bedroom apartment: $800 per month

Other areas to consider: Scottsdale is a sparkling jewel of the Sonoran Desert, with shopping, spas and golf as much a part of the landscape as saguaros. Paradise Valley may be just that, with only single family housing in this bedroom community, including many one-acre lots. The greater Phoenix area, ranked eighth largest in the country in terms of population, enjoys a high volume of tourism, but financial services and high-tech manufacturing are coming in at a record clip, thanks to the high cost of doing business in southern California. Phoenix suffers the same blights as Los Angeles in traffic and crime.

What things cost

ACCRA's national comparisons: The Phoenix/Scottsdale metro area has living costs about 7 percent below the national average (almost a 10 percent swing from 5 years ago), with housing about 19 percent higher, utilities almost 1 percent higher and healthcare more than 12 percent higher. Transportation and miscellaneous goods helped to bring down the overall factors.

Utilities: Phone: $25 per month; electric: $120 per month.

The tax ax

Sales tax: 8.9 percent

Property tax: $9.00 (est. property taxes paid per $1,000 of market value)

State income tax: 5.04 percent

Making the grade

Public education overview: School enrollment is seeing a steady increase of approximately 3 percent a year. The Fountain Hills Unified School District serves preschool through 12th grade and has earned a reputation for excellence in academics and earned respect throughout the state as a small, friendly, high-achieving district. The school district is considered progressive and well run. To date, reading and test scores at all grade levels have consistently ranked well above average for the state. At the Fountain Hills High School, 93 percent of graduates attend a two- or four-year college, they offer eight Advanced Placement courses, and have several special school-to-career programs. Several facilities offer Montessori and Christian education. There is a strong local homeschooling network in Fountain Hills.

Class size (student to teacher ratio): 18:1

Help for working parents: A number of local facilities offer quality education and have programs available for infant care, toddler programs, and preschool.

Boys and Girls Club: There is one center in Fountain Hills.

School year: School starts immediately after Labor Day and generally ends the second week of June. Children must be 5 years old on or before September 1 to enter kindergarten.

Special education/program for gifted students: Only those students with minor learning disabilities and can be mainstreamed have access to a special pull-out resource program for half the day. Children with more serious problems must look to larger school districts in Maricopa County. Gifted students also have access to a special pull-out program offering enrichment courses and individualized instruction.

Nearby colleges and universities: The American Institute of Design is within Fountain Hills city limits. There are seven colleges are within a 25-mile radius of Fountain Hills, including Arizona State University at Tempe.

Medical care

Hospitals/medical centers: Fountain Hills residents are within minutes of the finest healthcare providers and facilities in the country. The world-renowned Mayo Clinic at Scottsdale provides medical care in more than 60 medical and surgical specialties. The closest full-service hospital to Fountain Hills may be the Scottsdale Healthcare Shea (242 beds), which offers 24-hour emergency, pediatrics, obstetrics, and outpatient services, as well as cardiology, and women's and children's services. The Scottsdale healthcare system includes three campuses, two hospitals, outpatient centers, home health services, and a wide range of community health education and outreach programs.

Specialized care: The Headache/Stress Center, the Scottsdale Cardiovascular Center, and the Cambelback Behaviorial Services all offer specialized services.

Crime and safety

Police: Law enforcement services are contracted out with the Maricopa County Sheriff's Department. This community has the Town Marshall's Reservists, or the "Posse," comprised of local volunteers. Many provide their own horses and do everything from rescue people lost in the desert to enforce town ordinances. Crime prevention programs include Block Watch, S.M.A.R.T. Tents (Shocking Mainstream Adolescents into Resisting Temptation) designed to impress upon school-age children that the law is not "just for adults" or "the other guy." Another school-based program is STARS (Sheriff's Teaching Abuse Resistance to Students). The sheriff's department also has a "tank," a self-propelled Howitzer (donated by the Department of Defense) covered with anti-drug messages.

Fire: The Rural/Metro Fire Department of Maricopa County provides fire and emergency medical care to Fountain Hills. The town is assigned 25 firefighters including a chief, assistant chief, and two deputy fire marshals who staff the two, town-owned fire stations. Eight firefighters—four of whom are paramedics—are on duty each day. The department received the Life Safety Achievement Award in 2002 in recognition of their hard work for the community.

Let the good times roll

Family fun: Within a day's drive of Fountain Hills are some of the world's most spectacular sights: the Petrified Forest, the Painted Desert, and the Grand Canyon. Closer to home are more than 125 golf courses, and more boats per capita than any other state. Adjacent to Fountain Hills is the McDowell Mountain Regional Park, perfect for horseback riding and hiking. Saguaro Lake is just miles away for boating and swimming. A favorite pastime for staying cool is "tubing"—floating on an inner tube in the nearby Verde and Salt Rivers. Or enjoy WestWorld (an equestrian's delight with performances by world-famous contenders), hot-air ballooning, and cookouts at one of the "Old West" style restaurants. Don't forget to visit Fountain Park, a central meeting place for picnics, concerts, and community fun. Also of interest to kids are the Phoenix Zoo, the Heard Museum (natural history), and the Hall of Flame Museum, America's largest firefighting museum.

Sports: During spring training, local baseball fans are in heaven. The Phoenix metro area is packed with major league training camps. For professional action on the courts, Phoenix is home to the Phoenix Suns (NBA). The annual PGA Phoenix Open is a favorite. For hockey fans, the Phoenix Coyotes play in nearby Glendale. World-class tennis tournaments are also played here.

Arts and entertainment: Newcomers marvel at the number of cultural events and programs in the area with the largest being the Great Fair. This three-day event is recognized as one of the most popular and prestigious arts-and-crafts shows in the Southwest with more than 1,000 artists. The third day of the fair includes a hot-air balloon regatta. A 40-minute ride can bring you to the Phoenix Symphony, the Herberger Theater, the Museum of Fine Art, and dozens of opportunities to enjoy live performing arts. In Scottsdale you can enjoy the Kerr Cultural Center, the Gammage Center for the Performing Arts, and the Lyceum Theatre. With more than 100 galleries and a marvelous art school, Scottsdale is one of the preeminent art capitals in the Southwest.

Annual events: Fountain Hills Festival of Arts and Crafts, Specialized Cactus Cup Mountain Bike Race, Thanksgiving Day Parade, Avenue Christmas Tree Lighting, Community Luminaries Display, Farmer's Market.

Community life

A daily newspaper is one thing to give you reports on what's happening in your area. However, Fountain Hills also has a weekly community paper, where the best can shine with in-depth reporting and stories. Sit and relax at the Fountain Hills Public Library while you're reading, or go online and see what is happening around the world. Fountain Hills has a great neighborhood dog park where residents can take their pets to socialize.

The environment

How many places can say, "Happy holidays, and don't forget to wear your sunscreen" during December? Fountain Hills is clean from top to bottom. Air quality is excellent because of the town's higher elevations (at some peaks it is 2,500 feet above the valley floor). The McDowell Mountain range separates the community from Phoenix's smog. Water quality is rated very good. The town established two sources (ground wells and the Central Arizona Pipeline), so it can take from the best, one at a time.

In and around town

Roads and highways: I-17, I-10, SR 87

Closest airports: Mesa Falcon Field and Scottsdale Airport are approximately 12 miles. Phoenix Sky Harbor is 30 miles.

Public transportation: There is no public transportation available.

Average commute: 20 minutes

More Information

Town of Fountain Hills
16836 Palisades Boulevard
Fountain Hills, AZ 85268
480-837-2003
www.ci.fountain-hills.az.us

Fountain Hills Unified School District
16000 East Palisades Boulevard
Fountain Hills, AZ 85268
480-664-5000
www.fhusd.org

Fountain Hills Chamber of Commerce
16837 East Palisades Boulevard
Fountain Hills, AZ 85268
480-837-1654
www.fountainhillschamber.com

River of Time Museum/Public Library
02901 North La Montana Boulevard
Fountain Hills, AZ 85268
480-837-9793
www.riveroftimemuseum.org

SRP Customer Information Center
1505 North Project Drive
Tempe, AZ 85268
602-236-8888
www.srpnet.com

Chaparral City Water Company
12012 Panorama Drive
Fountain Hills, AZ 85268
480-837-9522
www.aswater.com

Southwest Gas Corporation
2200 North Central Avenue
Phoenix, AZ 85281
602-861-1999
www.swgas.com

Qwest Communications
9617 Metrocenter Parkway West
Phoenix, AZ 85051
800-544-1111
www.qwest.com

Fountain Hills Guide
343 West Lewis Avenue
Phoenix, AZ 85003
602-321-8277
www..fountainhillsguide.com

Fayetteville, Arkansas

3

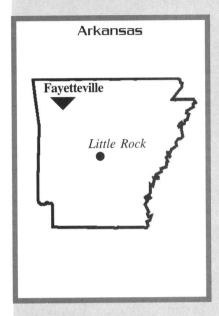

Fabulous features

First impressions of the Ozark Mountain region are indelible. Thanks to the unspoiled natural beauty and temperate year-round climate, residents have an invitation to spend their lives outdoors. Awaiting them are rolling hills, crystal-clear lakes, a majestic mountain backdrop, and crisp, clean air. Not that indoors is any less auspicious. The $7 million Walton Arts Center, a legacy of late billionaire retailer Sam Walton, is the region's first permanent home for theater, dance, and performing arts.

The hills may be alive with the sounds of chamber orchestras and symphonies, but more music to your ears is the sound of people at work, to the tune of a 97.5 percent employment rate. *Forbes* magazine (2005) rated Fayetteville seventh in "Best Places for Business and Careers." Area employment increased 20.4 percent in five years and employers in many industries now face serious labor shortages. Poultry processing is the largest employer in the area, led by Tyson Foods. One of the nation's leading retailers, Wal-Mart, Inc., is headquartered in Bentonville. Fayetteville is the fastest growing area in the state and one of the fastest growing places in the country.

Possible drawbacks: Arkansas is ranked 49th in the United States for family household income. While living costs are somewhat commensurate, many newcomers experience "paycheck shock." Growth in the area has been explosive and land values have increased substantially in recent years because of the influx of Fortune 500 companies.

▶ Local Population: 59,710

▶ County: Washington

▶ Population of surrounding metropolitan area: 157,715

▶ Region: Northwest Arkansas

▶ Closest metro area: Springfield, 73 miles

▶ Median home price: $130,150

▶ Median household income: $31,500

▶ Best reasons to live here: Breathtaking Ozark Mountain country, four delightful seasons, affordable housing, strong employment possibilities, and fabulous outdoor recreation in a laid-back college town.

Climate

Elevation 1,257'	Average temp. high/low (°F)	Average precipitation		Average no. days precipitation	Average humidity (%)
		rain (")	snow (")		
January	48/26	2.7	0	9	74
April	70/47	4.9	0	11	65
July	89/70	3.8	0	10	66
October	75/49	3.5	0	8	66
Number of days 32°F or below: 97			Number of days 90°F or warmer: 78		

Earning a living

Economic outlook: Fayetteville has seen explosive growth through most of the 1990s. Best known as a conservative college town, Fayetteville has emerged as a productive and attractive business community, underscored by a population jump of nearly 33 percent in the last 10 years. The Miliken Institute of Best Performing Cities rated Fayetteville metropolitan area the overall leader in top performance as well as first in job growth for 2003. The accolades continue with Fayetteville listed as one of the "Dazzling Dozen" by *Business Weekly* (2002), and one of America's hottest cities by *Expansion Management*, (2001). The unemployment rate seems to hover at or below 3 percent.

Where the jobs are: Major employers include University of Arkansas, Pinnacle Foods Corp., Superior Industries, Washington Regional Medical Center, Fayetteville Public Schools, Tyson's Mexican Original, and the city of Fayetteville

Business opportunities: The Genesis Business Incubator was created to attract new industry, particularly higher wage, higher skilled jobs by providing space and support services for new technology businesses. Participating companies have had an 85 percent survival rate. Fayetteville opened a new high-tech FiberPark, served by high-speed, high-capacity communications links. Areas to watch are Industrial Park South, the Fayetteville Municipal Airport, the Arkansas Research and Technology Park at Genesis, and the Business and Technology Park at Interstate 540, as the parks are magnets for attracting high-wage, high-tech, information-based companies. The city also boasts an active Small Business Development Center at the University of Arkansas, which advises new businesses on everything from financing to operations.

Local real estate

Market overview: "New Victorian" construction is popular, with wrap-around porches. Ranch style and southern colonials can be found.

Average rent for a two-bedroom apartment: $465 per month

Other areas to consider: Springdale has a big heart for families, sitting in the center of northwest Arkansas, and is home to the Rodeo of the Ozarks. Springfield is beautiful Ozark Mountain country. Take a trip under the mountain area by visiting the Fantastic Caverns, an underground riverbed. Tulsa lies to the west about two hours away, if you want bright lights and big city noise. However, don't expect to see New York-style people. Downtown Tulsa has skyscrapers and cowboys on the same street.

What things cost

ACCRA's national comparisons: Overall living costs are about 7 percent below the national average. Healthcare costs are 4 percent below average, housing is about 16 percent below average, utilities are 7 percent above, and goods and services run 7 percent below.

Utilities: Phone: $30 per month; water: $35 per month; gas: $45 per month (summer), $190 per month (winter)

The tax ax

Sales tax: 9.25 percent

Property tax: $47.30 (city $1, county $6.30, school district $40) per $1,000 valuation, with property assessed at 20 percent of market value. Tax on an $88,600 home in the city is about $838 a year.

State income tax: Graduated from 1 percent on first $3,000 income to 7 percent maximum on $25,000 and above.

Making the grade

Public education overview: Fayetteville's highly progressive school board has led the way in excellence through the explosive growth in Fayetteville. The Fayetteville public school system includes one senior high, a separate vocational-technical campus, two junior highs, two middle schools, and nine elementary schools. Fayetteville annually sends 80 percent of its graduates to college. *Expansion Management* magazine has awarded Fayetteville School District a gold medal for excellence in 1996, 2000, 2001, and 2002. No other school district in Arkansas has received a gold medal. The governor and television channel KTHV-TV named Fayetteville as one of the "Top 10 Gold Apple School Districts" in 2004. Policies such as zero tolerance of bullying and verbal abuse of a teacher help keep the schools a great and safe place to learn.

Class size (student to teacher ratio): 24:1

Help for working parents: Working parents can drop children off 30 minutes before school.

Boys & Girls Club info: There are nine centers available in Fayetteville.

School year: Last week of August through second week of June. Children must be 5 years old on or before October 1 to enter kindergarten.

Special education/programs for gifted students: One center offers educational opportunities for developmentally disabled children not provided for in the public school system. Fayetteville has the greatest representation at the annual Arkansas Governor's School for Gifted and Talented. The district's gifted and talented program was named the best in Arkansas in 2001, making it the fourth time they had won the award in the last 12 years.

Nearby colleges and universities: The University of Arkansas-Fayetteville is the only comprehensive doctoral degree granting institution in the state of Arkansas. UA offers more than 150 fields of study and new renovation and construction is planned for the remainder of the decade. Webster University offers undergraduate, graduate, and postgraduate studies. Other facilities are Northwest Technical Institute and Northwest Arkansas Community College in Bentonville.

Medical care

Hospitals/medical centers: The highly respected Washington Regional Medical Center is a nonprofit acute-care facility offering cardiac care, a trauma unit, physical therapy, hospice care, obstetrics, and oncology. Washington Regional hospital has a comprehensive cancer care program; the Walker Family Heart and Vascular Institute offers complete services in cardiology; and the Johnelle Hunt Women's Center services women and their families with five triage rooms, and a neonatal intensive-care nursery with parent-child rooms. These rooms allow infants to stay close to their families, while the parents are assisted by highly skilled medical teams. The North Hills Medical Park has many privately owned specialized clinics and same-day surgery facilities.

Specialized care: Northwest Arkansas Rehabilitation Hospital specializes in the treatment of strokes, spinal-cord injuries, and neurological disorders. The Northwest Arkansas Radiation Therapy Institute provides excellent cancer care.

Crime and safety

Police: To borrow from a baseball umpire, Fayetteville is S-A-F-E! Violent crime is not only low but has declined. In fact, the overall crime rate declined at the same time the population grew. The Fayetteville crime prevention and community policing units are active with programs such as Neighborhood Watch and Security surveys for both residential and commercial areas. Other events and programs include Red Ribbon Week, corporate safety fairs, car seat clinics, bike safety, and more.

Fire: The Fayetteville fire department has 89 full-time firefighters, with 80 percent EMT trained, working at five fire stations. The department's services include emergency medical (both basic and advanced life-support), fire suppression, fire rescue, hazardous materials response, prevention, public education events, and organization-wide disaster preparedness activities. The department has a mobile Safety House for educating children on what to do in case of an emergency. At Halloween, Station 1 has been know to give out bags of candy to the costumed trick-or-treaters.

Let the good times roll

Family fun: Who needs Disney World? The Ozark Mountains region is the ultimate in magic kingdoms! Start with the 500-mile shoreline of Beaver Lake, perfect for fishing, camping, and boating, and a natural playground with more than 30,000 acres of sparkling water and mountains. The famed Buffalo River is one of four in the country identified as a national river, a coveted status earned by its 95,000 acres of national parkland. Whitewater tubing and canoeing are just the start of the fun! Devil's Den, an exciting state park, offers spelunking, hiking, and camping in the beautiful Boston Mountains. Head south to the Ozark National Forest for hunting, hiking, and more picnicking. Trout and striped bass fishing in the White River is an angler's dream (professional bass fishing got its start here). The University of Arkansas Museum has Discovery Room, a special hands-on exhibit hall for kids. Out at Drake Field Airport, the Air Museum is a showcase for local aviation history.

Sports: Fayetteville was featured in the December 1, 2003, issue of *Sports Illustrated* as one of the "Top 50 Sports Towns in America." The Parks and Recreation department offers a large variety of sport activities for both children and adults, as well as helps local groups, such as the Boys and Girls Club, by offering additional programs including soccer, basketball, and youth baseball. The enthusiasm for sports is highlighted by the University of Arkansas champion teams competing in football, basketball, baseball, and track, giving Fayetteville residents a lot to cheer about.

Arts and entertainment: Fayetteville's favorite son, the late Sam Walton, died two weeks before the opening of his dream legacy, the Walton Arts Center. The 55,000 square foot complex is a regional performing arts, visual arts, and education center, bringing hundreds of exhibits, musical entertainment, theater, opera, and dance to the area. Visit the Joy Pratt Markham Gallery (exhibits change every four to six weeks). Concerts and performing arts are also presented at the Chi Omega Greek Theater, an outdoor amphitheater on the University of Arkansas campus.

Annual events: Hogeye Festival, Springfest, Arkansas Music Festival, Rodeo of the Ozarks, Washington County Fair, Prairie Grove Clothesline Fair, Arkansas Apple Festival and Fayetteville Autumnfest, War Eagle Arts and Crafts Fair, Lights of Ozarks

Community life

With more than 70 service clubs and organizations active in supporting community activities and interests, hometown spirit runs strong in Fayetteville. A wonderful Art Education Partnership Program through the Walton Arts Center is available for children. The recently opened Learning Center offers 20,000 square feet of educational facilities that will facilitate arts education for people of all ages.

The environment

Fayetteville's clean surroundings are the pride and priority of the area. In 2004 Fayetteville had 130 volunteers who dedicated 408 hours collecting litter and trash from Lake Fayetteville, South Fayetteville, and the Industrial trails clean-up activity. Companies wanting to relocate here must undergo a qualification process, and only those that do not pose a threat to air and water quality get the keys to the city. At present, water quality is excellent, thanks to a state-of-the-art treatment plant (the source water is nearby Beaver Lake). Air quality has never been an issue due to lack of smokestack industries.

In and around town

Roads and highways: US 62, 412, 71, Arkansas 16, 45, 112, 156, 180, 265, 471

Closest airports: Northwest Arkansas Regional Airport is served by various airlines with direct connections to Atlanta, Chicago, Dallas, Memphis, Kansas City, St. Louis, Charlotte, Little Rock, and LaGuardia. Drake Field in Fayetteville offers commuter service to major hubs as well.

Public transportation: Jefferson Bus Lines provides service throughout the city.

Average daily commute: 10 minutes

More Information

City of Fayetteville
113 West Mountain Road
Fayetteville, AR 72701
479-521-7700
www.accessfayetteville.org

City of Fayetteville Water Department
113 West Mountain Road
Fayetteville, AR 72701
479-575-1258
www.accessfayetteville.org

Fayetteville Public Schools
1000 West Stone Street
Fayetteville, AR 72701
479-444-3000
www.fayar.net

Arkansas Western Gas
1083 Sain Street
Fayetteville, AR 72702
479-521-5330
www.awgonline.com

Fayetteville Chamber of Commerce
123 West Mountain Road
Fayetteville, AR 72702
479-521-1710
www.fayettevillear.com

City of Fayetteville GIS
113 West Mountain Road
Fayetteville, AR 72701
479-575-8219
www.faygis.org

Southwestern Electric Power
300 North College Avenue
Fayetteville, AR 72702
479-521-2871
www.swepco.com

Fayetteville Promotional Commission
15 West Mountain Road
Fayetteville, AR 72702
479-587-9944
www.fayettevilletourism.com

Little Rock, Arkansas

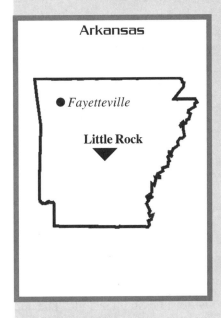

Arkansas

● *Fayetteville*

Little Rock
▼

Fabulous features

Little Rock has added a number of local flavors to the national scene. A few examples: Black Panther leader and author Eldridge Cleaver was born in Little Rock, as was Socks Clinton, First Feline of the Arkansas Governor's Mansion and the White House. Meyer's Bakery in Little Rock invented the brown-n-serve roll in the 1930s. Great things have come out of this southern river city.

Little Rock, capital of Arkansas and near the center of the state, where you could say "America comes together" at the junction of Interstate Highways 30 and 40. Sitting on the south bank of the Arkansas River, this central locality is only part of its economic package. Offering competitive wages and a right-to-work environment is why 28 Fortune 500 companies operate within the metropolitan area. *Expansion Management* magazine listed Little Rock in its "America's 50 Hottest Cities" for 2005.

Housing costs fare well under the national average, providing a boon for first-time buyers and those moving to Little Rock. And why not? The weather in Little Rock is great, there are wonderful people in the neighborhoods, and the downtown River Market District has something for everyone.

Possible drawbacks: Being a southern state, heat and humidity are natural effects. Every Wednesday afternoon the tornado siren is tested, yet most actual tornadoes go around the city.

▶ Local Population: 184,055

▶ County: Pulsaki

▶ Population of surrounding metropolitan area: 580,625

▶ Region: Central Arkansas

▶ Closest metro area: Memphis, 164 miles

▶ Median home price: $102,500

▶ Median household income: $37,572

▶ Best reasons to live here: Little Rock is centrally located, with strong job opportunities, a low cost of living, award-winning schools, great neighborhoods, and classic southern charm.

Climate

Elevation 350'	Average temp. high/low (°F)	Average precipitation rain (")	snow (")	Average no. days precipitation	Average humidity (%)
January	50/31	3.6	2.5	10	65
April	73/51	5.4	0	10	60
July	93/72	3.4	0	8	58
October	75/52	4.2	0	7	55
Number of days 32°F or below: 63			Number of days 90°F or warmer: 70		

Earning a living

Economic outlook: Little Rock has seen a steady increase in economic development activities due in large part to an active private sector and strong leadership of the Greater Little Rock Chamber of Commerce. Little Rock is one of the top 15 aggressive development markets in the nation, with projections indicating it will double during the next 20 years. Little Rock is home to several national companies including Dillard's, Alltel, and Stephens, Inc. The unemployment rate for this area averages 4.0 percent, which is below the national average. Job growth in the area is around 3.8 percent. In 2004, Little Rock was ranked second in the country for economic diversity by Moody's Investors Service by scoring 95.1 out of a possible 100.The Arkansas River runs past downtown, providing a 448-mile navigation channel for barge traffic from the Mississippi River. The Port of Little Rock is a designated Foreign Trade Zone and a United States Customs Port of Entry.

Where the jobs are: Top manufacturing employers are AFCO Steel, Inc., AGL Corporation, and AMERON Protective Coatings Group. The government, including local, state, and federal offices, is the largest employer, though Little Rock serves as the center of Arkansas' medical industry, with a number of excellent hospitals, including one of the top veteran's hospitals.

Business opportunities: The construction of the Alltel Arena, a 20,000 seat event center, across the river in North Little Rock, is in progress. The new Clinton Presidential Library, located in Little Rock, will provide business opportunities and tourist activity for decades to come. Completed in 2002, the Capital Commerce Center, a 86,500 square foot building downtown, is walking distance from the River Market District, plus it has immediate Interstate 30 access. Heifer International is constructing a new headquarters and global village to be a focal point for hunger education with a center for seminars and conferences. This is also adjacent to the new Clinton Presidential Library and the River Market District.

Local real estate

Market overview: From quaint neighborhoods to magnificent antebellum and red-brick Victorian, you'll find just about any style of home. Choose from loft apartments to two-story houses with sweeping, suburban-style lawns, in downtown Little Rock or its surrounding neighborhoods.

Average rent for a two-bedroom apartment: $538 per month

Other areas to consider: Cross over the bridge to North Little Rock for many of the same amenities in a smaller package. Check out the nearby towns of Sweet Home and College Station for southern hospitality. Say "Memphis" and usually the first image in your head is Graceland Mansion, which brings thousands of visitors every year through the area. This Tennessee metropolis is ranked in the Top 10 of the most mannerly cities.

What things cost

ACCRA's national comparisons: Overall living costs are about 8 percent below the national average. Health care costs are 12 percent below average, housing is about 20 percent below, utilities are 8 percent below, and transportation runs 3 percent below.

Utilities: Electricity $72.50 per month; natural gas $35 per month; phone $27 per month

The tax ax

Sales tax: 6.62 percent

Property tax: $13.80 est. property taxes paid per $1,000 of market value.

State income tax: 7.0 percent

Making the grade

Public education overview: The Little Rock School District operates 34 elementary schools, eight middle schools, five high schools, a career-technical center, an accelerated learning center, and two alternative centers. Students are offered more Advanced Placement (AP) and pre-AP courses than any other students in the state. The district regularly has more National Merit Semifinalists than any other school district in the state. Little Rock voters approved a tax increase in 2000 and this money has been used for building repairs, renovations, additions, and expansions; technology upgrades; and a dedicated building maintenance fund. Let's not forget that during the 2003 school year, more than 18,000 volunteers contributed 464,000 hours of volunteer time. The Volunteers in Public Schools program provides support and coordination for school volunteer programs and for connecting students to volunteers in the community.

Class size (student to teacher ration): 14:1

Help for working parents: The CARE program operates at most elementary schools providing before- and after-school programs and all-day on most school holidays. After-school programs are available at the eight middle schools, operating for 90 minutes on Tuesdays, Wednesdays, and Thursdays, offering academic tutoring and other activities.

Boys & Girls Club info: There are currently 14 centers available in Little Rock.

School year: Third week of August to the first week of June. Students must be 5 years old on or before September 15 to enter kindergarten. For the pre-K program, students must be 4 years old on or before September 15.

Special education/programs for gifted students: The Gifted and Talented Program is available in all schools. Students in grades six to 12 with behavioral difficulties are assigned to the Alternative Learning Center in lieu of long-term suspension or expulsion.

Nearby colleges and universities: Harding University, UA Law School, UA Medical School, UALR Graduate Institute of Technology, University of Arkansas-Little Rock, University of Arkansas-Pine Bluff, University of Central Arkansas, Weber University, Arkansas Baptist College, Philander Smith College, Pulaski Technical College

Medical care

Hospitals/medical centers: Healthcare is excellent in this area, with 11 medical hospitals providing approximately 3,582 patient beds. Some of the facilities are Arkansas Children's Hospital, the only pediatric medical center in Arkansas. Services include neonatal, transplants, and orthopedics, as well as an adolescent and sports medicine section, the first of its kind in the region. The University of Arkansas Medical Center is an award-winning teaching hospital, and was named one of the best hospitals by *U.S. New & World Report*. Some of their quality centers include the Arkansas Cancer Research Center and the Jackson T. Stephens Spine & Neurosciences Institute.

Specialized care: Arkansas Heart Hospital is an entire center dedicated to fighting heart disease. With all private-occupancy patient rooms, the hospital has the latest technology teamed with a highly trained staff.

Crime and safety

Police: Little Rock's police department consists of 150 sworn and civilian personnel (officers and other staff in non-police terms) providing public safety. Community Oriented Policing Program (COPP) officers are stationed directly in the neighborhoods, like a patrol beat, making positive, long-term rapport with residents. The S.T.A.R.T. Unit (Selective Traffic Accident Reduction Team) targets D.W.I violators to reduce traffic accidents. The Motorcycle Squad works on traffic enforcement and special events, such as parades and motorcades. LRPD has an airport detail responsible for security at the Little Rock National Airport and also has a highly trained SWAT team should they need to respond to hostage or high-threat situations.

Fire: The Little Rock fire department hired its first woman fire chief, overseeing the department's 20 Fire Stations. The department has four major divisions, currently being handled by more than 400 personnel. The fire department has several special operations companies including an aircraft rescue and fire fighting; a hazardous materials unit; an urban search and rescue unit with extended high angle rescue capability, low angle rescue capability, trench rescue capability, swift water rescue and collapse rescue capabilities; and a bomb squad with at least three members on duty at all times.

Let the good times roll

Family fun: Where do you start? The list for indoor and outdoor activities is long and varied. Perpetual Southern sunshine means plenty of time for recreation. With 50 parks of more than 5,000 acres, plus several lakes, you'll enjoy hiking, fishing, sailing, and more. Downtown has a cornucopia of venues from the Farmers Market to the Arkansas Repertory Theatre. There's the Riverfront Amphitheater or you can just enjoy the parks. From downtown you can journey to the Little Rock Zoo, or spend the day at the Children's Museum. Don't miss the IMAX theater inside the Aerospace Education Center. Located on the banks of the Arkansas River in downtown Little Rock's River Market District is the new William J. Clinton Presidential Center. The center includes a museum, educational, and research facilities. Next to the center is the University of Arkansas Clinton School of Public Service, located in a restored 1899 passenger train depot.

Sports: Little Rock's Ray Winder Field is the home of the Class AA minor league Arkansas Travelers, a farm club of the Los Angeles Angels. Several University of Arkansas Razorback football games are held each year at War Memorial Stadium.

Arts and entertainment: The Arkansas Symphony Orchestra, Ballet Arkansas, Chamber Music Society of Little Rock, Community Concerts Association, Little Rock Community Theatre, UALR Theatre Arts and Dance Department, Wildwood Park, and many others offer performing arts productions. Programs and performances are held throughout the year. Located in historic MacArthur Park, the Arkansas Arts Center features elegant art galleries that showcase the center's acclaimed collections.

Annual events: Cruisin' in the Rock, Riverfest, Art Market, Gully Park Concerts

Community life

There's nothing little about Little Rock. A part of history has returned to Little Rock by means of the restored historic trollies. RiverRail is a single-track trolley that winds over 2.5 miles. Trolleys share the street with automobile traffic, but in some cases run along the curb. The Little Rock loop service runs a clockwise adventure through the city. The second service goes over the river to North Little Rock Loop. Both have many sites to see. An extension going up to the President Clinton Center is being planned, with more routes and services in future plans.

The environment

The community's strong commitment to the environment is seen in a variety of ways from their curbside recycling program to the Arkansas River Trail. A total of 24 miles, the trail will let people walk or ride their bikes for errands and/or commuting to work. They can go from Little Rock to North Little Rock lessening the congestion created by cars and buses.

In and around town

Roads and highways: I-30, 40, 430, 440, 630, highways 167, 64, 65, 67, 70

Closest airports: The Little Rock National Airport, less than three miles from downtown, is served by 12 airlines, providing more than 80 departures and arrivals daily.

Public transportation: Central Arkansas Transit

Average daily commute: 17 minutes

More Information

Little Rock City Hall, Room #203
500 West Markham
Little Rock, AR 72201
501-371-4510
www.littlerock.org

Little Rock School District
810 West Markham
Little Rock, AR 72201
501-447-1000
www.lrsd.org

Little Rock Chamber of Commerce
1 Chamber Plaza
Little Rock, AR 72201
501-374-2001
www.littlerockchamber.com

Entergy Arkansas
900 South Louisiana Street
Little Rock, AR 72201
501-377-4000
www.entergyarkansas.com

Southwestern Bell
1111 West Capitol Avenue
Little Rock, AR 72201
800-464-7928
www.sbc.com

Central Arkansas Water
221 East Capitol Avenue
Little Rock, AR 72201
501-372-5161
www.carkw.com

CenterPoint Reliant Energy
2205 East Roosevelt
Little Rock, AR 72201
501-372-7552
http://centerpointenergy.com

Little Rock Boys and Girls Club
1201 Leisure Place
Little Rock, AR 72201
501-666-8816
www.lrbgc.org

The Children's Museum of Arkansas
1400 West Markham Street
Little Rock, AR 72201
501-374-4000
www.arkarts.com

Little Rock Zoo
1 Jonesboro Drive
Little Rock, AR 72201
501-666-2406
www.littlerockzoo.com

Chino, California

Fabulous features

Location, location, location—has this city got it! Smack in the middle of southern California, people of Chino are within an hour's drive of all the recreational amenities of beach, mountain, and desert. Athletics or amusement parks, these are the tough decisions Chinoans have to make. You want skiing? You have Mt. Baldy and Big Bear. You want desert? You can't get any better than Palm Springs, or the high desert of Hesperia/ Victorville. And the Pacific Ocean? You got it, dude, with Newport and Balboa due west. Disneyland, Knotts Berry Farm, and Magic Mountain round out the weekend or vacation festivity choices.

The Chino area, rich in agricultural heritage, has a strong Hispanic population. Surrounded by gently rolling hills to the south and west, the current and future growth in residential and industrial areas makes this one of the fastest growing cities in southern California. Chino is sitting in a four-corner area of the largest counties in the state, with easy freeway access, allowing for flexibility in the job market and recreational avenues.

The nomer "Where Everything Grows" originally referred to Chino's agricultural beginning, but today it applies to fabulous growth in families, business, and community.

Possible drawbacks: Southern California's smog can back up into the valley and hold the air quality in jeopardy for days at a time. It does rain in southern California, and if too much rain falls, there's flooding in the streets.

▶ Local Population: 72,054

▶ County: San Bernardino

▶ Population of surrounding metropolitan area: 1,859,678

▶ Region: Southern California

▶ Closest metro area: Anaheim, 19 miles

▶ Median home price: $391,000

▶ Median household income: $59,110

▶ Best reasons to live here: Chino is centrally located, with a southern California climate for year-round recreation. There is affordable housing in great neighborhoods, and a growing economic climate.

Climate

Elevation 750'	Average temp. high/low (°F)	Average precipitation rain (")	snow (")	Average no. days precipitation	Average humidity (%)
January	68/42	4.1	0	6	53
April	74/48	0.9	0	3	51
July	89/60	0	0	0	54
October	80/53	0.7	0	2	54
Number of days 32°F or below: 0			Number of days 90°F or warmer: 20		

Earning a living

Economic outlook: Ample access to major freeways makes industrial business flourish in this fast-growing community. Just about every type of business is represented in the city from large warehouses to small business. A healthy dose of retail keeps much of Chino's population working and spending money in the city. Looking at this part of the Inland Empire, you'll see a high-end growth of industries, such as financial, business services, and manufacturing. Employees and executives alike are migrating from the more expensive Los Angeles and Orange County areas, and raising their families where the cost of living is lower. Between 2000 and 2020, the Inland Empire is predicted to be the fastest growing area in southern California.

Where the jobs are: Major employers include the Chino Valley School District, Hussman Corporation, Sundance Spas, the city of Chino, American Honda, and the Fisher Scientific Corporation.

Business opportunities: Rumor has it that there will be more jobs than working-age people in this area. Downtown now has a transportation center next to City Hall. New businesses are attracted to the modern facilities, affordable lease rates, and access to the 60, 71, and 91 freeways, as well as the Ontario International Airport. Chino is also committed to their business retention program. Once a company relocates to this area, why would they want to go anywhere else?

Local real estate

Market overview: Older ranch-style homes in tree-lined tracts surround the Central Avenue corridor. Newer developments spread out, including two-story homes with open interiors, plus townhouses and condominiums.

Average rent for a two-bedroom apartment: $650 per month

Other areas to consider: Rancho Cucamonga, made famous by a Jack Benny routine, sits against the San Gabriel foothills, with palm tree-lined boulevards, minor league baseball, and great shopping malls. Riverside is a sprawling older area decorated in palm and eucalyptus trees. The University of Riverside provides a college town feel, and trainers from Guide Dogs of the Desert work their dogs on the main boulevards. Anaheim is a fast-paced, high-tech city in Orange County.

What things cost

ACCRA's national comparisons: Overall living costs are about 20 percent above the national average. Healthcare costs are 11 percent above average, housing is about 40 percent above, utilities are 11 percent below, and good and services run 1 percent above.

Utilities: Phone: $35 per month; electricity: $50 per month; gas: $35 per month; water: $40 per month

The tax ax

Sales tax: 7.75 percent

Property tax: Established through Proposition 13 as 1 percent of the purchase price plus limited locally approved bonds.

State income tax: 9.30 percent

Making the grade

Public education overview: The Chino Valley Unified School District services the cities of Chino, Chino Hills, and a portion of Ontario. The district currently has four high schools, one continuation high school, five junior high schools, 21 elementary schools, and two fundamental schools. This progressive district embraces a year-round calendar for many of their schools. Long before the No Child Left Behind Act, California voters wanted feedback from each of their schools, and in 1988 passed Proposition 98, the School Funding Initiative. The district has posted reports online for parents and the community to see how each school is doing. The St. Margaret Mary Catholic School has been open to the community's children since 1954. The school offers preschool and grades kindergarten through eight, with various programs such as computers, science, and fine arts, as well as competitive athletics. There is also extended care services available for working parents.

Class size (student to teacher ratio): 21:1

Boys & Girls Club info: There are no centers available in Chino.

School year: First week of September to mid-June on traditional schedule; check the individual schools for year-round tracks. Children must be 5 years old on or before December 2 to enter kindergarten.

Special education/programs for gifted students: GATE programs are available for gifted and talented students. Special education students may be enrolled in an individualized education program.

Nearby colleges and universities: Chaffey Community College, Cal Poly University of Pomona, Mt. San Antonio College, DeVry Institute of Technology, Claremont Colleges, and the University of LaVerne are just a few of the facilities within driving distance of Chino.

Medical care

Hospitals/medical centers: Chino Valley Medical Center (126 beds) in the heart of Chino provides 24-hour emergency care; 10 intensive care beds; full radiological and laboratory services; nuclear medicine; the Birthplace Center, where mothers have a single room alternative instead of moving from labor room to delivery room; pediatric unit; and surgical services. San Antonio Hospital, in nearby Upland, is a full service facility with emergency services, medical and surgical provisions, and maternity ward. Pomona Valley Hospital, 20 minutes to the west, is another full-service hospital providing medical and surgical care to the Inland Empire.

Specialized care: Canyon Ridge Hospital (59 beds) specializes in both inpatient and outpatient psychiatric care, as well as care for alcohol and drug abuse. Loma Linda University Hospital, a quality teaching hospital, is less than an hour away.

Crime and safety

Police: The Chino police department prides itself on keeping crime rates down and response times fast with a stellar department of 1.37 sworn officers per 1,000 people. Some grew up in the area and now serve the community. Community policing officers are assigned to regular areas and get to know the people and businesses. Patrol cars are equipped with mobile data computers. CPD has its own 911 dispatch center, and in 2005, will answer wireless E911 calls. Chino has a Citizen Police Academy, community support team, and Explorer Post. The crime prevention unit is involved with a variety of programs, such as Community Watch. How many urban crime units have their own mounted posse? The Chino Mounted Posse is composed of volunteers and sworn officers trained to assist in emergency situations or perform special services.

Fire: Chino Valley Independent Fire District is known for its high-quality services including emergency medical and paramedic services, hazardous materials response, and urban search and rescue. With six fire stations, more than 100 professional firefighters spend each day training themselves and the public about fire. The Urban Search and Rescue Team has received specialized training in swift water I and II level classes, vertical channel rescue, flood management, and boat handling. The Explorers program is part of the Boy Scouts of America, introducing the Explorer to fire services as a possible career through training and participation in actual situations.

Let the good times roll

Family fun: Chino's Recreation Services provides year-round quality activities and classes for children and adults. Whether it's softball or painting, there are things to do at all age levels. Or enjoy yourself at the various parks and playgrounds, such as Ayala Park. If golfing is your pleasure, you have found the place. Dozens of golf courses are nearby, and with Chino's climate, you can pretty much swing your clubs every weekend. The Planes of Fame Museum is a fun stop, whether you mark your calendar for the annual air show, or enjoy an afternoon walking around the aircraft carriers of history. The Children's Museum downtown has exhibits of Chino's past. The Neighborhood

Activity Center is a great place for all grade students to hang out, whlie seventh to ninth grade students can hang out at the Chino Experience, a state of the art teen center. Seasonal activities include enjoying delicious fresh apple cider in Oak Glen, or picking cherries in June out in Cherry Valley. Outside Chino are other treasures both in amusement parks and natural wonders. From the Pacific Ocean to Space Mountain, there is no reason to wonder what to do on a day off in the sunshine.

Sports: While no professional teams reside in Chino, southern California is home to the Dodgers and Angels (MLB), the Clippers and the Lakers (NBA), and the Kings and Mighty Ducks (NHL). Minor league baseball can be seen at the Quakes Stadium in Rancho Cucamonga.

Arts and entertainment: The Seventh Street Theater provides entertainment with their annual production season. Bridges Auditorium in Claremont provides big name entertainment and cultural events. The Los Angeles County Fairgrounds in Pomona holds various events and festivals all year long. An hour in travel time and you could be at any of the Los Angeles venues, such as the Hollywood Bowl or the Dorothy Chandler Pavilion.

Annual events: Pro Rodeo at the Chino Fairgrounds, Los Angeles County Fair, Festival of Lights

Community life

No matter how fast the community grows, it still has a small town heart. *The Chino Champion*, a great weekly newspaper, is at the core of keeping residents informed with in-depth stories or ongoing reports of various issues. People come together in a variety of ways to support and cheer each other on while enjoying the quality of life in the Chino Valley. Volunteering is strong in the community, whether it's helping out in a classroom, or pitching in at the senior center.

The environment

Water quality is very important to the City of Chino and the water department works hard to keep the drinking water clean and fresh. Recycling has been an important part of the community for decades. There is also a hotline to report graffiti, that is usually removed in 24 hours. Air quality can be an issue several times a year, and people with asthma or chronic breathing problems should be aware of the ecological conditions.

In and around town

Roads and highways: I-60, I-10, state route 71, 91, 66

Closest airports: The Ontario International Airport and Chino Municipal airport are both within driving distance of Chino.

Public transportation: OmniTrans bus service

Average daily commute: 20 minutes

More Information

City of Chino
13220 Central Avenue
Chino, CA 91710
909-627-7577
www.cityofchino.org

City of Chino Water Department
13220 Central Avenue
Chino, CA 91710
909-591-9820
www.cityofchino.org

Chino Valley Unified School District
5130 Riverside Drive
Chino, CA 91710
909-628-1201
www.chino.k12.ca.us

Southern California Gas Company
196 East Third Street
Pomona, CA 91766
800-427-2200
www.socalgas.com

St. Margaret Mary School
12664 Central Avenue
Chino, CA 91710
909-591-8419
www.stmargaretmaryschool.org

Planes of Fame Museum
7000 Merrill Avenue Suite 17
Chino, CA 91710
909-597-3722
www.planesoffame.org

Chamber of Commerce
13150 7th Street
Chino, CA 91710
909-627-6177
www.chinovalleychamber.com

Chino Rotary Club
PO Box 116
Chino, CA 91708
909-628-5501
www.planesoffame.org

Southern California Edison
1351 East Francis Street
Ontario, CA 91761
800-655-4555
www.sce.com

6 ▶ Pismo Beach, California

Fabulous features

Pismo Beach, better known as the "Clam Capital of the World," has 23 miles of unspoiled sandy beaches, dramatic rugged coastlines, and a 1,200-foot pier lined with fishing enthusiasts. One of the area's natural wonders are the regal orange and black monarch butterflies, which migrate annually from October through February, and bring in thousands of tourists. Tourism is one of the main industries of Pismo.

Located halfway between San Francisco and Los Angeles, Pismo Beach occupies the center of California's coastline. The mild marine weather and tons of recreational activities bring scores of tourists during the summer months, exploding Pismo's population. Main Street leads downhill straight to the ocean.

Job opportunities close to home are limited. Unless you work in the service industry or tourism trade, you're going to commute every day to nearby cities such as San Luis Obispo and Santa Maria. But when the working day is done, you can enjoy the fresh ocean air by golfing and bicycling to your heart's content.

All the benefits of small town life are found in Pismo Beach, where pollution and rush-hour traffic are unknown and residents call one another by their first names. Residents receive *The Clam Chronicle* on a quarterly basis, giving them highlights of the happenings in the city.

Possible drawbacks: The cost of living is high, and with the price of housing, you may have to camp out with the butterflies. New construction may be limited due to water restrictions.

▶ Local Population: 8,646

▶ County: San Luis Obispo

▶ Population of surrounding metropolitan area: 246,681

▶ Region: Central California

▶ Closest metro area: Santa Barbara, 94 miles

▶ Median home price: $313,100

▶ Median household income: $46,396

▶ Best reasons to live here: The beautiful seaside scenery, excellent schools, dedicated community, clean environment, and great year-round recreation.

Climate

Elevation 33'	Average temp. high/low (°F)	Average precipitation rain (")	Average precipitation snow (")	Average no. days precipitation	Average humidity (%)
January	65/43	3.6	0	8	61
April	69/46	1.1	0	5	61
July	71/51	0	0	0	62
October	73/51	0.6	0	2	62
Number of days 32°F or below: 0			Number of days 90°F or warmer: 0		

Earning a living

Economic outlook: Pismo Beach is largely a tourist economy, with the city's beach and golf courses drawing visitors throughout the year. Service industries based on tourism thrive, such as bicycle and kayak rentals, restaurants, hotels, and motels. In addition, you will find antique shops, start-up companies, light manufacturing, and industrial operations such as Western Pacific Elevator, a manufacturer of elevator and wheelchair lifts. The local sport-fishing fleet occasionally has need of workers with specialized skills. Also, the larger economy of San Luis Obispo is only nine miles away, and employees of California Polytechnic State University and other employers of the city often reside in Pismo. This helps keep the unemployment rate down to 3.4 percent.

Where the jobs are: Some of the major employers in the area are the county of San Luis Obispo, Cal Poly San Luis Obispo, Atascadero State Hospital, California Men's Colony, Pacific Gas & Electric Company, the Canyon Diablo Nuclear Power Plant, Cal Poly Foundation, the Lucia Mar Unified School District, and Paso Robles Public Schools.

Business opportunities: Although more than 8,600 people call Pismo Beach home, nearby cities such as Arroyo Grande, Shell Beach, and Oceano make Pismo Beach busier than you might expect. Opportunity may only be a stones throw away. Small business and entrepreneurs use technology and the Internet as their springboard to live in Pismo and conduct business around the world.

Local real estate

Market overview: You may or may not have a view of the ocean or nearby volcanic domes, but neighborhoods in Pismo are peaceful and quiet. A variety of housing styles are available. Older homes or condominiums may be more affordable than new models.

Average rent for a two-bedroom apartment: $910 per month

Other areas to consider: San Luis Obispo is an eclectic community, with Cal Poly and the Madonna Inn bringing in tourism and population growth. Santa Maria sits in a beautiful river valley, providing great vineyards and agriculture opportunities. Santa Barbara is still an ocean-side area, but with big-city amenities. How hard is it to study with the Pacific Ocean down the street? The University of California at Santa Barbara is known for its high quality of education. The mild climate and natural beauty is a magnet for artists and authors.

What things cost

ACCRA's national comparisons: Overall living costs are about 70 percent above the national average. Healthcare costs are 38 percent above average, housing is about 170 percent above, utilities are 18 percent above, and goods and services run 23 percent above.

Utilities: Electricity: $110 per month; natural gas: $50 per month; phone: $25 per month

The tax ax

Sales tax: 8.1 percent

Property tax: Established through Proposition 13 as 1 percent of the purchase price plus limited locally approved bonds.

State income tax: 6 percent

Making the grade

Public education overview: The Lucia Mar Unified School District is the largest in San Luis Obispo County. More than 10,900 students attend Lucia Mar's 10 elementary schools, three middle schools, two comprehensive high schools, one continuation high school, and adult education program. The district serves the communities of Arroyo Grande, Grover Beach, Pismo Beach, Shell Beach, Nipomo, and Oceano. In 2002, the district opened a second high school, Nipomo High School. A new elementary school in Nipomo, the Dorothea Lange Elementary School, is expected to open in the fall of 2005. The district has a progressive computer network and many of the teachers have classroom Websites, excellent for accessing information, calendars, and activities. Standardized testing consists of the California Achievement Test, and the district follows the state standards with highly successful results.

Class size (student to teacher ratio): 16:1

Boys & Girls Club info: There are no centers available in Pismo Beach.

School year: Last week of August to first week of June. Children must turn 5 years old on or before December 2 to enter kindergarten.

Special education/programs for gifted students: The Gifted and Talented Education program is available in the school district.

Nearby colleges and universities: California Polytechnic State University at San Luis Obispo is known for its agricultural and business schools, while Cuesta College is a quality community college.

Medical care

Hospitals/medical centers: Although Pismo Beach does not have its own facility, three hospitals are located in San Luis Obispo County, with more than 250 beds available. The Sierra Vista Regional Medical Center is the largest center, providing emergency services, coronary care, inpatient surgery, and a blood bank. The High Risk Infant Fol-low-up Program at Sierra Vista Regional Medical Center provides a team of professionals who work closely with your pediatrician. The service is offered at no cost to families. The Catholic Healthcare West/French Hospital Medical Center is another major facility (112 beds), that offers nuclear medicine and an open-heart surgery facility. Arroyo Grande Community Hospital is comprised of a surgical unit, transitional care unit, inten-sive care, radiology, cardiac rehabilitation, and one of the most complete sleep diagnostics laboratories in the area.

Crime and safety

Police: The Pismo Beach police department consists of 34 employees, 23 of whom are sworn officers. The Operations Division includes patrol, a K-9 unit, a motorcycle patrols, a bike patrol, and a citizen volunteer patrol. The Citizen's Academy is an excel-lent way to learn more about the daily operations and challenges, where graduates have the opportunity to serve the community by joining the Citizen Volunteer Patrol, a group that provides assistance to the police department during special events and times of increased tourist activity.

Fire: The city of Pismo Beach fire department, in a cooperative fire protection agreement with the California Department of Forestry and Fire Protection, employs a full-time staff including a battalion chief, three fire captains, and three fire apparatus engineers. Additionally, the department employs 20 reserve/paid call firefighters, and 18 seasonal lifeguards. The lifeguards protect the 1.5-mile stretch of beach with four life-guard towers and a patrol vehicle.

Let the good times roll

Family fun: People are often confused by the boundaries between the city of Pis-mo Beach and Pismo State Beach to the south. Activities allowed on each beach are different, so be aware of which sandbox you're playing in. Vehicles, horses, and camp-fires are allowed on Pismo State Beach, but are not allowed on the city's beach. Fishing from the pier generally results in some good catches of red snapper and ling cod. No license is required for pier fishing, making it fun for children of all ages, however licenses are required for deep sea or surf fishing. Dinosaur Cave Park, which covers 11 acres, is where you can observe dolphins, whales, and sea otters, as well as sea and shore birds. The park has been developed with trails and scenic overlooks, as well as off-street parking. A play area, restroom, and amphitheater have been proposed for the near future. Outside of Pismo you can travel to Solvang, a Scandinavian-themed town. Or visit Buellton, home of Anderson's Split Pea Soup. Mineral Springs at nearby Avila Beach are naturally heated mineral springs where you can swim in the pool or take a hot mineral bath.

Sports: Four golf courses are within a 10 minute drive of Pismo. Horseback riding, tennis, swimming, and hiking are year-round activities. Or you can enjoy afternoon bowling at Pismo Bowl.

Arts and entertainment: Spring to October, Art in the Park brings in local artisans including sculptors, jewelers, painters, potters and glass artists to display their crafts while music is performed by local musicians. Visit the galleries in town, such as the Seaside Gallery, which exhibits local talent.

Annual events: Art in the Park, KiteXPO, Annual Classic California Golf Tournament, Pismo Beach Classic Car Show, Fourth of July Fireworks on the Pier & Concert, Stride with the Tide 5K and 10K Fun Run, Annual Country Western Dance Festival, Annual Woodies and Rods Car Show, Annual Clam Festival, Jubilee By The Sea Jazz Festival, Monarch Butterfly Tours, Holiday Harmony and Tree Lighting Ceremony

Community life

The people of Pismo don't wait for the arrival of the monarch butterflies to go outside. Residents are often out walking, keeping an eye on the natural beauty of their area. This maybe a small town in area or population, but it's a great big community when it comes to support and appreciation. The city sponsors educational programs, events, and classes to educate children, adults, and seniors in everything from photography to wine tasting. Here in the "Clam Capital of the World," people come to dig the famed Pismo clam from the sand, and find a coastal haven for themselves.

The environment

Air quality is excellent with constant sea breezes. The Chamber of Commerce is working with a long-term vision in upgrading downtown with streetscapes, including park benches. The city has recently contracted with the California Highway Adoption Company to keep the roads into Pismo clean.

In and around town

Roads and highways: Highway 101

Closest airports: San Luis Obispo Airport provides regional and national service.

Public transportation: There is no public transportation currently available.

Average daily commute: 25 minutes

More Information

City of Pismo Beach
760 Mattie Road
Pismo Beach, CA 93449
805-773-4657
www.pismobeach.org

Lucia Mar Unified School District
602 Orchard Street
Arroyo Grande, CA 93420
805-473-4390
www.luciamar.k12.ca.us

Pismo Beach Chamber of Commerce
581 Dolliver Street
Pismo Beach, CA 93449
805-773-4382
www.pismochamber.com

Pismo Beach Visitor Information Center
581 Dolliver Street
Pismo Beach, CA 93449
805-773-4382
www.classiccalifornia.com

Sacramento, California

California

Sacramento

Pismo Beach

Chino

Vista

Fabulous features

Families who have recently moved to the city of Sacramento have something in common with the explorers of 150 years ago: they've struck gold—technology gold. Greater Sacramento is being populated by Silicon Valley refugees and young entrepreneurs. High-tech companies have poured into a corridor from Sacramento's trendy Old Town to the Sierra foothills.

As for small-town friendliness, you'll find dozens of communities in and around the capital city. From East Sacramento to Elk Grove, these towns boast houses with varying architectural styles and amenities. And with 16 school districts to choose from, parents can match their children's needs to the right environment. After school, there's exciting outdoor recreation to enjoy along the Sacramento delta, such as white-water rafting and windsurfing.

Walking across the Tower Bridge or enjoying a water-taxi ride on the river, it's easy to see why Disney's *Family Life* magazine called Sacramento one of the "Best Places for Vacation Spots for Families." Sperling's *Cities Ranked & Rated* (2004) has Sacramento listed in its Top 100 cities.

Possible drawbacks: Air quality and traffic congestion are the most notable complaints, which is common for large downtown areas. However, it's not the freeway parking-lot commute of Los Angeles (yet).

▶ Local Population: 406,000

▶ County: Sacramento

▶ Population of surrounding metropolitan area: 1,898,300

▶ Region: Northern California

▶ Closest metro area: San Francisco, 91 miles

▶ Median home price: $129,500

▶ Median household income: $38,903

▶ Best reasons to live here: Sacramento is one of California's most affordable big cities, with a stable economy, good job growth, broad range of recreational activities, and a vast choice of housing and neighborhoods.

Climate

Elevation 20'	Average temp. high/low (°F)	Average precipitation rain (")	snow (")	Average no. days precipitation	Average humidity (%)
January	55/40	4.0	0	10	70
April	73/48	1.1	0	5	44
July	93/60	.09	0	0	30
October	79/52	0.9	0	3	37
Number of days 32°F or below: 17			Number of days 90°F or warmer: 77		

Earning a living

Economic outlook: The area's employment base and pay scales continue to grow steadily. Industry is diverse, providing stability and an ever-growing number of employment opportunities. The latest survey information from *infoUSA* showed Sacramento in their Top 10 metro areas, with a 15.7 percent increase from 2000. Growth in education, healthcare, and social services is heading the top percentage of jobs at 19.1 percent. The high-tech industry is still a major player in the area, despite the fallout from the dot-com crash. The unemployment rate is 3.2 percent, well below the national average.

Where the jobs are: As the capital of California, it's no surprise the top employer for Sacramento is the state of California. The rest of the top five employers, listed by the *Sacramento Business Journal* in 2003, are the California State University Sacramento, Intel Corporation, UC Davis Medical Center, and CHW/Mercy Healthcare. Sacramento's private sector economy is diverse, from sole proprietor companies to corporate giants, such as Intel and Hewlett Packard. Service industries and retail supply about 25 percent of the area's job market.

Business opportunities: As of the summer of 2005, a new development of shops and entertainment may be going in at Bradshaw Road and Highway 50, where the Sacramento 6 drive-in movie theater once stood. Sacramento is a centrally located transportation hub, attracting R&D companies, manufacturing concerns, financial institutions, and construction businesses. A great place to look for jobs is at the Employment Development Department of the state of California *(www.caljobs.ca.gov)*.

Local real estate

Market overview: The California housing boom over the past 10 years has hit the Delta valley, where housing developments are blossoming. There is great diversity in the neighborhoods, from older, original ranch-style, to new developments.

Average rent for a two-bedroom apartment: $565 per month

Other areas to consider: Elk Grove, though incorporated in 2000, is rich in history and character. So many tourists have left their hearts in San Francisco that traffic may be difficult to navigate. Driving is rough if it's your first time on those steep hills. This is a fast-paced, diversified city. Activities are everywhere from Pier 39 to Ghirardelli Square, with a list of cultural influences as long as Lombard Street. Housing prices, however, are heartbreaking.

What things cost

ACCRA's national comparisons: Current number are not available. However, it appears that living costs in Sacramento are lower than other major markets in California.

Utilities: Phone: $30 per month; electric: $100 per month; natural gas: $45 per month; water: $30 per month

The tax ax

Sales tax: 7.75 percent

Property tax: Established through Proposition 13 as 1 percent of the purchase price plus limited locally approved bonds. Property tax revenue in Sacramento County alone is anticipated to increase by 11 percent in 2005.

State income tax: 9.3 percent

Making the grade

Public education overview: The 2005 school year will see a new tool of communication for the Sacramento City Unified School District. This high-tech program will allow school administrators to send messages to staff and parents quickly. Parents can provide up to six phone numbers (home, work, cell phone, or relative) for accessibility. This is a progressive program for the school district to involve the parents and keep the lines of communication open. Sacramento County, with 16 school districts, continues to struggle with overcrowding and budget cutbacks, though districts keep coming up with innovative solutions for providing quality education. Their formula seems to be working: 72 percent of graduating seniors go on to higher education, and Sacramento County has one of the lowest dropout rates in the state. The district makes safe schools a priority by fingerprinting new employee candidates. The three largest districts offer a special services program for Native American students who make up 1.4 percent of the student population.

Class size (student to teacher ratio): 22:1

Help for working parents: The district offers before- and after-school childcare on seven elementary campuses.

Boys & Girls Club: There are four centers available in Sacramento.

School year: Begins the end of August and ends in mid-June for traditional schedules. Check year-round school schedules on the district Website. Children must be 5 years old on or before December 2 to enter kindergarten.

Special education/programs for gifted students: Each school district provides special education programs for students up to 22 years old.

Nearby colleges and universities: California State University at Sacramento, University of California at Davis, and the Los Rios Community College District are all near the Sacramento area. The Los Rios nursing program at Sacramento City College, in partnership with Sutter Health, has developed a nursing program where students move seamlessly from community college, to a four-year college, and then into nursing positions throughout the community.

Medical care

Hospitals/medical centers: In the greater Sacramento area you'll find 18 acute-care hospitals. The largest, U.C. Medical Center in Davis (450 bed), has comprehensive emergency services, helicopter transport, cardiac services, kidney/corneal transplants, oncology, otolaryngology, pediatrics, and internal medicine. Equipped for treating major injuries, the hospital has the only trauma center in Sacramento. Three area hospitals are run by Mercy Healthcare Sacramento, two by Sutter Health (including the Sutter Cancer Center), and two by Kaiser-Permanente. The city is also home to Sacramento Women's Health Care Medical Group, Inc., which specializes in obstetrics/gynecology, and the Regional Center for Rehabilitation at American River Hospital.

Specialized care: Shriner's Children's Hospital (80 beds) is a major research center with medical-surgical services and a 25-bed pediatric intensive care unit, focusing on orthopedic and severe burns. Sierra Vista Hospital is an acute-care psychiatric hospital, providing both inpatient and outpatient services for adults and adolescents.

Crime and safety

Police: The Sacramento police department has implemented many programs to encourage the participation of citizens in keeping Sacramento safe. One such program is the Citizens Academy, a 10-week course designed to teach ordinary residents about the criminal justice system. The Community Recruiter program consists of community leaders from neighborhoods, associations, clubs, and businesses who assist the department in seeking out and recruiting police candidates. Another program is the citywide alert system, where the communities can sign up with their e-mail account to receive the latest in crime bulletins.

Fire: The Sacramento fire department is looking to add three new stations in the future. In 2005, the department entered into a partnership with the Wheelchair Foundation and other agencies to provide new wheelchairs to individuals in need.

Let the good times roll

Family fun: Between the American and Sacramento Rivers, 1,000 miles of waterways run through Sacramento, so it's no surprise that water recreation tops the list for outdoor activities. Six Flags Waterworld of Sacramento is home to the largest wave pool in northern California, and attractions such as Shark Attack and Hook's Lagoon. Though an amusement park by day, weddings, reunions, and more can take place under Fairytale Town's twinkling lights after hours. Can you imagine having your child's birthday party at King Arthur's castle? Beautiful landscaping and seasonal color surround 27 fairytale and nursery rhyme play sets. Step back into the Gold Rush days at Old Sacramento. Visit 53 historic buildings on 28 acres along the river. It's a fun place to relax, eat, and shop in the antique stores. Just a short drive away are exciting recreation opportunities in the Napa Valley wine country, San Francisco metropolitan area, Lake Tahoe, and Yosemite National Park.

Sports: Major league sports include the Sacramento Kings (NBA), the San Francisco 49'ers and Oakland Raiders (NFL); San Francisco Giants and Oakland Athletics (MLB). The nearest NHL hockey team is the San Jose Sharks. You don't want to miss the action of the Pacific Coast League Sacramento Rivercats playing at Raley Field or the fast pace of the Sacramento Monarch's women's basketball.

Arts and entertainment: Five major art organizations in the Greater Sacramento area include the Crocker Art Museum, the Sacramento Ballet Company, the Sacramento Theater Company, the Sacramento Opera Association, and the Sacramento Symphony. Yet more than 150 other organizations provide cultural and artistic entertainment in dance, music, literature, and theater. Sacramento has numerous museums including the Silver Wings Aviation Museum, and the California State Railroad Museum.

Annual events: Camellia Festival, Sacramento Jazz Jubilee, Folsom Rodeo, International Youth Soccer Festival, California State Fair, California International Marathon, and Art Second Saturdays.

Community life

The Volunteer Center of Sacramento has the scoop on volunteer opportunities in the area. Among the agencies relying on community volunteers are Meals on Wheels, Sacramento's Children's Home, Stanford Home Settlement, the Big Brother/Big Sister Program, and the Red Cross. Many cultural volunteer opportunities abound with the opera, symphony, and Sacramento History Museum.

The environment

Sacramento is concerned both about its air and land environment. Air quality is continuously monitored and the city encourages greener and more efficient building developments for the future. Recycling programs include regular curbside pickups and the education of young people how to be more environmentally aware.

In and around town

Roads and highways: I-5, I-80, state highway 99, 50

Closest airports: Sacramento International Airport is 12 miles northwest of downtown. The Sacramento Executive Airport is for private planes, while the Mather Airport in Rancho Cordova and Franklin Field are public use airports.

Public transportation: Regional transit includes bus routes and 26.9 miles of light-rail, covering over 400 square-miles of service area.

Average daily commute: 30 minutes

More Information

City of Sacramento
730 I Street
Sacramento, CA 95814
9116-808-5407
www.cityofsacramento.org

Sacramento City Unified School District
5735 47th Avenue
Sacramento, CA 95824
916-643-7400
www.scusd.edu

Sacramento Chamber of Commerce
917 Seventh Street
Sacramento, CA 95814
916-552-6808
www.metrochamber.org

Discovery Museum
3615 Auburn Boulevard
Sacramento, CA 95821
916-575-3941
www.thediscovery.org

Sacramento Philharmonic Orchestra
3400 3rd Avenue
Sacramento, CA 95817
916-732-9045
www.sacphil.org

Sacramento Zoo
3930 West Land Park Drive
Sacramento, CA 95822
916-264-5885
www.saczoo.com

Sacramento Rivercats
400 Ballpark Drive
West Sacramento, CA 95691
916-371-HITS
www.rivercats.com

Pacific Gas and Electric
5555 Florin-Perkins Road
Sacramento, CA 95826
800-743-5000
www.pge.com

Pacific Bell
4111 Marconi Avenue
Sacramento, CA 95821
916-972-2433
www.public.pacbell.net

City of Sacramento Utilities
730 I Street
Sacramento, CA 95814
916-808-5454
www.cityofsacramento.org

8 ▷ Vista, California

Fabulous features

Although she turned 40 in 2003, Vista isn't looking her age. The city is only seven miles from the Pacific Ocean, and seems to have it all. Why else would the population have nearly tripled in the past 20 years? Who wouldn't want to be in the "climatic wonderland of the United States," where the average daily temperature is 74° Fahrenheit? Children here go to top schools and have their pick of fun recreational activities. Vista boasts six times the national average number of parks within its 18 square mile border.

And speaking of schools, Vista has an excellent school system, that was made even better with the passing of a $140 million construction bond in March of 2002. Students often seek transfers into Vista's high schools because of its strong International Baccalaureate program.

Strict zoning has kept Vista's rolling hills and pleasant rural surroundings intact. Housing is readily available, with open designs and lush California vegetation. The days are picture perfect here, so head to the gorgeous state parks and beaches, or even go shopping in Mexico. If you're lucky, there might be a Vista on your horizon.

Possible drawbacks: All roads lead to Vista, but with accessibility also comes traffic congestion during rush hours. Weekday commuters can spend about 45 minutes traveling to San Diego.

▶ Local Population: 94,000

▶ County: San Diego

▶ Population of surrounding metropolitan area: 3,000,000

▶ Region: Southern California

▶ Closest metro area: San Diego, 35 miles

▶ Median home price: $487,000

▶ Median household income: $48,373

▶ Best reasons to live here: The absolutely perfect climate, strong job and business growth, great schools, wonderful outdoor recreation, and a strong community spirit.

Climate

Elevation 340'	Average temp. high/low (°F)	Average precipitation rain (")	snow (")	Average no. days precipitation	Average humidity (%)
January	68/45	3.1	0	7	58
April	72/50	0.9	0	5	59
July	82/61	0.2	0	0	66
October	78/56	0.4	0	2	64
Number of days 32°F or below: 0			Number of days 90°F or warmer: 3		

Earning a living

Economic outlook: The Vista Business Park will continue to grow over the next several years, adding square footage to the existing park, and increasing employment to approximately 19,000 employees working in the 650 national and international companies. Vista's retail sectors continue to look strong and, with the completion of the existing Vista Village project, should help generate 700 jobs and more than $500,000 in sales tax revenues. Several other retail projects are in the works and will be under construction in the near future. The city is revitalizing several historic areas, such as South Santa Fe and Mercantile, and hopes to develop additional residential and commercial uses for the area. The unemployment rate is 3.5 percent and expected to remain low.

Where the jobs are: The majority of businesses are manufacturing, education, and government. The largest employers are Vista Unified School District, Watkins Manufacturing Corporation, and the San Diego Superior Court.

Business opportunities: Vista has experienced the greatest economic boom in its history in retail sales and employment growth. The city's success in luring anchor stores such as Costco, Wal-Mart, Sam's Club, and Target Greatland has resulted in impressive sales tax revenues. Vista is easily accessible to more than 500,000 people living within a 10-mile radius. The Vista Economic Development Association notes their success with a 1,200-acre site developed in South Vista called the Vista Business Park. Initially, the association projected a 25-year time-table to develop the Business Park. But by 1999, original expectations were exceeded by a remarkable 10 years!

Local real estate

Market overview: Housing opportunities range from garden apartments to ocean view estates. Condominiums average between $170,000 and $290,000, while single-family home prices range from $250,000 to more than $1,000,000.

Average rent for a two-bedroom apartment: $950 per month

Other areas to consider: Camp Pendleton is a Marine Base of 200 square miles. San Marcos is a highly educated community with heart. San Diego, a strong tourism base with Sea World and the San Diego Zoo, brings in many new families. Most relocate because of the mild climate and great schools. From downtown skyscrapers to suburbs in rolling hills, the fresh air and cleanliness of San Diego will reel you in.

What things cost

ACCRA's national comparisons: Overall living costs for the nearby San Diego area are 45 percent above the national average. The major culprit is housing at a high 116 percent above the national average, followed by health care at 19 percent above, groceries at 14 percent above, and miscellaneous goods and services at 16 percent above. Only utilities are below average at 4.5 percent.

Utilities: Phone: $35 per month; water: $53 per month; electricity: $60 per month; natural gas: $40 per month

The tax ax

Sales tax: 7.75 percent

Property tax: Established through Proposition 13 as 1 percent of the purchase price plus limited locally approved bonds.

State income tax: Varies from 1 to 9.3 percent based upon income level.

Making the grade

Public education overview: The Vista Unified School District services 18 elementary schools, six middle schools, and six high schools. One of the many shining stars in this district is the commitment to technology. With more than 1,300 computers in the district and access to the Internet, more than 700 staff have e-mail accounts. Several schools develop and maintain their own Webpages. The school district has published their Educational Technology Plan. In 2002, the city passed a school construction bond supporting the construction of three new elementary schools, and upgrading of all school facilities. Several schools have earned National Blue Ribbon Award and California Distinguished School honors. The district offers a fully implemented International Baccalaureate program in the high schools. Ongoing programs such as Resolving Conflict Creatively Program are presented in a majority of classrooms. After–school tutoring is offered for students who need assistance with learning.

Class size (student to teacher ratio): 22:1

Help for working parents: The Children's Initiative provides after–school care in the San Diego County area.

Boys & Girls Club: There are two centers currently available.

School year: Mid-August to mid-June, check with schools whether single-track, modified traditional calendar or three–track year round schedule. Children must be 5 years old on or before December 2 to begin kindergarten.

Special education/programs for gifted students: The gifted and talented program is available for gifted and talented students. English language development and special educations programs are offered. "Advancement Via Individual Determination" is an elective class for students who would like to prepare for college.

Nearby colleges and universities: California State University at San Marcos, Mira Costa College, National University, Palomar College, and the University of Phoenix are all located in the Vista area.

Medical care

Hospitals/medical centers: Vista has access to some of the most outstanding healthcare facilities in the United States. Tri-City Medical Center, a 385-bed, acute-care district hospital offers a full range of primary care and medical-surgical services including emergency medicine, cardiovascular, and imaging services. Tri-City Medical Center has been designated as one of "100 Top Hospitals: Regional Benchmarks for Success" three years in a row by HCIA Mercer.

Specialized Care: The Vista Community Clinic is a private facility that provides quality healthcare where economic, social, or cultural barriers exist. The center has a full spectrum of both treatment and prevention services.

Crime and safety

Police: Although overall crime rates have risen slightly in the San Diego County area, Vista's crime rates have decreased due to the close working relationship between the sheriff's department and the Vista community. In addition to the main station located in the San Diego courthouse, the Vista sheriff's department maintains three neighborhood policing teams. Volunteer participation throughout the community is seen in the senior patrol, reserve deputy, and Explorer cadet programs. Vista has managed to achieve the greatest decreases in crime during the last six years of any of the 18 cities in the county of San Diego.

Fire: The Vista fire department has 63 suppression personnel divided among three shifts, including three battalion chiefs. Services include: firefighting, rescue, hazardous materials incident responses, and emergency medical services at the EMT and Paramedic level, with emergency transport. Tips on wildfires and wildfire season are a must-read for residents who live in the surrounding hills.

Let the good times roll

Family fun: Vista's central location offers quick accessibility to the Pacific ocean, mountains, Mexico, and world-famous attractions including the San Diego Zoo, Wild Animal Park, SeaWorld, Legoland, and Disneyland. Buena Vista Park and Guajome Regional Park are just two of the many places to play. Or get wet at the Wave Waterpark, the only family aquatic center in North San Diego County. Krikorian Premier Theaters, a magnificent 16-screen stadium-seating venue, opened in late 2003 and is part of the Vista Village Center, a variety of popular retail stores and restaurants. A farmers market is held each Saturday.

Sports: Sports fans travel 40 minutes to San Diego to watch professional games, such as the San Diego Padres (MLB), and the San Diego Chargers (NFL). Just 90 minutes away is Los Angeles, with additional professional teams as well as college sports. More than 20 public and private golf courses are located within a 45-minute drive.

Arts and entertainment: The Moonlight Amphitheatre, and the recently renovated Avo Playhouse, draw thousands of Southern Californians each year to experience award-winning productions. The Rancho Buena Vista Adobe provides students and visitors with hands-on educational and research programs of local history. The Antique Gas & Steam Engine Museum evokes nostalgic memories of rural lifestyles and family traditions.

Annual events: Highland Games at Brengle Terrace Park, Fourth of July at Brengle Terrace Park, Moonlight Stage Productions, Easter Egg Hunt at Brengle Terrace Park, Holiday Parade, Annual Duck Race, and the local farmers market.

Community life

Vista residents take a very active role in community life. Rotary, Soroptimist, and Elks organizations are popular, as is the Women's Club. The Public Arts Commission sponsored a city-wide utility box beautification project called "Vista in Bloom." The project involved painting designated utility boxes in Vista. Local artists designed and painted the boxes.

The environment

The Volunteer Vista Program is an active group and supports a variety of areas and issues. Coastal breezes help keep the air quality clean, while minimal manufacturing in the area helps to keep pollution down.

In and around town

Roads and highways: I-5, I-15, state highway 78, 76

Closest airports: San Diego International Airport is 37 miles south. John Wayne Airport in Irvine is 45 miles north, and Los Angeles International Airport is 93 miles north. Nearby Palomar and Oceanside Municipal airports handle smaller planes and provide frequent flights to Los Angeles.

Public transportation: The North County Transit District provides bus service.

Average daily commute: 26 minutes

More Information

Vista City Hall
600 Eucalyptus Avenue
Vista, CA 92085
760-726-1340
www.ci.vista.ca.us

Vista Unified School District
1234 Arcadia Avenue
Vista, CA 92084
760-726-2170
www.vusd.k12.ca.us

Vista Chamber of Commerce
201 Washington Street
Vista, CA 92084
760-726-1122
www.vistachamber.org

Moonlight Stage Productions
PO Box 1988
Vista, CA 92085
760-724-2110
www.moonlightstage.com

The Wave Waterpark
161 Recreation Drive
Vista, CA 92085
760-940-9283
www.thewavewaterpark.com

San Diego Gas and Electric Company
8330 Century Park CP31D
San Diego, CA 92123
800-411-7343
www.sdge.com

Southwestern Bell
101 West Broadway, Suite 1440
San Diego, CA 92101
800-750-2355
www.sbc.com

Vista Irrigation District
1391 Engineer Street
Vista, CA 92081
760-597-3100
www.vid-h2o.org

Colorado Springs, Colorado

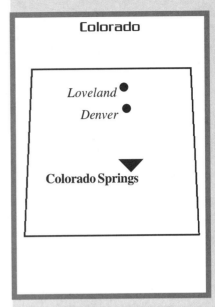

Colorado

Loveland
Denver
Colorado Springs

Fabulous features

Once known as the "City of Millionaires" because of the discovery of gold in nearby Cripple Creek, Colorado Springs lies at the foot of the majestic Pikes Peak. The city is over 6,000 feet in elevation, so give yourself time to get used to the thin air.

The area's low cost of living, stunning scenery, excellent sports, and recreational opportunities make this location a great place to live. Sperling's *Cities, Ranked & Rated* listed Colorado Springs as 18th, an excellent overall ranking. The city was ranked eighth on the "Best Cities for Women" list in the *Ladies' Home Journal* of 2002.

The Pikes Peak region plays host to about 5.4 million visitors yearly, which generates more than $740 million in revenue. At the southeast end of the city you'll find the Colorado Springs World Arena and Ice Hall. Home to the Colorado College Tigers hockey team, this shining star is touted as one of the finest training facilities in the world. Imagine taking lessons in the home of the United States National Short Track Speed Skating team! This entertainment area houses more than just an ice rink, it's calendar is filled with events from concerts to car shows.

Possible drawbacks: The high altitude may not be the best for someone who has trouble breathing. The job market is highly competitive, so you should probably secure a job before you move here.

▶ Local Population: 373,328

▶ County: El Paso

▶ Population of surrounding metropolitan area: 541,069

▶ Region: Central Colorado

▶ Closest metro area: Denver, 70 miles

▶ Median home price: $147,100

▶ Median household income: $50,646

▶ Best reasons to live here: Stunning scenery, a low overall cost of living, thriving arts community, and numerous schools, colleges, and universities.

Climate

Elevation 6,008'	Average temp. high/low (°F)	Average precipitation rain (")	snow (")	Average no. days precipitation	Average humidity (%)
January	36/11	0.4	5.2	5	46
April	54/27	1.9	6.7	8	35
July	80/49	3.1	0	13	39
October	60/30	0.9	3.4	5	37
Number of days 32°F or below: 162			Number of days 90°F or warmer: 15		

Earning a living

Economic outlook: Home to thriving businesses, high-tech companies, military installations, and nonprofit organizations, the Springs is proud of its healthy economy and high quality of life. The latest information from *infoUSA's* shows Colorado Springs in the Top 10 metro areas for job growth, showing a 14.7 percent increase from 2000. The military provides the area with a stable base of economic activity, employing defense, civil service, and military personnel. Colorado Springs has a labor force with better education and better training than the national average. The labor force growth rate for the next several years is expected to grow at more than 2 percent per year, creating over 4,000 jobs annually.

Where the jobs are: Major employment falls in military, tourism, space technology, printing, publishing, and manufacturing. Keep your eye on the Greater Colorado Springs Economic Development Corporation (EDC) (*www.coloradosprings.org*) for industry information. Over the next five years, EDC-assisted companies will generate more than 2,000 job opportunities with average salaries of $52,000 per year.

Business opportunities: High-tech companies continue to rule dominate Colorado Springs. The area's nickname, Silicon Mountain, means a lot more than looking over at Pike's Peak. Progressive Auto Insurance plans to build a 150,000 square foot data center, next to where the company has recently completed a 300,000 square foot call center.

Local real estate

Market overview: Houses generally have basements and front porches; ranch-style or two-story styles are available, and most are made of wood, stucco, or brick. Just make sure you have lots of windows to enjoy the scenery.

Average rent for a two-bedroom apartment: $650 per month

Other areas to consider: In southern Colorado you'll find Pueblo, known as the Home of Heroes, which is a great place for families. Fort Carson is home base for many of the country's finest army personnel. Denver is known as the mile-high city, because the elevation of the city is exactly 5,280 feet above sea-level. Colorado is rather dry, so drink plenty of liquids.

What things cost

ACCRA's national comparisons: Overall living costs are about 4 percent below the national average. Health care costs and transportation are 4 and 5 percent above the average, but the best news is housing is 5 percent below and utilities are 18 percent below the national averages. Miscellaneous good and services are approximately 5 percent below the average.

Utilities: Total of $181.74 per month, include electricity, natural gas, and water. Numbers are based on January 2005 billing information from Colorado Springs Utilities.

The tax ax

Sales tax: 6.4 percent

Property tax: $7.20 (est. property taxes paid per $1,000 of market value)

State income tax: 4.63 percent

Making the grade

Public education overview: A quality school district knows how to motivate students. Colorado Springs School District 11, with the Coca-Cola Bottling Company, gives scholarships to qualifying students each year, and one deserving high school student gets a new car. Qualifying means maintaining a 3.5 or above grade point average and having perfect attendance. This year, 131 high school students and 80 middle school students qualified to receive scholarship checks and savings bonds. Palmer High School was selected as a 2005 Hewlett Packard "Teaching for Technology" grant recipient. The school will receive an award package valued at more than $35,000. Midland International Elementary School has been officially authorized to offer the International Baccalaureate Primary Years Program. Colorado has the greatest number of schools authorized to offer the International Baccalaureate program in the United States. Buena Vista Elementary School is the first public Montessori School in Colorado Springs. The school will serve neighborhood children.

Class size(student to teacher ratio): 18:1

Help for working parents: Before- and after-school care is available at most elementary schools. Head Start is available at nine of the elementary schools.

Boys & Girls Club info: There are seven centers that serve the area.

School year: Mid-August to end of May. Children must be 5 years old on or before September 15 to enter kindergarten.

Special education/programs for gifted students: A gifted and talented program is available in the district. Special education is available in the schools, with tutoring services provided only when the direct special education services in the school are not sufficient to meet the student's needs.

Nearby colleges and universities: Colorado College is a private liberal arts and sciences college. The University of Colorado at Colorado Springs was ranked sixth among public master's universities by *U.S. News & World Report* (2005). The university has ranked in the top honors of this report for the last three years.

Medical care

Hospitals/medical centers: Memorial Hospital is a 477-bed general hospital owned by the city of Colorado Springs offering a wide range of services such as treatment for cancer, heart disease, and trauma. They've recently expanded their women's and emergency services. The Children's Hospital within Memorial offers a full range of services covering every healthcare need a child could have. Amenities such as private rooms and a toddler playroom are available. A Ronald McDonald House nearby provides support and lodging for families of hospitalized children who live out of the area. Penrose-St. Francis Health Services offers emergency, medical, and surgical services, as well as specialty services such as the Penrose Cancer Center.

Specialized care: Cedar Springs Behavioral Center offers inpatient and outpatient services for mental health issues, as well as substance and chemical dependency.

Crime and safety

Police: The Colorado Springs police department has a multitude of crime prevention services for the community, such as the Internet Crimes Against Children task force, Child Occupant Protection Program with car seat safety classes, neighborhood watch, and more. This proactive department has an air support unit with three helicopters to monitor safety from the air. The canine unit has seven handler teams ready to answer a call for help. The department also has a Community Alerts System in place to further enhance communications with the community.

Fire: The Colorado Springs fire department has 20 fire stations to protect and serve the community. The department has 18 companies specialized in emergency medical services. They have 10 wildland brush pumpers for fighting in areas of shrub. A heavy rescue truck provides special services, in case of cave-ins or building collapse rescues.

Let the good times roll

Family fun: If enjoying the scenery is not enough, the list of activities could be a book by itself. Just west of Colorado Springs is Old Colorado City, a historic and quaint shopping district. There's also the Colorado Springs Children's Museum. The Pikes Peak Cog Railway takes visitors on a trip to the 14,110 foot summit. Visit the Manitou Cliff Dwellings, just five miles west. The 940-acre Garden of the Gods Park is a perfect place for a nature walk or a picnic. The Flying W is a working cattle ranch with various museum buildings, rides, gift shops, cowboy "grub," and live country music. The North Slope Recreation Area at Pikes Peak includes opportunities for fishing, mountain biking, boating, and hiking.

Sports: There are professional sports teams in nearby Denver, including the Colorado Rockies (MLB), the Denver Broncos (NFL), the Nuggets (NBA), and the Colorado Avalanche (NHL). Closer to home, the Sky Sox, the Rockies' minor league team, play at Sox Stadium.

Arts and entertainment: The nationally-known Colorado Springs Symphony Orchestra plays year-round in the Pikes Peak Center. The Colorado Dance Theatre hosts a series of nationally recognized ballet, jazz and modern dance companies. The Fine Arts Center Repertory Theatre presents Broadway productions, and the arts center itself features collections of Native American and Hispanic art.

Annual events: Hummingbird Festival, Colorado Balloon Classic, Colorado Springs Jazz Festival, Territory Days, Imagination Celebration, the Fabulous Fourth, the Great Pikes Peak Cowboy Poetry Gathering

Community life

Colorado Springs is very focused on volunteerism. Thousands of people help the area churches, schools, government, hospitals, service groups, and nonprofit organizations every year. Volunteers in Parks help in the enhancements and support of the parks in the city. Various programs include Adopt-A-Park, Springs in Bloom, and Visitor Center Volunteers.

The environment

One of the great pleasures of living here is the fact that water comes straight from the sparkling snow of the Rocky Mountains. Colorado Springs gets its drinking water from Pikes Peak, as well as from snowmelt piped in from the continental divide. The water filtration and sewage treatment facilities meet or exceed all federal requirements. In 2005, drought measures were taken and residents were allowed to water their lawns only two days a week.

In and around town

Roads and highways: Interstate 25, US 85/87, 24, state highway 83, 94, 115, 122

Closest airports: Colorado Springs Airport has 100 flights daily.

Public transportation: The Colorado Springs City Bus provides scheduled bus service for the metropolitan service area.

Average daily commute: 19 minutes

More Information

City of Colorado Springs
107 North Nevada Avenue
Colorado Springs, CO 80901
719-385-2489
www.springsgov.com

Colorado Springs School District 11
1115 North El Paso Street
Colorado Springs, CO 80903
719-520-2000
www.d11.org

Greater Colorado Springs Chamber of Commerce
2 North Cascade Avenue, Suite 110
Colorado Springs, CO 80903
719-635-1551
www.coloradospringschamber.org

Colorado Springs Convention and Visitor's Bureau
515 South Cascade Boulevard
Colorado Springs, CO 80903
800-DO-VISIT
www.coloradosprings-travel.com

Colorado Springs Utilities
Customer Care Center
111 South Cascade Avenue
Colorado Springs, CO 80903
800-238-5434
www.csu.org

Loveland, Colorado

10

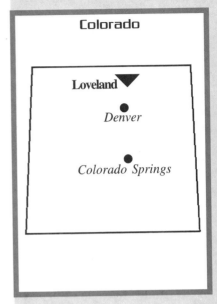

Fabulous features

Located at the foot of the Rocky Mountains, Loveland is billed as the "Arts and Hearts" capital of Colorado. Loveland was voted the number one place in the nation to "Revitalize your Life" by *AARP* magazine. Becoming a nationally renowned center for art (even the parks have bronze sculptures,) Loveland has been rated among the top eight "Great Art Destinations" in the United States by *U.S. Art* magazine. Thousands of people from around the world travel to Loveland the second weekend of August for the acclaimed Sculpture in the Park art show and sale, and on Valentine's Day, the post office is inundated with people who want to get a special Loveland stamp on their Valentine's Day cards.

Money magazine chose the Loveland region as one of the "Best Places to Live" in 2002. *Forbes* magazine ranked the Loveland area 49th on their list of "Best Places for 2002." And the Milken Institute selected Loveland as one of "America's Top Rated Smaller Cities" for the year 2002. Even the *Readers Digest* of 1997 has them ranked third on their "Top 50 Places to Raise a Family" list.

Possible drawbacks: The college population from Fort Collins has discovered the lower housing costs here, and have begun settling in the area. This creates a more transient culture. Traffic is also a growing concern.

▶ Local Population: 50,608

▶ County: Larimer

▶ Population of surrounding metropolitan area: 251,494

▶ Region: Northern Colorado

▶ Closest metro area: Denver, 46 miles

▶ Median home price: $155,900

▶ Median household income: $47,119

▶ Best reasons to live here: Incredible scenery, excellent schools, a growing economy, cultural amenities, and a tremendous sense of community spirit.

Climate

Elevation 4,982'	Average temp. high/low (°F)	Average precipitation		Average no. days precipitation	Average humidity (%)
		rain (")	snow (")		
January	42/14	0.4	6.3	6	51
April	61/32	2.1	8.9	10	47
July	87/55	1.7	0	11	38
October	65/34	1.0	3.7	6	42
Number of days 32°F or below: 163			Number of days 90°F or warmer: 32		

Earning a living

Economic outlook: During the first quarter of 2000, every major industry sector represented in Loveland experienced growth, with service, manufacturing, government, retail trade, and construction seeing the greatest expansion. The community has a diverse and highly-educated workforce. According to a new study by *American City Business Journals*, annual incomes in the Fort Collins/Loveland metropolitan statistical area grew by more than 180 percent between 1982 and 2002, the latest year for which official figures are available. The study considered not only the overall 20-year growth rate of incomes, but also the consistency of the growth rate within the 20-year period.

Where the jobs are: Agilent Technologies, Poudre Valley Health Systems, the Thompson School District, Larimer County, Wal-Mart Distribution Center, McKee Medical Center, and Woodward Governor

Business opportunities: The healthcare industry will see a new level of care when the Medical Center of the Rockies, a trauma level II hospital, is completed in 2007. Poudre Valley Health Systems will open its second Larimer County Hospital, located in the northeastern part of Loveland, in the fall of 2007. Group Publishing recently completed construction of a new building, an expansion of the publishing company's current campus.

Local real estate

Market overview: Loveland continues to offer high quality housing in a competitive market. New housing developments are being constructed in all corners of city. Home values are steadily increasing.

Average rent for a two-bedroom apartment: $746 per month

Other areas to consider: Fort Collins is the friendly, dependable, next-door neighbor. A great deal of agricultural business is done there, and almost everyone has a pick-up truck with a dog in the back. Boulder sits against the Rocky Mountains, and is a haven for high-tech industry and quality living, however it also has a large number of college students from the University of Colorado. Denver is known as the mile-high city, because the elevation of the city is exactly 5,280 feet above sea-level. Greeley is also within a short drive, and is home to the University of Northern Colorado.

What things cost

ACCRA's national comparisons: Overall, the cost of living is approximately 8 percent below the national average. Housing runs at 16 percent below average, with utilities 7 percent below average. Grocery items and transportation run about the same 4 percent below average. The only above average cost is health care at 11 percent above the national average.

Utilities: Electricity: $50 per month; natural gas: $40 per month; phone: $25 per month

The tax ax

Sales tax: 6.7 percent

Property tax: $7.20 (est. property taxes paid per $1,000 of market value)

State income tax: 4.63 percent

Making the grade

Public education overview: Loveland is in the Thompson School District, and has five high schools, five middle schools, and 19 elementary schools. Students can attend their choice of schools, as long as space and programs are available, and their parents agree to provide transportation. The district's Colorado Student Assessment Program test scores exceeded the state average at every grade level in 2003. Thompson students were awarded more than $12 million in post-secondary scholarships in 2004. More than 99 percent of Thompson's elementary and 91 percent of its secondary teachers are teaching the subject in which they received their degrees. In 2003, seven athletic teams received the Colorado High School Activities Association academic achievement award for having cumulative grade point averages of 3.59 or better. The Loveland High School marching band took the state 4A title in the fall of 2003 and 2004.

Class size (student to teacher ratio): 17:1

Help for working parents: Seven Early Childhood and Head Start Centers are available. All Early Childhood Centers have a Head Start program.

Boys & Girls Club: One center is available.

School year: Third week of August to the end of May. Children must be 5 years old on or before October 1 to enter kindergarten.

Special education/programs for gifted students: Gifted and talented programs exist in all Thompson schools.

Nearby colleges and universities: Loveland enjoys easy access to the state's three largest universities: Colorado State University in Fort Collins, the University of Northern Colorado in Greeley, and the University of Colorado at Boulder. Two community colleges also serve the Loveland area.

Medical care

Hospitals/medical centers: The McKee Medical Center (107 beds) has served as the only full-service hospital for more than 26 years. McKee Medical Center offers medical, obstetrical, pediatric, orthopedic, surgical, and critical care. McKee has the only labor, delivery, recovery, and postpartum suites in Northern Colorado. McKee Medical Center recently expanded by adding 124,000 square feet to their facility. Skyline Center for Health is a 79,000 square foot, $21 million medical complex located in east Loveland. Skyline was built to improve healthcare access and convenience for local residents. The new medical center offers an outpatient surgery center, an endoscopy center, a medical imaging center, MRI services, community urgent care, pediatric services, physical therapy, laboratory services, gastroenterology services, and physician offices.

Specialized care: When completed, the Medical Center of the Rockies will be a 570,000 square foot, five story, 134-bed regional hospital specializing in cardiac and trauma care. The Medical Center of the Rockies is scheduled to open in early 2007.

Crime and safety

Police: Loveland enjoys one of the lowest crime rates in the state of Colorado. The Loveland police department is nationally accredited and committed to community-oriented policing. Programs such as Colorado Watch Your Car, Citizen Academy, Santa Cops and Loveland Community Night are part of the crime prevention process. Patrol divisions include K-9, SWAT, a mounted unit, and a bicycle unit.

Fire: The Loveland fire and rescue department is a combination department that utilizes both career and volunteer firefighters. The staff consists of 58 career members and 80 volunteer members. The department also provides emergency medical services, dive rescue, hazardous materials, auto extrication, and high angle rope rescue.

Let the good times roll

Family fun: Right in Loveland's backyard is the Larimer County Parks and Open Space. Protected and cared for by staff and more then 2,000 volunteers, Loveland's county space includes the Devil's Backbone area and Carter Lake. Three golf courses (Cattail Creek Golf Course, Mariana Butte, and The Olde Course) are available, or you can visit the Chilson Recreation Center and enjoy the recreation facility for fitness, aquatic, and court sports. Outdoor swimming is at the Winona swimming pool or Lake Loveland beach. As the "Gateway to the Rockies," Loveland is nestled in a valley at the mouth of the beautiful Big Thompson Canyon. Rocky Mountain National Park and Trail Ridge Road are just a short drive away. For heart pumping excitement, take Trail Ridge Road over the continental divide. It's the highest paved road in the United States. It's more than 12,000 feet elevation at its highest point, so don't look down!

Arts and entertainment: Cultural events include the community choral, theatrical, and musical groups. There are free concerts throughout the summer at different locations. In the heart of downtown, the award-winning Loveland Museum is home to the past and the present. The Historic Rialto Theater, completely renovated to its original 1920 decor, is a centerpiece in downtown Loveland.

Sports: Northern Colorado is the place to be for great sports action. The Budweiser Events Center is home to the Colorado Eagles (CHL). The center is also home to the Colorado Chill (NWBL). And if you need the big leagues, Denver is home to the Denver Broncos (NFL), the Denver Nuggets (NBA), the Colorado Avalanche (NHL), the Colorado Rockies (MLB), and Colorado Rapids (MLS).

Annual events: Fourth of July festival, Sculpture in the Park, Sculpture Invitational, Art in the Park, Larimer County Fair, Corn Roast Festival

Community life

Loveland residents really reflect their town's name, by spending a lot of their time volunteering. Whether it's with the schools, seniors, or the fire department, their hours of commitment equal a ton of community spirit. The city of Loveland, Thompson School District, McKee Medical Center, United Way of Loveland in Berthoud-Estes Park, Volunteers of America, Senior Volunteer Program, and the House of Neighborly Services jointly recognize outstanding volunteers from the Loveland community.

The environment

In May of each year the community pulls together with the Parks and Recreation Department for River Cleanup Week. Residents can buy recycle bin wheel kits for only $5, which attach easily to the bottom of trash bins, so there's no more lugging and carrying bins to the curb. At the Loveland recycle center, they take old phone books, batteries, broken appliances, and more.

In and around town

Roads and highways: I-25, US 287, 34

Closest airports: The Fort Collins/Loveland Airport is a local airport. The Denver International Airport provides service to the rest of the United States and the world.

Public transportation: City of Loveland Transit offers a fixed route bus transportation Monday through Saturday.

Average daily commute: 18 minutes

More Information

City of Loveland
500 East Third Street
Loveland, CO 80537
970-962-2000
www.ci.loveland.co.us

Loveland Chamber of Commerce
5400 Stone Creek Circle
Loveland, CO 80538
970-667-6311
www.loveland.org

Thompson School District
800 South Taft Avenue
Loveland, CO 80537
970-613-5008
www.thompson.k12.co.us

Electric and Water Utilities
500 East 3rd Street
Loveland, CO
970 962-2111
970-962-2000
www.ci.loveland.co.us

Loveland Daily Reporter-Herald
201 East 5th Street
Loveland, CO
970-669-5050
www.lovelandfyi.com

Coral Springs, Florida

11

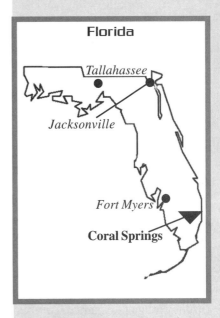

Florida

Tallahassee

Jacksonville

Fort Myers

Coral Springs

Fabulous features

Just as with a fine wine, some places get better with age. Coral Springs won the 2004 "Florida City of Excellence," the first award of its kind from the Florida League of Cities. This only highlights the city's well-deserved reputation for excellent schools, parks, and neighborhoods. With over a third of the population under the age of 18, Coral Springs is a young and thriving community.

Situated midway between Miami and West Palm Beach, Coral Springs is at the epicenter of Florida's growth. Since 1980, its population has increased by more than 150 percent. Today the community is active (about 600 organized teams play every competitive sport,) and a safe place to live (crime is the lowest of any city in the state with the same population). Both Fort Laudedale and the ocean are approximately 30 minutes away.

Coral Springs is unique among Florida cities because the city operates not like a government agency, but more like a business, with the residents as their stakeholders. They want the community to have a say in what takes places in Coral Springs. And it's working. Part of the city's mission statement is "to live, work, and raise a family." How fabulous is that?

Possible drawbacks: Florida summers are hot, humid, and rainy. Adjustment periods vary, but the first year is usually the worst for newcomers.

▶ Local Population: 126,711

▶ County: Broward

▶ Population of surrounding metropolitan area: 1,711,269

▶ Region: Southeast Florida

▶ Closest metro area: Miami, 23 miles

▶ Median home price: $267,795

▶ Median household income: $62,017

▶ Best reasons to live here: It's a successful planned community with beautiful neighborhoods, award-winning parks, endless family recreation, and great public schools.

Climate

Elevation 13'	Average temp. high/low (°F)	Average precipitation rain (")	Average precipitation snow (")	Average no. days precipitation	Average humidity (%)
January	76/59	3.0	0	8	59
April	82/67	3.9	0	7	55
July	90/76	6.6	0	15	64
October	86/72	6.3	0	13	63
Number of days 32°F or below: 0			Number of days 90°F or warmer: 30		

Earning a living

Economic outlook: The current job market is strong in all areas, from professional services to distribution and technology. Some commercial land remains to be developed. An innovative concept in the city has been "commercial condominiums." Using the condos as office space has been a boon for both the developer as well as the business owner. Cumber Professional Park and the Coral Springs Professional Campus are two examples of this new trend in Coral Springs, which probably contributed to the reasons *Money* magazine named Coral Springs to its 2004 "Hottest Towns" list.

Where the jobs are: Alliance Entertainment and First Data Merchant Services are big employers in the Coral Springs area.

Business opportunities: Redevelopment is the key word in Coral Springs. With a new downtown project and future redevelopment plans, new opportunities are presenting themselves in the form of redevelopment, technology, professional, and educational services. The Economic Development Foundation has been working very closely with the city and the developer of the "downtown Coral Springs" project. These opportunities will assist the city in moving economic development to a new level of competitiveness, and significantly increase the ability to recruit new companies to Coral Springs.

Local real estate

Market overview: The Florida look here is concrete block with stucco, although two-story models can be found.

Average rent for a two-bedroom apartment: $1,100 per month

Other areas to consider: Further north, Boca Raton has a Golden Bell Education Foundation to support the local school system. Fort Lauderdale keeps cool in the sun with a variety of inland waterways and ocean breezes. Miami is not all palm trees and pink flamingos; this busy urban area has historic districts and brand new developments. Known as the "Gateway to Latin America," Miami is 60 percent Latino, 22 percent African American, and 18 percent white and other. Southern Florida seems to have two seasons: hot and hurricanes.

What things cost

ACCRA's national comparisons: Total living costs are 12 percent above the national average, with the biggest chunk of that due to housing at 23 percent above average. Utilities break even, but transportation and groceries both are 12 percent higher than average. The only saving grace is healthcare, running 6 percent below the average.

Utilities: Electricity: $150 per month; water: $35 per month; phone: $30 per month

The tax ax

Sales tax: 6 percent in Broward County. (The city does not impose a sales tax.)

Property tax: Total millage in 2005 was $23.1953 ($4,059 on an average single family home assessed at $200,000 with homestead exemption) of which $4.2639 or 18.4 percent is from the city of Coral Springs

State income tax: There is no state income tax.

Making the grade

Public education overview: Coral Springs schools are widely regarded as some of the best in Florida. The city supports the schools through the Gang Resistance and Drug Awareness program; youth mentoring program, and police and fire Explorer posts. The city places a high priority on safety, and has assigned every school its own full-time officer. The city has aggressively pursued the addition of new classroom space for Coral Springs students, which includes new Coral Glades High School. The Coral Springs Charter Middle and High School received an "A" rating from the Governor's A-Plus Plan for Education, joining the distinguished list of 15 Coral Springs schools that earned the state's highest rating for academic performance in 2004. The Coral Springs Charter School offers a number of innovative programs, including the ACE Academy, which integrates accelerated academics with professional mentoring from corporate leaders. This project began when the city bought a nearly vacant mall and converted it into the Coral Springs Charter School. Children may have to make up "hurricane" days at the end of the school year.

Class size (student to teacher ratio): 22:1

Help for working parents: Before- and after-school care is available at most elementary schools.

Boys & Girls Club: No centers are currently available.

School year: Third week of August to first week in June. Children must be 5 years old on or before September 1 to enter kindergarten.

Special education/programs for gifted students: Exceptional Student Education is for the special education of eligible students, whether gifted or with a disability. Students attend their assigned school whenever possible.

Nearby colleges and universities: A University Partnership Program with two local universities (Barry University and Broward Community College) brings education to citizens and employees working within city limits. Classes are offered at a variety of locations, and programs range from education and nursing degrees to public administration.

Medical care

Hospitals/medical centers: Coral Springs Medical Center (200 beds) includes services such as level II neonatal unit, a high risk newborn follow-up clinic; a level II pediatric intensive care unit, and more. They offer drowning prevention classes and a women's diagnostic and wellness center. There are also several private hospitals in the Coral Springs area.

Specialized care: Camp KoralKids at the Coral Springs Medical Center is a summer camp for diabetic children. The VA Primary Care Clinic provides care for eligible veterans.

Crime and safety

Police: Coral Springs has had one of the lowest crime rates with 1.59 officers per 1,000 residents. The police department has its own full-service dispatch center, and also provides dispatch for fire and emergency medical services in the neighboring city of Parkland. Coral Springs places a strong emphasis on community-oriented policing with many different programs, including crime stoppers, safety programs in schools, and programs aimed at securing businesses.

Fire: The Coral Springs fire department is unique in many ways, most notably in its structure as a combination volunteer/career fire department. Emergency medical service is staffed by full-time personnel, and engine companies are staffed with career personnel, supplemented by volunteers. Volunteers are trained in the same manner as career personnel, and must pass the same state certification exams. Innovative technology is used to provide closest unit response, and all engines and rescue units are equipped to handle advanced life-support.

Let the good times roll

Family fun: The city's recreation department offers a variety of outdoor activities including basketball, baseball, softball, soccer, and much more. In addition, Coral Springs has a 30,000 square foot gymnasium; tournament-ready Tennis Center with red clay and hard courts; and world-class Aquatic Complex with competition pools, diving well, dry land training area, teaching pool, and fitness center. In 2004, Coral Springs had more than 20,000 participants in various youth sports programs, with more than 3,000 community volunteers. The city also has a thriving teen center. A new skate park for rollerbladers and skateboarders opened in 2004. Cypress Water Park includes a 120-foot flume slide in the main pool and three-tiered aquatic playground featuring a beach-like entrance, sprinklers, fountains, water cannons, tipping buckets, and small slides for children.

Sports: The excitement of professional sports is close by with the Miami Dolphins (NFL); the Miami Heat and Orlando Magic (NBA); the Florida Panthers (NHL); and the Florida Marlins (MLB). In nearby Palm Beach, some of the major league baseball teams come for spring training.

Arts and entertainment: The Coral Springs Center for the Arts is operated by Professional Facilities Management. The center features a 1,500 seat theater, a dance studio, and meeting rooms. The Center offers a Broadway series, comedy series, concert series, kid series, and other special engagements.

Annual events: Martin Luther King Jr. Celebration, Asian-Pacific Heritage Month, Fiesta Coral Springs, UniTown, UniKids, Our Town Festival, Waterway Cleanup, Taste of Coral Springs, EarthFest, Festival of the Arts, Holiday Parade, Veterans Day, Memorial Day, Fourth of July Celebration

Community life

In 2004, when not one, but four hurricanes ripped through Florida, Coral Springs was hard hit by Hurricane Frances. The city staff and community reacted quickly. Cleanup crews began immediately with both professional members and local volunteers. Hopefully a natural disaster like this will not happen again, but the great thing to know is this warm and welcoming community takes care of itself. The Tree Memorial program allows family or friends to dedicate a tree in memory of a loved one. The city has a list of trees that can be provided at cost, and will install the tree within a city park, on a space available basis.

The environment

The Coral Springs environment gets a clean bill of health. There are no landfills, because garbage is disposed of through nonpolluting incineration. Water quality meets all EPA requirements for both chlorinated and fluoridated. There are strict ordinances in place to preserve the woodlands, because Broward County borders the Everglades National Park. There has been a 90 percent response rate to curbside and drop-off recycling center programs. During a five-month period, the city recycled enough newspaper to save 20,000 trees.

In and around town

Roads and highways: I-95, US 1, SR 7, A1A, and the Sawgrass Expressway

Closest airports: The Palm Beach, Fort Lauderdale, and Miami International Airports are all within a 45 minute drive.

Public transportation: Commuting has improved since the Tri-Rail Monorail System opened. Broward County Mass Transit Division provides area bus transportation. Trains travel from Palm Beach to Miami in about 25 minutes.

Average daily commute: 20 minutes

More Information

City of Coral Springs
9551 West Sample Road
Coral Springs, FL 33065
954-344-1000
www.coralsprings.com

Broward County Public Schools
600 SE Third Avenue
Fort Lauderdale, FL 33301
754-321-0000
www.Browardschools.com

Coral Springs Chamber of Commerce
11805 Heron Bay
Coral Springs, FL 33076
954-752-4242
www.cschamber.com

Florida Power and Light
PO Box 025576
Miami, FL 33102
954-797-5000
www.fpl.com

BellSouth
Suite 19A01 Peachtree Street
Atlanta, GA 30309
888-757-6500
www.bellsouth.com

City of Coral Springs Water District
9551 West Sample Roar
Coral Springs, FL 33301
954-344-1825
www.coralsprings.com

12

Fort Myers, Florida

Fabulous features

If moving to a fast-growing area is a top priority for you, you might as well head to the one place projected to lead the country in job, income, and population growth in the 21st century. If you're under the impression that it's only retirees coming to Florida, think again! Lee County's median age is only 35.

Extensive renovation of the historic downtown waterfront is underway, with new restaurants, nightclubs, apartments, and artistic venues providing energy and growth. With no state income tax, reasonable real estate costs, and abundant job and business opportunities, this city can cure whatever ails you.

The quality of life in Fort Myers and Lee County is second to none. Many of the nations top business and life style magazines agree! *Expansion* magazine named Lee County a "Four-Star Community" in its annual quality-of-life scorecard (2003). *Money* magazine ranked Fort Myers-Cape Coral as one of the "Best Places to Live in America." *Self* magazine ranked the Fort Myers-Cape Coral metropolitan area "Number One in the Nation for Working Women" (2003). *Forbes* magazine ranked the Fort Myers-Cape Coral metro area 37th among the "Top 200" best metro areas for business and careers. *Forecast* magazine lists Ft. Myers-Cape Coral 15th in its "Booming 25" ranking of the fastest growing metro areas (2005).

Possible drawbacks: Not crazy about heat, humidity, or lightning? Maybe even a hurricane or two? You better check out another city. Wages and salaries are low, however the overall cost of living is low too.

- Local Population: 48,208
- County: Lee
- Population of surrounding metropolitan area: 244,292
- Region: Southwest Florida
- Closest metro area: Tampa Bay, 100 miles
- Median home price: $99,300
- Median household income: $29,241
- Best reasons to live here: The subtropical climate is great, plus the job market is hot. Fort Myers has affordable housing, a good school system, gorgeous Gulf Coast beaches, and no state income tax.

Climate

Elevation 10'	Average temp. high/low (°F)	Average precipitation rain (")	snow (")	Average no. days precipitation	Average humidity (%)
January	75/54	2.2	0	6	57
April	85/63	1.7	0	4	48
July	92/74	8.9	0	18	60
October	86/68	2.6	0	8	57
Number of days 32°F or below: 1			Number of days 90°F or warmer: 106		

Earning a living

Economic outlook: Lee County is located on the Gulf of Mexico, with easy access to Florida International Airport and Interstate 75. From Fort Myers, it's only a two hour drive to either Tampa or Fort Lauderdale. Fort Myers is home to the new Florida Gulf Coast University, and several junior colleges. Lee County's unemployment rate averages around 4 percent. The working age population (age 18-64) in southwest Florida increased 8.5 percent over the last four years. Currently, working age people (18-64) make up 55 percent of the population in Lee County.

Where the jobs are: Lee Memorial Health System, Publix Super Markets, Wal-Mart Corporation, Lee County Administration, SWFL Regional Medical Center, city of Cape Coral.

Business opportunities: Industries such as aviation and aerospace are the key to economic development in this area. Florida has more than 1,300 aviation industry businesses headquartered in the state. With more than 9,900 employees, the school district is the county's largest employer, and with the district's extensive construction program to build new schools and renovate existing buildings, the district is also the area's largest developer. Construction projects are underway, to ensure that the area's educational facilities keep up with the community's growth. Southwest Florida International Airport is the eighth fastest-growing airport in the country and is currently undergoing a $438 million expansion.

Local real estate

Market overview: The typical Florida home is a ranch-style concrete block with stucco exterior. Choices abound with condominiums, golf course communities, and plenty of diverse neighborhoods.

Average rent for a two-bedroom apartment: $800 per month

Other areas to consider: The city of Cape Coral is only 45 years old, and people under the age of 25 outnumber the people over the age of 65. Naples is a haven for salt-water and fresh-water fishing. Tampa has a diverse economy founded on tourism, construction, technology, and government.

What things cost

ACCRA's national comparisons: Fort Myers sits slightly below the national average in overall costs. Housing is nearly 7 percent below average, while utilities are a mere 1.3 percent below. Groceries are 2.7 percent below and healthcare is almost 12 percent below average.

Utilities: Electricity: $150 per month; water and sewer: $70 per month; phone $30 per month

The tax ax

Sales tax: 6 percent

Property tax: $18.00 (est. property taxes paid per $1,000 of market value)

State income tax: There is no state income tax.

Making the grade

Public education overview: Lee County School District is one of the largest in the country. Fort Myers has a total of 82 schools, including three alternative schools, seven charter schools, two high-tech centers, and seven special centers. Fort Myers High School was ranked 32nd in *Newsweek* magazine's list of 100 best high schools in the nation in 2003. Standardized testing consists of the Florida Comprehensive Assessment Test. Parents are encouraged to buy into the Florida Prepaid College Plan, where they can lock in the cost of tuition, local fees, and dormitory housing at a public Florida university or community college. A second opportunity called the Florida College Investment Plan helps save for other qualified college expenses.

Class size (student to teacher ratio): 19:1

Help for working parents: The Lee County Early Childhood Learning Services is recognized as a National Head Start Association Program of Excellence.

Boys & Girls Club: There are five centers currently available.

School year: Last week of August to mid-June. Children must be 5 years old on or before September 1 to enter kindergarten.

Nearby colleges and universities: *Consumer's Digest* has named Florida Gulf Coast University 11th among the "Top 50 Best Values" for public colleges and universities. Edison Community College was named one of the "Top 25" community colleges in the United States by *Community College Week* magazine in 2003.

Medical care

Hospitals/medical centers: In 2002, 2003, and 2005 Lee Memorial Hospital was ranked in the "Top 100 Best Hospitals" by *Solucient*. Lee provides 24-hour emergency care, general surgery, cancer care, and diabetes care. The HealthPark Medical Center has 360 beds, with additional beds in pediatrics, intensive care, and medical/surgical care. The center offers 24-hour emergency care, cardiac care, obstetrics and pediatrics, and integrates inpatient and outpatient services and physician's offices in one area. Columbia Regional Medical Center of Southwest Florida is an acute-care hospital, home to the Columbia Regional Heart Institute and the Patty Berg Cancer Center. It also has a 24-hour emergency room and walk-in Express Care center.

Specialized Care: The Children's Hospital of Southwest Florida has general pediatric beds, each with its own bath, shower, and parental sleeping area; a Ronald McDonald House on-site; and the only Regional Perinatal Intensive Care Center in the area.

Crime and safety

Police: The Fort Myers police department is an outstanding example of community policing and crime prevention programs. Over 60 Fort Myers communities have participated in Neighborhood Watch groups. The GRAMPA Cop Program (Getting Retirees Actively Motivated to Policing Again) has gained national recognition. GRAMPA cops are retired law enforcement officers who educate children about safety and drug prevention. The work of the school resource officers is supplemented by the GRAMPA cops, who work in the public and private elementary schools. Other youth activities are the Explorer program, Police Activities League, Do the Right Thing, DARE, and the Respect for Law camp.

Fire: The fire department is a full-service department, offering fire suppression, basic life-support, public education, code enforcement, hazardous material response, and mitigation, training, testing, and water response. The department, now known as Fire/Rescue, is also involved in summer youth programs that focus on at-risk youngsters.

Let the good times roll

Family fun: The expansive shoreline is all the invitation you need to enjoy water recreation in Fort Myers. Between the intoxicating Gulf of Mexico, the Caloosahatchee River, and Pine Island Sound, you can swim, sail, and fish to your heart's content. If shelling is more your style, the world's "Seashell Capital," Sanibel Island, is nearby. Back on land are beautiful parks, nature trails, and the Everglades Wonder Garden. There are four National Wildlife Refuges in the area. Get into the swing of things at the more than 27 private and public golf courses. Residents are also delighted with the Lee County Sports Complex in downtown Fort Myers, which has soccer and softball fields, jogging trails, and a fishing lake. The Imaginarium Hands-On Museum offers exciting interactive exhibits for all ages, including live animals, a hurricane simulator, wide-screen movie theater, dino dig, and an early-childhood area.

Sports: Speaking of the Lee County Sports Complex, that's where you'll batter up with the Minnesota Twins during spring training. The Boston Red Sox spring training camp is also here. According to the *National Golf Foundation*, Fort Myers ranks fifth in the nation for golfer-to-holes ratios. There are more than 27 golf courses open to the public. Or if you're interested in professinal sports, you can visit nearby Tampa Bay and watch the Buccaneers (NFL) or Lightning (NHL).

Arts and entertainment: From Bach to rock, the Barbara B. Mann Performing Arts Hall of the University of South Florida brings year-round shows, concerts, and entertainment. Fort Myers is also home to the Southwest Florida Symphony, the Nature Center and Planetarium, and the Fort Myers Historical Museum. The Lee County Civic Center brings in great family entertainment such as the circus, ice shows, and more. Welcome additions to the community are the $1.5 million Lee County Alliance of the Arts Cultural Arts Center and the restored Arcade Theater. The theater will offer an exhibit gallery, a library, and an exciting art education program. A great outing is to the Henry Ford and Thomas Edison winter homes.

Annual events: Edison Festival of Light, Sanibel Shell Fair, Caloosa Catch and Release Tournament, Arts in the Air.

Community life

The Fort Myers annual Edison Festival of Light is a month-long festival that culminates with the Pageant Parade. People put out chairs a month in advance! Other community efforts include Jimmy Carter's Habitat for Humanity and "Paint Your Heart Out" a program where volunteers paint the homes of elderly or low-income families.

The environment

The city of Fort Myers was recently named as a 2004 Tree City USA by the National Arbor Day Foundation. This is the 13th year Fort Myers has received this national recognition. Lee County meets or exceeds the EPA's Clean Air Act, insuring that air quality is good. Drinking water is often tested and is of excellent quality. Recycling efforts are innovative, with four recycling centers in the city. A curbside recycling program is in force. To educate students, schools have their own recycling programs and often take field trips to local landfills.

In and around town

Roads and highways: I-75, US 41, SR 80, SR 78, 31

Closest airports: Southwest Florida Regional Airport is served by 24 airlines.

Public transportation: LeeTran provides bus service throughout the county.

Average daily commute: 20 minutes

More Information

City of Fort Myers
2200 Second Street
Fort Myers, FL 33902
239-332-6700
www.cityftmyers.com

Fort Myers Utility Company
2200 Second Street
Fort Myers, FL 33902
239-332-6700
www.fortmyersutility.com

School District of Lee County
2055 Central Avenue
Fort Myers, FL 33901
239-334-1102
www.leeschools.net

Florida Power and Light
PO Box 025576
Miami, FL 33102
954-797-5000
www.fpl.com

Chamber of Commerce
2310 Edwards Drive
Fort Myers, FL 33902
800-366-3622
www.fortmyers.org

BellSouth
Suite 19A01 Peachtree Street
Atlanta, GA 30309
888-757-6500
www.bellsouth.com

TECO Energy
PO Box 111
Tampa, FL 33601
877-832-6747
www.tecoenergy.com

13 ▶ Jacksonville, Florida

Fabulous features

Jacksonville is featured as one of the "Top 10" place to live by *Money* magazine. Jacksonville is a city of surprises and delight. Though it is the largest city in square miles in the continental United States, its many distinct neighborhoods give it a small-town friendliness. Jacksonville is a major point of entry into Florida for many visitors—more than five million passengers travel through Jacksonville International Airport each year—offering a mild climate and abundant recreational, cultural, and educational opportunities. The city is also the home of several major sports and sporting events.

With a low unemployment rate of 3 percent, combined with strong job growth, Jacksonville has matured into a major financial center. A city serious about their commitment to children, check out the Jacksonville Children's Commission, a unique organization made up of mayor-appointed citizens from each of the seven school districts that offer a range of support for families.

Plenty of fun can be found in the downtown area, which has the Riverwalk shopping area, Jacksonville Landing, and shopping along the St. John's River.

Possible drawbacks: The winters are wonderful here, but the summers can be scorchers. Also, traffic can be heavy. Crossing the Buckman Bridge is said to take ages, even on a good day!

▶ Local Population: 690,052

▶ County: Duval

▶ Population of surrounding metropolitan area: 1,000,000

▶ Region: Northeast Florida

▶ Closest metro area: Orlando, 128 miles

▶ Median home price: $95,860

▶ Median household income: $40,792

▶ Best reasons to live here: The mild climate, reasonable cost of living, excellent housing prices, solid growing business economy, and year-round outdoor activities all make Jacksonville attractive.

Climate

Elevation 12'	Average temp. high/low (°F)	Average precipitation		Average no. days precipitation	Average humidity (%)
		rain (")	snow (")		
January	64/43	3.7	0	8	58
April	78/56	3.1	0	6	51
July	90/73	5.8	0	14	58
October	79/62	4.2	0	9	58
Number of days 32°F or below: 12			Number of days 90°F or warmer: 82		

Earning a living

Economic outlook: Jacksonville is a busy seaport city with a diverse economic structure. There is no shortage of labor, and job growth has been steady with unemployment typically below the national average. Few economists predict a true boom for Jacksonville, but that also means there is unlikely to be an economic downturn. More than 50,000 jobs have been created in the last five years. The city is home to more than 80 corporate and regional headquarters. The fastest-growing jobs are in technology, with occupations such as computer scientist, support specialist, and systems analyst.

Where the jobs are: The Top 10 employers include two United States Navy facilities at the Naval Air Station Jacksonville and Naval Station Mayport. Duval County Public Schools, Winn Dixie Stores Inc., Blue Cross and Blue Shield of Florida, the city of Jacksonville, the state of Florida, Publix Super Markets Inc., Baptist Health System, and Wal-Mart are also large employers.

Business opportunities: Jacksonville is one of the state's financial capitals, with nearly 10 percent of the Duval County work force employed in the finance, real estate, or insurance industries. Military spending is an important factor in the local economy. There are four modern seaport facilities, including America's newest cruise port, making Jacksonville a full-service international seaport.

Local real estate

Market overview: Older homes exist in a variety of styles. New models with master suites, or condominiums with additional amenities, can easily be found in areas surrounding Jacksonville.

Average rent for a two-bedroom apartment: $850 per month

Other areas to consider: St. Augustine may be the nation's oldest city, but it sports modern amenities and an active lifestyle for residents. Mayport is a beautiful city home to the Mayport Naval Base. Orlando is not just a city for Mickey Mouse, though Disney World takes up a big chunk of real estate. The Orlando Centroplex, including the Florida Citrus Bowl, Tinker Field, and TD Waterhouse Centre, helps keep this young community entertained.

What things cost

ACCRA's national comparisons: Overall cost of living is about 8 percent below the national average. Housing and utilities are both major factors for this with 11 percent and 19 percent below average. Healthcare is 11 percent below average, with groceries and transportation right at the standard.

Utilities: Phone: $25 per month; gas: $30 per month; electricity: $120 per month; water: $35 per month

The tax ax

Sales tax: 7 percent

Property tax: $18.00 (est. property taxes paid per $1,000 of market value)

State income tax: There is no state income tax.

Crime and safety

Police: Jacksonville's crime index shows over an 18 percent drop in the last 10 years. The Jacksonville sheriff's office has a geographic information system, where you can click on a specific area of Jacksonville and find out the reported crimes listed by type and date for that location. The Monitoring and Resourcing Students program puts a school resource officer on school campuses, where they can work directly with the most disruptive students. Individual substations serve the community in keeping officers close by to serve and protect.

Fire: The Jacksonville fire department responds to a variety of emergencies. These consist of building fires, wildland fires, automobile accidents, hazardous material incidents, marine emergencies, confined space incidents, and aircraft incidents. The department provides public safety and education, fire prevention, and emergency medical services.

Making the grade

Public education overview: The Duval County public school system has been named a model urban school district by the U.S. Department of Education. One of the nation's largest public school districts, Duval County serves 105 elementary schools, 26 middle schools, 17 high schools, three exceptional education schools, two academies of technology, and five special schools. Duval County has one of the country's largest magnet school programs. Online data is available for research on each school, listing test scores as well as school colors and staff information. The state of Florida passed a constitutional amendment in November of 2002 requiring a voluntary pre-kindergarten program for all 4 year old children by the fall of 2005. This program is designed to prepare kids for kindergarten and build a solid foundation for educational success.

Class size (student to teacher ratio): 20:1

Help for working parents: Most Duval County schools offer before- and after-school programs for a nominal charge.

Boys & Girls Club info: There are no centers currently available.

School year: Second week of August through the third week of May. Children must be 5 years old on or before September 1 to enter kindergarten.

Nearby colleges and universities: The University of North Florida, Florida Community College, Edward Waters College, Jacksonville University, Jones College, Luther Rice Bible College and Seminary, Trinity Baptist College, Webster University, Zoe College.

Medical care

Hospitals/medical centers: Major area hospitals include Baptist Medical Center/Wolfson Children's Hospital, Memorial Hospital, Methodist Medical Center, St. Luke's Hospital, St. Vincent's Medical Center, and the University Medical Center. The Mayo Clinic of Jacksonville, an extension of the Mayo Clinic in Minnesota, provides surgical programs, including computer-assisted sterotactic neurosurgery for removal of deep brain tumors, Mohs surgery for skin cancer, retinal surgery, reconstructive surgery, and otologic and neurotologic surgery.

Specialized care: Nemours Children's Clinic is an outpatient center for children with complex medical problems.

Let the good times roll

Family fun: Disney World and Universal Studios are just two hours away in Orlando, but don't miss out on all the great entertainment right in the neighborhood! You can enjoy outdoor recreation activities year-round. The Jacksonville Zoological Gardens feature more than 600 animals in beautiful settings. The Museum of Science and History features a 1,200-gallon marine aquarium, Science PODS (Personally Operated Discovery Stations), and Kidspace for the youngest visitors in their facilities. For water lovers, 19 public boat ramps and numerous marinas in Duval County provide opportunities for fresh-water and salt-water fishing. And Jacksonville is close to Amelia Island, Jacksonville Beach, and Neptune Beach.

Sports: The Jacksonville Jaguars (NFL) play in the 80,000-seat Jacksonville Municipal Stadium. The Jacksonville area is home to the PGA Tour World Headquarters, World Golf Village and the Golf Hall of Fame; it's also the home of the Players Championship at Sawgrass. There are 17 public courses, numerous private and semi-private club courses, and six resort courses. Tennis enthusiasts can choose from the many tennis courts around the area.

Arts and entertainment: More than 300 dance, theater, comedy, and musical events are showcased each year at the Florida Theatre. Listen to the Jacksonville

Symphony Orchestra or enjoy free, open air concerts from the St. John's River City Band. The Cummer Museum of Art, the Jacksonville Museum of Contemporary Art, Jacksonville Art Museum, the Alexander Brest Museum, and the Gallery at Jacksonville University feature permanent collections and traveling exhibitions of art.

Annual events: Soccer USA, River Run, and the USA 15K National Championship, the Bausch and Lomb Women's Association Championship, the DuPont All American Championships, the Players Championship and A Taste of Jacksonville, Fourth of July Festival, Association of Tennis Professionals Tour Classic, and Jacksonville Jazz Festival.

Community life

There's a robust volunteer spirit in the area, and newcomers can quickly immerse themselves in the life of the community through Volunteer Jacksonville, Esprit de Corps, Upbeat, the Foster Grandparents Program, and United Way of Northeast Florida. These groups bring people and organizations together to help those in need.

The environment

Strict ordinances preserve the woodlands, because Broward County borders the Everglades National Park. The Clean It Up, Green It Up campaign, started in 1996, helps residents work together with the city to beautify their neighborhoods. Other beautification programs exist, such as the Adopt-A-Road program, and a number of annual events provide additional volunteer opportunities. The Keep Jacksonville Beautiful Commission, created in 2003, works to develop recommendations on a variety of community beautification initiatives.

In and around town

Roads and highways: I-10, I-95, I-295, US 1, 17, 90, 301

Closest airports: Jacksonville International Airport provides national and international service, while Craig Municipal Airport serves corporate and private-use aircraft. Herlong Airport is the area's premier recreational and sport flying airport.

Public transportation: Bus service is provided by the Jacksonville Transportation Authority.

Average daily commute: 22 minutes

More Information

City of Jacksonville
117 West Duvall Street
Jacksonville, FL 32202
904-630-2489
www.coj.net

Duval County Public Schools
1701 Prudential Drive
Jacksonville, FL 32207
904-390-2000
www.educationcentral.org

Jacksonville Chamber of Commerce
3 Independent Drive
Jacksonville, FL 32202
904-366-6600
www.myjaxchamber.com

JEA Electric
PO Box 44297
Jacksonville, FL 32231
904-665-6000
www.jea.com

Florida Power and Light
PO Box 025576
Miami, FL 33102
954-797-5000
www.fpl.com

BellSouth
Suite 19A01 Peachtree Street
Atlanta, GA 30309
888-757-6500
www.bellsouth.com

TECO Energy
PO Box 111
Tampa, FL 33601
877-832-6747
www.tecoenergy.com

14 ▶ Boise, Idaho

Idaho

Boise ▼

Fabulous features

The Boise Chamber of Commerce hears from hundreds of people around the country who inquire about the good life. What Boise offers is a taste of the "great" life. In this city, where the majestic Rocky Mountains converge with the Boise River, residents know the inspirational power of natural resources. But because gorgeous scenery doesn't pay the rent, it's a good thing that employment opportunities are also bountiful. Hewlett-Packard, Albertsons, and Morrison Knudson are just a few firms in expansion modes.

Boise was ranked second in the "Best City in America to Do Business" listings by *Inc.* magazine (2005). It was ranked fifth city of its size in the nation for favorable business costs by *KPMG LLP* (2004), and ranked 13th best overall city by the National Policy Research Council's Gold Guide in May of 2004.

If Boise were a movie, they'd call it "Spirit of the Wild West Meets the Star Wars Generation." Some of today's most innovative computer technology was invented at Boise State University.

Possible drawbacks: There may be 100,000 trees in Boise, but don't expect to find jobs growing on them. Job satisfaction is so great, turnover is minimal (less than 3 percent per year). Boise's adolescent growing pains relate to rush hour traffic and housing prices going up.

▶ Local Population: 189,847

▶ County: Ada

▶ Population of surrounding metropolitan area: 403,817

▶ Region: Southwest Idaho

▶ Closest metro area: Salt Lake City, 336 miles

▶ Median home price: $120,700

▶ Median household income: $42,432

▶ Best reasons to live here: It's a sparkling clean mountain town with great recreation, diversified business base, affordable housing, friendly people, and low crime rate.

Climate

Elevation 2,730'	Average temp. high/low (°F)	Average precipitation		Average no. days precipitation	Average humidity (%)
		rain (")	snow (")		
January	37/21	0.7	6.5	12	70
April	61/37	1.0	0.6	8	36
July	91/59	0.2	0	2	21
October	65/39	1.3	0.1	6	38
Number of days 32°F or below: 124			Number of days 90°F or warmer: 43		

Earning a living

Economic outlook: *Forbes* ranked Boise number one in 2005 as the "Best Place for Business and Careers." Within the Boise area there are more than 18,000 businesses and a dozen corporate headquarters, four of which are Fortune 500 companies. The metro area consists of several cities and more than 512,000 people. All this, and the unemployment rate is only 4.7 percent. Nicknamed the "Treasure Valley," Boise's economy is strong due to a healthy mix of business, education, healthcare, retail, manufacturing, government, and the military—all working together to provide economic stability. The natural resource industries are central to the well-being of the area. Tourism is a major growth factor of the Idaho economy. People come to the area to ski, float the wild rivers, hunt, fish, and camp.

Where the jobs are: Simplot Corporation, Boise Cascade, Albertsons, Micron Technology, Hewlett-Packard, St. Luke's Medical Center, Boise State University, St. Alphonsus Medical Center, DirecTV, Boise Corporation

Business opportunities: The newest industry added to the diverse economic development is high-tech manufacturing, providing strong employment growth in recent years. A regional trade and commerce center, Boise draws people from three states— eastern Oregon, northern Nevada, and southern Idaho—a combined population of more than 550,000 people. The professional community is central to Boise's identity and integrity with some of the area's most talented professionals drawn here.

Local real estate

Market overview: Homes in the Boise area vary, with restored Victorian mansions, contemporary new construction, starter homes, condominiums, or apartment living.

Average rent for a two-bedroom apartment: $700 per month

Other areas to consider: Mountain Home, actually nestled between two mountain ranges, is home to an Air Force base. Fruitland's location on Highway 95 (the main route between Canada and Mexico), though of agricultural heritage, is diversifying into light industry. Salt Lake City, with its dramatic mountain range backdrop has clean and friendly neighborhoods.

What things cost

ACCRA's national comparisons: Overall costs of living are approximately 7 percent below the state average. Housing is 17 percent below, with groceries at 6 percent below, and healthcare riding around 8 percent below.

Utilities: Electricity: $60 per month; natural gas: $67 per month; phone: $27 per month

The tax ax

Sales tax: 6 percent

Property tax: $16.32 (est. property taxes paid per $1,000 of market value)

State income tax: 7.8 percent

Making the grade

Public education overview: *Expansion Management* magazine, in April of 2005, ranked Boise as fourth in the "Best Small" category and gave the city a Gold Medal rating. Standardized testing consists of the Idaho Standards Achievement Tests (ISAT). With the No Child Left Behind Act requirements, grades five, seven, and 10 will soon take a new science ISAT. In 2005, the Foothills Learning Center opened its doors. The center is for environmental education, land-use practice, natural resource conservation, and fire-wise construction practices. The Boise School Volunteer Program coordinates volunteers in the classroom, with over 10,000 volunteers contributing 300,000 hours annually. In 2004, the Treasure Valley Mathematics and Science Center opened, providing opportunities in math and science education unlike those found in traditional school settings. Initial financing came from the Micron Technology Foundation. Hewlitt-Packard donated over $300,000 in technology equipment supplies and start-up funds.

Class size (student to teacher ratio): 23:1

Help for working parents: Boise School District's child care program is called Just For Kids. Children ages 6 weeks to 12 years are eligible to enroll in the program.

Boys & Girls Club: There is one center available in Boise.

School year: Mid-August to the first week in June. Children must be 5 years old on or before September 1 to enter kindergarten.

Special education/programs for gifted students: The district offers a wide range of programs serving students from preschool through age 21. Program goals, curriculum, and materials are developmentally appropriate and focused towards meeting the individual needs of students.

Nearby colleges and universities: Boise State University, Idaho State University, George Fox University, University of Phoenix, University of Idaho

Medical care

Hospitals/medical centers: In 2004, the UnitedHealth Foundation's *America's Health Report* ranked Idaho as 18th healthiest state in the country. Because the state has a low prevalence of smokers and a low rate of cancer deaths or violent crimes, it's no wonder. The city boasts four hospitals of 810 beds and eight general clinics. Saint Alphonsus and St. Luke's Regional Medical Centers maintain the latest in technology and excellent nursing and support staffs. The centers also offer numerous health and wellness programs. The West Valley Medical Center, located in Caldwell, serves many western Idaho communities in Canyon County. Mercy Medical Center is a 152-bed acute-care facility located in Nampa.

Specialized care: The Mountain State Tumor Institute is a well-known cancer care facility. Other facilities include Northwest Passages Adolescent Hospital and the Veterans Administration Hospital.

Crime and safety

Police: The Boise police department is proud of their commitment to crime prevention and community policing, including programs like Crime Stoppers, Business Crime Prevention, Internet Crimes Against Children Task Force, and Neighborhood Watch. The Boise Police Activities League sponsors several ongoing events in the Boise area. The Parents And Youth Against Drug Abuse organization educates the community to prevent substance abuse. The Boise police school resource officers provide a valuable link between education and law enforcement in the school system. Specialized units include bike patrol, motor unit, K-9 patrol, and mounted patrol. The department also has a pipe and drum unit for special events.

Fire: The Boise fire department has 15 stations and celebrated its 100th anniversary in May of 2002. The department hosts an annual Firefighter Safety Symposium in May. The success of the symposium is the ability to deliver valuable training not only to Boise Fire Department personnel, but also to those attending from around the country.

Let the good times roll

Family fun: With a river flowing though the heart of Boise, and a 25-mile greenbelt, there is a lot to do outdoors during all four seasons. Southwest Idaho provides nature ala carte, just choose your pleasure in the nearby Rocky Mountains, canyons, sand dunes, and white-water rafting rivers. Enjoy every level of activity, including hiking, camping, or fishing around Boise's 91 parks. The area has a lot of indoor recreation as well. The Discovery Center of Idaho is a children's hands-on museum of fun and entertainment. Or spend an afternoon at the Basque Museum and Cultural Center, Idaho Anne Frank Human Rights Memorial, or the Idaho Black History Museum. The Boise Zoo is home to more than 175 animals. In nearby Meridian, take the kids to the Roaring Springs Water Park for cool fun in the summer.

Sports: Root for the home team from June to September as the Boise Hawks, a semiprofessional baseball team, plays at the Memorial Stadium. The Hawks are extremely active in the community. In the fall, fans can cheer on Boise State Bronco football. Idaho IceWorld was rated one of the "Coolest Rinks in America" by *American Hockey* magazine (2004). Boise was named "Idaho's Sportstown USA" by *Sports Illustrated* magazine (2004).

Arts and entertainment: Boise Little Theater is one of the longest running community theaters in the country. Boise Contemporary Theater has season tickets available for their productions. The Morrison Center for the performing arts is home to the Boise Philharmonic concerts, as well as ballet, opera, musical, and theatrical companies. Ballet Idaho performs September through March.

Annual events: Gene Harris Jazz Festival, Alive After Five, downtown events Wednesday evenings, Shakespeare Festival, Western Idaho Fair, Art in the Park, Christmas in the City, Humanitarian Bowl.

Community life

Volunteerism is the lifeblood of Boise. Some of the best examples are the annual Paint the Town program, Rake-up Boise, and Re-leaf Boise. Paint the Town includes residents and business leaders painting the homes of elderly citizens who can no longer maintain them. From the community centers to the beautiful scenery of this vibrant college town, people are happy in Boise.

The environment

Situated upstream at the start of the Boise River, the city gets first crack at the groundwater supply. Thanks to stringent bans and conservation, the quality and quantity of the water are excellent. Air quality is another matter. Because of the area's high elevation, wood smoke and other air pollution doesn't blow away, causing a natural phenomenon called "air inversions." Curbside recycling and the Recycle the Fall program help maintain the clean environment.

In and around town

Roads and highways: I-84, I-84B, US 20, 26, 30, state route 21, 44, 55

Closest airports: Boise Municipal is 10 minutes from downtown.

Public transportation: ValleyRide offers 17 weekday routes and seven Saturday routes.

Average daily commute: 20 minutes

More Information

City Hall
150 North Capitol Boulevard
Boise, ID 83702
208-384-4422
www.cityofboise.org

Boise Independent School District
8169 West Victory Road
Boise, ID 83709
208-338-3400
www.boiseschools.org

Chamber of Commerce
250 South 5th Street
Boise, ID 83702
208-472-5200
www.boisechamber.org

Idaho Power
1221 West Idaho Street
Boise, ID 83702
800-488-6151
www.idahopower.com

United Water
8248 West Victory Road
Boise, ID 83709
208-362 7304
www.unitedwater.com

Intermountain Gas
555 South Cole Road
Boise, ID 83709
800-342-1585
www.intgas.com

15 ▶ Naperville, Illinois

Illinois

Naperville

Springfield

Fabulous features

Does "follow the yellow brick road" sound familiar? The bricks along the Riverwalk in Naperville may not be yellow, but they do lead you through an historic and cultural community that has all the magic of Oz. Naperville will celebrate its 175th anniversary in 2006, and residents plan on celebrating all year long.

Money magazine in 2005 and 2003 listed Naperville as one of the "Best Places to Live." In 2004, *Money* magazine named it one of the "hottest cities" in the central United States. The Census Bureau identified the city as the "best place to raise kids" in communities with over 100,000 people.

The quality school district is one that real estate agents can boast about. Education is strongly supported in this community. The public library has taken the prize of being ranked the number one library in the country for the sixth year in a row.

The DuPage River flows through the heart of Naperville, and the residents created the splendid Riverwalk as a present for Naperville's 150th anniversary. Where else can you find a downtown location with covered bridges, an amphitheater, and a large sledding hill?

Possible drawbacks: When snow removal information is posted on the city's Website, you get the idea that this is not the balmy tropics.

▶ Local Population: 128,358

▶ County: DuPage

▶ Population of surrounding metropolitan area: 904,161

▶ Region: Northeast Illinois

▶ Closest metro area: Chicago, 25 miles

▶ Median home price: $254,200

▶ Median household income: $88,771

▶ Best reasons to live here: The high quality of education and lowest crime rate in the nation. Naperville has the best library in the country, beautiful scenery, and a cozy hometown atmosphere.

Climate

Elevation 700'	Average temp. high/low (°F)	Average precipitation		Average no. days precipitation	Average humidity (%)
		rain (")	snow (")		
January	31/13	1.8	11.2	11	58
April	61/37	3.8	1.6	12	51
July	86/62	4.1	0	10	58
October	65/41	2.7	0.4	9	58
Number of days 32°F or below: 119			Number of days 90°F or warmer: 21		

Earning a living

Economic outlook: Though many may think of this as a bedroom community to Chicago, Naperville includes high-tech research centers, national and international companies, and a highly educated workforce. With a low 2.4 percent unemployment rate, the majority of residents work in managerial, professional, service-related, or sales industries. Naperville is part of the area's East-West Corporate Corridor, with growing success in bringing in corporate giants. Being close to the Chicago metropolis and convenience of O'Hare airport provides an incentive for businesses to stay.

Where the jobs are: Lucent Technologies, Crate & Barrel, Ondeo Nalco Chemical Company, Kraft Foods, Nicor and Tellabs, Edward Hospital and Health Services, Argonne National Laboratory, Fermi National Accelerator Laboratory

Business opportunities: Recently, Naperville was ranked by *Home Computing* Magazine as one of the top five places in the country to start a home-based business. There is a thriving commercial and cultural district downtown. In nearby Downers Grove, the Sara Lee Corporation purchased a 534,000 square foot building in 2005 and will be relocating its corporate headquarters soon.

Local real estate

Market overview: Looking for historical charm or modern conveniences? This area has a bit of everything. Neighborhoods have ranch-style or traditional two-story, homes with or without attached garages, and older brick homes with basements.

Average rent for a two-bedroom apartment: $940 per month

Other areas to consider: Aurora, a diverse suburb community, is enjoying a strong increase in young families due to affordability. Oak Lawn has the charm and qualities of a small town, yet is minutes from big city conveniences. Chicago's known as the windy city for a reason! Gusts coming off Lake Michigan can be exhilarating or brutal, depending on your coat. The city offers diversity and entertainment from Rush Street to Lakeside Drive.

What things cost

ACCRA's national comparisons: Overall living costs, which include the city of Chicago, are 30 percent above the national average. The majority of this is due to housing at a whopping 67 percent above the average. Healthcare runs about 37 percent above the average and transportation and grocery items are in the teens above average.

Utilities: Electric: $59 per month; gas: $85 per month; phone: $27.50 per month

The tax ax

Sales tax: 6.75 percent

Property tax: $23.00 (est. property taxes paid per $1,000 of market value)

State income tax: 3.0 percent

Making the grade

Public education overview: The area is covered by two highly rated school districts. Indian Prairie Community Unit School District and Naperville Community United School District are touted as two of the leading school districts in the nation. Generations have attended these schools, and a large percentage of people move to the area because they want quality education for their children. District 204 has a new elementary school opening in 2006. District 203 uses the Illinois Standard Achievement Test for measuring math, reading, and writing. High school students must take the Prairie State Achievement Examination to graduate. Almost 97 percent of District 203 students graduate and 98 percent go on to attend higher education. *Expansion Management* magazine has awarded District 203 a "Gold Medal" ranking. The area also includes several parochial and private schools.

Class size (student to teacher ratio): 19:1

Help for working parents: Nearly all of the elementary schools have a YMCA sponsored before- and after-school care program.

Boys & Girls Club: There are no centers available.

School year: Late August to the first week of June. Children must be 5 years old on or before September 1 to enter kindergarten.

Special education/programs for gifted students: Special education resources are at all levels of schooling, from pre-kindergarten through high school. Honors and Enriched classes are available in a variety of grade levels.District 204 has pioneered the full-inclusion process for special needs children, where each child is given an IEP.

Nearby colleges and universities: North Central College is a private, nonprofit school, offering liberal arts and science degrees. A satellite branch of Chicago's well known DePaul University is located here, offering technology and business curriculums. Other venues are extension sites of College of DuPage and Northern Illinois University.

Medical care

Hospitals/medical centers: Edward Hospital and Health Services offers full-service healthcare, including a level II trauma center. The hospital is a leader in care for critically ill newborns, reproductive care, beating heart surgery, and general surgical and medical care. The Heart Hospital provides private rooms, which feel more like home than a hospital.

Specialized care: Linden Oaks Hospital offers mental healthcare and substance abuse services.

Crime and safety

Police: The Naperville police department's crime prevention unit has a lot to offer its citizens. Some of the programs include Neighborhood Watch, National Night Out, Citizen Police Academy, and DARE. Also in this unit is the Naperville Community Radio Watch program, which has specially trained volunteers acting as additional eyes and ears for the police. Officers are permanently assigned to a geographic location or beat. This allows for the patrol to become more familiar and experienced with their areas. Special units include the bicycle patrol unit, an organized dive team, two K9 units, and extra summer patrols of the Riverwalk area.

Fire: The Naperville fire department has eight fire stations with 200 full-time personnel. Emergency medical services are provided by six paramedic ambulances. All fire engines are also equipped with paramedic equipment, so the response time to an emergency call is generally under six minutes. The department is involved with the DuPage County Safe Kids Coalition, which helps educate the community about public safety.

Let the good times roll

Family fun: Pick a season and enjoy a variety of outdoor recreation. During warm weather, go swimming at Centennial Beach, which has a six-acre swim park and playground. Naperville has more than 100 fields for team sports. Visit the DuPage Children's Museum, with hands-on fun and exhibits. With 125 parks, you're almost always within walking distance of green space. Enjoy ice skating and roller rinks, tennis courts, and golf. The Forest Preserve District offers lakes, rivers, and miles of forested trails for jogging, biking, skiing, or horseback riding.

Sports: Professional sports are plentiful in Chicago, which is about 25 miles away. Root for the Chicago Bears (NFL), the championship playing Bulls (NBA), Blaze (NWBL), the Cubs and White Sox (MLB), or Blackhawks (NHL). Minor league baseball has the Kane County Cougars, too.

Arts and entertainment: The Summer Place Theatre produces three to four shows every year, performing in the Naperville Central High School Auditorium. The Magical Starlight Theatre is an annual show geared toward families, working with the Park District and the Summer Place Theatre. Enjoy the musical performances of the DuPage Symphony or the Naperville Municipal Band at the new downtown concert center. If choral is more your style, listen to the Young Naperville Singers, the Chorus of DuPage, or the men's glee club. The Naper Settlement gives you a chance to walk through a 19th century village, with shops, homes, and a charming church showing a collection of historical facts and features of the past.

Annual events: Naper Days, Women's Club Art Fair, Farmer's Market, Summer Concerts, Riverwalk Fine Arts Fair, Oktoberfest, Santa Train Ride

Community life

The community is gearing up for another big birthday bash in 2006. These people love to celebrate the great things of Naperville. With two-thirds of the workforce in white collar industry, the enthusiasm and commitment to their town is commendable. Service organizations abound, and there is no lack of opportunity to help out.

The environment

The community has a weekly recycled material pick-up with the regular trash removal services and centers for household hazardous waste materials. Residents can choose to participate in the Naperville Renewable Energy Option. This provision gives residential and commercial utility customers the opportunity to purchase emission-free, renewable sources of electricity from natural sources such as the wind, sun, and water. The renewable energy for the program is primarily wind energy from Illinois-based wind farms, with small amounts of hydroelectric and solar power, also generated within the state of Illinois.

In and around town

Roads and highways: I-355, I-88, I-55, I-294

Closest airports: The Chicago O'Hare International Airport is only 24 miles away, and Chicago Midway International Airport is 29 miles away.

Public transportation: Pace provides the city bus service. Or you can take the MetraRail lightrail to Chicago and Aurora.

Average daily commute: 27 minutes

More Information

City of Naperville
400 South Eagle Street
Naperville, IL 60566-7020
630-420-6111
www.naperville.il.us

Naperville Area Chamber of Commerce
55 South Main Street, Suite 351
Naperville, IL 60540
630-355-4141
www.naperville.net

Community Unit School District 203
203 West Hillside Road
Naperville, IL 60540
630-420-6300
www.ncusd203.org

Indian Prairie School District 204
780 Shoreline Drive
Aurora, IL 60504
630-375-3000
www.ipsd.org

City of Naperville
Electricity, Water, and Wastewater
400 South Eagle Street
Naperville, IL 60566
630-420-6059
www.naperville.il.us

Bloomington, Indiana

Fabulous features

Bloomington is a warm, friendly community nestled in wooded rolling hills. A quality college town with big city amenities, Bloomington tugs at the heart of all who live here. Offering a solid foundation for work (with one of the lowest unemployment rates in the state), recreation, leisure, and the arts, there's a lot of pride in this hometown.

Forbes magazine ranked Bloomington 10th in the "Best Smaller Metros" list for "Best Places for Business and Careers," with the city excelling in areas such as the cost of doing business and educational attainment. And when the working day is done, you can enjoy yourself outdoors. Home to Indiana's largest inland lake and National forest, you can relax by land or by water without having to drive for hours.

Indiana University provides abundant opportunities for live music and entertainment as well as sports, but Bloomington also has the Monroe County Convention Center that provides events. Your activity calendar can be as full as you'd like it to be with the wide variety of choices that are available here. In Bloomington, you may not be in a big city, but it will feel that way, without the crowds, traffic, high prices, and other urban hassles.

Possible drawbacks: How do you feel about tornados? It's a mid-west condition, and Bloomington has had its share over the years.

Indiana

▶ Local Population: 69,987

▶ County: Monroe

▶ Population of surrounding metropolitan area: 120,563

▶ Region: Central Indiana

▶ Closest metro area: Indianapolis, 47 miles

▶ Median home price: $126,000

▶ Median household income: $25,377

▶ Best reasons to live here: It's a friendly college town, with affordable housing, sports, a strong economy, and great recreational opportunities.

Climate

Elevation 745'	Average temp. high/low (°F)	Average precipitation rain (")	Average precipitation snow (")	Average no. days precipitation	Average humidity (%)
January	37/19	2.7	6.6	12	71
April	64/41	4.3	0.5	12	56
July	86/65	4.3	0	10	60
October	67/44	3.1	0.2	8	57
Number of days 32°F or below: 122			Number of days 90°F or warmer: 15		

Earning a living

Economic outlook: In Bloomington you have a strong public/private partnership creating quality development opportunities. The city's rapid information technology and medical/healthcare industry growth is a part of the economic success the area has seen in recent years. In the last 10 years, relocation of new companies to Bloomington and Monroe County, has resulted in more than 5,000 new jobs. The unemployment rate is approximately 4.7 percent for 2005. With more than 35,000 students attending Indiana University every year, Bloomington has a constant supply of highly educated labor. Over 82 percent of Bloomington's workforce is college educated.

Where the jobs are: Baxter Pharmaceutical Solutions LLC, Cook, Inc., Cornerstone Information Systems, Inc., Hirons and Company, Advance Design Corporation, Digital Media Inc., Technology Service Corporation

Business opportunities: Bloomington has all the tools and resources needed to continue growing the economy. The Bloomington Technology Incubator offers start-up companies a customized package of assistance services, providing lower costs with shared equipment, and access to conferencing facilities. Over the next several years, city hall will invest $23 million to improve its roads and sidewalks, encouraging biking, walking, and mass transit as the preferred means of transportation.

Local real estate

Market overview: A wide variety is available in affordable housing types from town houses, condominiums, and bungalows to lavishly detailed older homes.

Average rent for a two-bedroom apartment: $680 per month

Other areas to consider: With a skyline against the Illinois River, Peoria offers a bustling downtown and quiet neighborhoods. And believe it or not, there really is a Santa Claus, Indiana, with a Christmas Lake Golf Course and Lake Rudolph Campground. Housing costs in Indianapolis are consistently below the national average, and charming, tree-lined neighborhoods provide the finishing touch. This sports-happy town boasts some of the world's finest athletic facilities. Major sports brings in thousands of tourism dollars.

What things cost

ACCRA's national comparisons: Overall living costs are 9 percent below the national average, with housing at 18 percent below average being the major player. Utilities fall into the same category at 10 percent below average. Groceries and healthcare both run about 5 percent below the national average, with transportation close behind at 4 percent.

Utilities: Phone: $30 per month; electricity: $75 per month; natural gas: $40 per month; water: $25 per month

The tax ax

Sales tax: 6 percent

Property tax: $16.08 (est. property taxes paid per $1,000 of market value)

State income tax: 3.4 percent

Making the grade

Public education overview: Named "one of the best public school values" by *Expansion* magazine, Monroe County Community School Corporation offers a fabulous educational environment. Boasting top-notch, award-winning schools at the primary and secondary level, the district has 16 elementary schools, nine private schools, three middle schools, and three high schools. Online you'll find a five year technology plan available for parents to read. The corporation has two of the finest high schools (Bloomington North and Bloomington South) in the state of Indiana, offering a rigorous and challenging curriculum. Each year the high schools have students competing for National Merit Scholarships and earning the Indiana Academic Honors Diploma.

Class size (student to teacher ratio): 19:1

Boys & Girls Club: There are three centers currently available.

School year: Last week of August to the first week of June. Children must be 5 years old on or before June 1 to start kindergarten.

Special education/programs for gifted students: For gifted and talented students in grade school, parents can download and print out a nomination form and rating scale, submitting both to the appropriate office. The availability of special education faculty and their responsibilities are available online.

Nearby colleges and universities: Indiana University, The University of Indianapolis, Ivy Tech State College Central Indiana, Indiana University/Purdue University at Indianapolis, Depauw University

Medical care

Hospitals/medical centers: Bloomington Hospital has over 100 years of experience in serving Bloomington, and offers excellent services in cancer treatment, diabetes, cardiovascular, and medical and outpatient surgeries. In the Center for Women and Children, the OB unit has a birth options checklist, where you can plan ahead of time for things such as having the lights down low during birth, or having the baby sleep with you.

Specialized care: Bloomington Bone and Joint Clinic is southern Indiana's orthopedic and sports medicine clinic. The Indiana University Health Center provides medical services for students, their spouses, and dependents.

Crime and safety

Police: The Bloomington Police Department currently employs 112 full-time staff. The department's crime prevention programs include Neighborhood Watch, a strong and successful effort. The newest addition to the department is bicycle patrol. The department also participates in the Monroe County Dive Team. In 2003, the department established an Honor Guard, consisting of officers who volunteer their efforts at funerals and special memorial services.

Fire: The Bloomington fire department serves the city of Bloomington, Indiana University, as well as Salt Creek and Polk Townships. The department has 99 full-time firefighters devoted primarily to fire suppression and emergency medical services, with two to three minute response time in most cases. First responders provide emergency medical services for each of Bloomington's five stations.

Let the good times roll

Family fun: Home to Indiana's largest inland lake, Lake Monroe, Bloomington's natural beauty is perfect for hiking, fishing, boating, and more. Having the only National forest, and a variety of parks in the area, will give your family ample choices for outdoor recreation. Try hot-air ballooning with Balloon Safaris, or visit Barn Yard Friends, just east of Bloomington, for a petting zoo. Bryan Park Pool is Olympic-sized for cool, refreshing fun. Or try the Blackwell Horse Camp, a popular overnight camping area for equestrians. For indoor fun, take the family to WonderLab at the Museum of Science, Health, and Technology, which offers science adventures for all ages with permanent and temporary exhibits and science programs. The Hoosier Heights indoor climbing facility offers over 8,000 square feet of terrain suitable for all climbers. Or enjoy the Lazerlite Family Entertainment Center for laser tag enjoyment.

Sports: The Indiana Hoosiers provide continuous cheering and excitement all year, whether it's Big 10 football, NCAA basketball, or baseball. The Little 500 Race is so exciting, it's even inspired the movie *Breaking Away*. The magazine *Sports Illustrated* has called the race the "Greatest Intramural Event" in the country.

Arts and entertainment: From the world-renowned Indiana University School of Music to the many art galleries sprinkled around town, Bloomington has a lot of culture. Performances on campus include theater, ballet, opera, and music. Other museums include the Indiana University Art Museum, the Kinsey Institute, the Mathers Museum of World Cultures, the Hoagy Carmichael Room, and the Asian Culture Center.

Annual events: Chocolate Fest, Arts Fair on the Square, Bloomington ArtsWeek, Bloomington Beer Festival, Bloomington Early Music Festival, EastFest, Picnic with Pops, Fourth Street Festival of the Arts, Bubblefest, Canopy of Lights, Chimes of Christmas

Community life

You have to love a community with a program like SnowBusters, which is all about neighbors helping neighbors, and making sidewalks safe and clean for children and all pedestrians. The community of Bloomington uses various resources to maintain their successful Urban Forest program. Celebrate a child's birth by contributing a tree to be planted in one of Bloomington's city parks and receive a baby tree certificate suitable for framing. The Memorial/Honorary Tree program lets you plant a tree in memory of your lost loved ones.

The environment

Thousands of residents participate in the city of Bloomington Volunteer Network, which promotes and facilitates volunteer activities throughout the community. Recycling service is free to all those in the city trash pickup service. Every other week the pickup includes two categories, paper products and cans, glass, and plastic. The city's leaf collection program operates in November and December, where residents rake the leaves and bag them with bio-degradable leaf collection bags provided by the city.

In and around town

Roads and highways: state routes 46, 37

Closest airports: Monroe County Airport is about 7 miles away, while Indianapolis International Airport is about 42 miles away.

Public transportation: Bloomington Transit; Indiana University Campus bus services

Average daily commute: 18 minutes

More Information

City of Bloomington
401 North Morton Street
Bloomington, IN 47404
812-349-3409
www.bloomington.in.gov

Monroe County Community School
315 North Drive
Bloomington, IN 47401
812-330-7700
www.mccsc.edu

Bloomington Chamber of Commerce
PO Box 1302
Bloomington, IN 47402
812-336-6381
www.chamberbloomington.org

Wonderlab
308 West Fourth Street
Bloomington, IN 47404
812-337-1337
www.wonderlab.org

Indiana University
107 South Indiana Avenue
Bloomington, IN 47405-7000
812-855-4848
www.indiana.edu

Hoosier Energy
7398 North State Road 37
Bloomington, IN 47404
812-876-2021
www.hepn.com

Vectren/Indiana Gas Company
PO Box 209
Evansville, IN 47702-0209
800-227-1376
www.vectren.com

Indianapolis, Indiana

Fabulous features

Indiana's famous Circle City—Indianapolis—is quickly racing circles around cities twice its size, whether it's business opportunities, quality healthcare, affordable housing, or sports events.

Recently ranked fourth best city to expand or relocate a business by *Expansion Management* magazine (January 2005), Indianapolis was also ranked fourth on the magazine's "America's 50 Hottest Cities" list (November 2004). Indy ranked as the sixth best place to live and work in the country, (*BestJobsUSA.com*, 2002) and the number one professional sports city in the country (*ESPN.com, 2004*).

Housing costs in Indianapolis are consistently below the national average, and charming, tree-lined neighborhoods provide the finishing touch. High-quality educational opportunities abound with seven colleges and universities in the immediate area. This sports-happy town boasts some of the world's finest athletic facilities. Indy plays host each year to the world's largest sporting event, the Indianapolis 500. But there's more than sports here. *The Washington Post* notes that "Indianapolis has a surprising array of cultural and historical attractions," including the Children's Museum.

Possible drawbacks: Traffic congestion can make the daily commute seem longer and longer, and summer humidity can leave residents sweating like the Pacers at halftime.

▶ Local Population: 783,612

▶ County: Marion

▶ Population of surrounding metropolitan area: 860,454

▶ Region: Central Indiana

▶ Closest metro area: Louisville, 114 miles

▶ Median home price: $98,200

▶ Median household income: $40,051

▶ Best reasons to live here: The town has a growing economy, good job prospects, affordable housing, outstanding medical care, and exceptional higher education.

Climate

Elevation 717'	Average temp. high/low (°F)	Average precipitation		Average no. days precipitation	Average humidity (%)
		rain (")	snow (")		
January	34/18	2.3	6.8	12	71
April	62/41	3.7	0.5	12	56
July	85/65	4.6	0	10	60
October	65/43	2.8	0.2	8	57
Number of days 32°F or below: 122			Number of days 90°F or warmer: 15		

Earning a living

Economic outlook: Centrally located and popularly known as the Crossroads of America, Indianapolis is within one day's drive of 65 percent of the United States population, an excellent attribute for manufacturing or distribution. This is one of the reasons the city was ranked among the Top 20 cities for BioTech companies (*Business Facilities*, 2003), and ranked fifth among the least expensive large cities for doing business (*KPMG Competitive Alternatives*, 2004). Diversity and steady growth are hallmarks of the area's economic development, as well as low utility costs, affordable office space, and high-tech telecommunications. Being the capital, state government plays an important role in local employment. The unemployment rate hovers around 4.8 percent.

Where the jobs are: Eli Lilly and Company, Community Health Network, Clarian Health Partners, Inc., Indiana University/Purdue University at Indianapolis, St. Vincent Hospitals and Health Service, Marsh Supermarkets, Inc., Rolls Royce, FedEx, Allison Transmission/Div. of GMC, SBC Indiana, Wellpoint, Inc.

Business opportunities: Motor sport companies based in the Indianapolis region are a fast growing industry and provide a strong economic foundation for entrepreneurs, small businesses, and Indy's growing workforce. Also, efforts of the Indy Partnership, a privately-funded, nonprofit organization, resulted in creating more than 4,000 new jobs and retaining over 17,000 existing jobs in 2004. Formed in 2000, The Indy Partnership's completed economic development projects will have a positive effect on the community.

Local real estate

Market overview: Whether you are looking for an historic neighborhood, a low-maintenance condominium, or a new subdivision, Indianapolis has a variety of housing solutions to meet your needs.

Average rent for a two-bedroom apartment: $850 per month

Other areas to consider: The Indianapolis Motor Speedway actually sits in the town of Speedway, Indiana. This quality community is proud of its separateness from Indianapolis. Home of Indiana State University, Terre Haute is a fast growing city next to the Wabash River. Zionsville is conveniently located halfway between Indianapolis and Purdue, and has a unique downtown district with lots of modern amenities.

What things cost

ACCRA's national comparisons: Overall living costs are level with the national average. Housing and utilities both fall below average at 7 percent and 4.5 percent respectively. Healthcare is just below average at 2.5 percent. But grocery items transportation and miscellaneous goods are each about 4 percent above the average.

Utilities: Phone: $40 per month; water: $35 per month; electric: $50 per month; gas: $45 per month

The tax ax

Sales tax: 6 percent

Property tax: $21.42 (est. property taxes paid per $1,000 of market value)

State income tax: 3.4 percent

Making the grade

Public education overview: Whether it's with full-time kindergarten classes or their technology initiative, you can be assured that the Indianapolis public school system is pro-children. Since 2002, public school options in Indianapolis have expanded to include charter schools, with five in operation and another five scheduled to open by Fall of 2005. The district is restructuring their five high schools into "Small Schools," where each campus will include three to five learning communities of no more than 400 students grouped around specific academic themes. The district's online system allows parents and students to check assignments and stay in contact with teachers. Over 79 percent of Indianapolis high school graduates go on to higher education. Indianapolis is also served by over 50 private and parochial schools.

Class size (student to teacher ratio): 18:1

Help for working parents: After school programs are available.

Boys & Girls Club: There are 11 centers available.

School year: Mid-August to the end of May. Children must be 5 years old on or before June 1 to enter kindergarten.

Special education/programs for gifted students: Students are usually identified by the end of second grade using test scores from the Terra Nova Test or the Ravens Thinking Ability Test. The Elementary Gifted and Talented program provides learning experiences for students in grades three through five.

Nearby colleges and universities: Indiana University/Purdue University at Indianapolis offers more than 185 academic degrees, including undergraduate, graduate, and postgraduate programs. Butler University is a private, liberal arts and science university, with degrees offered in undergraduate, graduate, and postgraduate programs. Marion College is a Catholic college.

Medical care

Hospitals/medical centers: In addition to the Riley Hospital for Children (*Child Magazine* ranked it 18th Best Children's Hospital), a number of Indianapolis' 23 hospitals are nationally recognized. Clarian Health Partners (1,334 beds) offers a level I trauma center, organ transplant services, and cardiovascular center. Community Health Network (954 beds) offers the Indiana Heart Hospital, women's services, assisted fertility, orthopedics, and outpatient surgery. St. Vincent Health (895 beds) offers cardiology, pediatric care, pediatric emergency department, women and infants care, oncology, and sports medicine. St. Francis Hospital and Health Centers (472 beds) offers a regional heart center, bone marrow transplant program, level II neonatal intensive care unit, home health, and sleep disorders program.

Specialized Care: Wishard Health Services (275 beds) offers a level I trauma center, regional burn center, women's center, and an acute rehabilitation center.

Crime and safety

Police: The Indianapolis police department covers five districts with 1,175 officers. Special units include mounted patrol, canine team, and bicycle patrol. The bike patrol is full-time in the downtown area and part-time in other districts. As well as a Citizen's Academy, residents can also apply to the Civilian Volunteer Police, working with support services of the department. For the youth, the department has the Explorer program and the Police Athletic League, two programs designed to give the community's youth a chance to become directly involved with the department.

Fire: The Indianapolis fire department is located in Marion County and covers 93 of the 402 square miles constituting metropolitan Indianapolis and Marion County with 26 stations. The department's Website has a Survive Alive Village, an official fire safety Website for kids sponsored by Allstate Insurance. The department includes the Marion County Rescue Task Force, a national disaster response team staffed by 210 individuals who can be deployed to any type of natural or man-made disaster where people might be trapped, lost, or injured.

Let the good times roll

Family fun: Indianapolis has the nation's fourth largest city-owned park, Eagle Creek Park, with over 1,400 acres of water and 3,900 acres of land. Not only will you enjoy abundant outdoor recreation, but it is home to the world's largest Children's Museum, offering hands-on exhibits in science, natural history, and world culture. The Museum has a planetarium and an IWERKS theater. The Indianapolis Zoo features desert, forest, and plains animals, plus a whale and dolphin pavilion. With an extensive system of parks you'll find hiking trails, bike routes, rowing, sailing, swimming, cross-country skiing, and more.

Sports: Recognized as the Amateur Sports Capital of the World, Indianapolis hosts international events such as the Indianapolis 500, NCAA Final Four, Brickyard 400, and the United States Grand Prix Formula One race. Professional sports aren't left out either, with the Indianapolis Colts (NFL), Indiana Pacers (NBA), Indianapolis Indians (AAA baseball), and Indiana Fever (WBA). More than 40 public and private golf courses are available, plus hundreds of public and private tennis courts.

Arts and entertainment: The Indianapolis Museum of Art is the seventh-largest general art museum in the United States. The Eiteljorg Museum of American Indians and Western Art features Native American art and artifacts, as well as art celebrating the American West. The Indianapolis Art Center offers children and adult classes, lectures, and concerts. The Indianapolis Symphony Orchestra offers a full schedule of performances. Performing groups include the Indiana Repertory Theatre and the Phoenix Theatre. Dance Kaleidoscope, Indianapolis Ballet Theatre, and the Indianapolis Opera also stage performances.

Annual events: Earth Day, Indianapolis 500, Strawberry Festival, Indiana Black Expo, Indiana State Fair, Brickyard 400 NASCAR race, Penrod Arts Fair, Festival of Lights

Community life

The United Way of Central Indiana and the city of Indianapolis have partnered with *www.VolunteerMatch.org* to promote online access to volunteer opportunities. Volunteer Solutions helps connect individuals and families to volunteer opportunities in their community such as walk-a-thons, beautification days, tutoring, home building, meal deliveries, and more.

The environment

Knozone is Indianapolis' voluntary ozone-reduction program, educating area residents about man-made ozone pollution and encouraging voluntary actions to battle bad air at home, at work, and at play. With the support and participation of Central Indiana residents and businesses, Indianapolis has maintained Environmental Protection Agency standards.

In and around town

Roads and highways: I-465, I-65, I-74, I-70, I-69

Closest airports: Indianapolis International Airport is located approximately 12 miles from downtown.

Public transportation: The Indianapolis metro bus system (IndyGo) covers downtown and suburban areas.

Average daily commute: 25 minutes

More Information

City of Indianapolis
200 East Washington Street
Indianapolis, IN 46204
317-327-3601
www.indygov.org

Indianapolis Public Schools
120 East Walnut Street
Indianapolis, IN 46204
317-226-4000
www.ips.k12.in.us

Indianapolis Chamber of Commerce
111 Monument Circle, Suite 1950
Indianapolis, IN 46204
317-464-2200
www.indychamber.com

American Electric Power
101 West Ohio Street, Suite 1320
Indianapolis, IN 46204
317-822-6370
www.aep.com

SBC
240 North Meridian Street
Indianapolis, IN 46204
317-265-5965
www.sbc.com

Citizens Gas Utility
2020 North Meridian Street
Indianapolis, IN 46202
317-924-3341
www.citizengas.com

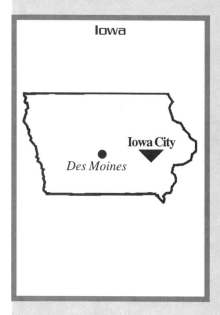

Iowa City, Iowa

Fabulous features

If Iowa City were a student, it would be voted class president. This heartland university town has already been voted to the top of the class on a variety of lists: *Forbes* "Best Small Places for Business and Careers" (2004, 2005); *Readers Digest* "Best Places to Raise a Family" (1998); *USA Today*'s "Best Educated Cities" (2004) and the *Milken Institute*'s best small metro economy. And the town's pride, the University of Iowa, scored tops on Kaplan's best value for your tuition dollar (2004), noting its outstanding medical program.

Even Iowa City's motto "Small-Town Atmosphere, Big-City Choices" gets high marks. Whether you're looking for great schools, a safe community, or low taxes, Iowa City offers an energetic combination of urban and rural environments with a high quality of life. Home to several Fortune 500 companies, and the University of Iowa, Iowa City's economic development is healthy and growing. The report card for Iowa City continues with high marks in some of the best schools in the country, from pre-kindergarten through high school. Being an "artist-friendly alternative" to such metropolitan centers as New York and Los Angeles means you have some of the best in your own neighborhood. This is an extra-credit city and a fabulous place to raise a family.

Possible drawbacks: If you're looking to wear shorts and flip-flops all year, keep searching. You'll be bundled up for more than 40 percent of the year in sweaters and coats.

▶ Local Population: 63,816

▶ County: Johnson

▶ Population of surrounding metropolitan area: 111,006

▶ Region: Eastern Iowa

▶ Closest metro areas: Madison, 176 miles

▶ Median home price: $147,525

▶ Median household income: $72,600

▶ Best reasons to live here: Iowa City is a university town, with excellent schools, friendly community, affordable housing, and abundant outdoor recreation.

Climate

Elevation 700'	Average temp. high/low (°F)	Average precipitation		Average no. days precipitation	Average humidity (%)
		rain (")	snow (")		
January	30/13	1.1	8.5	9	70
April	63/41	3.7	1.4	11	59
July	88/66	4.5	0	10	63
October	66/44	2.8	0.2	8	60
Number of days 32°F or below: 157			Number of days 90°F or warmer: 16		

Earning a living

Economic outlook: Iowa City's economy is as diverse as it is prosperous. Home to emerging and advancing entrepreneurs, this area has maintained fairly steady employment numbers. In 2005, *Forbes* magazine ranked the city ninth in it's "Best Smaller Metros for Business and Careers" list. The Iowa City area consistently ranks among the best places to live by *Places Rated Almanac*. While the state unemployment rate edged over 4 percent in recent years, Johnson County's rate remains around 3 percent.

Where the jobs are: The University of Iowa remains the area's largest employer, with 25,000 employees. The university heads one of the largest teaching hospitals in the nation and is the second largest employer in the city. ACT Inc., an independent nonprofit organization, comes in third. Proctor & Gamble is one of several Fortune 500 companies located in Iowa City.

Business opportunities: The city's new intermodial transit center will add new conveniences for those living and working in the downtown area. Plans for this transportation facility include 500 parking spaces , a Greyhound Bus station, a local bus depot, a daycare center, and bicycle storage. Construction is currently underway on the $10.5 million center.

Local real estate

Market overview: There is plenty of green space and lots of rolling hills. Housing runs from older, brick neighborhoods to new developments with two-story homes and open interiors.

Average rent for a two-bedroom apartment: $600 per month

Other areas to consider: The economy of Cedar Rapids includes Fortune 500 companies, high-tech industry, and agri-business. On the banks of the Mississippi River, Dubuque is like a Midwest San Francisco with steep hills and quality lifestyle. The capital of Wisconsin, Madison is a city bursting with energy and activity. Home of the University of Wisconsin Badgers, this community has a lot to cheer about, such as their stable, diverse economy. Bring your mittens, because it does get chilly during the winter.

What things cost

ACCRA's national comparisons: Overall the living costs are 5 percent below the national average. Housing is 4 percent below the average. Grocery items are the only rating in the double digits being 10 percent below the average. Healthcare is 2.5 percent below, and transportation is 5 percent below the average.

Utilities: Electricity: $60 per month; water: $38 per month; natural gas: $85 per month; phone: $20 per month

The tax ax

Sales tax: 5 percent

Property tax: $37.03 per $1,000 assessed value (consolidated tax rate)

State income tax: 0.36 to 8.98 percent

Making the grade

Public education overview: *Expansion Management* magazine (April, 2005) ranked Iowa City's school district as fifth in the "Best Overall Metro School District" (regardless of size of enrollment). *Offspring*, a journal for parents by the editors of the *Wall Street Journal*, recently ranked the Iowa City School District third in a regional comparison of school districts. The district currently has 17 elementary schools, two junior high schools, two senior high schools, one alternative school for seventh through 12th graders, as well as daycare and preschool facilities. In February of 2003, voters approved a $39 million bond referendum to build additional facilities and upgrade existing buildings. And district voters passed a $39 million referendum, "Yes for Kids," by a 71 percent margin to provide new classrooms and larger media centers at City High School and West High School.

Class size (student to teacher ratio): 18:1

Help for working parents: No information is currently available.

Boys & Girls Club: There are currently no centers available.

School year: Third week of August to first week of June. Children must be 5 years old on or before September 15 to enter kindergarten.

Special education/programs for gifted students: Support for special education in the schools is provided by Grant Wood Area Education Agency, and includes a variety of services. The Extended Learning Program is the elementary program for gifted and talented students in grades three through six.

Nearby colleges and universities: The University of Iowa at Iowa City, Kirkwood Community College

Medical care

Hospitals/medical centers: Mercy Iowa City includes the service Mercy On Call, a free, confidential phone service staffed by Mercy nurses, with a wide variety of resources and references to help you. The University of Iowa Hospitals and Clinics (775 beds) ranked overall as one of "America's Best Hospitals" with 12 of the hospital's specialties listed among the nation's Top 50 in the July 2004 issue of *U.S. News & World Report* magazine. Children's Hospital of Iowa provides care across a full spectrum, from health promotion and well-childcare to the crisis of traumatic injury and life-threatening illness.

Specialized care: Iowa City VA Medical Center provides medical and surgical care to veterans.

Crime and safety

Police: The Iowa City police department has 71 sworn and 28 nonsworn personnel. The officers are involved in many activities such as residential patrol, walking the downtown area, traffic enforcement, or education efforts, all effecting the quality of life. The community relations function includes participating in educational programs in the schools or participating in educational programs such as the Citizen Police Academy or Neighborhood Watch activities. The department has on their Website a blood alcohol concentration calculator if you are curious as to the effects of consumption and quantity of alcohol. The Johnson County Emergency Management tests the Emergency Warning Sirens on the first Monday of each month.

Fire: The Iowa City fire department has 57 full-time firefighters providing fire, medical, rescue, and hazardous materials emergency response. Their area of service includes the University of Iowa's main campus. The department also works in the community including fire safety education, fire station tours, a mobile fire safety education trailer, ride-along program, the Safety Village, and is a co-leader with Mercy Hospital of the Johnson County Safekids Coalition.

Let the good times roll

Family fun: Whether you're looking for something upbeat such as enjoying a theatrical performance, or low-key such as playing 18 holes of golf or camping along the Iowa River, Iowa City has a little of everything. Outdoor activities happen at 42 parks, with indoor and outdoor pools, tennis courts, ball fields, trails, picnic shelters, skate park, and outdoor theater. Or visit Coralville Lake, with 5,000 acres of water for pleasure boating, fishing, swimming, and waterskiing. Downtown is the University of Iowa campus and Old Capitol Museum. A two-block Literary Walk from the Iowa University Pentacrest recognizes some of the most notable entertainers and artisans (including John Irving and Kurt Vonnegut) who have a connection to the city. Completing the walk at Linn Street is the Clock Tower Plaza, with a skywalk. In nearby Coralville you'll find the Coral Ridge Mall, with a regulation-size ice arena, the Children's Museum, John Deere Play Plot, and an antique carousel.

Sports: The Iowa Hawkeye teams take center stage in this city. With men's and women's teams in 17 sports, the Hawkeyes offer thousands of fans the chance to watch championship-level athletics. The Old Capitol Youth Hockey Association is a nonprofit organization providing hockey instruction and opportunities for recreational play for members between 5 and 18 years of age.

Arts and entertainment: The Iowa City Community Theatre has many opportunities if you're interested in acting, working backstage, ushering, or playing in the orchestra. Housed in Macbride Hall, the Museum of Natural History includes more than one million specimens, from microscopic fossils of ancient pollen to mastodon skulls. The Museum of Art has a permanent collection of more than 9,000 paintings, prints, drawings, sculptures, photographs, and decorative art.

Annual events: Englert New Year's Eve Party, Farmers Market, Iowa City jazz festival, Iowa Arts Festival, Register's Annual Great Bicycle Ride Across Iowa

Community life

The University of Iowa keeps a fresh, young aura to the city as new freshmen come in every year. Yet this is not just a city for 15 to 30-year-olds. From downtown to the neighborhoods, you'll find a community working together to enhance the quality of life for everyone, young or old. Volunteer services are a vital part of the city and are welcomed in many venues.

The environment

Composting is encouraged in this university town, with how-to's posted on the city's Website. Water quality is important, and hundreds of tests a day are run to ensure the quality of drinking water in the city.

In and around town

Roads and highways: I-80, I-380, highway 6, 218, state highway 1, 965

Closest airports: The Eastern Iowa Airport in Cedar Rapids is 25 miles away.

Public transportation: There is no public transportation available.

Average daily commute: 16 minutes

More Information

Iowa City
410 East Washington Street
Iowa City, IA 52240
319-356-5000
www.icgov.org

Iowa City Community School District
509 South Dubuque Street
Iowa City, IA 52240
319-688-1000
www.iowa-city.k12.ia.us

Iowa City Chamber of Commerce
325 East Washington Street
Iowa City, IA 52244
319-337-9637
www.iowacityarea.com

Iowa City Community Theatre
PO Box 827
Iowa City, Iowa 52244
319-338-0443
www.iowacitycommunitytheatre.com

MidAmerican Energy
PO Box 657
Des Moines, IA 50303-0657
888-427-5632
www.midamericanenergy.com

MediaCom
702 South Gilbert Street
Iowa City, IA 52244
800-332-0443
www.mediacomcc.com

19 ▶ Overland Park, Kansas

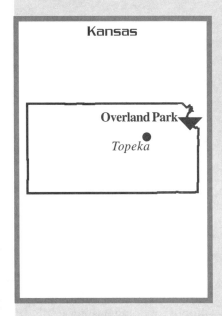

Kansas

Overland Park

Topeka

Fabulous features

Situated on rolling plains, Overland Park boasts outstanding parks, an active recreation department, three of the finest school districts in the country, and an extraordinarily low crime rate. Dorothy and Toto would have been amazed and in awe.

Even a partial list of accolades for this community in recent years is impressive: Overland Park ranked first out of 74 similar cities nationwide, earning it an A-plus on the "Kid Friendly Cities Report Card" from *Zero Population Growth's Kid Friendly Cities Study* of 2001. The Deanna Rose Children's Farmstead earned an extra credit, as a quality kid-friendly feature of the community. *Money* magazine in 2004 listed Overland Park as the third "Hottest Place to Live" in the central region with a population over 100,000. *Business Development Outlook* in 2001 ranked Overland Park the second best city in America to live. Overland Park made the Top10 list of "America's Best Cities for Women" in the 2001 *Ladies Home Journal* survey.

With four distinct seasons, the city of Overland Park offers numerous recreational outdoor choices including 77 parks, six municipal pools, more than 50 miles of bike/hike trail, three public golf courses, and more. A number of people have discovered that you don't need to click your ruby slippers together three times. Overland Park is as nice a place as any over the rainbow.

Possible drawbacks: Kansas is landlocked, so the only thing that comes from the Gulf of Mexico is humidity.

▶ Local Population: 167,000

▶ County: Johnson

▶ population of surrounding metropolitan area: 486,515

▶ Region: Northeastern Kansas

▶ Closest metro area: Kansas City, 8 miles

▶ Median home price: $220,722

▶ Median household income: $62,116

▶ Best reasons to live here: Overland Park has a stable economy, low rates of unemployment, superb public schools, affordable housing, and excellent healthcare.

Climate

Elevation 1,000'	Average temp. high/low (°F)	Average precipitation		Average no. days precipitation	Average humidity (%)
		rain (")	snow (")		
January	38/20	1.3	5.6	7	67
April	56/35	3.7	0.8	11	59
July	89/69	4.0	0	9	64
October	69/48	3.4	0.1	8	60
Number of days 32°F or below: 106			Number of days 90°F or warmer: 40		

Earning a living

Economic outlook: Job availability is above average in this region, and from 1981 to 2003, the number of jobs more than tripled. The workforce is nationally ranked with above-average education and skills. Long-range planning by the city has allowed for developing residential, commercial, and office projects. On average, 3,000 new residents move to the city each year. The Kansas City metropolitan area has more lane-miles of freeway per capita than any other metro area in the United States, which helps lower the cost of doing business. Jobs have doubled in the last 10 years, and unemployment stands at 3.7 percent.

Where the jobs are: Sprint, Applebee's International, Blue Valley School District, Data Systems International, Disney Marketing, Farmers Insurance Group, Gentiva Health Services, Primedia Business Magazines, Waddell & Reed, Yellow Roadway Corporation

Business opportunities: Already home of the Overland Park Convention Center, a $151 million Events Center and Entertainment District has been proposed that would bring minor league sports, moderate-sized concerts, and family entertainment programs. A new high-end shopping mall complex is launching construction. This would be the third regional mall in Overland Park. Johnson County has a business incubator program for start-up operations where companies locate within a facility run by incubator officials, receive tips and advice from peers, and grow their business, eventually moving into their own office or building.

Local real estate

Market overview: In 2003 residents extended the one-eighth cent sales tax for five years to construct new neighborhood streets and make thoroughfare improvements. Older homes include split-levels and ranch-styles, with basements and double garages. New developments are plentiful to choose from.

Average rent for a two-bedroom apartment: $900 per month

Other areas to consider: Shawnee combines a solid economic base with quiet residential neighborhoods. Independence's quality schools and activities make for a family friendly community, with the annual Neewollah celebration attracting more than 80,000 people. Going to Kansas City is a pretty nice. Headquartered companies such as Hallmarks Cards, Sprint, and Russell Stover Candies are a few examples.

What things cost

ACCRA's national comparisons: Overall living costs are 3 percent below average, with grocery items being the lowest percentage at 9 percent below. Housing is 2.5 percent below and health care runs about 7 percent below. Utilities are 3 percent above average, with transportation around 4 percent below.

Utilities: Gas: $65 per month; electricity: $75 per month; water: $27.50 per month; phone: $23 per month

The tax ax

Sales tax: 7.525 percent (city, county, and state)

Property tax: $2,189 (average for a $200,000 home)

State income tax: 3.5 to 6.45 percent

Making the grade

Public education overview: Overland Park is served by three public school districts—Blue Valley, Olathe, and Shawnee Mission—and several private schools. All school districts serving Overland Park have received *Expansion Management* magazine's Gold Medal Education Quotient, and countless state and national awards for educational excellence. Results from national standard tests place all districts well above the national average. The graduation rate of students is 93 percent or higher. The Blue Valley School District was recognized as a Sprint Showcase School in 2002 as well as recipient of the Presidential Award for Excellence in Math and Science in 2003. Shawnee Mission Schools had an elementary school win a No Child Left Behind Blue Ribbon of Excellence Award and named one of the 100 Best Communities for Music Education. Olathe Schools have had students with perfect ACT scores in 2004, 2003, 2000 and 1999; and the only district in the state to achieve a level III Kansas Award for Excellence.

Class size (student to teacher ratio): 15:1

Help for working parents: After school programs are provided in most elementary schools, generally supervised by the YMCA or other agencies.

Boys & Girls Club: There are no centers available.

School year: Middle of August to first week of June. Children must be 5 years old on or before September 1 to enter kindergarten.

Special education/programs for gifted students: Mainstreaming and "class within a class" programs are used in the districts.

Nearby colleges and universities: University of Kansas Edwards Campus has more than doubled in size in less than 10 years. Construction has begun on another addition. Johnson County Community College is a two-year college. The college will open the Nerman Museum of Contemporary Art in 2007.

Medical care

Hospitals/medical centers: There are six major medical centers available in the area: Children's Mercy, Health Midwest Menorah Medical Park, Health Midwest Overland Park Regional Medical Center, St. Luke's Shawnee Mission Medical Center, Carondelet Center, and St Luke's South Campus. All six hospitals have full-staffed, 24-hour emergency centers and provide a variety of specialized programs, including wellness and community education classes. Several healthcare centers affiliated with St. Luke's Shawnee Mission are set up in Overland Park shopping malls. These facilities, staffed by physicians, provide non-trauma healthcare services. Children's Mercy South specializes in pediatric outpatient surgical procedures.

Specialized care: Caring for the mental well-being of Overland Park residents are the Johnson County Mental Health Center and Johnson County Developmental Supports.

Crime and safety

Police: The Overland Park police department is very active with crime prevention programs such as VIN Etch programs, babysitting classes, preschool visits, Teen "Drive-Right" Classes, robbery prevention/survival, shoplifting/theft prevention training, financial fraud prevention training, workplace violence presentations, and road rage presentations. The department works with Homes Association annual meetings and Neighborhood Conservation meetings. All this with a ratio of 1.44 sworn officers per 1,000 residents.

Fire: The Overland Park fire department has won international awards and has an exchange program with departments in France. The department acquired hazardous material response equipment and serves as a regional responder in the Midwest. There are five firestations and a fire training facility. Not only is the fire department always on the alert for public safety, but public compassion as well. In 2005 the department had a Fun Day event for children with special needs, with firetruck rides and equipment displays.

Let the good times roll

Family fun: Overland Park offers many attractions, including downtown Overland Park, the New Theatre Restaurant, 300-acre Overland Park Arboretum and Botanical Gardens, Deanna Rose Children's Farmstead, and Dick Clark's American Bandstand Grill. Overland Park maintains more than 2,000 acres of green space with 63 beautifully maintained parks, a children's petting farm, and Indian Creek, a gorgeous, 10-mile bike and hike trail that will eventually connect with adjacent communities. At Deanna Rose Farmstead, there is a miniature farm created for children, and residents can reserve plots in which to grow their own garden. Great fun awaits on the Missouri side of Kansas City at Worlds of Fun and Ocean of Fun water parks.

Sports: Professional sports enthusiasts can head to Kansas City for year-round action. The Kansas City Royals (MLB), the Chiefs (NFL) and the Attacks (MLS) are here. Collegiate sports fans are delighted with the NCAA's national headquarters and visitors' center in Overland Park.

Arts and entertainment: Music in the Park is found during the summer at Santa Fe Commons Park. At the Overland Park Convention Center, a unique gallery space will show six art exhibitions a year.

Annual events: Fall for the Arts, Halloween Concertfest, Seasonal Lighting Display Contest

Community life

Any community that has a New Arrivals Greeting Service and the theme "Welcome home to Overland Park" shows that this is a great place to raise your family. Friendliness and generosity are the hallmarks of this city. Hundreds of volunteer opportunities are available from the Aboretum to the Deanna Rose Children's Farmstead, OP Arts, and Help-A-Neighbor. There's a place for everyone in Overland Park.

The environment

Overland Park is green and clean. For most years it has been recognized a Tree City, USA. And with few manufacturing plants, Overland Park's air quality has been excellent. Water quality is also good with respect to abundance and purity (the Missouri and Kansas rivers meet or exceed all state and national regulations). Several neighborhoods participate in curbside recycling and composting.

In and around town

Roads and highways: I-35, I-435, US-69, I-635, highway 56

Closest airports: Kansas City International Airport is about 40 minutes away. There are also two business/commuter airports: Johnson County Executive Airport and New Century Air Center.

Public transportation: Johnson County Transit (The Jo) provides bus routes including express service to downtown.

Average daily commute: 12 minutes

More Information

City Hall
8500 Santa Fe Drive
Overland Park, KS 66212
913-895-6000
www.opkansas.org

Blue Valley Schools
15020 Metcalf Street
Overland Park, KS 66283
913-239-4000
www.bluevalleyk12.org

Olathe Schools
14160 Black Bob Road
Olathe, KS 66063
913-780-7000
www.olathe.k12.ks.us

Shawnee Mission Schools
7235 Antioch Road
Shawnee Mission, KS 66204
913-993-620
www.smsd.org

Chamber of Commerce
9001 West 110th Street, Suite 150
Overland Park, KS 66210
913-491-3600
www.opks.org

Economic Development
9001 West 110th Street, Suite 150
Overland Park, KS 66210
913-491-3600
www.opedc.org

Convention and Visitors Bureau
9001 W 110 Street, Suite 100
Overland Park, Kansas 66210
800-262-7275
www.opcvb.org

Kansas City Power and Light
1201 Walnut Street
Kansas City, MO 64106
888-544-4852
www.kcpl.com

Southwestern Bell
5400 Foxridge Drive, Room 310
Mission, KS 66202
888-294-8433
www.sbc.com

Johnson County Water District 1
5930 Beverly Street
Mission, KS 66202
913-895-1800
www.waterone.org

Kansas Gas Service
11401 West 89th Street
Overland Park, KS 64106
800-794-4780
www.kgas.com

Bowling Green, Kentucky

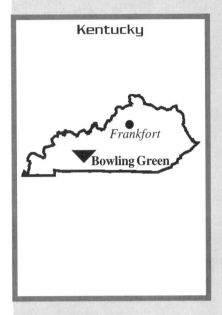

Kentucky

Frankfort

Bowling Green

Fabulous features

The sun does shine bright on the ol' Kentucky homes in Bowling Green. This bluegrass community offers an outstanding quality of life for its residents, with a healthy dose of retail services and a record-breaking number of restaurants per capita. If you want something a little more racy, you have the General Motors Corvette Plant and Museum. Or, in the slow lane, don't miss the annual BB&T Soap Box Derby races.

Continued economic growth offers increased job opportunities as a number of industry corporate headquarters relocate. For the past five years, *Site Selection* magazine has ranked Bowling Green as one of America's top five small towns to relocate or expand a corporate facility.

The educational system in Bowling Green includes Western Kentucky University, Bowling Green Technical College, and an award-winning school system. With four distinctive seasons, the school children can enjoy the sweet anticipation of the odd snow day. Bowling Green's venues from downtown to green, open spaces allow a great deal in recreational opportunities.

Possible drawbacks: Centrally located, Bowling Green becomes the "big city" for the many rural communities around it. During the weekend increased traffic makes it almost impossible to get anywhere on the main thoroughfares. City officials have recently voted in a new 20-year traffic plan which should help ease the congestion.

▸ Local Population: 49,296

▸ County: Warren

▸ Population of surrounding metropolitan area: 92,522

▸ Region: Southern Kentucky

▸ Closest metro area: Nashville, 61 miles

▸ Median home price: $111,000

▸ Median household income: $36,428

▸ Best reasons to live here: Bowling Green has beautiful scenery, a delightful year-round climate, low crime, a range of housing options, good school system, and abundant outdoor recreation.

Climate

Elevation 547'	Average temp. high/low (°F)	Average precipitation		Average no. days precipitation	Average humidity (%)
		rain (")	snow (")		
January	43/25	4.1	4.1	11	66
April	69/45	4.2	0.1	11	56
July	89/68	4.2	0	10	61
October	70/46	3.2	0	7	57
Number of days 32°F or below: 76			Number of days 90°F or warmer: 51		

Earning a living

Economic outlook: With the recent location and expansion of Bowling Green Medal Forming, 1,100 new jobs were created in 2003 and 2004. Recent growth in Bowling Green has developed with new industrial parks and a revitalized downtown area. Warren County is the only county in Kentucky to have no special taxing districts, making them the lowest taxed county in the state. Where else will you find the world-famous General Motors Corvette Assembly Plant and National Corvette Museum?

Where the jobs are: Commonwealth Health Corporation, BANDO USA, Inc., Georgia-Pacific Corporation, Holley Performance Products Headquarters, Western Kentucky University, Warren County Board of Education, Fruit of the Loom, DESA Heating, Eagle Industries, Country Oven Bakery

Business opportunities: The Kentucky Transpark, an environmentally friendly high-tech business park, is centrally located, within 600 miles of 43 percent of the United States population and less than a mile from Interstate 65, the busiest north/south corridor. In cooperation with the Kentucky Community and Technical College System and Western Kentucky University, the Transpark will feature onsite educational and research centers. These facilities will provide customized workforce training and specialized services for not only Transpark tenants, but newly created, existing, or expanding regional businesses as well. A 25,000 square foot training facility is planned for future construction at the Transpark.

Local real estate

Market overview: Everyone from first-home buyers to those ready to invest in more luxurious homes will have lots to choose from.

Average rent for a two-bedroom apartment: $580 per month

Other areas to consider: Somerset, home to the Center for Rural Development, sits on the banks of Lake Cumberland. Bardstown, the Nelson county seat, is steeped in history and Kentucky charm. If you are raising a family in a city where it's getting harder to face the music, Nashville will put more than a song in your heart, it will put extra money in your pocket! The overall tax burden and living costs are lower than in any other major city in the country.

What things cost

ACCRA's national comparisons: Overall living costs are 7 percent below the national average with housing costs being the catalyst with a whopping 25 percent below average. Health care and grocery items are even with the numbers, with transportation and utilities only 2 or 3 percent below average.

Utilities: Phone: $45 per month; natural gas: $20 per month (summer) and $190 per month (winter); electricity: $70 per month; trash: $14 per month

The tax ax

Sales tax: 6 percent

Property tax: $3.76 (est. property taxes paid per $1,000 of market value)

State income tax: 2 to 6 percent

Making the grade

Public education overview: The Bowling Green Independent School District serves six elementary schools, one junior high school, and one senior high school. *Offspring* magazine has recognized the district as one of the 100 best school districts in the nation. Approximately 21 different languages are spoken by students and teachers in the district. This diversity provides students with an opportunity to see what they will experience out in the world. The district recently opened the new Bowling Green Junior High School, and a new elementary school is scheduled to open in 2005. Technology in the district is important, and there are a lot of resources on Internet for parents and students to access. Links to KidBiz3000 can help improve reading skills. Kentucky uses the Commonwealth Accountability Testing System as their standardized testing, and each school's report card scores can be found online. The awards and credits these schools have accumulated would be too long to list. Private schools are also available, such as Bowling Green Christian Academy, which celebrated its 10th anniversary in 2004.

Class size (student to teacher ratio): 16:1

Help for working parents: The preschool program for economically-disadvantaged children is designed for children who will be 4 years old by October 1, and who qualify for free school lunches under federal guidelines.

Boys & Girls Club: There are currently two centers available.

School year: First week of August to the last week of May. Children must be 5 years old on or before October 1 to start kindergarten.

Special education/programs for gifted students: The district's early start program is an important step in getting at risk 3 and 4 year olds off to the best start. Special education programs are tailored to each child. Gifted programs are widely available.

Nearby colleges and universities: Western Kentucky University at Bowling Green offers excellent undergraduate and graduate programs. Western's school of journalism and broadcasting achieved national prominence by placing in the top three of the William Randolph Hearst Foundation national academic rankings in each of the past five years. Bowling Green Technical College offers accredited certificate, diploma, and two-year programs.

Medical care

Hospitals/medical centers: Greenview Regional Hospital (211 beds) provides level II emergency services. The hospital has recently added a StealthStation Treatment Guidance System to their surgical services. The new technology is used to locate tumors with minimal disruption. The after-hours clinic provides additional services to the community. The Medical Center (402 acute-care beds and 110 extended-care beds) offers cardiac care, maternity, cancer treatment, and emergency care. In 2004 a $30 million expansion and renovation was completed, providing a new emergency room, an expanded surgery area, and a consolidated diagnostic imaging center. The community also benefits from their extensive wellness programs.

Specialized care: The Heart Institute at the Medical Center offers the region's only comprehensive cardiac program, including 24-hour emergency intervention for open-heart surgery. The Cancer Treatment Center for Southern Kentucky offers a caring staff and the highest quality in service.

Crime and safety

Police: Bowling Green police department has 155 officers, and recently enlarged their facility by 16,000 square feet to add additional space for communication, evidence, and increased patrol facilities. The communications center was recently awarded the highest audit award from the Kentucky State Police and the FBI. A new addition to the patrol division is the motorcycle unit. Harley-Davidson of Bowling Green leased the motorcycles to the department for $1 a year. The department has a cadet program, offering 15 positions for full-time students at Western Kentucky University to work part-time at the department. The department has also increased its technology power with a GPS monitoring system. Dedication to crime prevention programs include Crimestoppers and Neighborhood Watch.

Fire: The Bowling Green fire department employs 106 workers, 93 of whom actively respond to fires. The department has a dynamic prevention program, working with approximately 14,000 children a year. The department has also upgraded technology with gas detection devices to indicate hazardous materials and thermal imaging devices at all company buildings in the city. The department purchased a platform truck in 2004, providing an elevator-like platform for firefighting.

Let the good times roll

Family fun: Whatever your idea of fun, you can probably find it in the Bowling Green area. From Fountain Square Park to beautiful lakes, you'll find a vast array of recreational opportunities including swimming, fishing, skating, golfing, tennis, canoeing, or horseback riding. Go down in the cavern of Lost River Cave for cool, interesting fun. The river is both the shortest, and the deepest, in the world. Greenwood Park offers 36 holes of unique and challenging mini-golf on their Jungle Village Golf Course. Race the family on the Rolling Thunder Go-Kart track, or cool off in the bumper boat pool. The Russell Sims Aquatic Center has a 50-meter pool with large play structures poviding fun for all ages. Beech Bend Park & Splash Lagoon is an amusement park offering more than 40 rides and attractions. Visit Holley Performance Products, celebrating 50 years in Bowling Green, for a free tour of the facility where they make the carburetors for all NASCAR vehicles. Bowling Green's Parks and Recreation Department was named the 2003 Kentucky Parks and Recreation "Department of the Year."

Sports: For professional excitement, head down the highway to Nashville and cheer on the Tennessee Titans (NFL); Nashville Predators (NHL); Nashville Kats (arena football); Nashville Dream (Women's Professional Football League), or the Nashville Sounds (AAA baseball). Or enjoy the excitement at home with Western Kentucky, which fields teams in 20 varsity sports. Beech Bend Raceway offers racing from March to November.

Arts and entertainment: While it's not your average historical attraction, the National Corvette Museum showcases America's favorite car, with more than 75 models. You'll see classics in mint condition, unique prototypes that never went into production, and racetrack champions. The Barren River Imaginative Museum of Science is a fun hands-on museum for the whole family with over 40 exhibits. The Capital Arts Center features two art galleries and a 840-seat theatre. The Public Theater of Kentucky, Phoenix Theater is located in historic downtown with an intimate 147-seat facility.

Annual events: Southern Kentucky Book Festival, BB&T Soap Box Derby, Concerts in the Park, Holley NHRA National Hot Rod Reunion, National Corvette Homecoming, Duncan Hines Festival, Houchens Industries Winter Light at Basil Griffin Park

Community life

From volunteering to neighborhood associations, Bowling Green lends itself to a southern, gentle way for residents to take pride in their community and offer their services. The Bowling Green Coalition of Active Neighborhoods has its own Website and keeps everyone current with newsletters, e-mails, and support.

The environment

In April of 2004, First Lady Laura Bush announced that Bowling Green was one of 31 Kentucky cities designated as a "Preserve America" community. At the time the award was received, only 65 cities across the nation had earned this distinction. Created in March of 2003, Preserve America is designed to encourage and support community efforts for preservation and enjoyment of America's cultural and natural heritage.

In and around town

Roads and highways: I-65, highway 68, 31, 231, 185

Closest airports: Nashville International Airport is 65 miles away. Bowling Green-Warren County Airport is a municipality center.

Public transportation: Bowling Green Public Transit department has fixed route bus and shuttle services.

Average daily commute: 35 minutes

More Information

City of Bowling Green
1001 College Street
Bowling Green, KY 42102
270-393-3000
www.bgky.org

Bowling Green City Schools
900 Campbell Lane
Bowling Green, KY 42102
270-746-2200
www.b-g.k12.ky.us

Warren Rural Electric Cooperative
951 Fairview Avenue
Bowling Green, KY 42102
270-846-3774
www.wrecc.com

Bowling Green Municipal Utilities
801 Center Street
Bowling Green, KY
270-782-1200
www.bgmu.com

Southwestern Bell
5400 Foxridge Drive, Room 310
Mission, KS 66202
888-294-8433
www.sbc.com

Warren County Water District
523 US 31-W Bypass
Bowling Green, KY
513-695-1337
www.warrenswcd.com

Atmos Energy
2850 Russellville Road
Bowling Green, KY
800-621-1867
www.atmosenergy.com

Bangor, Maine

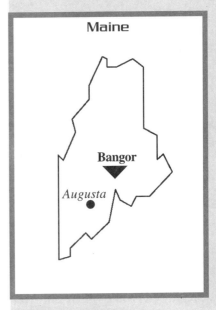

Fabulous features

On the eastern edge of the country, you'll find not only one of the greatest places to raise your family, but one of the safest. *Reader's Digest* of 1998 named Bangor as 19th in the "Top 50 Places to Raise a Family" in the United States. With low crime rates, excellent educational opportunities, a steady economy, and plenty of things to do, Bangor has all the benefits of a large city with none of the problems.

World Trade magazine recognized Bangor as being among its "Top 10 Quality of Life" places to live. With affordability, education, healthcare, and transportation as just some of the factors that determined its selection, Bangor made the grade! In 2004, Bangor was rated sixth in the top safest metropolitan areas in the country by Morgan Quitno. In *Macmillan Travel*'s 1999 and 1997 "Places Rated Almanac," Bangor captured the highest rating of any metropolitan area with less than 100,000 people.

Students growing up in Bangor, Maine have the experience of a rich and varied educational program in a large school district, while enjoying the advantages of a small town childhood. The municipally-owned Bass Park Complex annually brings approximately 100,000 visitors, with such attractions as fairs, expositions, conventions, and concerts.

Possible drawbacks: Maine seems to have four seasons: summer, fall, winter, and mud. With a Nor'easter thrown in every now and then for good measure, if you're not one to snuggle indoors on a cold night, Bangor is probably not the city for you.

▶ Local Population: 31,473

▶ County: Penobscot

▶ Population of surrounding metropolitan area: 125,393

▶ Region: Central Maine

▶ Closest metro area: Boston, 234 miles

▶ Median home price: $105,500

▶ Median household income: $42,047

▶ Best reasons to live here: Bangor offers a low crime rate, excellent schools, a hometown community, beautiful scenery, and a strong economy.

Climate

Elevation 158'	Average temp. high/low (°F)	Average precipitation		Average no. days precipitation	Average humidity (%)
		rain (")	snow (")		
January	28/8	3.4	20	12	62
April	53/33	3.3	4	13	54
July	80/59	3.3	0	11	58
October	57/38	3.5	0.5	10	59
Number of days 32°F or below: 155			Number of days 90°F or warmer: 94		

Earning a living

Economic outlook: The unemployment rate for the Bangor region is consistently below the state average. In the six year period from 1998 to 2003, the unemployment rate ranged from 2.5 to 3.2 percent. The workforce grew steadily from 49,500 in 1998 to 54,025 in 2003. *Business Week* recognized this when naming Bangor as one of "Dazzling Dozen" metro areas constituting America's 12 pockets of prosperity. The workforce is highly educated, with fresh, diverse graduates from the six colleges and universities in the area. Bangor has successfully revitalized its downtown using incentives and support for arts and cultural organizations. Bangor is also enjoying a residential development boon. The number of building permits issued in 2003 was 50 percent more than in 2002.

Where the jobs are: Affiliated Healthcare Systems, Eastern Maine Healthcare, Bangor Mall, University of Maine, General Electric Power Systems, Bangor Savings Bank, St. Joseph's Hospital, city of Bangor, Bangor school district

Business opportunities: Bangor is a commuter town, with a lot of the workforce coming from the surrounding areas as well as in the city itself. Bangor continues its prominence as a retail, entertainment, cultural, and service center for a large portion of the state of Maine, as well as portions of Atlantic Canada. Within 30 miles of Bangor are three ports, transporting commodities to points in the United States, Canada, and offering shorter routes for European-bound cargo. With more than 110,000 miles of fiber optic cable and 100 percent digital phone switching, technology is in place for this state. Maine leads the country with its telecommunications infrastructure.

Local real estate

Market overview: Houses come in just about every size, and with choices from lakefront, shorefront, streamfront, residential, single family, apartments, condos, farms, manufactured, and modular homes.

Average rent for a two-bedroom apartment: $650 per month

Other areas to consider: Waterville, on the banks of Kennebec River, is a diverse and active community. Or you can follow the river to the capital of Maine, Augusta. Enjoy cultural events and variety of higher educational choices. Celebrating 375 years in 2005, Boston's looking pretty good. More than 12 million visitors per year come to tour the cobble-stoned streets and admire the campus of Harvard University.

What things cost

ACCRA's national comparisons: Overall costs of living are about even with the national average. Housing is a double digit 15.9 percent below the average, with utilities counteracting that with 29.3 percent above average. Health care is 12 percent above and grocery items are about 2 percent above.

Utilities: Current information is not available.

The tax ax

Sales tax: 5 percent (food and prescriptions are exempt)

Property tax: Tax rate per $1,000 of valuation is $23.35

State income tax: Individual rates vary from 2 to 8 percent

Making the grade

Public education overview: The Bangor School System provides students with a wide range of academic programs, from Advanced Placement courses at Bangor High School to services for students with special needs. The arts are a key part of Bangor education, and visual arts and music programs are offered at many levels. The Metropolitan Achievement Test has been part of the assessment process in Bangor since 1979, and is the only test given every year to all students. The Maine Educational Assessment underwent significant revisions in 1998. The Performing Arts Program lets all students receive classroom music instruction, choral instruction, string instruction, and band instruction. Bangor region also has eight private primary and secondary schools and the regional Vocational Technology High School.

Class size (student to teacher ratio): 11:1

Help for working parents: Kids Connection is a before- and after-school program supervised by the YMCA.

Boys & Girls Club: There are no centers currently available.

School year: First week of September to the middle of June. Children must be 5 years old on or before October 15 to be eligible for kindergarten.

Special education/programs for gifted students: The Bangor school department provides comprehensive special education programs and accommodations for children with disabilities.

Nearby colleges and universities: The University of Maine offers 91 baccalaureate, 62 masters, and 25 doctoral programs. Husson College offers two- and four-year degrees. Eastern Maine Community College offers one-year certificates, and one-and two-year diplomas. The University of Maine at Augusta Bangor campus confers bachelor degrees in dental hygiene and associate degrees in various programs. The Maine Maritime Academy has an international reputation for excellence in preparing men and women for position of leadership in marine-related fields.

Medical care

Hospitals/medical centers: Eastern Maine Medical Center (411 beds) provides specialty and intensive care services to the northern part of the state and is one of three designated centers in the Maine Trauma System. The center offers cancer treatment, dialysis, a heart center, orthopedics, and women's services. St. Joseph Hospital (100 beds) is operated by the Felician Sisters with a 24-hour emergency room, surgery center, cardiology, and nuclear services.

Specialized care: The state-operated Bangor Mental Health Institute is also located in the city.

Crime and safety

Police: The Bangor police department has a sworn staff of 76 and a civilian staff of 22. The department prides itself as one of the lowest violent crime rates for metropolitan areas of 100,000 population or less. Crime prevention programs are active and successful, including school liaison officers and DARE. The department employs 10 full-time dispatchers, all of whom are certified. The Bangor Police Athletic League has been in existence for 13 years, helping to bring area youth and police officers together through a variety of sports and activities.

Fire: The Bangor fire department is staffed by 88 career firefighters who work a 42 hour schedule per week. The department operates from three stations. With ambulances and paramedics located at all three stations, department staff can be on scene anywhere in Bangor in less than five minutes. Heart defibrillators are on each ambulance and engine. The department recently established a paramedic bike team serving public events where traditional responses might be delayed. Ready to handle any emergency, the department has a technical rescue team for high-angle rescues, confined space/below grade rescues, plus swift and cold water rescues.

Let the good times roll

Family fun: With 30 park and play areas, life outdoors is never dull. The city forest is 650-acres, with miles of walking, biking, and cross-country trails. Or if water is more to your liking, there is the Kenduskeag Stream or the Penobscot River for canoeing or fishing. You can also enjoy two municipal outdoor swimming pools, or the 7,000 square foot Pancoe Pool, featuring two water slides, a zero-entry area, and several water spray features for youngsters. Recreation in Bangor is family-friendly even in the winter with skiing, snowmobiling, and ice-fishing. Just outside of Bangor are some of the country's most beautiful nature sites, such as Mt. Katahdin, Maine's highest peak and the fabled end of the Appalachian Trail.

Sports: According to W-ZON Sports-Zone Radio, Bangor residents cheer for the Boston Red Sox. Collegiate and high school sports pull in the crowds, and fans root for the home teams.

Arts and entertainment: Would you believe the Bangor Symphony Orchestra is the oldest community orchestra in the United States? The symphony has provided continuous service since 1896. The symphony will mark its 110th season in 2006. Check out the Maine Discovery Museum, the largest children's museum north of Boston. The University of Maine Museum of Art houses a permanent collection and changing exhibits. Other venues include the Bangor Museum and Center for History, Robinson Ballet, and Penobscot Theatre Company. Even the Bangor police department has a museum featuring interesting items from the law enforcement past.

Annual events: American Folk Festival, Winter Weekend, Downtown Art Studio Tour, Cool Sounds , Kenduskeag Stream Canoe Race, Bangor State Fair, Bangor Garden Show, soapbox derby, Cascade Park Celebration

Community life

Bangor is one of the few places left in the country where you can let your children play outside and not worry. Children often walk or ride their bikes downtown, to the pool, to the YMCA, or to school. People are so darned nice they usually won't take no for an answer, and if you are asked over to dinner, you'll have no choice but to accept. The community is full of family-type friends, where the wives and husbands enjoy each other's company, and the children all play together.

The environment

Since 1990, Keep Bangor Beautiful has been promoting recycling and beautification programs such as Adopt-A-Park, where business and community organizations may adopt one of Bangor's parks, or Bangor Community Garden, where green-thumbed volunteers plant and care for a garden that everyone may enjoy.

In and around town

Roads and highways: I-95, I-395, state 1-A, 9

Closest airports: Bangor International Airport

Public transportation: Cyr Bus Line and the BAT Community Connector.

Average daily commute: 15 minutes

More Information

City of Bangor
73 Harlow Street
Bangor, ME 04401
207-992-4200
www.bgrme.org

Bangor School System
73 Harlow Street
Bangor, ME 04401
207-992-4152
www.bangorschools.net

Bangor Chamber of Commerce
519 Main Street
Bangor, ME 04401
207-947-0307
www.bangorregion.com

Bangor Hydro-Electric Company
PO Box 932
Bangor, ME 04402
207-945-5621
www.bhe.com

Bell Atlantic
1 Davis Farm Road
Portland, ME 04103
207-797-1438
www.bellatlantic.com

Bangor Gas Company
PO Box 980
Bangor, ME 04402
207-941-9595
www.bangorgas.com

Bangor Water District
614 State Street
Bangor, ME 04401
207-947-4516
www.bangorwater.org

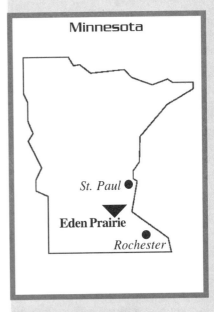

Minnesota

St. Paul •

▼
Eden Prairie
• *Rochester*

Eden Prairie, Minnesota

22

Fabulous features

Eden Prairie owes its name to author Elizabeth Fry Ellet, who, upon visiting this area's bluffs and prairies in the mid-1800s, proclaimed this to be the garden spot of the territory. *Money* magazine calls Eden Prairie the sixth best place in the United States to live and work.

Situated in the vibrant southwestern suburbs of Minneapolis/St. Paul, Eden Prairie boasts very low crime rates and outstanding schools. The city has a strong job market, terrific shopping options, and a variety of restaurants. Eden Prairie is a community of people committed to family recreation, the arts, and community involvement.

Being so close to the Twin Cities, residents have cultural and recreational choices from theater, orchestras, and art museums to major college and professional sports teams, For some of the best indoor recreation, don't miss the Mall of America in nearby Bloomington.

Eden Prairie is only 12 miles from the Twin Cities International Airport, so your family and friends can visit often. This is truly the Eden of the Midwest.

Possible drawbacks: Many newcomers experience the Goldilocks syndrome, crying "this day is too hot" one day, and "this day is too cold" the next. Subzero temperatures can last from November to March, and summer humidity is no picnic either.

▸ Local Population: 60,981
▸ County: Hennepin
▸ Population of surrounding metropolitan area: 2,642,056
▸ Region: Southeast Minnesota
▸ Closest metro area: Minneapolis, 10 miles
▸ Median home price: $325,000
▸ Median household income: $93,258
▸ Best reasons to live here: It's a beautiful lakefront city, with outstanding healthcare and great public schools. Residents are committed to family recreation and the arts.

Climate

Elevation 830'	Average temp. high/low (°F)	Average precipitation		Average no. days precipitation	Average humidity (%)
		rain (")	snow (")		
January	23/3	0.9	10.7	9	69
April	59/35	2.4	2.8	10	55
July	84/62	4.3	0	10	59
October	61/38	2.1	0.5	8	61
Number of days 32°F or below: 158			Number of days 90°F or warmer: 15		

Earning a living

Economic outlook: Thanks to a long-standing and diversified business base, the economic climate of Eden Prairie remains vibrant. The fastest growing city in Minnesota in terms of residential building permits issued between 2000 and 2003, Eden Prairie's building permit activity for retail and commercial property remains very strong. The Twin Cities are headquarters to 13 Fortune 500 companies and Eden Prairie is home to two Fortune 500 companies. Barring unforeseen economic shifts, unemployment should remain at a low 2.8 percent. The Mall of America employs 10,000 people, and will continue to have a ripple effect for other business as it brings shoppers to the area.

Where the jobs are: The Eden Prairie school district, MTS Systems, Inc., Magnetic Peripherals, Rosemount Engineering, CPT, Minnesota Vikings Football, GE Capital Fleet Services, ADC Telecommunications

Business opportunities: Eden Prairie is home to more than 2,200 businesses large and small. Computer firms, printing and publishing, and wood products are some of the fast-growing local industries. Minnesota's famed "Medical Alley" includes hundreds of large corporations. Shopping by Canadian neighbors helps to fuel retail sales.

Local real estate

Market overview: Houses are well-built, most properties are good size, and neighborhoods are beautifully maintained. The appeal of this suburb is the large percentage of land allocated exclusively for parks and green space.

Average rent for a two-bedroom apartment: $900 per month

Other areas to consider: Minnetonka has four distinct seasons and three great school districts. Farmington is a fast growing community with an agricultural heritage. The best of both worlds, large scale business and residential areas, comes with the Twin Cities. With a stable and growing economy, you also have the benefits of five major league sports teams to relax with on the weekends.

What things cost

ACCRA's national comparisons: Overall costs of living are 9 percent above the national average. Housing takes the brunt of the costs at 16.5 percent above the average, with utilities right behind at 14.5 percent above average. Healthcare is 13.9 percent above.

Utilities: Electricity: $65 per month; natural gas: $140 per month (winter) and $30 per month (summer); water: $35/mo; and phone: $25 per month

The tax ax

Sales tax: 7 percent

Property tax: $12.50 (est. property taxes paid per $1,000 of market value)

State income tax: 6 to 8.5 percent

Making the grade

Public education overview: The Eden Prairie school district boasts one of the largest student activities, intramurals, and athletic programs in Minnesota. In 2002, 99 percent of seniors graduated, and 95 percent went on to two- or four-year colleges. And when you start them out at Partners Preschool, you have a quality Eden Prairie education right from the beginning. Parents are receiving important district information by e-mail. Another new attitude in the district is a group called Citizens for Eden Prairie Schools. The members work to preserve and promote high quality education in Eden Prairie through communication with the community and lobbying the legislature. Eden Prairie Schools have been awarded the 2004 "What Parents Want" Award by SchoolMatch, an independent nationwide organization. The International School of Minnesota is a private school located in Eden Prairie that serves students preschool through high school.

Class size (student to teacher ratio): 16:1

Help for working parents: After-school care is provided by the YMCA, or parents of elementary students can choose private centers such as Children's World Learning Centers.

Boys & Girls Club: There are none available.

School year: After Labor Day through mid-June. Children must be 5 years old on or before September 1 to enter kindergarten.

Special education/programs for gifted students: The district's program is for gifted and talented students. Eden Prairie Schools provides a comprehensive program for students with disabilities. Most students receive services in their neighborhood school, and when possible in their regular class setting.

Nearby colleges and universities: The Twin Cities metropolitan area is home to 22 universities, colleges, community colleges, and technical colleges. Hennepin Technical College trains students from among their 45 diverse programs and degrees, the most popular being transportation and nursing.

Medical care

Hospitals/medical centers: When a state can boast of having the second-highest average life expectancy in the country, it's a safe bet that the quality of healthcare is exceptional. The internationally acclaimed Mayo Clinic in Rochester and the University of Minnesota Hospital have some of the finest facilities, diagnostic programs, medical research, and physician care available. The University Hospital is considered the transplant capital of the world. The first open-heart surgery was performed here almost 40 years ago. In the seven-county metro area, there are 32 full-service hospitals.

Specialized care: Minneapolis Children's Medical Center, Shriner's Hospital for Crippled Children, and VA's Medical Center.

Crime and safety

Police: The Eden Prairie police department has 65 sworn officers on staff, and a ratio of 1 officer per 1,000 residents. Emergency service is provided through the city of Eden Prairie for police, fire, and emergency medical services. Many crime prevention programs are promoted such as National Night Out, Community Emergency Response Teams, Neighborhood Watch Groups, school liaison programs, CounterAct, Safety Camp, and the Citizen's Academy.

Fire: The city of Eden Prairie fire department has 4 full-time and 75 highly trained volunteer firefighters. This professional and devoted group staffs fire prevention, fire suppression, and emergency preparedness divisions for the community. In 2004, the department raised $60,000 through private donations to purchase automatic external defibrillators for every public building and school in the community. A fourth fire station will open to serve the southwest quadrant of the city in mid-2006.

Let the good times roll

Family fun: No matter the weather, go outside and play. Eden Prairie has 43 parks, wetlands, and special use areas, five historical sites, and 15 conservation areas covering more than 2,500 acres, and over 90 miles of bike trails. The Parks and Recreation department offers over 130 programs for youth and family, serves more than 550 teams and 9,500 participants each year through adult athletic programs; and serves more than 500-600 participants with disabilities with therapeutic recreation and adaptive recreation programs. The Eden Prairie Community Center has an indoor pool and two indoor skating rinks, fitness center, and snack bar. Nearby in the Twin Cities you have at least 1,000 lakes, plus four state parks available for skiing, swimming, boating, and golf.

Sports: "Tickets" is Minneapolis's middle name. Spectator sports include the major league Minnesota Twins (MLB), Vikings (NFL), Minnewosota Wild (NHL), Timberwolves (NBA), plus all the Big 10 action at the University of Minnesota. And guess where the Viking's training camp is? Eden Prairie! Minnesotans are rabid golfers, and far be it to let a little thing such as winter get between them and their beloved game. For more than 20 years, armed with golf clubs, hockey sticks, sleds, snowmobiles, and tennis balls (which are easier to see in the snow), golfers have been traipsing out onto the ice of Lake Minnetonka to play ice-golf in the annual Chilly Open.

Arts and entertainment: With more than 90 performing arts organizations, Minneapolis is second only to New York City in terms of the number and diversity of cultural offerings. Theater, ballet, dance, and opera tickets are affordable and available. Ordway Music Theater, Orchestra Hall, the Guthrie Theater, and Walker Arts Center are just a few places to enjoy the Minnesota Orchestra, the St. Paul Chamber Orchestra, and the Minnesota Opera. Also for families are two resident children's theater groups, the Children's Museum, and the hands-on Science Museum of Minnesota.

Annual events: July Fourth Celebration, Sunbonnet Days, St. Paul Winter Carnival, Wayzata Chilly Open, Minneapolis Aquatennial, Festival of Nations, Twin Cities Marathon

Community life

When you say "Put your hands up" in this town, no one bats an eye. They know it's not a robbery in action, it's a call for volunteers! And people respond! The city of Eden Prairie operates three municipal liquor stores. The liquor stores generate more than $8 million in sales and provide upward of $650,000 in profits to the city. The profits generated by the liquor stores are used to fund several city projects, including the pavement management program, facility maintenance, and replacement of playground equipment.

The environment

Eden Prairie has a Community Clean Up Day once a year. Hennepin County is again making backyard composting bins and kitchen food waste buckets available to residents at a 57 percent discount. Hennepin County has scheduled three neighborhood collections for household hazardous waste and problem materials for county residents.

In and around town

Roads and highways: I-94, I-35, highway 62

Closest airports: Minneapolis/St. Paul International Airport is approximately 20 minutes away.

Public transportation: Metro Transit Commission covers the entire metro area. Minnesota Ride-share encourages carpools.

Average daily commute: 17 minutes

More Information

City of Eden Prairie
8080 Mitchell
Eden Prairie, MN 55344
952-949-8300
www.edenprairie.org

Independent School District 272
8100 School Road
Eden Prairie, MN 55344
952-975-7000
www2.edenpr.org/wps/portal

Eden Prairie Chamber of Commerce
11455 Flying Cloud Drive Suite 200
Eden Prairie, MN 55344
952-944-2830
www.epchamber.org

Minnesota Valley Electric Cooperative
125 Minnesota Valley Electric Drive
Jordan, MN 55352
952-492-2313
www.mvec.net

23

Rochester, Minnesota

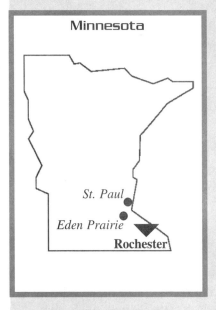

Minnesota

St. Paul

Eden Prairie

Rochester

Fabulous features

Rochester is home to the world-famous Mayo Clinic, whose tradition of caring and compassion extends far beyond the hospital walls. *Redbook* magazine cited Rochester as one of the Top 10 cities for working mothers because of its excellent network of childcare services and the many businesses offering flexible workdays. Rochester was ranked by *Readers Digest* in the Top 50 "Best Places to Raise a Family" in 1998. *Money* magazine recently said it best, "One thing to remember about Rochester is that it has the sophistication of a larger metro area, but not the congestion or the complications." Named "Best Small City" in America by *Money* magazine, Rochester merges a cosmopolitan atmosphere with Midwestern hospitality.

The city's population is diverse, with a large number of immigrants. Rochester is attractive, with beautiful walkways and bike trails winding through the city along the Zumbro River. All of the buildings in downtown are connected by pedestrian subways or skyways, so it's possible to get around comfortably in any weather. And the employment scene? Currently the jobless rate is an enviable 2.5 percent.

Possible drawbacks: Temperatures can drop to 30 degrees Fahrenheit below zero in winter, and a string of below-zero days is not uncommon. Though the area receives heavy snow, the highway department is diligent about clearing the roads and keeping them sanded.

- ▶ Local Population: 95,000
- ▶ County: Olmsted
- ▶ Population of surrounding metropolitan area: 135,000
- ▶ Region: Southeast Minnesota
- ▶ Closest metro area: Minneapolis, 75 miles
- ▶ Median home price: $167,000
- ▶ Median household income: $92,931
- ▶ Best reasons to live here: Abundant healthcare, a clean environment, and a low crime rate. Rochester maintains a small-town friendliness.

Climate

Elevation 988'	Average temp. high/low (°F)	Average precipitation rain (")	snow (")	Average no. days precipitation	Average humidity (%)
January	20/3	1.0	10.7	9	75
April	55/34	3.1	3.8	12	62
July	81/60	4.8	0	11	64
October	57/37	2.2	0.7	9	64
Number of days 32°F or below: 158			Number of days 90°F or warmer: 15		

Earning a living

Economic outlook: The Rochester area population grows at a rate of 1 to 1.5 percent each year, fueling a corresponding rate of job growth. Unemployment here has been historically low, between 2.5 and 3.5 percent for the past 20 years. More than 70 large manufacturing firms and service companies support a strong, diverse business economy. A large food and dairy industry is a significant part of the economy, with service and medical sector opportunities right behind.

Where the jobs are: Mayo Clinic, IBM, St. Mary's Hospital, Rochester Methodist Hospital, Rochester School District, Western Digital, Pemstar, Chocase Software

Business opportunities: Rochester's continued service and medical opportunities will prevail, and there are potential bioscience/technology job opportunities ahead. Rochester International Airport, owned by the city, is increasing its capacity and ability to accept additional flights by extending the primary runway. Increased air cargo has made the airport more competitive. The Rochester Area Economic Development, Inc., supplies assistance to emerging and expanding companies.

Local real estate

Market overview: A diversity of styles, locations, and costs are available. From older colonials to the new developments with multi-gabled luxury homes, there's something for everyone.

Average rent for a two-bedroom apartment: $850 per month

Other areas to consider: Think history plus community and you'll come up with the family-friendly city of Winona. Along highway 90 is Fairmont, with a chain of five lakes running through the city. Who's job is it to count all the lakes in the area? The Twin Cities have a stable and growing economy, and you'll also have the benefits of five major league sports teams to relax with on the weekends.

What things cost

ACCRA's national comparisons: Overall living costs are 4 percent below the national average. Housing holds at 7 percent below average with utilities at 3 percent below. Health care is double digits at 11 percent over the average.

Utilities: Gas: $100 per month; electric: $68 per month; water: $50 per month; phone: $40 per month

The tax ax

Sales tax: 7 percent

Property tax: $10.00 (est. property taxes paid per $1,000 market value)

State income tax: 5.35 to 7.85 percent

Making the grade

Public education overview: Rochester's public schools serve students at 16 elementary schools, four middle schools, and three high schools. The district's three strategic aims are high student achievement; safe and welcoming learning environment; and efficient and effective operations. Student achievement levels are consistently above state and national averages with more than 85 percent of graduating seniors pursuing higher education. The Rochester Public School Foundation, founded in 1988, has awarded a number of grants over the years enhancing the platform of education with community involvement. Rochester also has 11 parochial elementary and one parochial high school. The district uses the Minnesota Basic Skills Tests for standardized testing.

Class size (student to teacher ratio): 25:1

Help for working parents: All elementary schools offer on-site before- and after-school care.

Boys & Girls Clubs: There are two centers currently available.

School year: Third week of August to first week of June. Children must be 5 years old on or before September 1 to enter kindergarten.

Special education/programs for gifted students: A gifted and talented program is active and successful in testing and providing a program matched to the student's abilities. Independent studies and advanced placement programs are available.

Nearby colleges and universities: Rochester Community Technical College, University of Minnesota, Winona State, Crossroads College

Medical care

Hospitals/medical centers: The Mayo Clinic, one of the largest and most respected medical facilities in the United States, is located in Rochester. A seven-time winner of the "100 Top Hospital" recognitions, the Mayo Clinic, Rochester Methodist Hospital, and Saint Mary's Hospital together comprise the center. Mayo physicians staff both hospitals. The medical center has 45 buildings with 1,595 beds, 22,000 employees, and 3,400 physicians. Rochester Methodist Hospital complex is an acute-care hospital with 794 licensed beds and a staff of more than 1,300. St. Mary's Hospital provides more than 1,000 beds and is one of the world's largest private nonprofit hospitals.

Specialized care: The Zumbro Valley Mental Health Center, and the Mayo Clinic's Urgent Care Center provides nonemergency healthcare for adults and children.

Crime and safety

Police: The Rochester police department has 124 sworn officers, supported by 46 nonsworn members. The Communications Center, staffed by nonsworn personnel under non-sworn management, serves the police, sheriff's department, the Rochester fire department, and several small rural fire and first responder organizations. Crime prevention includes DARE and Neighborhood Watch, Business Watch, Explorers post, Citizen Police Academy, the Police Activity Leage, and McGruff Houses. A McGruff House is a temporary safe haven for children who need help while walking in a neighborhood. Operation Identification is a program of permanently marking and registering valuable property and notifying potential thieves and burglars that this action has been taken. In 2002, the department won the National Center for Early Defibrillation Award for achieving excellence in defibrillation.

Fire: Rochester fire makes full use of a mobile fire safety house and the official "Sparky Fire Dog" character to deliver fire and life safety messages. Classes are taught by firefighters in schools and other community events. Rochester fire provides emergency vehicle extrication, confined space, high angle, water, ice, and agricultural accident rescue services. Rochester has been designated a State Regional Chemical Assessment Team, and as such may be dispatched to hazardous material incidents anywhere in southeastern Minnesota.

Let the good times roll

Family fun: Rochester has over 64 parks for outdoor fun and enjoyment, with 12 miles of hike and bike trails, pools, tennis courts, and skating rinks. Chester Woods Park, with its 188-acre reservoir, is where to go for fishing, boating, and a swimming beach. In the winter time, cross-country skiers are out at the Douglas Trail. Take the kids to Quarry Hill Nature Center for the interactive displays and exhibits of the area's wildlife and natural beauty, but especially to see the 1,700-gallon native-fish aquarium.

Sports: You can either head over to the Twin Cities for Minnesota professional action with the Vikings (NFL), Timberwolves (NBA), Minnesota Wild (NHL), or Twins (MLB), or root for the home team with the Rochester A's (single A baseball) or the Rochester Giants (semi-professional football). You have nothing to lose but your voice!

Arts and entertainment: There are 10 art galleries in Rochester, offering visitors a variety of styles and experiences. The Mayo Clinic allows walking tours of their artwork and sculptures. The Rochester Art Center, besides providing gallery space for local and national artists, provides art courses and art education. The Southeastern Minnesota Visual Artists features a gallery with a collection including everything from pottery to oil paintings by regional artists. Rochester Civic Theatre offers seven productions each year.

Annual events: Rochesterfest, Winterfest, Down by the Riverside Concerts

Community life

Every kind of volunteer program and service club exists here. Rotary Clubs, Kiwanis Clubs, and the American Association of University Women raise money for scholarships for young people in need. With nearly half a million people seeking medical care at the Mayo Clinic each year, Rochester has become the city with a heart.

The environment

Rochester is under the Olmsted County smoke-free restaurant ordinance, where smoking in dining establishments that earn more than half their revenue from food sales is prohibited. The county also has an aggressive recycling program, a hazardous household waste facility, and a waste-to-energy facility that creates steam and electricity from garbage.

In and around town

Roads and highways: I-90, I-35, US 14, 52, 63, state highways 30, 40, 296

Closest airports: Rochester Municipal Airport. Rochester Direct provides van service to Minneapolis Airport.

Public transportation: Limited bus service is available.

Average daily commute: 15 minutes

More Information

City of Rochester
201 4th Street SE
Rochester, MN 55904
507-285-8086
www.ci.rochester.mn.us

Independent School District #535
615 7th Street SW
Rochester, MN 55902
570-285-8551
www.rochester.k12.mn.us

Rochester Area Chamber of Commerce
220 South Broadway, Suite 100
Rochester, MN 55904
507-288-1122
www.rochestermnchamber.com

Rochester Public Utilities
4000 East River Road NE
Rochester, MN 55906
507-280-1500
www.rpu.org

Qwest Communications
320 2nd Avenue SW
Rochester, MN 55902
800-475-7526
www.qwest.com

24

Columbia, Missouri

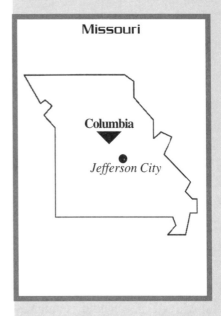

Missouri

Columbia

Jefferson City

Fabulous features

Click on Columbia's Convention and Visitors Bureau Website and at the top you'll see "Columbia, the smart, innovative, artsy, eclectic, clever, savvy, vibrant, too-dynamic-to-fit-into-a-short-tagline city." What's left to say? This is a fast-growing Midwest city, packed with quality culture, and great people. You get small town friendliness with big city features for a high quality of life.

Some of Columbia's many attributes are an excellent school system, outstanding healthcare facilities, plenty of entertainment opportunities, bundled with a low cost of living in a clean, green environment. It's also centrally located with quick access to St. Louis and Kansas City, and the beautiful Lake of the Ozarks.

At every turn, this quiet city is infused with life and brains. Home to the University of Missouri, Columbia offers a vitality as natural as the rolling hills. A university town with a variety of flavors and activities, Columbia was ranked number one "Best Town to Live In" in the 2005 Reader's Choice Awards published by *Rural Missouri* magazine. Columbia ranked 15th "Least Stressful City" in which to live by Sperling's *Best Places* study of 2004.

Possible drawbacks: Columbia provides healthcare to the entirety of central Missouri, so although there are many doctors in the area, it's not always easy to get an appointment. Also, air service to the area is limited, so you'll have to drive two hours to the airport.

▶ Local Population: 84,531

▶ County: Boone

▶ Population of surrounding metropolitan area: 135,454

▶ Region: Central Missouri

▶ Closest metro area: St. Louis, 145 miles

▶ Median home price: $118,500

▶ Median household income: $33,729

▶ Best reasons to live here: Columbia offers award-winning schools, outstanding medical care, affordable housing, green space, and a booming job market.

Climate

Elevation 758'	Average temp. high/low (°F)	Average precipitation rain (")	snow (")	Average no. days precipitation	Average humidity (%)
January	37/18	1.7	5.9	8	69
April	66/43	4.2	0.7	11	59
July	89/67	3.7	0	8	63
October	68/44	3.2	0	9	62
Number of days 32°F or below: 108			Number of days 90°F or warmer: 39		

Earning a living

Economic outlook: Wal-Mart co-founder Sam Walton was a Columbia native, a graduate of Hickman High School, and the University of Missouri-Columbia. Columbia could soon end up with four Wal-Mart Supercenters. Columbia Transload Inc. is an 84,000 square foot storage and transportation facility that opened in March of 2004. Freight can be taken into Columbia by rail, using the facility for storage. Because a single rail car can hold as much as three or four heavy trucks, fewer trucks will be on the road because of the warehouse, which means less wear and tear on the roads.

Where the jobs are: University of Missouri, University of Missouri HealthCare, Columbia Public Schools, Boone Hospital Center, City of Columbia, Shelter Insurance

Business opportunities: Columbia's median age is 26, so is it any wonder *Forbes magazine* listed Columbia as the 38th "Best Small Metro for Business" in 2004? And *Expansion Management* magazine rated Columbia a five-star city in their 2005 *Quality of Life* study? Note that Missouri is not a right-to-work state, and has a very small presence of organized labor in general.

Local real estate

Market overview: On the heels of a record-setting year for home-financing rates, Columbia in 2003 had its third straight year of more than 2,000 homes sold.

Average rent for a two-bedroom apartment: $570 per month

Other areas to consider: Jefferson City is the state's capital, and has all the amenities of a family-friendly community. Imagine raising your child in Hannibal, the hometown of Mark Twain, where the phone number to the Visitors Bureau is 1-TOM-AND-HUCK! Resting up against the mighty Mississippi, St. Louis is moderately flat with a gentle rise or two, and home to a lot of people. Parts of the 1904 World's Fair can be seen every day.

What things cost

ACCRA's national comparisons: Overall costs of living are 6 percent below the national average. Housing is down in the double digits at 10.3 percent below average. Utilities are 7 percent below, with healthcare right next to it at 5 percent below. Transportation and miscellaneous goods both come in at 2 percent below the average.

Utilities: Electricity: $55 per month; natural gas: $60 per month; phone: $27 per month

The tax ax

Sales tax: 7.22 percent

Property tax: $14.90 (est. property taxes paid per $1,000 of market value)

State income tax: 1.5 to 6.0 percent

Making the grade

Public education overview: *Expansion Management* magazine's 2004 study rated the Columbia Public School District a "Blue Ribbon District." Columbia is very supportive of education, as evidenced by such community programs as Partners In Education, Parents As Teachers, Caring Communities, Adventure Club, and the city's Career Awareness and Related Experience Program. The dropout rate for the district is 4 to 5 percent. Approximately 80 to 90 percent of high school graduates go on to higher education. The Missouri Assessment Program is the district's standardized testing. In 2005, groups of elementary school students in bright yellow shirts participated in a pilot Walking School Bus program. Parents will take turns in leading the "buses" to and from school. Walking to school is an easy way for children (and adults) to get the 30 to 60 minutes of daily physical activity recommended by the Centers for Disease Control to maintain a healthy weight and reduce the risk of chronic disease.

Class size (student to teacher ratio): 15:1

Help for working parents: All elementary schools offer before- and after-school care. Adventure Clubs are operated by the Extension Division of the University of Missouri. Children 3 to 5 years old from anywhere in the district can qualify for a free half-day preschool program.

Boys & Girls Club: There are two centers available

School year: First week of September to mid June. Children must be 5 years old on or before July 1 to enter kindergarten.

Nearby colleges and universities: The University of Missouri Columbia is both an acclaimed research institution and a state land-grant university. The "America's Best Colleges 2005" study by *U.S. News & World Report* ranked the univerity in the top tier of national universities. Columbia also has two private liberal arts colleges: Stephens College and Columbia College.

Medical care

Hospitals/medical centers: Boone Hospital Center (344 beds) is a full-service facility. The University of Missouri Health Sciences Center includes University Hospital, Children's Hospital, Ellis Fischel Cancer Center, Columbia Regional Hospital, and the University of Missouri-Columbia's School of Medicine, Nursing, and Health Related Professions.

Specialized care: The Harry S. Truman Memorial Veterans Hospital is an affiliated acute-care teaching hospital with services for veterans.

Crime and safety

Police: The Columbia police department Community Action Team was created in 1998 to assist officers in solving chronic problems, and to address crime trends. The Community Action Team also uses non-traditional methods of policing and works closely with many units within the police department, other city departments, and other law enforcement agencies. The Crime Free Multi-Housing program was first offered in Columbia in March of 2000 as a way to reduce the number of calls for service at rental properties. The Neighborhood Response Team consists of various city agencies that work together in an effort to address quality of life. Other crime prevention programs include DARE, Neighborhood Watch, Citizens on Patrol, Youth Academy, Citizens Police Academy, and Crime Stoppers.

Fire: The Columbia fire department has 124 firefighters. When a citizen calls 911, a computer aided dispatch system helps identify the location of the incident; any special information about that location such as the closest fire hydrants, cross streets, special hazards such as chemicals or gasoline stored on site; or even if small children live at the residence. The Honor Guard continues their impressive quality with three more National Championships (1993, 1999, and 2000) as well as a second place finish (1998) and a third place finish (1997). The Honor Guard continues to be recognized as one of the finest fire department Honor Guards in the nation.

Let the good times roll

Family fun: Recreational opportunities in the Columbia and mid-Missouri area are plentiful. Within 10 miles of Columbia, there are 3,000 acres of state park lands. The city itself has 1,500 acres of beautiful parks. Federal forests and wildlife refuges are nearby, as is the Katy Trail, a hiking and biking trail that stretches across Missouri and is accessible throughout Columbia. Hunting and fishing opportunities abound in central Missouri and the Ozarks. Columbia is only a few hours' drive from scenic lakes and streams that are ideal for float trips, camping, and backpacking.

Sports: For the sports enthusiast, Kansas City and St. Louis both have major-league sports teams, including the Chiefs and Rams (NFL), the St. Louis Blues (NHL), and the Royals and Cardinals (MLB). Don't forget the university offers Big 12 Conference football, basketball, baseball, and other sports. The Health Sciences Center complex is close to a 65,000-seat stadium, a 15,000-seat multipurpose auditorium, an 18-hole golf course, an indoor recreation building, tennis courts, racquetball courts, squash courts, and indoor and outdoor swimming pools.

Arts and entertainment: Music lovers will enjoy performances at the Missouri Symphony Society and appearances by acclaimed ballet, dance, and choral groups. Plays and musicals are staged at the university's Rhynsberger Theater, and Stephens

College offers outstanding productions at its Playhouse and Warehouse theaters. The Twilight Festivals in June and September bring thousands of people to the district. Art in the Park and the Fall Festival of the Arts are also a big hit. And who can forget the Blind Boone Ragtime and Early Jazz Festival, honoring one of Columbia's most renowned citizens, John William "Blind" Boone?

Annual events: Martin Luther King Jr. celebration, Salute to Veterans Air Show, Twilight Festival, Art in the Park, J.W. Boone Ragtime and Early Jazz Festival, Fire in the Sky, Boone County Fair, Columbia Festival of the Arts, Downtown Holiday Festival, First Night Columbia

Community life

An active student population and a large pool of senior citizens are reasons why the number of volunteers and total number of hours contributed to the community are higher in Columbia. Sororities and fraternities have given back to the community, donating $15,000 to each of six local agencies. More than 200 senior citizens keep the roles of Columbia's RSVP program filled, giving piano lessons, making quilts and blankets for needy children, delivering food for the Central Missouri Food Bank, tutoring local students, and assisting in blood drives.

The environment

Columbia's recycling program, called the "Blue Bag Program," enables residents to have recycled items picked up with their regular trash collection once a week. Columbia has one of the most progressive environmentally sensitive city governments in the Midwest, contributing to excellent air and water quality. Stringent bans on land disturbance and burning and billboard control show the city's commitment.

In and around town

Roads and highways: I-70, US 63

Closest airports: Columbia Regional Airport offers direct service to St. Louis.

Public transportation: Columbia Transit Authority

Average daily commute: 15 minutes

More Information

City of Columbia
701 East Broadway
Columbia, MO
573-874-7111
www.gocolumbiamo.com

Columbia #93 School District
1818 West Worley Street
Columbia, MO 65203-1038
573-214-3400
www.columbia.k12.mo.us

Chamber of Commerce
300 South Providence Road
Columbia, MO 65203
573-874-1132
http://chamber.columbia.mo.us

Columbia Water and Light Department
725 East Broadway
Columbia, MO
573-874-7380
www.gocolumbiamo.com

Boone Electric Cooperative
1413 Rangeline Road
Columbia, MO 65203
573-449-4181
www.booneelectric.com

CenturyTel
625 East Cherry
Columbia, MO
800-201-4099
www.centurytel.com

25

Billings, Montana

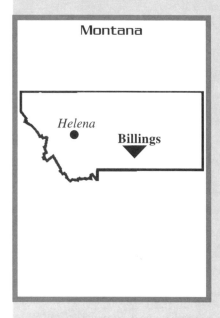

Fabulous features

What do you think of when someone says Montana? Big skies? Wide open spaces? Now add to that vision a cultural hub with views of four incredible mountain ranges, great schools, and a stable economy. Guess what you have? Billings, Montana!

Not only will you find natural beauty here, but you'll find great man-made views as well. In 2002 a great downtown gathering place and Billings landmark was constructed. They call it Skypoint. Part of their downtown revitalization includes streetscape elements.

A beauty with brains, Billings has enjoyed a rapid growth rate, supported by various economies, including energy, agriculture, and transportation. Commercial interests have brought a lot more people, creating a center for quality education plus additional choices for higher learning, medical facilities, and cultural activities.

Land of the Big Sky? You betcha! With big fun and comfortable living thrown in, too. Billings is a fabulous place to raise a family.

Possible drawbacks: Limited manufacturing opportunities may be an issue if your career is centered on heavy or major manufacturing. But then you have some of the cleanest air possible in Big Sky country, so it's a toss-up.

▶ Local Population: 89,847
▶ County: Yellowstone
▶ Population of surrounding metropolitan area: 129,352
▶ Region: Central Montana
▶ Closest metro area: Salt Lake City, 386 miles
▶ Median home price: $99,900
▶ Median household income: $35,147
▶ Best reasons to live here: Billings has incredible natural scenery, affordable housing, and a relatively milder climate.

Climate

Elevation 3,124'	Average temp. high/low (°F)	Average precipitation		Average no. days precipitation	Average humidity (%)
		rain (")	snow (")		
January	33/15	0.8	9.3	8	57
April	58/35	1.7	8.1	10	42
July	86/58	1.3	0	8	32
October	59/37	1.3	3.6	6	43
Number of days 32°F or below: 152			Number of days 90°F or warmer: 28		

Earning a living

Economic outlook: Billings is one of the largest centers for retail, medical, and convention services, drawing people from Montana, Wyoming, South Dakota, and North Dakota. The undeniable hub for the distribution of goods and services in this large area, Billings has excellent transportation networks set up. Billings was ranked eighth best small city for creating and sustaining jobs, in the Milken Institute's 2004 report. The unemployment rate for Yellowstone County runs at an average of 3 percent, partly due to the Business Expansion and Retention program. The program is a collaborative community effort providing assistance to expand business, increase employment, and maintain a healthy economy. Can you imagine having your convention in Billings surrounded by Yellowstone National Park and mountain ranges? Their facilities include more than 750,000 square feet, perfect for any annual summit.

Where the jobs are: The Deaconess Billings Clinic, St. Vincent Healthcare, Diversified Transfer and Storage, Billings School District, Montana State University, the city of Billings

Business opportunities: Future plans for Billings concentrates on creating housing in the downtown area including lofts, townhouses, and luxury housing. A community effort among Realtors, developers, and the residential departments at Montana State University at Billings will provide the efforts in developing and planning new housing downtown. The new Regional Operations Center is a 44,000 square foot, two-story facility in southwest Billings. The center is expected to bring over 100 new jobs to Billings within the next year, with more jobs planned in the long term. The total economic impact of the project on the community over a 10 year period may be approximately $65.6 million in additional wages and income.

Local real estate

Market overview: If variety is the spice of life, housing in Billings is one spicy dish! Ranch style, two-story, duplexes, condos, and more are all available.

Average rent for a two-bedroom apartment: $580 per month

Other areas to consider: High-tech is icing on the cake to the Bozeman's agricultural economy. Laurel is a rural community compared to Billings. Salt Lake City, with its dramatic mountain range backdrop, has clean and friendly neighborhoods.

What things cost

ACCRA's national comparisons: Overall living costs is 1.7 percent below the national average. The rest of the numbers fluctuate from housing at 13.6 percent below average to healthcare at 13.1 percent above average. Grocery items, utilities, and miscellaneous goods are all about 2 to 3 percent above average, and transportation runs about 3.8 percent below.

Utilities: Electricity: $57 per month; gas: $68 per month; phone: $29 per month

The tax ax

Sales tax: There is no sales tax in Billings.

Property tax: $13.60 (est. property taxes paid per $1,000 of market value)

State income tax: 1 to 2 percent

Making the grade

Public education overview: Billings high schools consistently rank in the top percentile nationwide in score achievement for the American College Test. Students participate in the Iowa Test of Basic Skills for standardized testing. Endowments, scholarships, grants, and special events are what the Education Foundation provides for students and educators. Programs include: Saturday Live, a fund-raising carnival; Partners in Education, matching businesses and schools as partners; and Reading Rocks, a summer reading program. There is also the Billings Catholic School District, with a reputation for providing an excellent academic education. Typically, the elementary students test at or above grade level on national basic skills tests. Nearly all of the St. Francis students remain in the Billings Catholic Schools following eighth grade by enrolling at Central Catholic High School. Central Catholic High School has a graduation rate of almost 100 percent. Over 90 percent of Central graduates enroll in a college or university.

Class size (student to teacher ratio): 18:1

Help for working parents: KIDS After School Care is available on a fee-based program.

Boys & Girls Club: There are three centers currently available.

School year: Mid-August to Mid-June. Children must be 5 years old on or before September 10 to enter kindergarten.

Special education/programs for gifted students: Both services are available in the school district.

Nearby colleges and universities: Montana State University at Billings offers associate and bachelor degrees. Rocky Mountain College is Montana's oldest and first institution of higher learning, with quality liberal arts and professionally orientated majors.

Medical care

Hospitals/medical centers: Two hospitals handle medical and surgical needs for Billings. Deaconess Billings Clinic (272 beds) is a level II trauma center with services including cardiovascular, medical neurological, psychiatric, and pulmonary. St. Vincent Healthcare (302 bed) has a level II trauma center, and offers services in cardiology, general internal medicine, neonatology, orthopedic care, pediatrics, rehabilitation, and women's services.

Specialized care: Northern Rockies Cancer Center is the foremost treatment center in the region. Rimrock Foundation offers treatments for various addictive disorders, such as chemical dependency and eating disorders.

Crime and safety

Police: The Billings police department has five canine units. The department participates in the McGruff Safety House, a national program to provide temporary safe havens for children. The volunteer program recruits, trains, and places volunteers throughout the department to help and strengthen innovative public safety programs for the needs of the community. Crime prevention programs include participation in National Night Out, Neighborhood Watch, and more.

Fire: The city of Billings fire department is staffed with 97 shift personnel providing fire suppression and emergency response. The biggest community achievement in 2004 was the passing of the Public Safety Levy, which will enable the fire department to catch up with the continual growth of the city. The levy will provide 16 firefighters and a new station over the next five years. The department's partnership with Montana State University at Billings in providing a fire science degree program is beginning to provide qualified applicants for the fire department.

Let the good times roll

Family fun: Billings knows how to throw a party, either downtown or at the Metra-Park, you'll find something for everyone. MetraPark, seating 12,000, is a multi-purpose facility serving as an auditorium, exhibition hall, stadium, and fairgrounds for such events as live concerts, trade expositions, rodeos, horse racing, and the Montana State Fair. Sporting events include basketball, football, wrestling, and hockey. Pictograph Cave State Park is a few miles south of Billings, where in prehistoric times, Indians camped at the cave and added some 106 primitive paintings to the cave's sandstone walls. There are three national parks within a day's drive of Billings: Yellowstone, Glacier, and Grand Teton.

Sports: Billings Mustangs baseball is located just minutes north of downtown Billings. Cobb Field has been the home of the Billings Mustangs since the club's inaugural season of 1948. Originally known as Athletic Park, the 4,200 seat stadium was renamed

Cobb Field. The Billings Mavericks are entering into their fifth season with the National Indoor Football League. The Mavericks play in the MetraPark Arena, which holds 8,700 fans.

Arts and entertainment: The Alberta Bair Theater hosts ballet, plays, children's theatre, and chorale productions, as well as the Billings Symphony and the Rimrock Opera Company. Yellowstone Art Museum houses more than 2,000 pieces and focuses on regional and western art.

Annual events: Strawberry Festival, Alive After 5, Harvestfest, Holiday Parade, Christmas Stroll

Community life

Billings may be one of the best kept secrets west of the Mississippi, because the people are busy working and playing in an almost self-contained community. With a busy downtown sector, there's no end of entertainment. Volunteering can be just about anything you can imagine, from the police department to the elementary schools. Billings is a friendly, genuine community.

The environment

For the number of people in Billings, they have a large number of recycling centers. Their community is important to them and residents have made the quality of life a priority. Earth First Aid has a curbside recycling program, providing three bins per household with their service. On their Website is a list of "green" businesses, those that recycle with their service. Clean air and water are almost taken for granted around here.

In and around town

Roads and highways: I-90, I-94, state highway 87, 3

Closest airports: Logan International Airport has 35 scheduled flights daily with seven passenger airlines.

Public transportation: Metropolitan Transit offers local and regional bus service.

Average daily commute: 16 minutes

More Information

City of Billings
210 North 27th Street
Billings, MT 59103
406-657-8433
www.ci.billings.mt.us

Billings Public Schools
415 North 30th Street
Billings, MT 59101
406-247-3777
www.billings.k12.mt.us

Billings Catholic Schools
PO Box 31158
Billings, MT 59107
406-252-0997
www.billingscatholicschools.org

Billings Area Chamber of Commerce
815 South 27th Street
Billings, MT 59107-1177
406-245-4111
www.billingschamber.com

Downtown Billings
2906 3rd Ave. North
Billings, MT 59101
406-294-5060
www.downtownbillings.com

Northwestern Energy
40 East Broadway
Butte, MT 59701
888-467-2669
www.northwesternenergy.com

Yellowstone Valley Electric
150 Cooperative Way
Huntley, MT 59037
800-736-5323
www.yvec.com

Montana Dakota Utilities
2603 2nd Avenue North
Billings, MT
800-638-3278
www.montana-dakota.com

OneeightyCommunications
206 North 29th Street
Billings, MT 59101
406-294-4000
www.oneeighty.com

City of Billings Water
2251 Belknap Avenue
Billings, MT
406-657-8331
www.ci.billings.mt.us

Bresnan Communications
1124 16th Street W, Suite 6
Billings, MT
406-238-7700
www.bresnan.com

26

Henderson, Nevada

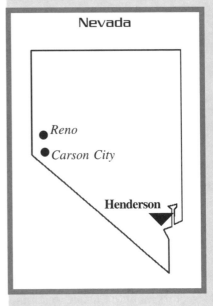

Nevada

● Reno
● Carson City

Henderson

Fabulous features

For a great place to live, look to Henderson's excellent healthcare, award-winning parks, recreation, and schools. The lights from Las Vegas play shadow games on the mountains, adding to the sweet dreams of this community.

Located in the center of three of the greatest man-made attractions in the country, Henderson is just minutes from the neon glitter of Las Vegas, the splendor of the Hoover Dam, and the tranquility of Lake Mead. Known for having small town values with big city efficiencies, Henderson has one of the lowest property tax rates and no state tax. Many new residents and businesses choose to relocate here every year.

Henderson is a suburb with lots of sunshine, mild winters, very little rain, and a mountain range 45 minutes away. No wonder it's been ranked for being "Kids Friendly" and one of the "Top 50 Safest Cities to Live."

Henderson is the home of chocolate (Ethel M. Chocolates), marshmallow (Kidd and Company), and ice cream (Gold Bond) makers. One official has mused that Henderson might be the "Sweet Tooth Capital of Nevada." No wonder the city slogan is "A Place to Call Home."

Possible drawbacks: The desert climate is totally unique. Winters drop down into the 20s, while summers can sizzle with continuous 100-plus days. Some love the roller coaster variety, while others yearn for a more "normal" climate.

▶ Local Population: 229,985

▶ County: Clark

▶ Population of surrounding metropolitan area: 1,715,337

▶ Region: Southern Nevada

▶ Closest metro area: Las Vegas, 18 miles

▶ Median home price: $156,000

▶ Median household income: $55,949

▶ Best reasons to live here: It's a fast growing area, with fabulous culture and recreation, a dry desert climate, no state income tax, and excellent medical care.

Climate

Elevation 1,940'	Average temp. high/low (°F)	Average precipitation rain (")	snow (")	Average no. days precipitation	Average humidity (%)
January	56/37	0.6	0.9	3	32
April	77/53	0.2	0	2	16
July	103/78	0.5	0	3	15
October	80/57	0.3	0	2	20
Number of days 32°F or below: 41			Number of days 90°F or warmer: 131		

Earning a living

Economic outlook: Henderson is no longer a bedroom community to Las Vegas. More than 35 percent of employed residents work in Henderson, exceeding the goal set in the 1996 Henderson Comprehensive Plan for 25 percent in-town employment. In fact, three times more residents work locally within the city limits than commute to the nearby Las Vegas Strip. Home to a variety of industries, the predominant business sectors include finance, insurance, and real estate firms. Henderson has also become home to a number of new colleges. In 2002, Nevada State College opened its doors, making Henderson home to the first state college in Nevada. With the addition of Touro University College of Osteopathic Medicine, and National University in the past year, Henderson is now home to 13 colleges and universities. Positions in highest demand in the area include those in healthcare fields.

Where the jobs are: St. Rose Dominican Hospital/Siena Hospital, Ford Credit, Good Humor-Breyers Ice Cream, Ethel M. Chocolates, Berry Plastics, Ocean Spray Cranberries, Inc.

Business opportunities: The I-215 Beltway linking to I-15 serves Henderson in interstate transportation, making the city part of the CANAMAX trade corridor, developed to facilitate the movement of goods, services, people, and information between Canada, America, and Mexico. The 2004 *Kosmont-Rose Cost of Doing Business Survey* rated Henderson as a "Low Cost City," creating an outstanding business environment with one of the lowest tax systems in the nation featuring neither state corporate income, nor personal income taxes. In addition, Henderson's property tax rates are among the lowest in the state of Nevada.

Local real estate

Market overview: Construction is mainly frame, stucco, and concrete block with minimal landscape or desertscape to endure the summer sun.

Average rent for a two-bedroom apartment: $600 per month

Other areas to consider: Boulder City lies in the shadow of Hoover Dam. There is no gambling allowed in this oasis. Paradise is a growing community within commuting distance of Vegas. Future job growth predictions for Las Vegas are over 42 percent, helping it to become the premiere entertainment destination.

What things cost

ACCRA's national comparisons: The overall cost of living is 13 percent above the national average. The one-two punch comes from housing being 30 percent above average and healthcare at 20 percent above average. Utilities is the only area that drops below the nation's average at a mere 3.4 percent.

Utilities: Water: $33.63 per month; Gas: $74.16 per month(winter) or $28.99 per month (summer); electric: $123.26 per month; phone: $15.64 per month

The tax ax

Sales tax: 7.5 percent

Property tax: For every $100 of assessed valuation on a home, a person will pay $2.94 in property taxes. The assessed value is 35 percent of taxable value.

State income tax: There is no state income tax.

Making the grade

Public education overview: Henderson public schools are part of the Clark County School District, one of the largest school districts in the United States. All public schools serving Henderson youth are in the district's southeast region, which also includes schools in southeastern Las Vegas, Searchlight, Boulder City, and Laughlin. Of their current operating schools, 18 elementary school and six junior high school sites encompass 460 total acres. The land was donated to the school district as part of the city's development process. People Promoting Literacy Efforts is a true community partnership between the city of Henderson, Clark County School District, and community partners including the Henderson District Public Libraries, Henderson Community Foundation, and numerous other private businesses.

Class size (student to teacher ratio): 21:1

Help for working parents: The Parks and Recreation Department offers Safekey, a before- and after-school recreational program at all Henderson elementary schools.

Boys & Girls Club: There are currently six centers available.

School year: The last week of August to the first week of June. Children must be 5 years old on or before September 30 to enter kindergarten.

Special education/programs for gifted students: Children identified as special education students have an individualized educational program developed for them. When possible, children are mainstreamed with support services in the classroom. Gifted and talented students are tested before being enrolled in gifted and talented education program.

Nearby colleges and universities: The Community College of Southern Nevada offers associate degrees. Nevada State College specializes in four-year degrees. The University of Nevada offers undergraduate, graduate, and doctoral programs. The Art Institute of Las Vegas offers degrees specializing in the applied arts.

Medical care

Hospitals/medical centers: St. Rose Dominican Hospital (143 beds) offers labor/delivery suites, laser surgery, 24-hour emergency, and extensive outpatient services including cardiology, oncology, and home health services. The HealthSouth Rehabilitation Hospital of Henderson (60 beds) offers acute-care, inpatient rehabilitation, outpatient surgery, and occupational medicine.

Specialized care: Sunrise Children's Hospital recently announced the certification of Sunrise Children's Hospital's pediatric dialysis unit. The new unit is the first and only pediatric end-stage renal disease unit of its kind in Nevada.

Crime and safety

Police: The Henderson police department is the largest full-service department in the state of Nevada, providing centralized 911 emergency services which dispatches all police, fire, and ambulance emergency calls. The department uses a community policing philosophy with crime prevention activities such as National Night Out, Every 15 Minutes, and DARE. Other programs include Safe At Home Program, Watch Your Car Program, Adopt a School Program, Business Watch, and Neighborhood Watch.

Fire: The Henderson fire department employs 186 people, operates nine fire stations, and one fire training center. The department is the only full-service department in the Las Vegas Valley. Emergency response times average 5 minutes, 40 seconds. The local Explorer Post recently celebrated its 14th anniversary. An automatic external defibrillator program has trained casino security personnel in the use of this new equipment. The Christmas Bicycle Program gives away bicycles and helmets to children ranging in age from 3 to 18. The firefighters assembled all the bikes and enlist the support of many area businesses.

Let the good times roll

Family fun: Henderson is a golfer's paradise, offering 11 championship golf courses. Outdoor enthusiasts will enjoy the soft-water rapids of the Colorado River, the hiking trails of Lake Mead, and the biking and walking trails found throughout the city. The Multigenerational Center campus of Liberty Pointe opened in 2002 and includes the Henderson Pavilion facility for music, dance, and theater, as well as the Promenade for outdoor events such as the annual Book Fair. The Center includes a 12,000 square foot gym; elevated jogging track; 3,000 square foot fitness room; climbing wall; indoor lap pool, game room; dance, fitness and aerobics rooms; adult lounge; classrooms, computer lab and demonstration kitchen; arts and crafts room; child care and romper room. The Aquatic Complex is highlighted by an activity pool complete with water play features, slides, and zero-depth entry, and as well as a 50-meter competitive pool with diving area.

Sports: As the largest sports complex in Nevada, the Arroyo Grande Sports Complex spans 60 acres. In addition to nine lighted ball fields, the center provides lighted basketball courts, horseshoe pits, a playground, and a walking fitness course.

Arts and entertainment: A variety of cultural events include a little of everything from ArtFest to the Henderson Civic Symphony to Missoula Children's Theatre to Concerts in the Park. The Made in Nevada Art Fair and the Annual Shakespeare in the Park are big local attractions. The Henderson Pavilion at Liberty Pointe will also be scheduling annual events, or check out the Henderson Writers Group.

Annual events: Springsational Heritage Parade and Festival, Bark in the Park, ArtFest, WinterFest, Henderson Halloween, All Abilities Expo

Community life

Henderson has the Volunteer Connection, an organized volunteer service increasing resident involvement in the daily operations of the city government. You can volunteer to work at the animal control shelter, or help out at the convention center with visitor services. Both the police and fire departments encourage volunteering to help out in their community programs.

The environment

Recognizing that water is one of the most precious resources in a desert environment, Henderson is committed to preserving water by adopting a drought plan. In addition, the city continually identifies ways to internally conserve water, and elicits residents' aide and compliance in the conservation of water. The city formed the Henderson Water Watchers, city employees dedicated to helping citizens weather drought conditions by providing educational resources, including conservation workshops, Webpages, and printed materials.

In and around town

Roads and highways: I-15, I-215, US 95, 93

Closest airports: Henderson Executive Airport is 10 minutes away. McCarran International Airport is 12 minutes away.

Public transportation: Citizens Area Transit (CATRIDE) serves Clark County.

Average daily commute: 15 minutes

More Information

City of Henderson
200 Water Street
Henderson, NV 89009
702-267-2171
www.cityofhenderson.com

Sprint Telephone Nevada
330 South Valley View
Las Vegas, NV 89107
702-244-7400
www.sprint.com

Clark County School District
2832 East Flamingo Road
Las Vegas, NV 89121 USA
702-799-1072
www.ccsd.net

Southwest Gas Corporation
4300 West Tropicana Avenue
Las Vegas, NV 89103
702-365-1555
www.swgas.com

Henderson Chamber of Commerce
590 South Boulder Highway
Henderson, NV 89015
702-565-3115
www.cityofhenderson.com

City of Henderson, Utility Services
240 Water Street
PO Box 95050
Henderson, NV 89009
www.cityofhenderson.com

Nevada Power Company
227 South Water Street
Henderson, NV 89015
702-367-5555
www.nevadapower.com

City of Henderson Writers Group
Paso Verde Branch
Henderson Library
www.hendersonwritersgroup.org

27 ▶ Reno, Nevada

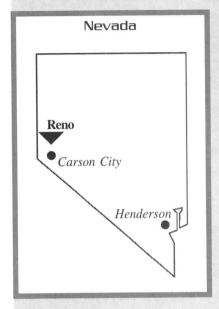

Nevada

Reno

Carson City

Henderson

Fabulous features

In your search for a great place to raise your family, you may want to take a gamble on Reno. For a long time Reno, Nevada has been a vacation destination, but more and more people are choosing to call the city home, thanks to its beautiful natural surroundings, strong economy, great neighborhoods, mild climate, and low taxes. The bonuses, of course, are the sparkling alpine lakes and tantalizing view of the Sierra Nevada mountains.

Two of the many accolades for Reno include Sperling's *Cities Ranked & Rated,* where Reno took ninth place, and the May, 2003 issue of *Men's Journal,* where Reno ranked third out of 50 cities in America as a great place. You can choose to do almost anything in Reno, from hang-gliding to horseback riding, but most residents enjoy the spectacular skiing. Culture, entertainment, and special events are year-round fixtures, as Reno has its own ballet, opera, and orchestra.

The Reno area has been dealt a generous economic hand. Business growth is strong, and the last decade has seen numerous companies relocate here or set up distribution networks and warehouses. The gateway to the Sierra Nevada region, Reno is a city that has it all. Known as "The Biggest Little City in the World," Reno is the center of commerce and culture in northern Nevada.

Possible drawbacks: Although the taxes are low, the overall cost of living is a bit on the high side, with real estate taking a sizable bite out of the city budget. Real estate sprawl is a growing problem.

▶ Local Population: 189,388

▶ County: Washoe

▶ Population of surrounding metropolitan area: 339,486

▶ Region: Western Nevada

▶ Closest metro area: Sacramento, 140 miles

▶ Median home price: $179,300

▶ Median household income: $40,530

▶ Best reasons to live here: With low taxes, great outdoor recreation, an expanding job base, fabulous scenery, and excellent public transportation, Reno has the royal flush.

Climate

Elevation 4,498'	Average temp. high/low (°F)	Average precipitation		Average no. days precipitation	Average humidity (%)
		rain (")	snow (")		
January	45/22	1.2	5.8	6	50
April	64/34	0.3	1.2	4	28
July	90/52	0.2	0	2	18
October	69/34	0.5	0.3	3	27
Number of days 32°F or below: 189			Number of days 90°F or warmer: 52		

Earning a living

Economic outlook: With its gambling industry squeezed between Las Vegas at one end and Indian casinos at the other, Reno's leaders know the smart money is moving away from gambling and toward high-tech. The University of Nevada is jazzing up its nanoscience and engineering programs to attract scientists, engineers, and research grants. *Time* magazine reported in November of 2003 that "Where the Jobs Are" can be found in small to mid-sized cities like Reno. Companies are finding lower costs of living and higher pools of educated workers in the smaller regions. *Inc.* magazine ranked Reno number one of "Best Places to do Business in America." *Dun and Bradstreet* reported Reno as the "Best Small City in America for Small Business." In the last five years. companies such as *Amazon.com* and PC-Doctor have located distribution warehouses and offices in Reno.

Where the jobs are: Washoe County School District, University of Reno, Reno Hilton, Washoe Medical Center, Inc.

Business opportunities: Tanamera Commercial Development developed an 850,000 square foot technology park, with miles of conduit for fiber-optic cable. Many people are bailing out of the higher priced areas of California and moving their families and businesses east. If homes are less expensive, square footage for office buildings is, too. And Reno has ample transportation opportunities, making warehousing and distribution centers financially viable.

Local real estate

Market overview: Housing in the Reno area includes apartments, condos, single-family homes, and large and small ranches. Several new developments have been built west of Reno.

Average rent for a two-bedroom apartment: $900 per month

Other areas to consider: From the Old West to the 21st century, Carson City has a little of everything, including a short drive to Virginia City. Truckee sits up in the Sierra Nevada mountains next to Donner Lake. As the capital of California, Sacramento's small-town friendliness comes in the dozens of communities in and around downtown. From East Sacramento to Elk Grove, these communities boast houses with varying architectural styles and 16 school districts.

What things cost

ACCRA's national comparisons: Overall living costs are 6 percent above the national average. Transportation takes the biggest chunk at 20 percent above the average, with housing breaking even. Utilities come in at 14 percent above average and groceries a little lower at 9 percent. Healthcare is 2.5 percent above.

Utilities: Electricity: $70 per month; natural gas: $87 per month; phone: $28 per month

The tax ax

Sales tax: 7.25 percent

Property tax: $26.30 (est. property taxes paid per $1,000 of market value)

State income tax: There is no state income tax.

Making the grade

Public education overview: *Expansion Management* magazine (April 2005) ranked Reno-Sparks fifth in the "Best Small" category for school districts. Washoe County School District's annual dropout rate has continued to decline, hitting an all-time low in 2002. The school district receives strong support from the business and professional community. The district has nineteen elementary schools operating on a nontraditional calendar. Of those schools, eight follow a multi-track schedule, and nine operate on a single-track, year-round schedule. The district is one of the largest school districts in the United States mandating that all students enrolled in Advanced Placement (AP) courses take the AP exams for those courses. The district sponsors eight charter schools, seven of which are in Reno. The Early Childhood Preschool program is made up of two components: the Classroom on Wheels (COW Bus) and the Pre-K Program. Both programs provide free quality preschool services and adhere to the same guidelines.

Class size (student to teacher ratio): 22:1

Help for working parents: Before- and after-school daycare is available at more than half the elementary schools, generally from 6:30 a.m. to 6 p.m. Costs are involved, and some have breakfast programs.

Boys & Girls Club: There are five centers currently available.

School year: Traditional schedules start the week before Labor Day through the second week in June. Children must be 5 years old on or before September 30 to enter kindergarten. However, many elementary schools are on year-round calendars. Check the district Website for specific calendar sessions per school.

Special education/programs for gifted students: Mainstreaming is emphasized for those with learning disabilities, although special resource programs are available at almost every school.

Nearby colleges and universities: The University of Nevada at Reno offers degrees in 72 baccalaureate, 28 doctoral, and 67 other graduate programs. In 2001, the *US News & World Report* ranked the University of Nevada as one of "America's Best Colleges." Other facilities include National Judicial College, Truckee Meadows Community College, Western Nevada Community College, and Sierra Nevada College.

Medical care

Hospitals/medical centers: Northern Nevada Medical Center offers comprehensive medical care, specializing in diabetes, pediatrics, and patient rehabilitation services. St. Mary's Hospital offers acute, comprehensive medical care, specializing in maternity, cardiac surgery, home care, rehabilitation, and chemical dependency. Washoe Medical Center has comprehensive medical care, specializing in rehabilitation, psychiatric services, a trauma unit, renal dialysis, women's care, and the Washoe Pregnancy center.

Specialized care: The Veterans Administration Medical Center offers a nursing homecare unit, psychiatric unit, alcohol drug treatment, and medical/surgical care.

Crime and safety

Police: The Reno police department is nationally recognized as a model for community oriented policing and problem solving. The Senior Auxiliary Volunteer Effort provides additional resources to the department. The downtown enforcement team includes the horse mounted unit, reserve officer program, homeless evaluation liaison program, and river patrol. The newest aspects of the downtown enforcement team are the crisis intervention team and the motel interdiction team. Both units have been developed to effectively target and assist problems areas within downtown Reno.

Fire: The city of Reno fire department has programs such as the community risk reduction program, where the department works to provide public education to the local community and schools. For a city of less than 200,000 people, the department is responsible for a very large number of high-rise buildings. The Reno fire department utilizes a network of 17 fire stations throughout the city of Reno and Washoe county to help keep their response times fast. The department is a wildland/urban interface department, with seven brush trucks in the metro division, six brush trucks in the rural division, and volunteer stations scattered throughout Washoe County.

Let the good times roll

Family fun: Set in the surreal beauty of the Sierra Nevada mountains, Reno and Lake Tahoe's season of fun lasts all year. With more annual snowfall than Utah or Colorado, Lake Tahoe's ski resorts guarantee fun into late spring. Think about hitting the slopes in the morning and then golf in the afternoon at one of 39 golf courses, even in March! The only facility of its kind in the world, the National Bowling Stadium is dedicated to the sport of bowling. *The Los Angeles Times* called it the "Taj Mahal of Tenpins." Living up to its name, the stadium was elegantly designed with the tournament bowler in mind. The stadium features 80 lanes and permanent seating for more than 1,100 spectators. Downtown Reno has the Riverwalk and amphitheater, with scheduled concerts and other performances. The area also has the Fleischmann Planetarium and Science Center. And don't forget about Great Basin Adventure, a children's theme park with "old-fashioned fun," including a petting zoo, log ride, and a mine where you can actually pan for gold. The kids can even climb a dinosaur or two. Just 35 minutes from downtown is Virginia City, where the family can sample the days of wooden sidewalks and old-fashion saloons.

Sports: While no professional teams are in the area, you don't have to pay high prices for high excitement. The University of Nevada Wolfpack plays all intercollegiate sports. Other teams to cheer about include the Reno Rattlers (soccer) and Reno Diamonds (minor league baseball). Professional boxing matches are often held at the convention center.

Arts and entertainment: Reno has a philharmonic orchestra, Reno chamber orchestra, Nevada Opera Association, and the Nevada Festival Ballet. A number of community groups perform in the area, including the Washoe County Community Concert Association and the Sierra Nevada Chorale.

Annual events: Artown, Hot August Nights, Great Reno Balloon Races, National Championship Air Races, Tour de Nez

Community life

Residents of Reno love to celebrate anything and everything. Community life, therefore, revolves around community spirit and a busy social calendar, one in which all age groups can find something in which to participate. Even City Hall has open doors in this city. Residents can sign up for the Reno Citizens Institute, a free 10-week, in-depth course on Reno's local government, where you can meet and greet department heads and understand the workings of city hall. The Youth City Council is always looking for youth participation and involvement.

The environment

The Desert Research Institute's ongoing cloud seeding program has successfully increased precipitation in the Tahoe Truckee Basin. The institute, and the University of Nevada Reno, have shown that wildlife detection dogs may provide a real advantage in surveying populations of the threatened species of the Mojave Desert tortoises. And environmental efforts to protect the air quality include oxygenated fuels used during winter months. Spring clean-up of parks and wildlife areas are part of an active calendar of events.

In and around town

Roads and highways: I-80, US 395, 50, 95

Closest airports: Reno Tahoe International Airport is 4 miles from downtown. Reno Stead Airport is a general aviation airport.

Public transportation: Citifare is operated by the Regional Transportation Commission (RTC). The RTC also operates Citilift, a paratransit service providing door-to-door service for the disabled.

Average daily commute: 22 minutes

More Information

City of Reno, Nevada
PO Box 1900
Reno, NV 89505
775-334-2099
www.cityofreno.com

Downtown Enforcement Team
11 North Sierra Street
Reno, NV 89505
775-334-2446
www.cityofreno.com

Washoe County School District
425 East Ninth Street
Reno, NV 89520
775-348-0200
www.washoe.k12.nv.us

Reno Chamber of Commerce
One East First Street Suite 1600
Reno, NV 89501
775-337-3030
www.reno-sparkschamber.org

Artown
165 West Liberty Street
Reno, NV 89501
775-322-1538
www.renoisartown.com

Sierra Pacific Resources
6100 Neil Road
Reno, NV 89511
800-962-0399
www.sierrapacific.com

Truckee Meadows Water Authority
PO Box 30013
Reno, NV 89520
775-834-8080
www.tmh20.com

28 ▶ Portsmouth, New Hampshire

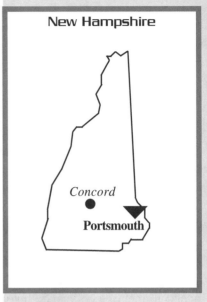

New Hampshire

Concord

Portsmouth

Fabulous features

The quality of life in Portsmouth is hard to beat. Young professionals, especially entrepreneurial types and highly skilled technical workers, have been particularly attracted to all that Portsmouth offers. The city has something for everyone, with a working port combined with natural landscapes, parks, and proximity to New Hampshire's lakes and mountains.

The city has grown over the last 10 years, yet every effort has been made to preserve the quality of life, including cultural roots and history. Take a trip downtown and you'll be within 10 to 15 minutes of art galleries and performing arts theaters. Check out the Music Hall (which celebrated its 125th birthday in 2005), or any of the other arts venues that are highly regarded. If you're not going downtown, within five minutes you can enjoy more than 17 miles of coastline and beaches.

Portsmouth is one of the healthiest places in the country to raise a family. More than five major hospitals in the area are responsible for the lowest infant mortality rate in the country. This is one of the reasons *Money* magazine ranked Portsmouth in their "Top 10 places to Live" for five years in a row. As the "City of the Open Door," come check out all that Portsmouth has to offer.

Possible drawbacks: If you're a sun bird who needs temperatures above 68 degrees Fahrenheit, this is not the town for you. Winters can seem long. In some years, the city gets over 100 inches of snow!

- ▶ Local Population: 20,789
- ▶ County: Rockingham
- ▶ Population of surrounding metropolitan area: 277,359
- ▶ Region: Southeast New Hampshire
- ▶ Closest metro area: Boston, 50 miles
- ▶ Median home price: $168,000
- ▶ Median household income: $45,195
- ▶ Best reasons to live here: A stable economy with strong technology base, a delightful downtown, cultural activities, and all the amenities of a cosmopolitan city in a small town package.

Climate

Elevation 100'	Average temp. high/low (°F)	Average precipitation rain (")	snow (")	Average no. days precipitation	Average humidity (%)
January	34/15	4.1	17.3	11	59
April	57/34	4.3	2.3	11	50
July	83/59	3.4	0	10	54
October	61/39	4.3	0.1	9	55
Number of days 32°F or below: 99			Number of days 90°F or warmer: 12		

Earning a living

Economic outlook: Portsmouth has many unique assets, including its role as New Hampshire's only deep-water port and a central role as a high-tech hub for northern New England. The region is commonly knows as the e-coast, because of the vital role software, hardware, Web design, and e-commerce companies have come to play in the economic landscape of the region. Portsmouth has a youthful and technologically adept workforce. Many educational institutions, including the University of New Hampshire and a number of technical colleges, produce workers who thrive in the technological business climate that has characterized much of Portsmouth's new economic growth. New Hampshire has one Foreign Trade Zone consisting of five distinct sites, three of which are located in Portsmouth. Unemployment rates average around 4.6 percent.

Where the jobs are: Liberty Mutual Insurance, Columbia HCA Hospital, Lonza Biologics, Erie Scientific/Sybron Lab Products, Pan-Am Airlines, Portsmouth Naval Shipyard

Business opportunities: The Pease International Trade Port, established following the 1990 closure of Pease Air Force Base, is one of the most successful military redevelopments in the country. A number of Portsmouth's largest employers are located at the Trade Port, including several corporate headquarters, manufacturing, biotech, and information technology firms. The port is also charged with overseeing the operation of the Port of New Hampshire. Tourism is a powerful economic force in Portsmouth year-round. The New Hampshire Seacoast, where Portsmouth is the anchor, generates millions of dollars in revenue for the state and local government.

Local real estate

Market overview: A variety of available housing includes one-bedroom condos, single-family homes in historic districts, and red-brick duplexes that served as housing during World War I. Modern developments are available from apartments to luxury homes.

Average rent for a two-bedroom apartment: $900 per month

Other areas to consider: Celebrating its 375th birthday, Boston's looking good in 2005. Over 12 million visitors per year come to tour the cobblestone streets and admire the Harvard University campus. Portland, Maine is a tapestry of skyline and shoreline. With a strong economy, the city offers the ease of city living without the stress.

What things cost

ACCRA's national comparisons: The overall cost of living is high at 20 percent above the national average. Housing and utilities take the biggest bite at 31.6 percent and 30 percent respectfully. Health care is even high at a hefty 36 percent above the average.

Utilities: Current information is not available.

The tax ax

Sales tax: There is no sales tax in Portsmouth.

Property tax: $19.27(est. property taxes paid per $1,000 of market value)

State income tax: There is no state income tax in New Hampshire.

Making the grade

Public education overview: The community awarded the Portsmouth school department a $38 million bond in 2002, concurring their commitment to continuing the high quality of education. Upgrades have already been made to Portsmouth High School, including an expanded central library, a renovated auditorium, a new science wing, and a new technical education wing and New Franklin Elementary School. A unique program for the elementary schools is Exchange City, a national program where teachers present an eight-week economics and entrepreneurship curriculum to fifth and sixth grade students. The highlight of the course is a visit to Exchange City, where students use the principles and practices they've learned to run the "city" for a day. Portsmouth's Exchange City, the first in New England, draws students from all over the region. The department has a Veterans Diploma program for veterans of World War II or the Korean War who left Portsmouth High School to enlist or were drafted and did not complete high school, and they may be eligible to receive a diploma during the next ceremony held in June. What a wonderful example to set for the children!

Class size (student to teacher ratio): 16:1

Help for working parents: Before- and after-school care is available at all elementary schools.

Boys & Girls Club: There are currently two centers available.

School year: Last week of August to mid-June.

Special education/programs for gifted students: There is no information currently available.

Nearby colleges and universities: The University of New Hampshire in Durham was rated number one for value in education in New Hampshire and 15th in the country by *Kiplinger's Personal Finance* in January of 2003. It's a comprehensive research university known for, among other things, its school of engineering and the nationally recognized Whittemore School of Business.

Medical care

Hospitals/medical centers: With more than five major hospitals in the area, Portsmouth has one of the lowest infant mortality rates in the country. Portsmouth Regional Hospital and Pavilion has developed a solid reputation for providing high quality healthcare services for seacoast residents. It has become a regional center of excellence in cardiac care, neurosurgery, and obstetrics. The hospital is an international training center for orthopedic surgery, one of only five such programs in the country.

Specialized care: There is no specialized care in Portsmouth.

Crime and safety

Police: The Portsmouth police department has 71 full-time officers, 28 auxiliary officers, and 25 full- and part-time civilian support staff personnel. The patrol division consists of uniformed field personnel, accident investigation team, emergency response team, canine unit, motorcycle patrol, parking enforcement, animal control, and a police Explorer post. Members of the Bureau of Investigative Services are responsible for major crime investigations, juvenile investigations, DARE, Crime Stoppers, and the undercover narcotics unit. The department includes crime prevention programs such as Crime Watch, National Night Out, and community policing.

Fire: The Portsmouth fire department provides Fire Protection, Advanced Life Support Ambulance, Fire Prevention, Hazardous Materials Response, and Special Rescue Services. PFD has 42 Firefighters, 12 Fire Officers, 1 Fire Marshal, 3 Chief Officers and an Administrative Secretary. The department maintains three fire stations staffed 24 hours a day.

Let the good times roll

Family fun: Outdoor adventure is available everywhere in and around Portsmouth. Water sports are plentiful during the summer, and the mountains for skiing are only an hour's drive away. Water Country is the largest water park in New England for summer fun. The New Heights Youth program provides excitement for young people at no or little charge. The Children's Museum of Portsmouth features a variety of entertaining and educational exhibits. Seacoast Science Center, dedicated to environmental preservation, has lots of activities for kids. Enjoy ice rinks and a rollerskating rink. Or head downtown for various entertainment and activities.

Sports: Portsmouth is an hour away from Boston, where you can cheer professional sports teams such as the 2004 World Series Champion Red Sox. Or stay close to home and head for a Little League game. A local Portsmouth team recently won the national Little League championship.

Arts and entertainment: The Button Factory Artist Studios, the Children's Museum, the Music Hall, New Hampshire Theatre Project, Players Ring, Pontine Movement Theatre, and the Seacoast Repertory Theatre are all entertaining opportunities.

Annual events: Market Square Day, Music by the Sea, Harbor Arts Jazz Festival, Portsmouth Harbour Trail 5k Road Race, Seacoast Jazz Festival, Bowstreet Artisans Fair, Historic Homes at Twilight, First Night Portsmouth

Community life

The per capita rate of community involvement is quite high. Most efforts are managed by the Seacoast United Way Volunteer Program. When news broke of potential military base closures, the community took action by setting up the Website *www.saveourshipyard.org*. Portsmouth was successful in turning around the Pease Air Force Base closure to become a positive thing for the community.

The environment

Mandatory recycling programs are in effect for businesses and residents in most or all of Portsmouth. Phases have slowly been implemented. Failure to recycle could result in a citation or fine up to $100. Household Hazardous Waste Days are held every year.

In and around town

Roads and highways: I-95, SR 1A, 33, federal route 1, 4

Closest airports: Pease Airport is in Portsmouth; Logan Airport is in Boston.

Public transportation: Free trolley transportation is available downtown. Wildcat Transit is the University of New Hamshire's transportation service.

Average daily commute: 22 minutes

More Information

City of Portsmouth
1 Junkins Avenue
Portsmouth, NH 03801
603-431-2000
www.cityofportsmouth.com

Portsmouth School Department
50 Clough Drive
Portsmouth, NH 03801
603-431-5080
www.cityofportsmouth.com

Portsmouth Chamber of Commerce
500 Market Street
Portsmouth, NH 03802
603-436-3988
www.portsmouthchamber.org

Public Service of New Hampshire
PO Box 330
Manchester, NH 03105
800-662-7764
www.psnh.com

Morristown, New Jersey

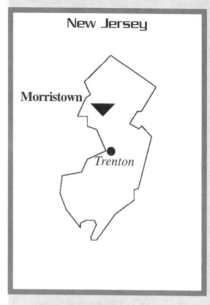

Fabulous features

You may have seen the funny signs that say, "General Washington slept here," but in Morristown, it's no joke! Amid the rolling hills of Morris County is the historic Jacob Ford Mansion, which was Washington's winter headquarters during the Revolutionary War. In fact, Morris County is surrounded by historical landmarks. But it is the future of this area that grabs attention.

Morris County is the third fastest growing county in the tri-state (New York, New Jersey, Connecticut) region, because many multinational firms have world headquarters or major operations along the I-287 corporate corridor. With a large presence of foreign labor, the Morristown schools offer strong foreign language programs. The town itself is a mix of wonderful antique shops and charming tree-lined streets. There are stately, old homes and high-rise condominiums within a stone's throw of each other.

One of the city's most prestigious residents is the Seeing Eye campus. For over 70 years this school has matched seeing eye dogs with the visually handicapped, giving them more independence in their lives. In April of 2005, a bronze statue of Frank Morris and his dog, Buddy, was unveiled in the middle of a traffic island near the Morristown Green.

Possible drawbacks: If you've never driven in New Jersey, be prepared for a shock. You should drive with a co-pilot if possible, because the on/off ramps take some getting used to.

▶ Local Population: 18,831

▶ County: Morris

▶ Population of surrounding metropolitan area: 470,212

▶ Region: Northeast New Jersey

▶ Closest metro area: New York City, 30 miles

▶ Median home price: $224,400

▶ Median household income: $57,552

▶ Best reasons to live here: It's a prosperous, fast-growing county, with New England-style charm, wonderful parks, progressive schools, great medical care, and a lovely historic area.

Climate

Elevation 327'	Average temp. high/low (°F)	Average precipitation		Average no. days precipitation	Average humidity (%)
		rain (")	snow (")		
January	38/19	4.1	7.5	11	59
April	62/38	4.3	0.7	11	49
July	86/62	4.9	0	10	52
October	65/41	4.0	0	8	54
Number of days 32°F or below: 87			Number of days 90°F or warmer: 20		

Earning a living

Economic outlook: The Morristown Partnership, a special district organization started in 1995, is active in recruiting and retaining businesses in Morristown. As a marketing agent, a Business Expo is held every year, encouraging local businesses to network. Land at Morristown Airport, and you are a quick ride to the headquarters of 54 Fortune 500 companies.

Where the jobs are: Bayer Corporation, Consumer Care Division, Colgate-Palmolive Co., Watson Pharma, Dendrite International, C3i

Business opportunities: From the smallest shops along South Street, the medium-sized firms on the Green, or the largest corporations on Madison Avenue, Morristown is home to hundreds of businesses. Morristown is the county seat of Morris County, and situated on the Whippany River. Check with Morris Area Development Group for up to date economic data for the region.

Local real estate

Market overview: Historic districts are found throughout the county. Many are all-brick, or brick with wood shingles. Garages and basements are common.

Average rent for a two-bedroom apartment: $1,000

Other areas to consider: More than a just a bedroom community, Montclair holds its own with a state university and cultural population.

What things cost

ACCRA's national comparisons: The overall cost of living is 34 percent above the national average. Housing is mainly the culprit at 78 percent above the average. After that, the rest of the categories level back, but are still in double digit figures. Utilities are 15 percent higher, healthcare is 18 percent higher, and grocery items are 16 percent higher.

Utilities: Electricity: $84 per month; natural gas: $78 per month; phone: $30 per month

The tax ax

Sales tax: 6 percent

Property tax: $7.03 (est. property taxes paid per $1,000 of market value)

State income tax: 1.40 to 6.37 percent

Making the grade

Public education overview: The Morris School District serves the communities of Morristown and Morris Township. Morristown High School has a Homework Hero section on their Website where parents, students, and teachers can view and update assignments. Hillcrest Elementary has a special event when students write and illustrate a book. The students and parents will be invited to a "Publishing Tea" where they can read their book and receive a special ribbon in recognition.

Class size (student to teacher ratio): 18:1

Help for working parents: The school-age child care program serves after-school care for ages 5 through 13, and when the district's public schools are closed. The Community School also provides a before- and after-school childcare program.

Boys & Girls Club: There are no centers available.

School year: Begins after Labor Day to mid-June. Children must be 5 years old on or before October 31 to enter kindergarten.

Special education/programs for gifted students: The Morris School District provides services to students with identified disabilities. The district also operates a preschool program for children with special educational needs.

Nearby colleges and universities: The College of St. Elizabeth includes a women's college with undergraduate studies, and School of Graduate Studies and Center for Theological and Spiritual Development.

Medical care

Hospitals/medical centers: Morristown Memorial Hospital offers specialized services and many community health programs, such as a level II trauma center, a level III regional perinatal center, and a regional pediatric center. It operates the largest photopheresis center in the United States and the only one in New Jersey.

Specialized care: Greystone Park Psychiatric Hospital offers specialized services for mental healthcare.

Crime and safety

Police: The Morristown police department has a visible presence patrolling by foot, bicycle, and car. Response times average less than two minutes. The department has 60 officers. Crime prevention programs include DARE and Neighborhood Watch.

Fire: The Morristown fire department is comprised of 26 full-time firefighters, many of whom are emergency medical technicians and/or fire inspectors, manning four shifts, with six to eight staff per shift.

Let the good times roll

Family fun: Being the Garden State, you can enjoy endless hours in the parks of the community. West of Morristown, children will enjoy Fosterfields Living Historical Farm, an example of a working farm. At Loanaka Brook Park, visitors can relax after sightseeing with a quiet picnic lunch or a bike ride on one of the park's superb trails.

Sports: The New Jersey Meadowlands is home to the New Jersey Devils (NHL), the Jets and Giants (NFL), and the New Jersey Nets (NBA). The New York Yankees and New York Mets are the Major League Baseball teams in the area.

Arts and entertainment: The Community Theatre Musical Theatre Workshop is for children. The New Jersey State Council on the Arts designated the Morris Museum a major arts institution for 2004 to 2006. The Morris Museum has received this accolade every year since 1997.

Annual events: St. Patrick's Day Parade, Public Reading of the Declaration of Independence, Christmas Festival, Annual Gingerbread Wonderland, First Night

Community life

You can get involved in Morristown in a number of fun and exciting ways, such as beautification, marketing, promotions, advertising, or cleanliness. You can immortalize yourself, a friend, a relative, or a business in the streets of Morristown, when you Adopt-a-Light. They'll engrave your name on a bronze plaque and mount it on a streetlight.

The environment

Morristown's bevy of environmental programs prove it is very aware of the ecology. Morristown has annual clean-up days and programs. The Upper Raritan River Water Association ensures that there is clean water for the community.

In and around town

Roads and highways: I-287, 80, 280

Closest airports: Newark International Airport is only 20 minutes away.

Public transportation: NJ Transit trains can take you to Hoboken or Manhattan.

Average daily commute: 20 minutes

More Information

City of Morristown
200 South Street
Morristown, NJ 07963
www.morristown-nj.org

Morris County Chamber of Commerce
25 Lindsley Drive
Morristown, NJ 07960
www.morrischamber.org

Morris School District
31 Hazel Street
Morristown, NJ 07963
www.morrisschooldistrict.com

The Seeing Eye, Inc.
PO Box 375
Morristown, NJ 07965
www.sweeingeye.org

30 ▶ Albuquerque, New Mexico

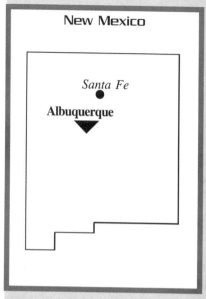

New Mexico

Santa Fe
●
Albuquerque
▼

Fabulous features

This year marks the historic 300th birthday of one of the most remarkable cities: Albuquerque. From April of 2005 through October of 2006, the city will celebrate this extraordinary milestone with literally hundreds of events honoring Albuquerque's rich history and tradition. You may not be able to spell it, you may even have a hard time saying it, but once you see Albuquerque, you'll never forget it! This "Land of Enchantment" is nestled beneath the spectacular Sandi mountains, adjoining the famed Rio Grande Valley.

True to its Mexican, Spanish, and Native American heritage, there is a spirit of cooperation that unified this city long before it started growing at twice the rate of the nation. In fact, it was the hard-working, highly educated workforce that inspired America Online, Inc. and Intuit software technical support services to locate their facilities here. It's also why dozens of others have expanded here in the past. *Entrepreneur* magazine named it one of the 10 "hottest" cities in America for business. Albuquerque was ranked the most creative mid-size city in the United States by Dr. Richard Florida, author of *The Creative Class*, and in 2005 was named the fifth "Best City in the Nation for Doing Business" by *Forbes* magazine.

Wrap together free university tuition available to New Mexico high school graduates, a rich cultural and ethnic diversity, with unprecedented ethnic harmony, abundant recreation, reasonable taxes and living costs, great medical services, excellent schools and you have quite a package.

Possible drawbacks: If you shrivel from too much sun, think again before moving out here.

▶ Local Population: 477,194
▶ County: Bernalillo
▶ Population of surrounding metropolitan area: 589,033
▶ Region: Central New Mexico
▶ Closest metro area: Phoenix, 391 miles
▶ Median home price: $141,000
▶ Median household income: $42,373
▶ Best reasons to live here: Albuquerque has low taxes and living costs, a pleasant year-round climate, ethnic and cultural diversity, excellent schools and universities, and abundant outdoor recreation opportunities.

Climate

Elevation 4,955'	Average temp. high/low (°F)	Average precipitation rain (")	snow (")	Average no. days precipitation	Average humidity (%)
January	48/22	0.4	2.5	4	39
April	71/38	0.5	0.6	3	19
July	92/62	1.3	0	9	27
October	71/41	0.9	0.1	5	30
Number of days 32°F or below: 123			Number of days 90°F or warmer: 61		

Earning a living

Economic outlook: The film and media industry, the aerospace/aviation industry, and the growing real estate industry have all led to strong economic growth for the Albuquerque area. Jobs with the most vacancies are within retail, healthcare, and construction, as well as scientific research and business support services. Many job opportunities for engineers in various disciplines are also available. Tourism is a strong factor in the city's economy, bringing in skiers, balloonists, and retirees.

Where the jobs are: Some of the major employers are Albuquerque Public School System, the University of New Mexico, the city of Albuquerque, Sandia National Laboratories, and Presbyterian Hospital.

Business opportunities: The growth of the area's aviation cluster will be at the forefront of the city's economic growth. The area has a good concentration of high-tech industries, particularly in electronics, optics, biotechnoloy/biomedics, nanotechnology, and microsystems, which will continue to fuel the economy. Tourism continues to be a strong component of the local economy. There is a growing film and digital media industry, fueled by the state's incentives for film production. The area is becoming more attractive to major manufacturing companies because of increasing operation costs on the east and west coasts.

Local real estate

Market overview: Realtors have been punching overtime cards, showing off new construction in the city. *Kiplinger's Personal Finance* magazine said the Albuquerque area has the most affordable housing in the United States.

Average rent for a two-bedroom apartment: $750 per month

Other areas to consider: At the southern end of the Rocky Mountains lies Santa Fe, New Mexico's state capital. Skiing and tourism go hand-in-hand here. The village of Los Lunas has abundant petroglyphs, showing a diverse Native American history. Phoenix is Arizona's capital, and in size is bigger than Los Angeles. Growing pains include traffic and crime with the influx of more people. Tourism is a large part of the economy, including major league sports.

What things cost

ACCRA's national comparisons: The overall cost of living is about even with the national average, coming in at 100.8 percent. Utilities are the biggest skew at 127 percent above the average, with housing at 0.8 percent below. Miscellaneous goods rides at 4 percent below average, and transportation is right behind it at 3.2 percent below.

Utilities: Gas: $25 per month; electricity: $25 per month; water: $40 per month

The tax ax

Sales tax: 6.025 percent

Property tax: $9.80 (est. property taxes paid per $1,000 of market value)

State income tax: The highest bracket is 7.7 percent, but tax cuts phased in over five years will drop the top bracket to 4.9 percent by 2007.

Making the grade

Public education overview: The Albuquerque Public School District has had 21 schools recognized by the United States Department of Education as Centers for Excellence or Blue Ribbons Schools, more than any other district in the nation. Various Albuquerque high schools, in conjunction with such organizations as Sandia National Labs, University of New Mexico, and Albuquerque Technical Vocational Institute, are operating and developing programs providing students with more hands-on and accelerated learning environments. Such programs include a Photonics Academy and Advanced Technology Academy. In 2005, students will be able to attend the newly formed Math, Science, and Technology high school, which will offer students accelerated math and science courses. The area is also home to several private and parochial schools.

Class size (student to teacher ratio): 17:1

Help for working parents: Before- and after-school care programs are available with services provided by Campfire, Albuquerque Parks and Recreation, Bernalillo County Parks and Recreation, and the YMCA. Many middle schools also have after-school programs giving students a safe, mentally-active environment until their parents or guardians come home from work.

Boys & Girls Club: There are currently three centers available.

School year: Traditional schools run from mid-August to he end of May. Check the Website for the year-round school calendar. Children must be 5 years old on or before September 1 to enter kindergarten.

Special education/programs for gifted students: Special education offers a full continuum of services for students with disabilities and giftedness who meet eligibility criteria established by state and federal laws. Services for identified students are available at all grade levels, including preschool.

Nearby colleges and universities: The University of New Mexico at Albuquerque is a quality campus, and is one of the top research and scientific developments centers. In 2002, the *U.S. News & World Report* had three programs in the university's School of Medicine listed in the Top 10. Other schools include Albuquerque Technical Vocational Institute, University of Phoenix, and the National American University.

Medical care

Hospitals/medical centers: The University of New Mexico Hospital, ranked as one of the top performing hospitals in the United States, offers a level I trauma center, surgical services, rehabilitation services, and women's health services. Lovelace Sandia Health System includes the Women's Hospital, Albuquerque Regional Medical Center, and Lovelace Medical Center.

Specialized care: The Children's Hospital Heart Center of pediatric cardiology provides heart care for children. There is a Ronald McDonald House as part of the Children's Hospital. The Children's Psychiatric Center provides treatment to children through age 17.

Crime and safety

Police: The Albuquerque police department, sporting 2.04 officers per thousand residents, provides crime prevention programs such as Neighborhood Watch, crime free multi-housing, and crime free overnight lodging. The department is proud of the low crime rates and fast response times. The voters enacted a quarter cent public safety tax in 2004 that is now enhancing police, fire, and corrections facilities, as well as greatly augmenting prevention and intervention programs.

Fire: The Albuquerque fire department is comprised of 568 uniformed personnel and 29 stations. The department was the first urban department in the country to be entirely cross-trained in wildland firefighting techniques. Another division is the mounted search and rescue team, a unique group with skills in emergency, medical, horsemanship, and mountain rescue.

Let the good times roll

Family fun: With all the sunshine, outdoor activities are plentiful. Competitive and recreation leagues for children and adults are available in a variety of sports. Los Altos Skate Park, rafting classes, fishing clinic, caving adventures, WOW campout, cross-country skiing, and rappelling adventures are some of the activities. Other entertainment includes Cliff's Amusement Park, Beach Water Park, and the Hinkle Family Fun Center. With some 800 parks and more than 80 miles of running and biking trails, Albuquerque has purchased and dedicated nearly 20,000 acres as permanent open space. In keeping with the tricentennial celebration, the grand opening of one of the world's most remarkable collections of balloon-related artifacts and memorabilia—the Anderson-Abruzzo Albuquerque International Balloon Museum—is scheduled to open. Just minutes from

Albuquerque, enjoy a panorama of 11,000 square miles of central New Mexico, as seen from the world's longest tramway. Ascend from the desert floor to the top of 10,378-foot Sandia Peak. Sandia Peak is home to snowboarding and skiing in the winter, and hiking and mountain biking in the summer.

Sports: Enjoy the University of New Mexico's athletic events, or take in an exciting game with the Albuquerque Isotopes (AAA baseball). For indoor action, check out the New Mexico Scorpions (minor league hockey). Spectators can also enjoy quarterhorse and thoroughbred racing at the Albuquerque Downs on the state fairgrounds.

Arts and entertainment: Albuquerque has several theatrical companies, including an excellent children's theater. Other offerings include the New Mexico Symphony Orchestra, Chamber Orchestra of Albuquerque, Albuquerque Ballet Company, and more. More than 100 galleries display original works of art ranging from traditional to contemporary.

Annual events: International Balloon Fiesta, Gathering of Nations Powwow, New Mexico State Fair, Duke City Marathon

Community life

Integration is a key to the community life of Albuquerque. People enthusiastically share backgrounds, ideas, and customs at the many festivals. These celebrations reflect a wide diversion of community backgrounds. The Mayor's Office of Volunteerism and Civic Engagement is a cooperative venture between ¡VOLUNTEER! Albuquerque and the city. Did you know New Mexico has a state cookie? The Biscochito is a small, anise-flavored cookie used during special celebrations. In 1996, New Mexico made "Red or green?" the official state question. This refers to a person's preference of red or green chili when ordering food.

The environment

Albuquerque's plentiful water supply is from deep wells, which pump water from the Rio Grande Basin. The Albuquerque municipal water system is generally recognized as one of the country's most technologically advanced. Albuquerque is the nuclear capital of the United States, with much of the nation's nuclear research conducted here. Air quality is good, and the community works hard to remain below EPA ozone guideline standards.

In and around town

Roads and highways: I-25, I-40, highways 85, 66

Closest airports: Albuquerque International Airport provides flights daily.

Public transportation: ABQ Ride bus system provides regional routes and bus service throughout Albuquerque.

Average daily commute: 22 minutes

More Information

City of Albuquerque
PO Box 1293
Albuquerque, NM 87103
505-768-3000
www.cabq.gov

Albuquerque Public Schools
725 University Boulevard Southeast
Albuquerque, NM 87106
505-842-8211
www.aps.eud

Greater Albuquerque Chamber of Commerce
PO Box 25100
Albuquerque, NM 87125
505-764-3700
www.gacc.org

City of Albuquerque Public Works Department
One Civic Plaza NW
Albuquerque, NM 87103
505-768-3000
www.cabq.gov

Public Service Company of New Mexico
414 Silver Avenue SW
Albuquerque, NM 87158
505-768-3000
www.cabq.gov

31 ▶ Raleigh, North Carolina

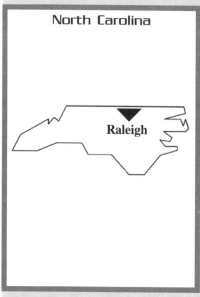

North Carolina

Raleigh

Fabulous features

Some of the country's best minds have moved to the Raleigh/Durham/Chapel Hill area known as the Triangle, for its concentration of universities, medical centers, and research facilities. Don't worry though, Bohemians want a piece of the Triangle as much as doctors and techies. Legions of writers, artists, and musicians electrify the creative scene and keep it buzzing.

Forbes magazine ranked Raleigh second in the "Best Place for Business and Careers" (2005). The Triangle is home to three nationally acclaimed research universities, several medical facilities, and Research Triangle Park (one of the largest planned research centers in the world,) the economic opportunities are endless. North Carolina's capital city offers a high quality of life, from education to recreation.

This Triangle should definitely be in your box of blocks. Raleigh, North Carolina is a great place to raise a family.

Possible drawbacks: Wake County has grown so fast, the infrastructure is always playing catch up. When the growing pains will stop is anyone's guess, but the ones complaining the most are the newcomers. They'd hate for growth to ruin this wonderful area.

▶ Local Population: 276,093
▶ County: Wake
▶ Population of surrounding metropolitan area: 627,846
▶ Region: Northern North Carolina
▶ Closest metro area: Charlotte, 130 miles
▶ Median home price: $156,000
▶ Median household income: $46,612
▶ Best reasons to live here: A world-renowned research center, outstanding medical care, low unemployment, and low crime.

Climate

Elevation 350'	Average temp. high/low (°F)	Average precipitation rain (")	snow (")	Average no. days precipitation	Average humidity (%)
January	49/30	4.4	2.8	10	55
April	71/48	3.0	0	9	46
July	88/69	4.4	0	11	58
October	70/49	3.7	0	7	53
Number of days 32°F or below: 82			Number of days 90°F or warmer: 25		

Earning a living

Economic outlook: What attracts the attention of such renowned national publications as *Money*, *Forbes*, *FORTUNE*, and *Entrepreneur* year after year? A strong and diverse economic climate, high quality of life, skilled workforce, and highly acclaimed academic institutions are a few reasons why the Triangle has landed on so many Top 10 lists. (Best Hottest Job Market, *Business 2.0*, March 2004. Second Best Place for Business, *Forbes*, May 2004 and 2005. Fourth Best City for Entrepreneurs and Small Business, *Gold Guide*, May 2004.) The Raleigh Convention and Conference Center has over 130,000 square feet of meeting space with the latest technology, making this a great amenity to businesses.

Where the jobs are: Aqua America, Inc., Ascom Wireless Solutions, Credit Suisse First Boston

Business opportunities: The Raleigh area provides employment for over 94 percent of its citizens who seek work. Over the past decade, the unemployment rate has been below the state and national rates. Construction has begun for the Dorothy and Roy Park Alumni Center, and is expected to be complete in the spring of 2006. The 56,000 square foot building, made possible by a 5 million dollar donation from Dorothy Park and her late husband, will be located on Main Campus Drive on Centennial Campus and will be owned by the North Carolina State Alumni Association.

Local real estate

Market overview: From older neighborhoods to new developments, you have a choice of just about anything in this region.

Average rent for a two-bedroom apartment: $700 per month

Other areas to consider: Cary is part of the Research Triangle, and very family friendly. More young professionals are calling this home. Winston-Salem has accrued accolades from "most livable" to "Top 10 Digital City" over the last few years. Charlotte runs the gamut from screaming NASCAR engines and the roar at the Carolina Panthers' games, to quiet culture and beautiful museums. This same mixture has carried over into the school district. The Charlotte Mecklenburg Schools have been recognized for its academic quality with a large dose of arts and humanities.

What things cost

ACCRA's national comparisons: The overall cost of living is 2.3 percent below the national average with housing almost in the double digits at 9.4 percent below average. Utilities run 6.8 percent above average, with grocery items and health care both about 6 percent above average.

Utilities: Electricity: $130 per month; phone: $30 per month

The tax ax

Sales tax: 7 percent

Property tax: $11.38 (est. property taxes paid per $1,000 market value)

State income tax: 6.0 to 8.25 percent

Making the grade

Public education overview: Wake County's public school system is consistently ranked as one of the top in the state. Approximately 85 percent of graduates go on to pursue higher education, and SAT scores in this city are significantly higher than both the state and national averages. Raleigh also has several private, parochial, and special-needs schools to round out the choices in primary and secondary education.

Class size (student to teacher ratio): 16:1

Help for working parents: After-school care is available at 17 elementary schools. All elementary schools offer early arrival programs starting at 7 a.m.

Boys & Girls Club: There are four centers available.

School year: Last week in August to first week in June. Year-round elementary schools and middle schools run class for 45 days and then take a 15 day break. To enter kindergarten, children must be 5 years old on or before October 16.

Special education/programs for gifted students: The Wake County School System boasts one of the best state special education programs, because they work in conjunction with the local universities and state-funded centers.

Nearby colleges and universities: Raleigh is home to five colleges and universities, including Meredith College (one of the South's largest women's colleges,) North Carolina State (one of the triangle's three major research universities,) and the University of North Carolina at Chapel Hill. Altogether, the Triangle has eight colleges and universities.

Medical care

Hospitals/medical centers: The university medical centers are among the nation's best. Physicians trained at these universities are likely to set up practice here. Duke University Medical Center is one of the finest and most respected medical, teaching, and research hospitals in the country. Its Heart Center boasts one of the largest cardiac groups in the country, performing major cardiac surgery. Duke has a cancer center, AIDS center, and Alzheimer's research center, and a world-renowned diet center, as well. University of North Carolina Medical Center is known for its treatment of cystic fibrosis as well as a comprehensive transplant program for heart, lung, liver, and kidney. The Columbia-Raleigh Community Hospital offers general medical and surgical services. Rex Hospital is known for cancer care, obstetrics, same-day surgery, and a wellness center.

Specialized care: The Lenox Baker Children's Hospital provides care for the area children. The Dorothea Dix Hospital is a comprehensive psychiatric hospital.

Crime and safety

Police: Raleigh often appears on lists of safe places to live. Some of the Raleigh police department's special operations divisions include the selective enforcement unit, the drug enforcement unit, the traffic enforcement unit, the special projects unit, the canine unit, the animal control unit, the police desk operations, school safety patrols, and taxi inspections.

Fire: Raleigh's fire department personnel are highly visible goodwill ambassadors for the city. At any hour of the day, Raleigh firefighters can be seen outside any of the 26 fire stations cleaning and maintaining the emergency vehicles and equipment. In addition to fire suppression, the department also provides first responder EMT services and child safety seat inspections. Additionally, the department is part of a regional urban search and rescue team that is trained to respond to technical rescue situations involving structural collapse, confined space, trench and high angle rescue, vehicle extrication, or land and water search and rescue. The department also serves as one of the state's regional response teams, providing hazardous materials response within Raleigh and surrounding counties.

Let the good times roll

Family fun: Raleigh gives you lots of choices for activities at community centers, pools, gymnasiums, fields, greenways, weight rooms, and lakes. With a temperate climate, you can spend most of your free time outdoors canoeing, biking, climbing, camping, and fishing. Find a racquet and head for one of the 112 courts. Grab the kids and head out to one of 58 ballparks. Find out about the walking paths nearby, with 41 miles of greenway with 24 different trails throughout Raleigh. Check out Arts Together, Inc. an arts school with fun classes for all ages.

Sports: Cheering can go all year long with the dynamic collegiate sports at the University of North Carolina Tar Heels, North Carolina State Wolfpack, and Duke Blue Devils. Or go watch some hockey with the Carolina Hurricanes. Baseball is covered with the Durham Bulls and Carolina Mudcats (minor league).

Arts and entertainment: With no lack of avenues to pursue, try the Raleigh Little Theater, Theater in the Park, University Players productions, Opera Company of North Carolina, the Raleigh Boychoir, Raleigh Chamber Music Guild, Raleigh Civic Symphony, or the Carolina Ballet. The Raleigh Convention and Conference Center offers productions in their auditorium.

Annual events: Artsplosure, Raleigh Arts Festivals, Summerfest

Community life

Raleigh is indeed a "pitch-in" city. Residents volunteer in soup kitchens, help to spruce up the city, and roll back their sleeves with no questions. Whether it is with the Red Cross or the Museum of National Sciences, there are volunteer opportunities everywhere. Enjoy the recreation and celebration events as a reward for living in such a quality town.

The environment

Xeriscaping is an approach to landscaping that uses small amounts of water while still maintaining a traditional look. While xeriscape translates to mean "dry scene," in practice xeriscaping means simply landscaping with slow growing, drought tolerant plants to conserve water and reduce yard trimmings. Raleigh has a booklet available to learn how to xeriscape.

In and around town

Roads and highways: I-40, I-95, US 64, highways 1, 70

Closest airports: The Raleigh-Durham International Airport is only 15 miles from downtown Raleigh.

Public transportation: The Capital Area Transit offers local bus service. A free trolley service on the Showtime Trolley runs on Thursdays, Fridays, and Saturdays.

Average daily commute: 25 minutes

More Information

City of Raleigh
222 West Hargett Street
Raleigh, NC 27601
919-664-7000
www.raleigh-nc.org

Wake County Public School System
3600 Wake Forest Road
Raleigh, NC 27609
919-850-1600
www.wcpss.net

Chamber of Commerce
222 West Hargett Street
Raleigh, NC 27601
919-664-7000
www.raleighchamber.org

Progress Energy
PO Box 1551
Raleigh, NC 27602-1551
800-452-2777
www.progress-energy.com

City of Raleigh, Utility Billing
222 West Hargett Street
Raleigh, NC 27601
919-664-7000
www.raleigh-nc.org

32

Cincinnati, Ohio

Ohio

Columbus

Cincinnati

Fabulous features

Cincinnati is one of the country's shining stars, where you'll find big city comforts with small town friendliness. With excellent educational opportunities, safe neighborhoods, rich cultural and recreational offerings, and a wide range of attractions, Cincinnati a great place to raise your family.

Cincinnati is known for its natural beauty with steep hills and wooded suburbs, a picturesque downtown on the wide Ohio River front, and four distinct seasons. Acclaimed by *Fortune* magazine as one of the Top 10 places to live and work, Cincinnati has friendly neighbors, great job opportunities, excellent schools, diverse religions, shopping, safety, and lots of things to do. All this, and it's affordable, too! The *Special Millennium Edition of Places Rated Almanac* ranked Greater Cincinnati 11th, in the top 3 percent of metro areas. In 2004, Cincinnati was second on the "America's Most Livable Cities" list.

Whether you're cheering on the Cincinnati Bengals and the Reds, or along the sidelines of Little League and pee-wee soccer, there's a lot of excitement and heart in this city. In the April 2004 issue, *Esquire* magazine put Cincinnati seventh on its Top 10 list of "Cities that Rock."

Possible drawbacks: Urban sprawl can become a problem in large cities. And because Ohio is a landlocked state, Cincinnati is not a good place for beach fans.

► Local Population: 331,285

► County: Hamilton

► Population of surrounding metropolitan area: 845,303

► Region: Central Ohio

► Closest metro area: Chicago, 287 miles

► Median home price: $93,000

► Median household income: $29,493

► Best reasons to live here: There are lots of amenities, great schools, a strong economy, beautiful riverfront views, friendly communities, and a low crime rate.

Climate

Elevation 683'	Average temp. high/low (°F)	Average precipitation rain (")	Average precipitation snow (")	Average no. days precipitation	Average humidity (%)
January	37/19	3.1	7.2	12	69
April	64/40	4.2	0.5	13	54
July	86/64	4.3	0	10	58
October	66/43	3.1	0.3	8	56
Number of days 32°F or below: 98			Number of days 90°F or warmer: 28		

Earning a living

Economic outlook: *Employment Review* and *Outlook* magazine both list Cincinnati among the 20 best cities in which to live and work. The region is home to nearly 400 Fortune 500 firms, with eight headquartered here. Being a central location with various transportation avenues, foreign investment has been a boon to the economy. More than 300 foreign-owned firms are located here. The closeness of an international airport has increased the deciding factors for many companies. The Port of Cincinnati is the country's fifth largest inland port for domestic barge loads. Home to two major barge companies, the port provides links to 140 other barge lines. Small businesses are thriving alongside large corporations in the region. Ranked 16th for entrepreneurship and number one for lowest failure rates according to *Entrepreneur* magazine, Cincinnati is a good bet for small business growth.

Where the jobs are: The University of Cincinnati, Procter & Gamble, the Kroger Co., Toyota Motor Manufacturing North America, Inc., Fifth Third Bank, the University of Cincinnati's Genome Research Institute

Business opportunities: With the diversity of this community, several specialized chambers of commerce have emerged. You want to check out the Greater Cincinnati's Women's Chamber of Commerce, Hispanic Chamber of Commerce of Greater Cincinnati, the Greater Cincinnati and Northern Kentucky African American Chamber of Commerce, and the newest addition, the French-American Chamber of Commerce. New businesses are flourishing at the Hamilton County Business Center incubator, a hotbed for high-tech start-ups, and BIO/START, a biotechnology incubator on the University of Cincinnati Medical Center campus.

Local real estate

Market overview: With 52 neighborhoods to choose from, you might want to start your search for the perfect dreamhome at the home ownership center of Great Cincinnati *(www.cincinnatihome.org)*.

Average rent for a two-bedroom apartment: $700 per month

Other areas to consider: Dayton was home to the Wright Brothers, and this city has been flying high ever since. Take a streetcar through downtown, or relax on the river. Away from the hustle of big city light's, try Trenton for quiet suburb living and a friendly community.

What things cost

ACCRA's national comparisons: Overall living costs are about 6.2 percent below the national average. Housing is the sweetest asset running 17.5 percent below average, though utilities are over 9 percent above average. Healthcare is 6.2 percent below average and grocery items are 7.3 percent below.

Utilities: Electricity: $67 per month; natural gas: $76 per month; phone: $28 per month

The tax ax

Sales tax: 7 percent

Property tax: $88.12 (est. property taxes paid per $1,000 market value)

State income tax: 0.74 to 7.5 percent

Making the grade

Public education overview: In April of 2005, the Cincinnati public schools held its first Showcase of Schools, a district-wide open house where parents and the community could come in and learn about each of the schools' programs. Families have a multitude of school choices for their kids: public, private, parochial, Christian, Islamic, and Jewish schools, as well as military academies or vocational training. The graduation rate jumped to 72.1 percent for the class of 2004, up 11 percentage points from the previous year and up 25 percentage points since 1999. The district adopted a voluntary school-uniform policy to require or strongly encourage students to wear uniforms. Quite a few of the schools have adopted a variation of blue and white for their students. "Schools of Choice" is the name covering magnet schools that offer different programs. Incoming high school students must pick a high school to attend, as the district no longer has attendance boundaries that say where a student will attend.

Class size (student to teacher ratio): 18:1

Help for working parents: After-school care is available.

Boys & Girls Club: There are four centers currently available.

School year: Third week of August to first week of June.

Special education/programs for gifted students: The Gifted Programming Department identifies children who perform at exceptionally high levels, as well as children who show potential to do so.

Nearby colleges and universities: More than 20 area colleges and universities offer everything from associate degrees to doctoral programs at campuses large and small. A few samples are Cincinnati State Technical and Community College, the College of Mount St. Joseph, University of Cincinnati Xavier University, and the Union Institute and University.

Medical care

Hospitals/medical centers: Cincinnati has excellent healthcare facilities, including Bethesda North Hospital (309 beds) with top-rated maternity and emergency care. Cincinnati Children's Hospital Medical Center (340 beds) services pediatrics from infants to adolescents, and was rated two years in a row in the "100 Top Hospitals." The Jewish Hospital (200 beds) has the only adult stem cell transplant program in the area. Good Samaritan Hospital (700 beds), is a level III newborn intensive care unit and delivers more babies than any area hospital. It's the largest private teaching and specialty facility in the area.

Specialized care: Summit Behavioral Health Care (283 beds) provides mental healthcare. Shriners Hospital for Children (30 beds) serves critical pediatrics.

Crime and safety

Police: The Cincinnati police department currently employs 1,057 sworn officers and 281 non-sworn employees. The department serves with the community oriented policing philosophy, implementing such programs as: computer aided dispatching, school resource officers, DARE, mountain bike patrol, citizens police academy, student police academy, and the Cincinnati neighborhood action strategy. Plus there are 45 sworn and one civilian member of the park unit. The unit is comprised of the mounted squad, park squad, and canine squad.

Fire: The Cincinnati fire department consists of 785 uniformed men and women staffing 26 firehouses, with 26 engines. The department also has one heavy rescue/hazmat unit, four ALS rescue units, six ambulances, and four boats.

Let the good times roll

Family fun: In the summer families flock to theme parks, including Paramount's Kings Island; Coney Kids Town, a mini city of 10 buildings, including a town hall, ice cream shop, schoolhouse, and a market; the Beach Waterpark; and LeSourdsville Lake Amusement Park. Go a few minutes from downtown, and you'll find acres of parks and woodlands perfect for hiking, biking, and camping. Boating and water activities are available on the Ohio River. Go further north to Trenton for drives in the countryside. Year-round fun comes with the Cincinnati Zoo, Krohn Conservatory, the UnMuseum for children at the new Contemporary Arts Center, or Newport Aquarium.

Sports: Cincinnati baseball is an all-time favorite, as the Cincinnati Reds continue to excite loyal fans at the new Great American Ball Park. The professional sports lineup includes the Bengals (NFL); Riverhawks (soccer); Mighty Ducks (AHL) and Cyclones (IHL) hockey. Plus horse and car racing at nearby Kentucky Speedway and Lawrenceburg Speedway.

Arts and entertainment: Galleries, theaters, and museums, including the new Contemporary Arts Center, are everywhere. In 2006 mark your calendars for Tall Stacks

Music and Arts Festival. The Lois and Richard Rosenthal Center for Contemporary Art, the Cincinnati Opera, the Cesar Pelli-designed Aronoff Center for the Arts, and the National Underground Railroad Freedom Center are also great places to explore. Schedules can be found for the Cincinnati Ballet, the Cincinnati Opera, and Cincinnati Pops Orchestra.

Annual events: Fine Arts Sampler, Oktoberfest-Zinzinnati, Kidsfest at Sawyer Point, Riverfest, Summer on the Square, Balloonfest, Jazz Festival, Chilifest, Kids' Expo

Community life

Whether you live in the suburbs or downtown, the people here are friendly and helpful. And children are put at the top of the list most of the time. In 2002, a program called 1,000 Hands asked for volunteers and built a playground for all children, including extensive ramping for wheelchair access, in just six days. This kind of commitment is what Cincinnatians are about.

The environment

Keep Cincinnati Beautiful is spreading the positive message in connection with the "Don't Trash the 'Nati" campaign, by empowering local youth to take pride in their community. The campaign's kickoff was on October 1, 2004.

In and around town

Roads and highways: I-71, I-75, I-74

Closest airports: Cincinnati/Northern Kentucky International Airport, Cincinnati/ Blue Ash Municipal Airport, Cincinnati Municipal/Lunken Airport, and Cincinnati West Airport.

Public transportation: The Metro and TANK provide local bus service.

Average daily commute: 25 minutes

More Information

City of Cincinnati
801 Plum Street
Cincinnati, OH 45202
513-352-3000
www.cincinnati-oh.gov

Cincinnati Public Schools
2651 Burnet Avenue
Cincinnati, OH 45219
513-475-7000
www.cps-k12.org

Cincinnati Chamber of Commerce
300 Carew Tower, 441 Vine Street
Cincinnati, OH 45202
513-579-3100
www.gccc.com

Cincinnati Gas and Electric Company
513-421-9500
Cincinnati Water Works
513-591-7700
www.cincinnati-oh.gov

Bend, Oregon

33

Fabulous features

In majestic Bend, nestled at the base of the Cascade Mountain Range, residents are thriving on steady diets of fun. You can ski Mt. Bachelor even in July, rock climb at Crooked River Canyon, mountain bike through the Swampy Lakes, fish at Lake Chinook, or raft down the Deschutes.

The Bend-LaPine schools are brimming with outstanding teachers and progressive programs. With beautiful schools, strong ties to businesses, and numerous program innovations, Bend proves that big cities don't corner the market on quality education.

Speaking of the market, local Realtors are busy assisting the constant block of new buyers coming to take a look at the great selection of homes. There is something for every kind of buyer in Bend, where land is wide, open, and inexpensive. An added bonus to consumers is that there is no sales tax.

What gets the checkbooks out are the convenient neighborhoods. This is a real walking community, where you can walk to school, shopping, the park, even work, with perpetual sunshine and breathtaking scenery. *Sperling's Cities: Ranked & Rated* (2004) rated Bend second in "Emerging Metropolitan Areas."

Possible drawbacks: Unfortunately, job growth hasn't kept pace with the growing population. State aid for schools has declined and forced cutbacks throughout Oregon. Frigid winters and high pollen counts in spring and fall have many residents never leaving home without a box of tissues.

▶ Local Population: 59,779

▶ County: Deschutes

▶ Population of surrounding metropolitan area: 135,450

▶ Region: Northwest Oregon

▶ Closest metro area: Portland, 137 miles

▶ Median home price: $227,500

▶ Median household income: $57,800

▶ Best reasons to live here: The scenic beauty is on a grand scale. It's a year-round recreation paradise, with low crime, a clean environment, and friendly atmosphere.

Climate

Elevation 3,628'	Average temp. high/low (°F)	Average precipitation		Average no. days precipitation	Average humidity (%)
		rain (")	snow (")		
January	40/23	1.8	5.1	15	78
April	57/30	0.7	0.3	12	57
July	81/46	0.6	0	3	41
October	62/32	0.6	0.2	9	61
Number of days 32°F or below: 54			Number of days 90°F or warmer: 15		

Earning a living

Economic outlook: Tourism is one of the larger industries, however, it tends to be seasonal, so the town's economic foundation is based on healthcare and social assistance services. Wood product manufacturing and scientific/technical services are important players as well. Originally a small mill town, Bend has emerged as Oregon's fastest growing high technology area. Between 1995 and 2004, the Central Oregon population grew by an incredible 46 percent. For existing and new employers, there is a large labor pool of applicants vying for available jobs.

Where the jobs are: St. Charles Medical Center, Mt. Bachelor, Inc., Beaver Motor Coaches, iSKY Inc., JELD-WEN Windows and Doors, Bend Memorial Clinic, the Lancair Company, and Lifewise, Inc.

Business opportunities: Bend's downtown remains a vital and sought-after location for retail, commercial, and business offices. An aggressive $22 million urban renewal district has been established to expand the downtown core, provide additional parking, new building construction, and renovation of existing historic structures. Near downtown, the Old Mill District, a 240-acre mixed-use development along the banks of the Deschutes River is near completion. The area is just north of Bend's newest bridge, the Southern River Crossing, which arches across the Deschutes River between southeast and southwest Bend. The Department of Transportation's largest construction project in two decades, the $100 million Bend Parkway was completed in 2001. This new "freeway" section eases demand on the local streets by keeping through traffic flowing.

Local real estate

Market overview: Most older homes have wood exteriors without basements. Contemporary designs with vaulted, opening ceilings are becoming more popular.

Average rent for a two-bedroom apartment: $920 per month

Other areas to consider: Corvallis, tucked in the Willamette Valley, is home to Oregon State University and a regional medical center. This community has created a 2020 Vision Statement of their goals. Roseburg, in southwest Oregon, enjoys mild but definite seasons and no extreme temperature changes. Portland is Oregon's big city, with a skyline of great architecture, trolleys, and a world-class lightrail system.

What things cost

ACCRA's national comparisons: Overall living costs are 12 percent above the national average. Housing and healthcare are 30 percent and 20 percent above the average. Utilities are 9 percent below the average, with grocery items only 1 percent below the average.

Utilities: Electricity: $53 per month; natural gas: $89 per month; phone: $23 per month

The tax ax

Sales tax: There is no sales tax in Oregon.

Property tax: $11.60 (est. property taxes paid per $1,000 of market value.)

State income tax: 9 percent

Making the grade

Public education overview: Bend is the largest of the communities served by the Bend-La Pine School District. Enrollment is served in 10 elementary schools, three middle schools, and three high schools. Magnet schools are available in Bend. Students continuously score above state and national averages on assessment tests. The high school graduation standards, and new Honors Diploma, ensure graduates will have a defined set of skills, rather than completing a required amount of class time. At the high schools, students can participate in the School-to-Career program, a business partnership between students and the chamber of commerce. Students receive credit and payment while working for local companies.

Class size (student to teacher ratio): 23:1

Help for working parents: The Bend Parks and Recreation Department provides before- and after-school programs.

Boys & Girls Club: There are two centers currently available.

School year: Starts around Labor Day and ends early June. Children must be 5 years old on or before September 1 to enter kindergarten.

Nearby colleges and universities: Central Oregon Community College is located in the Bend area.

Medical care

Hospitals/medical centers: Top-notch professionals and superb facilities are the hallmark of Bend's healthcare system. The St. Charles Medical Center (181 beds) offers a level II trauma center, and specialties such as radiation, oncology, neurology, neurosurgery, open-heart surgery, pathology, and men's and women's health services. St. Charles also operates Air Life, the helicopter ambulance service.

Crime and safety

Police: Crime rates, another measure of livability, have been falling in Bend for the past two years. The Bend police department has 70 sworn officers and 24 staff. The citizen's academy program and community policing strategies are just two of the programs increasing effectiveness. Currently four canine units are with the department, one unit for each patrol shift. Volunteers are an important part of operations, assisting with the handicapped parking patrol, speed watch, courier services, and event volunteers. A Volunteer must attend the Bend police citizen's academy and complete a background check.

Fire: The Bend fire department and Rural Fire District #2 includes 76 paid staff, 20 volunteers, 4 stations, and a variety of operational needs. In 1995 the entire fleet of vehicles was replaced, which included over 20 pieces of fire and EMS equipment. In addition, the department has the only five-story training tower in Oregon on the east side of the Cascade Mountains.

Let the good times roll

Family fun: Nestled at the eastern base of the scenic Cascade mountain range, Bend is a wonderland for year-round recreation. Snow activities are tantamount at Mt. Bachelor. With 24 premier golf courses within a 15-mile radius, Bend is known as the "Palm Springs" of the Pacific Northwest. There are 37 developed city parks, including Drake Park, with 11 acres of lawn and trees bordering the Deschutes River. Camping, fishing, biking, and whitewater rafting seem more fun here. For indoor fun, INCLIMB rock gym offers 8,000 square feet of climbing terrain with bouldering rooms. Or Working Wonders Children's Museum is an extraordinary place where innovative programs and activities inspire curiosity and creativity in children.

Sports: Bend Elks baseball, a summer collegiate baseball league, has taken root in the Pacific Northwest and will open play in June of 2005. The summer amateur league is a first of its kind on the West Coast, as the newly formed West Coast Collegiate Baseball League. The league will feature only college players and apply for NCAA certification this winter. The new league features the 2004 NBC World Series champion Aloha Knights and the Pacific International League 2004 champion Bend Elks.

Arts and entertainment: Two theater groups provide plays and entertainment year-round. Concerts are held throughout the year outdoors at Drake Park. Two museums feature exhibits portraying the cultural and natural heritage of the area. There is a thriving art community supporting more than 10 art galleries, juried expositions, and art walking tours. The Children's Music Theatre Group provides classes in theater skills, voice, dance, and all aspects of music theater production.

Annual events: Pole, Pedal, or Paddle race; Cascade Festival of Music; Old Fashioned Fourth of July Celebration; Bend Summer Festival; Sunriver Music Festival

Community life

Maybe it's the clean air, but this community works hard to help their neighbors, their children, and their city. Volunteer needs are everywhere, but so are the residents, always willing to help out. From parents volunteering at the schools to Bend Aid, assistance program for low-income working families, the support and caring are here.

The environment

Water supplied by the city of Bend, through deep wells and its extensive watershed, has been ranked as some of the highest quality municipal water in the country. The annual Commute Options Week campaign is a vital resource for educating the central Oregon community on better ways to use transportation, and ensures the region will continue to be a desirable place to live and work.

In and around town

Roads and highways: US 97, US 20

Closest airports: Bend Municipal Airport is only 5.5 miles northeast of the city. Redmond Municipal Airport is 16 miles north, and is serviced by Horizon, Skywest, and Delta airlines.

Public transportation: Bus service is available through Greyhound and Central Oregon Breeze, but there is no other public transportation.

Average daily commute: 20 minutes

More Information

City of Bend
710 Northwest Wall Street
Bend, OR 97701
541-388-5505
www.ci.bend.or.us

Bend-La Pine School District
520 Northwest Wall Street
Bend, OR 97701
541-383-6000
www.bend.k12.or.us

Bend Chamber of Commerce
777 Northwest Wall Street
Bend, OR 97701
541-382-3221
www.bendchamber.org

Central Electric Co-Op
PO Box 846
Redmond, OR 97756
541-389-1980
www.cec-co.com

Pacific Power
1033 NE 6th Avenue
Portland, OR 97256
888-221-7070
www.pacificorp.com

34 ▶ Milwaukie, Oregon

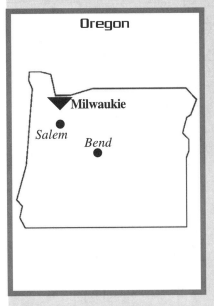

Oregon

Milwaukie

Salem

Bend

Fabulous features

Whatever happened to the kids from high school who defied the dress code and organized sit-ins? You'll probably find them in the Portland area (only now they own restaurants and program computers.) Milwaukie is an older, revitalized community with award-winning schools. The district sends more students to the Odyssey of the Mind competition than any other in the United States.

In spite of a population growth, this is still one of the best areas of the country to work and play. Rapid growth in high-tech, international trade, retail, and film and TV production are propelling the economy. The Milwaukie area is the home of the Bomber, an authentic World War II B17G bomber, located on McLoughlin Boulevard, serving as a local landmark.

Above all, this area guarantees vigorous, year-round recreation. Travel 80 miles to the ocean or 70 miles to Mt. Hood. Or head towards Portland and windsurf on the Columbia River Gorge, hike the wilderness in Forest Park, attend the Oregon Symphony, or root for the champion Trail Blazers.

Possible drawbacks: State aid for Oregon schools has declined, forcing cutbacks throughout the Milwaukie school district. Gray skies and

▶ Local Population: 20,490

▶ County: Clackamas

▶ Population of surrounding metropolitan area: 338,391

▶ Region: Northwest Oregon

▶ Closest metro area: Portland, 20 miles

▶ Median home price: $154,800

▶ Median household income: $43,635

▶ Best reasons to live here: The clean environment, good schools, scenic beauty, and variety of cultural and visual arts.

Climate

Elevation 3'	Average temp. high/low (°F)	Average precipitation rain (")	snow (")	Average no. days precipitation	Average humidity (%)
January	46/36	6.2	3.2	18	76
April	62/43	3.2	0	15	55
July	80/57	0.8	0	4	45
October	64/47	3.3	0	12	62
Number of days 32°F or below: 44			Number of days 90°F or warmer: 10		

drizzle are constant. Just when you think they're gone, they're back.

Earning a living

Economic outlook: Marquis Health Services, a senior-care provider in a four-state region, relocated their main office to Milwaukie in 2005. Also in 2005, three bridges will be installed to span the Union Pacific Railroad, Johnson Creek, and McLoughlin Boulevard. Strong concentrations of metals fabrication, machinery, distribution, and computer software and hardware firms are part of the economic foundation. Several clusters of professional service firms and corporate headquarters exist in the southern and central parts of the county.

Where the jobs are: United Grocers, Oregon Cutting Systems Division of Blount, Warn Industries, Providence Milwaukie Hospital

Business opportunities: North Main Village is a mixed commercial and residential development across from city hall. Many commute to the Portland area, which opens up the door to a variety of job industries and employment.

Local real estate

Market overview: Pre-1975 homes tend to be bungalows and ranch styles with single-car garages. After 1975 came split levels and Victorian models. Because the land is hilly, homes may be on slopes with little or no yard.

Average rent for a two-bedroom apartment: $870 per month

Other areas to consider: Eugene is the second largest city in Oregon, and many residential areas include neighborhood associations. There really are communities called Happy Valley and Sunnyside in Oregon. Both enjoy beautiful scenery and mild seasons. Portland is Oregon's big city, with a skyline of great architecture, trolleys, and a lightrail system.

What things cost

ACCRA's national comparisons: Overall living costs are 16 percent above the national average. Housing costs are 30 percent above the average with transportation and healthcare 23 percent above the average. Utilities come in 19 percent below the national average.

Utilities: Current information is not available.

The tax ax

Sales tax: There is no sales tax in Oregon

Property tax: $12.30 (est. property taxes paid per $1,000 of market value)

State income tax: 5 to 9 percent

Making the grade

Public education overview: Ranking sixth in the state in student enrollment, North Clackamas School District #12 serves the incorporated cities of Milwaukie, Happy Valley, and Johnson City, as well as the neighborhoods of Oak Grove, Concord, Clackamas, Sunnyside, Mount Scott, Southgate, and Carver. Dropout rates are at a 10-year low at 3.12 percent. More than 5,000 volunteers and 600 local businesses contribute to the education of NC12 students. More than 67 percent of high school graduates go on to college after graduation. The Sabin Skills Center is a professional-technical school. Homeschooled and private school students can take NC12 classes by contacting the local school counselor or principal. Many homeschool families enjoy taking electives, such as music.

Class size (student to teacher ratio): 22:1

Help for working parents: Elementary schools provide before- and after-school care up to 6 p.m. Winter, spring, and summer break care is also available and open from 6:30 a.m. to 6 p.m.

Boys & Girls Club: There are no centers available.

School year: Starts around Labor Day and ends mid-June. Children must be 5 years old by September 1 to enter kindergarten.

Special education/programs for gifted students: Talented and gifted programs are available for students.

Nearby colleges and universities: Portland State University, Oregon Health Sciences University, Marylhurst College, Mt. Hood Community College, Clackamas Community College, Lewis & Clark College, the University of Portland, Reed College, and the Pacific Northwest College of Art are all in the Bend area.

Medical care

Hospitals/medical centers: Providence Milwaukie Hospital is a full-service hospital with a 24-hour emergency department, chemical dependency services, and family maternity center. In 2003 and 2001, Providence Milwaukie was awarded the national *Solucient* "100 Top Hospitals" award. In 2001, the North Clakamus Chamber of Commerce named the hospital its "Large Business of the Year." Kaiser Sunnyside Hospital (187 bed) offers cardiology, neurology, obstetrics/gynecology, orthopedics, and emergency care.

Specialized care: Doernbecher Children's Hospital is in Portland at Oregon Health Sciences University.

Crime and safety

Police: In 2001, the Milwaukie police department expanded its community policing philosophy by transitioning into geo-based policing. This concept provides for a close partnership between police, citizens, and the neighborhoods, an accountability to a geographic area which have been identified as the city's neighborhood associations. With two officers assigned to each of these associations, the department moves towards greater communication, education, identification, and problem solving in the community. This is an innovative approach, and more cities may follow Milwaukie's lead in the future.

Fire: Clackamas County Fire District #1 has 15 fire stations and more than 170 fire fighters, paramedics and volunteers. Their swift water rescue team has earned a reputation as a leader in swift water rescue on the west coast. Additionally, the department employs a highly skilled nurse to train, educate, and ensure that the paramedics and EMTs are providing quality medical care to the community.

Let the good times roll

Family fun: Milwaukie will be a prominent destination for BMX racers when Willamette Valley BMX opens its track in a previously vacant warehouse in the North Industrial Area. The track will be the third indoor facility in all of Oregon. Milwaukie River Fest, held on Milwaukie's riverfront near the Jefferson boat ramp, offers lots of family fun. Held in July, events include a parade, live music, food, crafts, community vendors, entertainment, a beer garden, and Dragon Boat races. The main Riverfront event is a giant fireworks display, held on Saturday evening. A mere 15 miles east of Milwaukie is a wonderful campus called Guide Dogs for the Blind. Adults and children over the age of 9 can volunteer to be puppy raisers for Guide Dogs, and share in the incredible process of raising a dog who will one day give independence to a visually handicapped person. Attend one of the graduations on this 27-acre campus and you'll never forget the experience.

Sports: Portland is home to the Trailblazers (NBA); the Winter Hawks (Western Hockey League), and the Beaver baseball team (minor league). There's the Portland 200 Indy car race in June, bicycle races at Portland International Raceway, and thoroughbred racing from October to April at Portland Meadows. The Portland State University Vikings play football at Portland Civic Stadium.

Arts and entertainment: Milwaukie's Historical Museum features local history and artifacts and provides a wealth of research material for historians and students. The museum's authentic, 1872 horse-drawn streetcar is a unique attraction. The Sara Hite Rose Garden is a floral treasure across from the Milwaukie Center. Outside town you'll find nearly 150 nonprofit arts organizations fanning the community's interest in the arts. The Portland Center for the Performing Arts is home to many performing arts groups, including the nationally acclaimed Oregon Symphony and the Portland Opera Association. Also enjoy the Oregon Ballet Theatre, the Rose Theatre, Musical Company, Storefront Theatre, and the Oregon Shakespeare Festival.

Annual events: Milwaukie Cherry Festival, Milwaukie Festival Daze, Riverfest

Community life

The Milwaukie Center provides services to older people, and more than 500 volunteers help run the programs. Down to Earth Day is in May, when local Scout groups and service clubs clean up the downtown area. Supply Our Schools is a project that connects businesses who donate discarded or discontinued inventory and supplies, and teachers who need supplies for the classroom. Chamber partners in the project are the North Clackamas and Gladstone School Districts, local governments, and local businesses.

The environment

Residents can take an 8-week course to become a "Master Recycler," including such topics as waste prevention and alternatives to hazardous household products. Participants agree to volunteer at least 30 hours after completing the course. The neighborhood associations hold work parties on a regular basis throughout the year, which includes removal of invasive plant species, planting native trees and plants, and removing trash. Milwaukie has weekly curbside recycling of glass, metal, and newspaper, and picks up lawn debris for compost.

In and around town

Roads and highways:I-5, I-84, US 26

Closest airports: Portland International Airport is 20 minutes away.

Public transportation: TRI-MET system serves the three counties surrounding Portland. Also, MAX, the lightrail system, runs every 15 minutes from downtown Portland east to the suburb of Gresham.

Average daily commute: 25 minutes

More Information

City Hall
10722 Southeast Main Street
Milwaukie, OR 97222
503-786-7555
http://cityofmilwaukie.org

North Clackamas Schools
4444 Southeast Lake Road
Milwaukie, OR 97222
503-653-3601
www.clack.k12.or.us

North Clackamas Chamber of Commerce
7740 SE Harmoney Road
Milwaukie, OR 97222
503-564-7777
www.yourchamber.com

Portland General Electric
121 Southwest Salmon Street
Portland, OR 97204
503-228-6322
www.portlandgeneral.com

Pacific Northwest Bell
PO Box 3881
Portland, OR 97251
503-242-7428
www.qwest.com

Northwest Natural Gas
220 Northwest Second Avenue
Portland, OR 97207
503-226-4211
www.nwnatural.com

Salem, Oregon

Oregon

● *Milwaukie*

▼ **Salem**

● *Bend*

Fabulous features

Sitting on the 45th parallel, Salem is exactly halfway between the North Pole and the Equator. It's also the end of the famous Oregon Trail, that arduous path that many settlers braved to reach the "promised land." This central location, with one foot firmly planted in a rich, historical past, and the other pointed into the 21st century, offers residents the best of everything.

With the majestic Willamette River flowing by, families enjoy the benefits of one of the most agricultural areas in the country. This fertile valley grows the finest in fresh vegetables, flowers, and flavorful wines. Living in Salem gives you the beauty of the rugged Oregon wilderness, yet the conveniences of city life. No wonder Salem was selected an "All-America City" several times and ranked as one of the best places to raise a family by *Readers Digest* (1998).

The friendly feel of a small town nestled in a beautiful serene setting, plus easy access to big-city activities, is what brings people to the Oregon capital city. An excellent education system, low crime, and a growing economy with wide ranging recreation opportunities all year long keeps them here.

Possible drawbacks: State aid for Oregon schools has declined and forced cutbacks throughout the state. Unemployment is a little high, as the rates of government employment fluctuate.

▶ Local Population: 141,151

▶ County: Marion

▶ Population of surrounding metropolitan area: 291,000

▶ Region: Western Oregon

▶ Closest metro area: Portland, 49 miles

▶ Median home price: $131,100

▶ Median household income: $38,881

▶ Best reasons to live here: Salem has a mild climate with four distinct seasons, friendly neighborhoods, year-round recreation, and excellent schools.

Climate

Elevation 154'	Average temp. high/low (°F)	Average precipitation		Average no. days precipitation	Average humidity (%)
		rain (")	snow (")		
January	47/34	6.0	2.9	18	76
April	61/39	2.8	0	14	57
July	81/52	0.6	0	3	41
October	65/42	3.1	0	12	60
Number of days 32°F or below: 69			Number of days 90°F or warmer: 17		

Earning a living

Economic outlook: Salem was rated number one in manufacturing growth in an "exurban area," according to a 2001 study by Cleveland State University. "Exurban" is defined as a rural county adjacent to a metropolitan area. The Willamette Valley is rich and fertile, perfect land for vineyards and vegetables. Some of the top manufacturers are in food processing. Not only is Salem the capital, but also the county seat for Marion County, meaning thousands of jobs are in government positions. Salem has a variety of attributes attracting new industries and retaining existing businesses, such as a central location, main rail lines, and a municipal airport. The city also has close proximity to Portland International Airport and the port of Portland for cargo shipping.

Where the jobs are: Historically, the Salem economy has been based on government employment, agriculture, food processing, wood and paper products, and light manufacturing. The food products industry is the largest single manufacturing sector with Norpace Foods, Inc. and Agripac employing as many as 10,000 people during the peak of the processing season. Salem Hospital is a major employer, as well as Mitsubishi and Silicon America.

Business opportunities: The Salem Conference Center, a full-service facility with both meeting rooms and the adjoining Phoenix Grand Hotel, make this an excellent asset for businesses. Another project in the works is the Mill Creek Industrial Park, scheduled for August of 2005, bringing warehouse and distribution firms within easy access of the I-5 corridor.

Local real estate

Market overview: Mid-valley construction of single- and multiple-unit dwellings have kept pace with the population growth. The area offers a large variety of housing options from rental units and dwellings for first-time buyers to luxury estates.

Average rent for a two-bedroom apartment: $775 per month

Other areas to consider: Newport is a small fishing community on the coast with an economy shored by oyster farms and tourists. Dallas is a family community with an aquatic center and active parks and recreation department.

What things cost

ACCRA's national comparisons: Overall costs of living are 6.8 percent above the national average. Health care is the largest chunk to this at 20 percent above average. Housing and transportation are 8 percent and 10 percent above average. Utilities are below average by 16 percent.

Utilities: Electricity: $53 per month; natural gas: $89 per month; phone: $23 per month

The tax ax

Sales tax: There is no sales tax in Oregon.

Property tax: $13.20 (est. property taxes paid per $1,000 of market value)

State income tax: 5 to 9 percent

Making the grade

Public education overview: Salem-Keizer public schools (District 24-J) provides for students in kindergarten through grade 12 with 45 elementary schools, 11 middle schools, seven high schools, and several alternative programs. Salem students consistently score above the national average. A number of parochial and private schools, including Blanchet Catholic School, Salem Academy, and Western Mennonite, are available. More than 90 percent of Blanchet graduates go on to higher education or join the military. The Business Partnership in Education is a program where business employees, school staff and students become strongly involved as an integral part of each other's organization. There is emphasis on career education and the practical applicability in the work world. The annual conference "Expanding Your Horizons" exposes middle-aged school girls to careers in math and science, and is sponsored by the American Association of University Women.

Class size (student to teacher ratio): 24:1

Help for working parents: Preschool classes are available at certain elementary schools with a schedule from mid-September to the third week of May.

Boys & Girls Club: There are currently four centers available.

School year: First week of September to mid-June. Children must be 5 years old by September 1 to enter kindergarten.

Special education/programs for gifted students: The school district provides comprehensive, specialized, educational services for children who are deaf or hard of hearing in a setting that is communication-accessible through the use of American Sign Language by all staff. A talented and gifted program serves about 9 percent of all students.

Nearby colleges and universities: Chemeketa Community College, Chemeketa's Training and Economic Development Center, George Fox University, and Western Baptist College are all within Salem's reach. Tokyo International University of America opened its campus across from Willamette University in 1989.

Medical care

Hospitals/medical centers: Salem Hospital (454 beds) is one of the largest of Oregon's 63 acute-care hospitals. The hospital is the city's largest private employer, with approximately 2,900 full- and part-time employees. More than 500 volunteers provide nonmedical support for the hospital. The Center for Outpatient Medicine, located just east of the main hospital, houses the hospital's Regional Cancer call services, outpatient surgery, imaging, sleep disorders center, and a number of other outpatient programs. The building is connected to the main hospital and a seven-story parking structure by skybridges.

Specialized Care: There is no specialized care available in Salem.

Crime and safety

Police: The Salem police department employs 180 officers and 55 civilian personnel and subscribes to the community-oriented policing model. The department offers opportunities for citizens to ride along with police officers. The department has a citizen's police academy and is seeking volunteers for its new, expanded program, which will include citizen foot patrols in downtown, and assist code enforcement and the radar reader board in monitoring speed violators, plus monitor disabled parking spaces. The Youth Services Unit works with the school district to provide a safe learning environment for the children. Other crime prevention programs include Neighborhood Watch and National Night Out. Bringing Law Enforcement and Students Together Camp is a cooperative effort of the police department and the Marion County sheriff's office for middle school students who pledge to be drug free, crime free, and gang free.

Fire: The Salem fire department has nine stations and a total of 171 employees. The department has a 30 member water rescue team with specialized training in swift water and shore-based rescue activities. In 2004, the department purchased a water rescue boat, allowing the team to provide emergency aid on the boat, instead of waiting until the victim is brought to shore. The fire and life safety division presents public safety education courses starring firefighter Bill and Flash "The Fearless Fire Dog," with fire safety games. The department, with ambulance providers, has a program called Capital FireMed, where for a small annual fee everyone in a household receives unlimited emergency ambulance service.

Let the good times roll

Family fun: For outdoor enthusiasts, Salem has everything from golfing and cycling to fishing and boating. With mountains all around and the ocean only an hour away, skiing, hiking, scuba diving, surfing, beach combing, and much more can all be done within a day's drive. Nestled in the forests of the south Salem hills just off I-5, the Enchanted Forest theme park offers fun for all ages. Thrillville USA is an amusement park offering water slides, roller coasters, and more. Salem's downtown Riverfront Park, with an outdoor amphitheater and the Willamette Queen sternwheeler, is host to a variety of events. Don't miss the carousel, with exquisite wooden horses hand-carved and painted by hundreds of community volunteers.

Sports: Sports enthusiasts can enjoy minor-league baseball at the Salem-Keizer Volcanoes Stadium, or catch the Cascade Surge Soccer team at McCulloch Stadium in the 24-acre Bush's Pasture Park. The Wallace Sports Complex, which sits along the Willamette River, regularly hosts many local, regional, and national softball and soccer competitions, bringing in over $3.5 million to the local economy.

Arts and entertainment: The Children's Educational Theatre has dramatic arts program for children that includes classroom instruction, performance, and technical training. The arts are well represented through a variety of organizations like the Reed Opera House, Salem Ballet Association, Salem Youth Symphony Association, and A.C. Gilbert's Discovery Village.

Annual events: Salem Saturday Market, the World Beat Festival, Keizer's Iris Festival, the Bite of Salem, the Marion County Fair, the Oregon State Fair, Art Fair and Festival, Festival of Lights Holiday Parade

Community life

No matter what your interest, ability, age, or how much time you have to give, volunteering is a way to make a difference in Salem. The community of Salem's volunteers provide a powerhouse of skills, time, talent, and energy. Volunteers make Salem a quality place to call home.

The environment

Salem's water, originating high in the Cascade Mountains, is very soft and very pure, far exceeding the standards of the State Health Department. The community is supportive of keeping the community clean and green.

In and around town

Roads and highways: I-5, highway 22

Closest airports: McNary Field provides service to Portland International Airport.

Public transportation: Salem Mass Transit District provides local bus service.

Average daily commute: 20 minutes

More Information

City of Salem
555 Liberty Street Southeast
Salem, OR 97301
503-588-6161
www.cityofsalem.net

City of Salem (water)
555 Liberty SE
Salem, OR 97301
503-588-6161
www.cityofsalem.net

Salem-Keizer Public Schools
2450 Lancaster Drive
Salem, OR 97305
503-399-3000
www.salkeiz.k12.or.us

Portland General Electric
121 Southwest Salmon Street
Portland, OR 97204
503-228-6322
www.portlandgeneral.com

Salem Area Chamber of Commerce
1110 Commercial Street
Salem, OR 97301
503-81-1466
www.salemchamber.org

Pacific Northwest Bell
PO Box 3881
Portland, OR 97251
503-242-7428
www.qwest.com

Children's Educational Theatre
710 Howard Street S.E.
Salem, OR 97301
503-399-3398
www.childrensedtheatre.org

Northwest Natural Gas
220 Northwest Second Avenue
Portland, OR 97207
503-226-4211
www.nwnatural.com

Salem Electric
633 7th Street NW
Salem, OR 97304
503-362-3601
www.salemelectric.com

36 ► Providence, Rhode Island

Fabulous Features

Providence remains a virtually undiscovered city with a distinctive hometown feel, providing diversity and culture without seeming too crowded or hurried. Combining the best of urban life with a community feel, Providence is a truly inviting place to raise a family.

Nicknamed "America's Renaissance City," Providence has been undergoing major remodeling. In the past 10 years, the two beautiful rivers running through downtown have been uncovered. Although pavement once buried them, graceful bridges now arc over the streets, and pedestrians can meander along the cobblestone sidewalks, watching gondolas glide on the river. Once an abandoned freight yard, breathtaking Waterplace Park now sits in the center of the city, with a series of canals, fountains, and walkways.

Even though it's the capital of the state, Providence has a laid back personality. Ivy-covered Brown University dominates the city's east side, adding to the intellectual and cultural landscape. Cosmopolitan high rises create a majestic skyline, mixing new- and old-world architecture. Providence is also a city of 22 neighborhoods and simple charm. Boston is only 50 miles away, and families can enjoy the amenities of Providence with larger city aspects only a short drive away.

Possible drawbacks: The cost of living and housing is more than the national average, but the amenities and quality community more than make up for it.

Rhode Island

► Local Population: 174,000
► County: Providence
► Population of surrounding metropolitan area: 955,500
► Region: Coastal Rhode Island
► Closest metro area: Boston, 50 miles
► Median home price: $190,000
► Median household income: $47,646
► Best reasons to live here: One of the East Coast's best kept secrets, small-town atmosphere, with vast choices of unique housing and neighborhoods.

Climate

Elevation 51'	Average temp. high/low (°F)	Average precipitation		Average no. days precipitation	Average humidity (%)
		rain (")	snow (")		
January	37/20	3.9	10	11	58
April	58/39	4.1	1	11	51
July	82/63	3.2	0	9	58
October	63/43	3.6	0.1	8	58
Number of days 32°F or below: 6			Number of days 90°F or warmer: 9		

Earning a living

Economic overview: Located within the area's borders are a variety of business-es representing nearly every possible industry, from biotechnology firms to software and communications companies. Providence has a diverse range of employment opportuni-ties. Its central location is another benefit for corporations, with excellent transportation facilities including highway, rail, air, and port. With the highest number of skilled workers per square mile of any state, Providence's unemployment rate stays below the national average.

Where the jobs are: Fleet Financial Services, Citizens Financial Group, the Dio-cese of Providence, local government

Business opportunities: During the renaissance 1990s came the Rhode Island Convention Center and the Providence Place Mall, bringing in thousands of tourists and businesses. Also, the area boasts the largest centers of jewelry design and manufac-turing in the country. Economic initiatives and resources can be found with the Providence Foundation, the Rhode Island Economic Development Corporation, and the Providence Department of Planning and Development.

Local real estate

Market overview: Each neighborhood in Providence helps foster preservation of family traditions in this ethnically diverse city. This lends culture and flair to the city.

Average rent for a two-bedroom apartment: $950 per month

Other areas to consider: Centrally located Warwick is made up of 30 villages, each special in its own way. South Kingston offers something for the whole family, whether culture at the Court Center for the Arts, or fun at the Enchanted Forest.

What things cost

ACCRA's national comparisons: The overall costs of living are 27.2 percent above the national average. Housing is the largest piece, at 68 percent above average. Utilities are at 25 percent above. Transportation is below the average by 1 percent.

Utilities: Electricity: $80 per month; natural gas: $98 per month; phone: $29 per month

The tax ax

Sales tax: 7 percent

Property tax: $22.60 (est. property taxes paid per $1,000 of market value)

State income tax: 25 percent

Making the grade

Public education overview: An important change in the school district has been the adoption of the Rekindling the Dream program: "…in conjunction with the community to rekindle the dreams of Providence children, student by student, dream by dream." The district offers programs involving the entire community such as mentoring courses and family literacy programs.

Class size (student to teacher ratio): 26:1

Help for working parents: After-school care is available in some of the schools.

Boys & Girls Club: There are five centers available.

School year: First of September to the third week of June in traditional calendar. Some use a 230-day calendar.

Nearby colleges and universities: Brown University, Providence College, Rhode Island College, the University of Rhode Island, and Johnson and Wales. The Rhode Island School of Design is famous for the quality of education in artistic venues.

Medical care

Hospitals/medical centers: Newport Hospital includes services such as the birthing center, diagnostic imaging, and surgical facilities. Recently renovated floors have control systems, including separate heat controls in a room, bedside computers for caregivers, and no overhead paging. Hasbro Children's Hospital includes a family-centered environment with expert staff. The Providence area includes seven hospitals.

Specialized Care: Bradley Hospital is a children's mental-health facility.

Crime and safety

Police: The patch on their uniforms says "Semper Vigilans" or "Always Vigilant." That's what a great department does, and as the state's largest police department, the Providence police department keeps watch over the city. The city is divided into nine districts, each with its own substation.

Fire: The Providence fire department is one of our country's oldest units. Since the 1700s the departments motto has been "In Omnia Paratus" or "In All Things Ready." These dedicated firefighters have unique names for their engine and ladder companies, a tradition that has been passed down from generation to generation.

Let the good times roll

Family fun: Our smallest state in the union, Rhode Island's capital boasts 100 miles of coastline, making water sports a way of life. The best sailing is located minutes away in popular Newport, and snowboarders and skiers can head for the mountains of northern New England just a few hours drive away. The Providence Children's Museum is an adventure for children from ages 1 to 11. At any time enjoy the Providence Place Mall for hundreds of shops and restaurants.

Arts and entertainment: Performing arts play a large part in the beauty and culture of Providence. The Museum of Art has a collection of over 100,000 works. WaterFire has a season schedule of performances.

Sports: For die-hard sports fans, the New England Patriots at Foxboro Stadium is a half hour drive north. If you'd rather root for the home team, other local sports include the Pawtucket Red Sox, the Providence Bruins, and the Rhode Island Sting Rays.

Annual events: Rhode Island Film Festival, Verizon Jazz Festival

In and around town

Airport: T. F. Green, though not an international airport, carries passengers to most major cities across the United States. Otherwise, Boston's Logan Airport is only 41 miles north.

Public transportation: Providence LINK has a fleet of trackless trolleys running on compressed natural gas. Daily ferries shuttle between Providence and Newport, creating additional opportunities for families to enjoy.

Average daily commute: 19 minutes

More Information

Providence City Hall
25 Dorrance Street
Providence, RI 02903
401-421-7740
www.providenceri.com

Providence Schools
797 Westminster Street
Providence, RI 02903
401-456-9100
www.providenceshools.org

Providence Chamber of Commerce
30 Exchange Terrace
Providence, RI 02903
401-521-5000
www.providencechamber.com

Pawtucket Red Sox
1 Columbus Avenue
Pawtucket, RI 02904
401-724-7300
www.pawsox.com

Providence City Water
552 Academy Avenue
Providence, RI 02908
401-521-6300
www.provwater.com

New England Gas Company
100 Weybosset Street
Providence, RI 02901
800-544-4944
www.negasco.com

Charleston, South Carolina

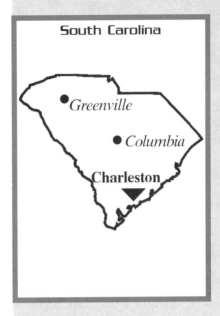

South Carolina

Greenville

Columbia

Charleston

Fabulous features

C is for charm in this picturesque, coastal city, with narrow cobblestone streets, horse-drawn carriages and antebellum homes. **H** is for the rich history of this colonial port. As the first United States city to serve as a model for preservation, there are 1,000 homes, gardens, and buildings, from circa 1670 to the 1840s. **A** is for the Armed Forces. More than 13,000 residents are employed by the Navy, Air Force, and Coast Guard, pouring $4.5 billion into the local economy. **R** is for religious freedom in this, the "Holy City." Charleston's founding constitution guaranteed religious choice, and the city is the home of the oldest existing reform Jewish congregation. **L** is for luxury homes at affordable prices. **E** is for the burgeoning economy that helped Charleston "dance" past the last recession. Tourism brings in $1.2 billion, the Port of Charleston is at 100-percent capacity, and construction is always booming. **S** is for the delightful seasons, with average daily temperatures ranging from 54 to 75 degrees Fahrenheit. **T** is for the tax bite, which is more like a whimper. **O** is for the ocean breezes on the 90 miles of unspoiled Atlantic beaches. And **N** is for the new business moving in. Accolades such as 2004 *Men's Journal*'s favorite place to live, and *Atlanta Journal Constitution's* 2004 "Best Place to Hit the Beach" keep Charleston at the top of the tourists' lists. Put it all together and what do you have? One fabulous place to call home!

Possible drawbacks: Charleston has a large number of bridges and public transportation options, but in a limited number of areas. A new bridge spanning the Cooper River should be completed in 2005.

▶ Local Population: 96,650

▶ County: Charleston

▶ Population of surrounding metropolitan area: 306,969

▶ Region: Southern South Carolina

▶ Closest metro area: Charlotte, 177 miles

▶ Median home price: $139,700

▶ Median household income: $35,295

▶ Best reasons to live here: It's a charming Southern city with an exciting history, great climate, affordable real estate, favorable economy, and exciting recreation and culture.

Climate

Elevation 118'	Average temp. high/low (°F)	Average precipitation		Average no. days precipitation	Average humidity (%)
		rain (")	snow (")		
January	57/41	3.8	.1	10	56
April	73/57	2.6	0	7	49
July	89/76	5.5	0	14	62
October	76/60	3.1	0	6	56
Number of days 32°F or below: 36			Number of days 90°F or warmer: 47		

Earning a living

Economic outlook: Charleston is the largest business and financial center in the southeastern section of the state, and the largest containerized cargo port on the Southeast and Gulf coasts. Charleston has become a leading tourist destination, with 4.6 million visitors adding more than $5 billion each year to the local economy. *Travel & Leisure* magazine has named Charleston the fourth "Top City in the U.S. and Canada" and Travelsmart named Charleston number one safest and most culturally fascinating city in 2004.

Where the jobs are: The Medical University of South Carolina, Navy, Air Force, Charleston and Berkeley County Schools, Roper St. Francis Healthcare, Piggly Wiggly Carolina Corporation, Columbia/HCA Healthcare

Business opportunities: The Charleston digital corridor is a creative effort to attract, and nurture technology and knowledge-based companies and industry professionals to the city of Charleston through a combination of initiatives and business incentives. With the goal of offering tangible resources to the business community, the digital corridor serves as a portal to government, infrastructure, real estate, education, venture capital, professional resources, and a trained workforce. The corridor consists of four geographic areas, offering a diverse range of options to meet the unique size, personality, price, and infrastructure requirements for all types of knowledge-based industries.

Local real estate

Market overview: You can find it all, from antebellum mansions to luxury townhouses, and beautiful new single-family homes.

Average rent for a two-bedroom apartment: $750 per month

Other areas to consider: The town of Summerville, known as "Flowertown in the Pines," has southern charm and historic landmarks. Myrtle Beach is not only a great place to live, but comes with its own ghosts and pirate stories. Charlotte runs the gamut from screaming NASCAR engines to quiet culture and beautiful museums.

What things cost

ACCRA's national comparisons: Overall living costs are 2.7 percent below the national average. Even better, housing is 11.1 percent below, transportation is 4.9 percent below and healthcare is 1.7 percent below. Goods and services run 3.4 percent above average.

Utilities: Electricity: $146 per month; phone: $23 per month

The tax ax

Sales tax: 5 percent

Property tax: $12.40 (est. property taxes paid per $1,000 of market value)

State income tax: 2.5 to 7.0 percent

Making the grade

Public education overview: The Charleston County school district is divided into eight districts, with the city central serviced under District 20. Test scores of college-bound students are very competitive (all the high schools have advanced placement courses), and an average of 57.5 percent of students go on to four-year colleges. One possible drawback is that with the area being rather transient (military and corporate transfers) many teachers stay a few years and then leave. But Charleston area schools can hold their own in terms of nationally accepted standards or better. Retired persons can apply for membership in the Gold Pass Club for free admission to all school-related activities.

Class size (student to teacher ratio): 16:1

Help for working parents: After-school care is available at most of the schools.

Boys & Girls Club: There are nine centers available.

School year: Mid-August to the end of May. Children must be 5 years old on or before November 1 to enter kindergarten.

Special education/programs for gifted students: Special education programs include the low incidence team.

Nearby colleges and universities: The College of Charleston is located downtown and is state supported. The Medical University of South Carolina is on the Charleston peninsula. This state university is for healthcare professions and ranked among the top 100 institutions in the country. The Citadel is a state-supported military college, and other post-secondary schools include Trident Technical College, Johnson and Wales University, and Charleston Southern University.

Medical care

Hospitals/medical centers: There are four major joint-accredited hospitals within an eight-block radius of downtown. The Medical University of South Carolina Med Center is the state's largest teaching center and has a highly respected heart and kidney transplant program. It is the only tertiary care and level I trauma center in the area. Charleston Memorial, St. Francis Xavier, Roper Hospital, and the VA Medical Center are also downtown. Trident Regional Naval Hospital is a private facility specializing in coronary care.

Specialized care: Charter Hospital specializes in psychiatric care, and Fenwick Hall Hospital offers drug and alcohol rehabilitation. There is also a Ronald McDonald house.

Crime and safety

Police: Charleston proper actually has the highest ratio of police for every 10,000 citizens of any city in the United States. Some of the divisions with the Charleston police department are the traffic division, harbor patrol, foot patrol, bicycle patrol, canine unit, mounted horse patrol, school liaison/truancy office, and safe streets unit. The underwater recovery unit works in conjunction with the marine patrol unit. The aviation unit consists of an experienced team of pilots and observers utilizing both a jet ranger helicopter and a cessna fixed-wing aircraft. The program "Operation Midnight" is a planned partnership between police and parents to keep children and young teens off the street between midnight and 6 a.m.

Fire: The city of Charleston fire department is a class I rated department, consisting of 19 fire companies located throughout the city. In 2004, the new Daniel Island public safety facility opened, housing a ladder company and engine company. The ladder company is a new addition to the firefighting force on the island. Berkeley County placed an ambulance a police substation there as well.

Let the good times roll

Family fun: The Charleston area has 90 miles of beaches, many freshwater lakes, and more than 160 parks for outdoor activities. With a mild southern climate, sailing, fishing, and camping are enjoyable throughout the year. Golf is a year-round treat on more than 34 public and private golf courses. The list of quality things for kids to do in Charleston is lengthy, including the Children's Museum, the South Carolina Aquarium, Charles Towne Landing with a replica of first Colonial ship, Magnolia Garden petting zoo, Carolina Ice Palace, and Charleston Hanger Skateboard Park.

Sports: There's plenty of excitement with the Charleston RiverDogs Professional Baseball and the Charleston Swamp Fox Arena Football; South Carolina Stingrays Hockey Team; Charleston Battery Professional Soccer; and the North Charleston Lowgators minor league NBA. The Family Circle Tennis Center (one of many tennis centers in the area) is home of the Family Circle Cup tournament.

Arts and entertainment: Charleston, North Carolina is home to the Charleston Symphony Orchestra, Sottile Theatre, Charleston Ballet Theatre, Robert Ivy Ballet, Footlight Players and the Dock Street Theatre/Charleston Stage Company, one of America's first playhouses. Historic museums continue to fascinate residents and visitors alike. These include the Gibbes Museum of Art (which offers a splendid showcase of American art and Southern history, as well as one of the finest collections of miniatures in the world), the Charleston Museum (the oldest in the country, with a wonderful "Discover Me" room for children) and Patriot's Point (the world's largest maritime and naval museum).

Annual events: Strawberry Festival, Spoleto Festival, Piccolo Spoleto, Southeastern Wildlife Expo, farmers market, Holiday Magic

Community life

The Mayor's Office for Children, Youth, and Families focuses on improving the conditions for children, mobilizing resources in the community to work on their behalf, and developing strategies to support them. The office was created in 1994 to focus attention on improving the lives of children, mobilizing resources in the community to prepare them for success in life, and ensure that they become productive members and future leaders.

The environment

Air and water quality are considered excellent, with a good distance between the industrial and residential areas keeping pollution at a minimum. Air quality meets both EPA standards and Clean Air Act requirements. Ocean sea breezes contribute to clean air as well. The Clean City Commission sponsors neighborhood clean-ups and citywide drives.

In and around town

Roads and highways: I-26, I-95, I-526, US 17, 52, 78, 176, 701

Closest airports: Charleston International Airport is only 8 miles from downtown.

Public transportation: Charleston's bus service is operated by SCE&G.

Average daily commute: 20 minutes

More Information

City of Charleston
75 Calhoun Street
Charleston, SC 29401
843-722-3366
www.ci.charleston.sc.us

Charleston Metro Chamber of Commerce
2750 Speissegger Drive, Suite 100
North Charleston, SC 29405
843-577-2510
www.charlestonchamber.net

Moultrie Constituent District 2
665 Coleman Boulevard
Mt. Pleasant, SC 29464
843-849-2878
www.ccsdschools.com

Moultrie Constituent District 20
75 Calhoun Street
Charleston, SC 29401
843-937-6598
www.ccsdschools.com

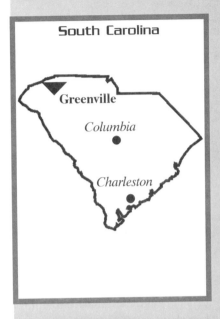

South Carolina

Greenville
Columbia
Charleston

38 ▶ Greenville, South Carolina

Fabulous features

If you know Greenville at all, you know the mountain scenery, fresh air, and rushing streams are the greatest possible wake-up call. Sitting in the foothills of the Blue Ridge Mountains, more than a few bluegrass songs will go through your mind.

Greenville County has the largest school district in South Carolina and is home to the International Baccalaureate program, the South Carolina Governor's School for the Arts, and the Roper Mountain Science Center. The economy has been zooming past the rest of the state. The upstate area is a designated foreign trade zone and is home to more than 240 international firms from 23 nations, including BMW, Hitachi, and Michelin.

Though Greenville has a history of diverse living environments and neighborhoods, the downtown area is experiencing a boom in new housing development, becoming one of the most popular places to live.

Residents roll out the green carpet for great recreation. The Peace Center for the Performing Arts will fill your social calendar. The name Peace is appropriate, because this is a community in peaceful accord. Race relations are enviable (there is minority representation on every elected board).

Possible drawbacks: There's a battle between the older generations who enjoy the status quo and young newcomers who want beautiful and new facilities. The views are fabulous, though.

▶ Local Population: 56,002

▶ County: Greenville

▶ Population of surrounding metropolitan area: 379,616

▶ Region: Northern South Carolina

▶ Closest metro area: Charlotte, 110 miles

▶ Median home price: $118,100

▶ Median household income: $33,144

▶ Best reasons to live here: Affordable living, low taxes, mountain views, pleasant climate, great education, and growing cultural arena that is environmentally sound.

Climate

Elevation 966'	Average temp. high/low (°F)	Average precipitation rain (")	snow (")	Average no. days precipitation	Average humidity (%)
January	51/31	5.1	3.9	11	58
April	72/47	3.8	0.4	10	49
July	89/69	4.7	0	12	61
October	72/49	4.1	0	8	55
Number of days 32°F or below: 68			Number of days 90°F or warmer: 29		

Earning a living

Economic outlook: As one of the south's leading manufacturing areas, Greenville is headquarters to many national and international companies such as BMW, Michelin, and Dunlop Slazenger Corp. The upstate region of South Carolina, with Greenville at its center, boasts more than 2,200 manufacturing facilities. In fact, *Site Selection* magazine has rated Greenville one of the "Top 10 Metro Areas for New Plants and Expansions." Greenville-Spartanburg International Airport, located 12 miles from downtown Greenville on I-85, has undergone a $40 million modernization and expansion. Unemployment rates have been averaging 4.4 percent.

Where the jobs are: General Electric, Kemet, Hitachi, and BMW Manufacturing all call the Greenville area home.

Business opportunities: Is it any wonder that Greenville is internationally known as a hub of new generation manufacturing? Originally owned and operated by Textile Hall Corporation, the Palmetto Expo Center was purchased by the city of Greenville in September of 2001. The Palmetto Expo Center is one of the largest exposition facilities in the southeast.

Local real estate

Market overview: In the past 10 years, Greenville experienced over $160 million in new residential construction and an additional $100 million in renovations in the city's older neighborhoods.

Average rent for a two-bedroom apartment: $750 per month

Other areas to consider: Spartanburg has local colleges and international businesses. You've got to love a community named Pumpkintown, and yes, they have a Pumpkin Festival the second Saturday in October.

What things cost

ACCRA's national comparisons: Overall living costs are 9.1 percent below the national average. Housing is in double digits holding at 19.6 percent below average. Utilities comes right behind that with 7.3 percent below. Groceries are 3.5 percent below and healthcare breaks even with the national average.

Utilities: Electricity: $115 per month; phone: $25 per month

The tax ax

Sales tax: 6 percent

Property tax: $134.60 (est. property taxes paid per $1,000 market value).

State income tax: 2.5 to 7.0 percent

Making the grade

Public education overview: Greenville County has the largest school district in South Carolina. Fork Shoals Elementary School received official notification that the school has become a fully authorized International Baccalaureate School. Taylors Elementary School is one of seven schools nationwide to be recognized by the National School Public Relations Association with an Award of Excellence for their school Website. Eight magnet academies offer unique educational opportunities at the elementary, middle, and high school levels. Each academy offers distinct programs in foreign language, communication arts, engineering, health professions, international studies, science, and technology. Greenville has a number of highly accredited private schools as well.

Class size (student to teacher ratio): 17:1

Help for working parents: Before- and after-school childcare is available for elementary-aged children. Fees vary.

Boys & Girls Club: There are three centers currently available.

School year: Third week of August to first week of June. Children must be 5 years old on or before September 1 to enter kindergarten.

Special education/programs for gifted students: The district has faculty and staff of more than 800 teachers, therapists, and other specialists trained to provide instruction and assistance to meet the individual needs of children. The Greenville County Gifted Center serves students in grades three through eight.

Nearby colleges and universities: Greenville Technical College, North Greenville College, Bob Jones University, University Center of Greenville, Clemson University

Medical care

Hospitals/medical centers: The Greenville Hospital System has a children's hospital with Greenville's only level III neonatal intensive care unit, plus a dedicated emergency center. In early 2005 the Children's Hospital was given a half million dollar gift from the new Donald A. Gardner Family Center for neurological disorders. The Heart Institute provides the most innovative and comprehensive cardiac care in the state. The St. Francis Hospital (257 beds) is an all-private-room facility located near downtown, offering comprehensive surgical services, open-heart surgeries, neurosurgery, bone marrow transplants, and a 24-hour emergency room. St. Francis Women's and Family Hospital (62 beds) is a facility on the east side, providing obstetrics, gynecology, pediatrics, general medical, surgical care, and critical care.

Crime and safety

Police: The Greenville police department has a staff of over 230 employees with 179 sworn officers. The department works closely with children through a variety of programs including a summer youth softball league, a Christmas bicycle gift program, and a substance abuse awareness course. There's even a student e-mail address set up for students who need to talk to an officer. Residents can participate in the citizens education academy. "Operation: Bear Hug" provides stuffed animals to comfort children during traumatic situations.

Fire: The Greenville fire department carries out its duties with an emphasis on fire prevention and public education, in addition to fire and rescue response. The department responds to other emergency situations including vehicle extrications, medical emergencies, hazardous materials incidents, high-angle rescue, structural collapse, swift water rescue, and any natural or man-made disasters. Greenville was one of the first fire departments in South Carolina to build and utilize a Safety House.

Let the good times roll

Family fun: The Peace Center for the Performing Arts hosts major productions on three stages, including an outdoor amphitheater. For the sports-minded, the Greenville area offers 30 semi-private and public golf courses including signature designs by Gary Player, Willard Byrd, and Tom Jackson. Carved out of the Blue Ridge Mountains, many area courses offer spectacular scenery with challenging play. Other recreational opportunities include camping, hiking, or skiing in the Blue Ridge Mountains; water sports on Lakes Hartwell, Keowee, and Jocassee; and whitewater rafting along the scenic Nantahala and Chattooga rivers. For the spectator, Greenville's new 16,000-seat Bi-Lo Center houses a full schedule of sports, concerts, and special events. Don't forget the beauty and entertainment downtown, though. The Falls Park has two amphitheaters and tree-shaded walking trails.

Sports: The Greenville Grrrowls (AA hockey league) play at the Bilo Center.

Arts and entertainment: Greenville's Peace Center for the Performing Arts is home to the Greenville Symphony, the Greenville Ballet, and more. Local college and universities present exciting performances as does the popular Theater on the Green. The Greenville Museum of Art and the Bob Jones University Art Gallery offer revolving and permanent exhibitions.

Annual events: Art in the Park, Jazz Concerts, Farmers Market, Moonlight Movies

Community life

Volunteering is a way of life for many people here. Personal involvement is the reason that many annual events are such big successes. From hot-air ballooning festivals to the city-wide New Year's Eve fireworks display and party, Greenville residents speak of giving small tokens and getting huge returns.

The environment

Greenville prides itself on its ability to keep the city clean from top to bottom. Water quality is excellent (and many say great tasting) and although air quality has sometimes approached EPA limits, it has never exceeded the guidelines. (Most cities would be thrilled with that record).

In and around town

Roads and highways: I-85, I-185, 385, US 25, 123, 29, 276

Closest airports: Greenville-Spartanburg International Airport is 12 miles from downtown on I-85. The Greenville Downtown Airport, the third busiest airport in the state, offers a full range of services.

Public transportation: Greenville Transit Authority provides service Monday through Saturday.

Average daily commute: 18 minutes

More Information

City of Greenville
PO Box 2207
Greenville, SC 29602
864-232-2273
www.greatergreenville.com

Greenville County School District
PO Box 2848
Greenville, SC 29602
864-241-3100
www.greenville.k12.sc.us

Chamber of Commerce
24 Cleveland Street
Greenville, SC 29601
864-242-1050
www.greenvillechamber.org

BellSouth Telephone
1155 Peachtree St. NE
Atlanta, GA 30309-3610
888-757 6500
www.bellsouth.com

Greenville Water and Sewer
407 West Broad Street
Greenville, SC 29601
864-241-6000
www.greenvillewater.com

Piedmont Natural Gas
1915 Rexford Road
Charlotte, NC 28233
864-233-7966
www.piedmontng.com

39 ▶ Nashville, Tennessee

Fabulous features

If you are raising a family in a city where it's getting harder to face the music, Nashville will put more than a song in your heart. It will put extra money in your pocket! The overall tax burden and living costs are lower than in any other major city in the country.

In Nashville, you can not only afford the keys to the door, you can keep up with mortgage payments. Employment opportunities are outstanding, thanks in large part to the services of Partnership 2010 (originally named Partnership 2000). Over 350 companies have relocated their corporate headquarters to Nashville, Tennessee. It's why *Expansion Management*'s survey of America's "50 Hottest Cities" ranked Nashville number one for 2005. *Kiplinger's Personal Finance* Magazine recently identified Nashville as one of 15 "supercities," and is one of the best places to look for work, own a business, and enjoy a high quality of life.

With beautiful rolling hills, a sparkling clean environment (newcomers say the first thing they notice is how nice the air smells), incredibly easy access (30 minutes is a long commute) and lots of fantastic family entertainment and recreation, Nashville is a great place to raise a family.

Possible drawbacks: Growing pains? The city's infrastructure is trying to keep up with all the newcomers. Do you like heading to the beach? Better gas up the car. The closest one is in the Florida panhandle, more than five and a half hours away by car!

▶ Local Population: 580,450

▶ County: Davidson

▶ Population of surrounding metropolitan area: 1,271,890

▶ Region: Central Tennessee

▶ Closest metro area: Memphis, 212 miles

▶ Median home price: $113,300

▶ Median household income: $39,232

▶ Best reasons to live here: Big-city living in a country setting, with affordable housing, a mild year-round climate, clean environment, great entertainment, and an excellent school system.

Climate

Elevation 550'	Average temp. high/low (°F)	Average precipitation		Average no. days precipitation	Average humidity (%)
		rain (")	snow (")		
January	42/27	4.0	3.7	11	66
April	70/46	3.9	0	11	56
July	89/69	3.8	0	10	61
October	71/48	3.1	0	7	58
Number of days 32°F or below: 75			Number of days 90°F or warmer: 37		

Earning a living

Economic outlook: This is a market with a low unemployment rate of 3.1 percent. Careful planning has paved the way for a resounding success. From 1996 to 2002, the list of new and expanding businesses included Dell Computer, HCA, Dollar General Corporation, PRIMUS Financial, and Sprint PCS. In 2004 the High-Tech Institute, Inc., built a 36,000 square foot facility to replace its existing 27,000 square foot space. Boise Cascade relocated part of their business with an 86,000 square foot industrial warehouse at the Cumberland Distribution Center in Nashville.

Where the jobs are: Nashville's Opryland Hotel is now the seventh-largest hotel in the nation. Some of the major employers in the area are: Vanderbilt University and Medical Center; Saint Thomas Health Services; Nissan North America, Inc.; and Gaylord Entertainment Company.

Business opportunities: Because of low personal and corporate taxes, commercial space, and the population boom, it's an ideal city of launching or relocating a business. Partnership 2010 (formerly Partnership 2000) is the economic development initiative for the Nashville region. Their goals for the next four years include creating more than $10 billion in economic impact for the region's economy and creating 50,000 new jobs for the Nashville region, which translates to more new housing units being added and more new consumer spending.

Local real estate

Market overview: Brick-styled homes are available, as are condos, capes, and colonials. Homes are spacious but not too many have fireplaces.

Average rent for a two-bedroom apartment: $800 per month

Other areas to consider: Clarksville, next to Cumberland River, offers upscale amenities. Fort Campbell is close by, too. Knoxville is the home of Mountain Dew and the University of Tennessee. When you say Memphis, usually the first image to pop in your head is Graceland Mansion, bringing thousands of visitors through the area. But this Tennessee metropolis is full of southern charm, ranked in the Top 10 of the most mannerly cities in the country.

What things cost

ACCRA's national comparisons: Overall living costs are 5.5 percent below the national average. The healthiest drop is due to housing at an incredible 21.8 percent below the average. Utilities are also in double digits at 10.7 percent below. Healthcare is at 9.3 percent below average and miscellaneous goods is the only one above at 7.3 percent.

Utilities: Electricity: $50 per month; natural gas: $42 per month; phone: $30 per month

The tax ax

Sales tax: 9.25 percent

Property tax: $45.80 (est. property taxes paid per $1,000 market value)

State income tax: There are no state taxes in Tennessee.

Making the grade

Public education overview: Although the state of Tennessee is ranked 49th in the nation in persons 25 and older with a high school diploma, the metropolitan Nashville school district is busting its classrooms to change that. The commitment from staff, parents, and the community is putting the need and responsibility for education at the top of the "To Do" list. Since 1997, $439 million have been dedicated to construction costs. As of 2005, 79 out of the 131 district schools have been modernized. Every elementary school has a physical education teacher, an art teacher, a music teacher, and a reading specialist. Nashville is in the first year of a five-year school improvement plan, which will fundamentally restructure where children go to school. Also, a new Website should be up in 2006 to provide more information to parents. Currently, 11 magnet schools offer a variety of options to students from kindergarten through high school in specialized areas such as the arts, literature, languages, business, communication, science, engineering, and advanced academics.

Class size (student to teacher ratio): 16:1

Help for working parents: Before- and after-school care is available to parents.

Boys & Girls Club: There are eight centers available.

School year: Last week of August through mid-June. Children must be 5 years old on or before September 30 to enter kindergarten.

Special education/programs for gifted students: An excellent special education program works to meet the needs of the students. The average expenditure in the special schools is $26,000 per child.

Nearby colleges and universities: Nashville has 18 colleges and universities, two law schools, and two medical schools (second only to New York City), including the prestigious Vanderbilt University, as well as Fisk University, Tennessee State University, and Middle Tennessee State, plus 21 community colleges.

Medical care

Hospitals/medical centers: Nashville's second largest industry is healthcare. Vanderbilt University Hospital (658 beds) is one of the most respected research facilities in the country, a six-time winner of the "100 Top Hospital" awards ranked by *Solucient*. The hospital offers 86 specialty clinics. The Monroe Carell, Jr. Children's Hospital at Vanderbilt (206 beds) opened in February of 2004. It also offers 36 intensive care beds, 60 neonatal intensive care beds, 25 emergency department beds, and 12 operating rooms. Construction is underway on an 11 story Outpatient Center. Saint Thomas Health Services is also a six-time winner of the "100 Top Hospitals" in America by *Solucient*. Nashville General Hospital at Meharry is city-owned and is governed by the Metropolitan Nashville Hospital Authority. Centennial Medical Center offers 24-hour emergency care, a transplant center, diabetes treatment center, and a research center.

Specialized care: The Vanderbilt Psychiatric Hospital provides inpatient, partial hospitalization, and intensive outpatient services to children, adolescents, and adults. Vanderbilt LifeFlight is the critical-care air medical transport service of Vanderbilt University Medical Center.

Crime and safety

Police: Davidson County is divided into six patrol precincts. The north precinct was opened in 2004. The horse mounted patrol is within the central precinct, under the special events detail. Bicycle patrols are a part of both west and central precincts, with the downtown bikes that most everyone sees assigned under the central precinct's special events detail. Youth programs and crime prevention services include DARE, GREAT, and Police Explorers. Neighborhood Watch and the citizen police academy are provided as well as BOLO (Be on the Lookout), a program for citizens with training to make observations in their neighborhoods and report suspicious activity to patrol officers in their area.

Fire: The Nashville fire department has 36 stations and 1,121 personnel. One of the EMS programs is "The Heartbeat of Nashville" or public access defibrillation, ensuring that automatic external defibrillator are available in public places where large numbers of people gather. The Nashville Fire Explorers Post 417 offers youth between the ages of 14 and 20 the opportunity to experience and train in fire and emergency services, and to provide various services to the community.

Let the good times roll

Family fun: For 80 years the Grand Ole Opry has been bringing entertainment and music to locals and the world. Activities can be as varied as the colors of the rainbow. Historical Civil War or the Zoo? IMAX Theater or the General Jackson Showboat? Take in the Adventure Science Center, planetarium, or Chaffin's Barn Dinner Theatre, Nashville's oldest professional theatre. Remember those lush, green, rolling hills outside? They're perfect for outdoor fun. Don't miss out on golfing, or rent a jet-ski for some water action.

Sports: Three professional sports teams will keep you hoarse from cheering: the Nashville Predators (NHL), Tennessee Titans (NFL), and the Nashville Dream (NWF). Watch AAA baseball with the Nashville Sounds and the Nashville Rhythm, the newest addition to Nashville (ABA). Enjoy Busch and Indy series car racing. The Tennessee Sports Hall of Fame Museum (located inside the Gaylor Entertainment Center) celebrates the amateur and professional athletes of Tennessee.

Arts and entertainment: Opryland USA, home to the Grand Ole Opry, theme park, and world-famous Music Row, brings the best sounds around. Cultural offerings are not overshadowed with the Tennessee Performing Arts Center, home to the Nashville Symphony, ballet, opera, and Tennessee Repertory Theater. The Parthenon (built as the world's only full scale replica of the original Parthenon in Greece) is the city's most visible art museum.

Annual events: Iroquiois Steeplechase, International Country Music Fan Fair, Kidsfest at Opryland, Nashville Country Holidays

Community life

Keeping downtown Nashville clean and safe for employees, residents, and visitors is the primary focus of a team of ambassadors managed by the Nashville Downtown Partnership. Every day, they pay attention to many details that help create an attractive and welcoming downtown environment.

The environment

Air quality is excellent, thanks to an abundance of light manufacturing, service industries, and an innovative thermal transfer plant. Nashville burns its garbage for energy, heating and cooling commercial buildings throughout downtown (everyone comments on how fresh the air smells). Water quality is crystal clear out of the tap (the Cumberland River is the main source, providing ample supply). Recycling efforts consist of curbside pickups, community compost heaps, and an annual drive to collect out of date phone books.

In and around town

Roads and highways: I-440, I-65, I-265, I-24, I-40

Closest airports: Nashville International Airport is eight miles east of downtown.

Public transportation: Metro Transit Authority provides bus service throughout the entire metro area.

Average daily commute: 21 minutes

More Information

City of Nashville
225 Polk Avenue
Nashville, TN 37203
615-862-6000
www.nashville.gov

Metropolitan Nashville Public Schools
2601 Bransford Avenue
Nashville TN 37204
615-259-8400
www.mnps.org

Nashville Area Chamber of Commerce
225 Polk Avenue
Nashville, TN 37203
615-862-6000
www.nashvillechamber.com

Nashville Electric Service
1214 Church Street
Nashville, TN 37246
615-736-6900
www.nespower.com

BellSouth
1155 Peachtree Street NE
Atlanta, GA 30309-3610
615-557-6500
www.bellsouthcorp.com

Nashville Gas Company
665 Mainstream Drive
Nashville, TN 37228
615-734-0734
www.nashvillegas.com

40 ▶ Austin, Texas

Texas

Plano ●
Austin ▼
Galveston ●

Fabulous features

Located along the banks of the Colorado River along the eastern edge of the Texas Hill Country, Austin is renowned for its natural beauty. The scenery in Austin is atypical of other Texas towns. Most people are amazed they're in Texas when they drive in for the first time, because the area is very hilly and very green. And yet this is as much a corporate, political, and educational arena as the largest cities in the country. As the Texas capital, home of the University of Texas, and headquarters for scores of high-tech firms, there is more "intelligence" here than at the CIA.

You'll find liberal attitudes and cutting-edge technology, but also people getting back to basics. The great indoors of Austin is promising, with continuous live entertainment and great activities for the family. What other city delivers "live" local music in a variety of locations, including at the airport, greeting visitors and home-coming Austinites?

Listing accolades for Austin is like counting the number of bands playing Saturday night. Too many. Yes, Texas has tornadoes. And yes, tornadoes are bad. But if you're concerned about moving to Austin because of tornadoes, don't be. Central Texas gets a fair number but Austin itself is rarely the site of a tornado touchdown. The extra bonus to living here (like you needed one) is no personal income tax. Austin is indeed a "capital" city.

Possible drawbacks: Housing costs and taxes are on the rise, as in most of the country. Direct flights to New York and California are limited, making air travel out of Austin more difficult. The summer months can be hot and humid.

▶ Local Population: 680,899

▶ County: Travis

▶ Population of surrounding metropolitan area: 812,280

▶ Region: Central Texas

▶ Closest metro area: San Antonio, 79 miles

▶ Median home price: $156,700

▶ Median household income: $42,689

▶ Best reasons to live here: With phenomenal business growth, wonderful schools, exciting family recreation, affordable housing, beautiful lakes and hills, no state income tax, and mild winters, Austin is the place to be.

Climate

Elevation 501'	Average temp. high/low (°F)	Average precipitation		Average no. days precipitation	Average humidity (%)
		rain (")	snow (")		
January	60/40	1.9	0.5	8	63
April	79/58	2.5	0	7	60
July	95/73	2.0	0	5	56
October	81/63	4.1	0	7	59
Number of days 32°F or below: 23			Number of days 90°F or warmer: 101		

Earning a living

Economic outlook: Austin's economy is anchored by state government and the University of Texas. Commercial industry is headed by Dell, Motorola, and AMD. Austin is known as a "chip" town, because of Motorola and other successful silicon companies. Austin's economy was severely hurt by the burst of the technology-bubble back at the beginning of the decade, yet the semiconductor industry, too, is very cyclical, and was cycling down when the bust hit. It's cycling up again at this point. *Forbes* magazine ranked Austin third as a "Best Place for Business and Careers" in 2005.

Where the jobs are: AISD, Dell, federal and state government, IBM, Seton Healthcare Network, St. David's Healthcare Partnership, Freescale Semiconductor, University of Texas at Austin

Business opportunities: Austin gets its large share of high ratings from being third on *Forbes* magazine's "Best Places to Do Business," and fourth on *Business 2.0*'s "Boomtown" ratings, with more than 1,000 tech companies. Austin's renowned business environment is nurturing a fast-growing wireless industry and the kind of innovative collaboration that has earned the region a reputation as "Number One in Creativity" according to the *Harvard Business Review*.

Local real estate

Market overview: Every day sees the arrival of more and more newcomers to Austin. With this steady increase in population comes a correspondingly high demand for both new and existing housing.

Average rent for a two-bedroom apartment: $1,000 per month

Other areas to consider: Waco, home of Baylor University, is a hot place to live, but you can cool down in Lake Waco. Did you know there's a glass bottom boat ride at the Aquarena in San Marcos? San Antonio is a rich blend of history and the future, Texas style. The Alamo sits stoically downtown, silently echoing the cry "Remember the Alamo." Take a stroll along the Riverwalk, or enjoy the fun at the new Sea World. A growing economy and world class culture make these Texans stand tall.

What things cost

ACCRA's national comparisons: Overall living costs are about 6 percent below the national average. Housing is a double digit figure at 13.5 percent below the average with utilities just 2 points higher. Grocery items take the cake at 22 percent below the average. Healthcare is 2.5 percent below and transportation is even.

Utilities: Electricity: $75 per month; natural gas: $33 per month; phone: $18 per month

The tax ax

Sales tax: 8.25 percent

Property tax: $4.66 (est. property taxes paid per $1,000 of market value)

State income tax: There is no state income tax in Texas.

Making the grade

Public education overview: *Expansion Management* (April 2005) ranked Austin Independent School District as number one in the "Best Medium" category. District students come from homes in which 57 different native languages are spoken. The district had five of *Newsweek*'s top 600 high schools in the nation, more than any other district in Texas. The dropout rate has been cut by more than two-thirds over the past four years, and last year's rate was 1.1 percent. The "Gear Up Austin" program, in conjunction with federal grants, works with a section of students in high school with intense college preparation studies, providing the skills they will need for success in the 21st Century. The Austin Nature and Science Center provides homeschool programs.

Class size (student to teacher ratio): 23:1

Help for working parents: The Greater Austin area has nearly 200 childcare facilities. Nearly every elementary campus offers early drop-off and after-school programs. The YMCA and Extend-A-Care run many of the programs, and prices are on a sliding scale.

Boys & Girls Club info: There are five area locations.

School year: Third week of August to last week in May. Students must be 5 years old on or before September 1 to start kindergarten.

Special education/programs for gifted students: "Aim High" is one of the most innovative gifted programs for elementary grades, focusing on learning how to think rather than simply being a consumer of information. There are more than 20 special education services, such as content mastery centers and regular classroom support.

Nearby colleges and universities: The University of Texas at Austin, Huston-Tillotson College, St. Edward's University, Concordia University at Austin, Southwest Texas State University, Austin Community College, Southwestern University

Medical care

Hospitals/medical centers: Options in healthcare are abundant, with 12 major hospitals including Brackenridge Hospital, with a 24-hour regional trauma center. St. David's Health Care System offers cardiology services, a Women's Health Resource Center, and centers for diabetes and in-vitro fertilization. Seton Medical Center, a large regional facility, offers heart and transplant centers and a critically ill newborn program. Other hospitals include Central Texas Medical Center, Georgetown Hospital, and Round Rock Hospital (with a Family Birthing Center).

Specialized care: The Austin Diagnostic Clinic and the Seton Northwest Healthy Plaza treat sports-related injuries, radiation therapy, and same-day surgical care. The Rehabilitation Hospital of Austin has services for pain, pediatrics, and injuries.

Crime and safety

Police: The Austin police department has strong crime prevention programs such as citizens academy, a trading cards program, and capital area Crime Stoppers. Officers of the Coahuila, Mexico, state police department have been in Austin to receive SWAT training. And then there's Austin, a 3-year-old golden retriever. Austin is a special dog with a special story: he was rescued as a puppy in the woods east of Houston. He was then turned over to the Golden Retriever Rescue Group of Houston, where Texas Hearing and Service Dogs purchased him and provided testing and training before donating him to the police department in 1999. Austin has been trained to rescue people, and is currently certified in advanced tracking, area search, disaster search, evidence search, cadaver search, and air operations.

Fire: The Austin fire department consists of 40 stations plus an aircraft firefighting/rescue station at Bergstrom International Airport. More than 1,000 firefighters and 50 civilians work and support in fire suppression, emergency medical response, and fire protection. Additional services include hazardous materials response, serach and rescue, and water rescue.

Let the good times roll

Family fun: "Free Admission" are the two most famous words in the Austin language, with more than 12,000 acres of parks and some of the most sparkling lakes in the region. Town Lake Hike and Bike Trail is a spectacular five-mile stretch looping the Colorado River. Highland Lakes is the largest concentration of freshwater lakes in Texas (with more than 700 miles of shoreline). Must-do's are the Austin Symphony's Instrumental Petting Zoo (musical instruments dangle on ropes so kids can "fiddle" around), the Austin Children's Museum, Austin Nature Center, and the Jourdan/Bachman Pioneer Farm. The annual Lance Armstrong's Ride for the Roses is a plus, but it doesn't matter if you are a beginner or a Tour de France champion, the rolling hill country provides some of the best cycling terrain in the world. Home to the country's largest urban bat population, up to 1.5 million Mexican free-tail bats can be seen nightly flying from under the Congress Avenue Bridge from April through October.

Sports: The Dallas Cowboys training camp is here. The "Austin Ice Bats," a WPHL pro hockey team, play at the Travis County Expo Center. Austin is home to the 2005 Rose Bowl Champions, the Texas Longhorns. National Basketball Development League has awarded teams to four southwest cities for the 2005 season, including Austin. The new NBA minor's team will feature players on the verge of making it to the majors in an affordable, family-oriented atmosphere.

Arts and entertainment: Touted as the real musical capital of the country (with more than 100 clubs, there are more live performances on a given night than in any other city). Other offerings include Ballet Austin, the Paramount Theater of Performing Arts, and dozens of museums, galleries, and live theater. Austin caters to the small, unknown bands, who play in various venues across town. The Austin Art in Public Places program is a fun way for artists to display their works. Austin's Children's Museum has over 7,000 square feet of gallery space for children to play, learn, and explore.

Annual events: Austin's farmers market, Kite Festival at Zilker Park, South by Southwest Music and Media Conference, Texas Food and Wine Festival, Capital 10,000, Fourth of July Fireworks and Symphony, Austin City Limits Music Festival, Ride for the Roses

Community life

Austin City News is an online community newsletter of events and happenings around the city. Past issues are archived online for fast, fun information.

The environment

Austin straddles the state of Texas's most vulnerable water supply, the Edwards Aquifer, which is home to more endangered species than any other urban area of the nation. Keep Austin Beautiful, a nonprofit organization, includes more than 10,000 volunteers committing tens of thousands of hours to projects involving the clean up and beautification of Austin's public spaces. The Tool Shack, a tool-lending library, is available for groups to check out shovels, rakes, and more for clean-up projects.

In and around town

Roads and highways: I-35, 71, US 183

Closest airports: Austin Airport is not a hub for any airlines, but the upside is that the airport is new and you get live music. All the vendors must be Texas-owned.

Public transportation: Capital Metro serves riders daily. Capital Metro is investigating a lightrail alternative for commuter traffic connecting downtown, points far north and south, and the new airport.

Average daily commute: 30 minutes

More Information

City of Austin
PO Box 1088
Austin, TX 78767
512-974-2000
www.ci.austin.tx.us

Austin Independent School District
1111 West 6th Street
Austin, TX 78703
512-414-1700
www.austinisd.org

Austin Convention Center
500 East Cesar Chavez Street
Austin, TX 78701
512-404-4000
www.austinconventioncenter.com

The Greater Austin Chamber of Commerce
210 Barton Springs Road, Suite 400
Austin, TX 78704
512-478-9383
www.austin-chamber.org

Austin Energy
City of Austin
PO Box 2267
Austin, TX 78783
www.austinenergy.com

Galveston, Texas

Fabulous features

Ever vacation in a picturesque beach resort and wonder what it's like to live there? If you're ready to take the plunge, think Galveston Island. This sparkling Gulf Coast city is on the cutting edge. From organizing the annual Victorian Christmas celebration to school tutoring by FRIENDS (Fantastic, Resourceful, Interested in Education, Note-worthy Dedicated Seniors), volunteers make the city hum. No wonder Galveston ranked 21st in the *Readers Digest's* (1998) "Best Places to Raise a Family."

Residents have time to give back to the community, because the average commute is a cakewalk (35 minutes to Houston) and most parents aren't working several jobs. With no state income tax, Galveston is the most affordable housing market in the country relative to income levels, and living costs are generally 10 percent below average. And with 32 miles of sandy beaches, a charming historic district, and Victorian architecture, Galveston is a great place to raise a family.

There's no waiting for first-rate medical care (the state's oldest, most prestigious medical school is here, with seven hospitals and 90 clinics) or educational opportunities (no other Texas city has branches of both the University of Texas and Texas A&M). Many people have discovered that a "short" vacation stay in Galveston Island can last a lifetime.

Possible drawbacks: High humidity and the threat of hurricanes are reminders that Gulf Coast living has its hazards.

Texas

► Local Population: 57,247
► County: Galveston
► Population of surrounding metropolitan area: 250,158
► Region: Eastern Texas
► Closest metro area: Houston, 50 miles
► Median home price: $73,800
► Median household income: $33,109
► Best reasons to live here: This coastal island has glorious scenery, a semi-tropical climate, tremendous ethnic diversity, a close-knit community, good schools, and excellent medical care.

Climate

Elevation 10'	Average temp. high/low (°F)	Average precipitation		Average no. days precipitation	Average humidity (%)
		rain (")	snow (")		
January	62/49	4.1	0	10	77
April	75/64	2.6	0	6	75
July	89/80	3.5	0	9	70
October	80/66	3.5	0	7	65
Number of days 32°F or below: 4			Number of days 90°F or warmer: 11		

Earning a living

Economic outlook: Galveston has a strong economic base, covering a wide range of industries, from tourism to medical technology. A 30-minute drive up Interstate Highway 45 finds the Johnson Space Center and many support industries with opportunities in engineering, electronics, and aeronautical research. Go a little further up the highway to Houston, the fourth largest city in the United States. If you don't mind a longer commute, working in Houston and living in Galveston may seem to be the best of both worlds. Galveston is a foreign trade zone, and the Port of Galveston, at 30 minutes from open water, is ideal for cargo shipments. The Historic Downtown/Strand Partnership is the key to the revitalization of downtown and increased business viability. Unemployment for the area still remains high at 8.8 percent.

Where the jobs are: Major employers include the University of Texas Medical Branch, the Port of Galveston facilities, Texas A&M Campus, and the tourist or hospitality industry. The American National Insurance Company and Galveston Independent School District provide other employment opportunities.

Business opportunities: As a major vacation destination with more than 4,000 hotel rooms and condominiums, as well as numerous restaurants and attractions, Galveston's hospitality industry generates more than $350 million annually and a growing number of jobs. The Port of Galveston, the western Gulf of Mexico's gateway for international cruise vacations, is home to Carnival Cruise Line's *Ecstasy* and Royal Caribbean International's *Rhapsody of the Seas*. In 2004, Galveston became the seasonal homeport for Princess Cruises and Celebrity Cruises.

Local real estate

Market overview: Victorian styles are popular and found in two historic areas. Beach front and resort homes have traditional styles. Most older homes do not have a garage.

Average rent for a two-bedroom apartment: $700 per month

Other areas to consider: Port Arthur is a diverse, fun community with plenty of water to keep you cool. Corpus Christi is another waterfront community with mild year-round weather. Houston is the fourth largest city in the United States. Space City has more than 20,000 acres of green city parks for outdoor pleasures. The Johnson Space Center and Mission Control are always on the visitor's list.

What things cost

ACCRA's national comparisons: Overall costs of living are 10 percent below the national average, with housing a low 28 percent below the average. Utilities and transportation are about even with the national average, and healthcare is 9 percent above.

Utilities: Electricity: $100 per month; natural gas: $40 per month; phone: $22 per month

The tax ax

Sales tax: 8.25 percent

Property tax: Not available, though county, school district, and special amenity taxes may vary widely depending on the district.

State income tax: There is no state income tax in Texas.

Making the grade

Public education overview: The Galveston Independent School District serves nine elementary schools, four middle schools, one high school, two alternative schools and an accelerated instruction program. Eight private schools are also available. On the Bolivar Peninsula, the new Crenshaw Elementary and Middle School will be open for the 2005 school year. Third and fifth grade students are given the Texas Assessment of Knowledge and Skills test in reading and math, and must pass to be promoted to the next grade. Full-day kindergarten is available. The district has an electronic newsletter to keep parents informed about events, and an educational channel, GISD-TV, is available to local cable subscribers.

Class size (student to teacher ratio): 17:1

Help for working parents: After-school care is provided through the YMCA on a fee-based program.

Boys & Girls Club: There are two centers currently available.

School year: Mid-August to the end of May. Half-day pre-kindergarten classes are available for children who are 4 years old on or before September 1, and full-day kindergarten is available at all elementary schools for children who are 5 years old on or before September 1.

Special education/programs for gifted students: Gifted students go through a nomination and screening program with services available from kindergarten through grade 12. In special education, over 18 services are provided for students with disabilities from preschool to age 21.

Nearby colleges and universities: The University of Texas Medical Branch includes four schools and two institutes on a 100-acre campus; Texas A&M University at Galveston is an ocean-oriented, research branch of the main campus; Galveston College is a two-year community college; and the University of Texas Medical Branch has four schools and two institutes.

Medical care

Hospitals/medical centers: Galveston Island is recognized worldwide for its health-care and medical research. The University of Texas Medical Branch, the state's oldest medical school, has six hospitals and a variety of specialized clinics. Facilities include a level I trauma center and a specially designed Children's Emergency Room. Clinical areas include the heart center, behavioral health, and diabetes care. The Mainland Medical Center has gone through recent $35 million improvement, including the new bone and joint institute and opening a new patient wing. Services include cardiac care, diabetes management, and emergency services with a heliport.

Specialized care: Shriners Burn Center is a world-renowned research and treatment center operated by the Shriners of North America, with an eight-story, 30-bed facility.

Crime and safety

Police: The Galveston police department provides exceptional community services. A few of the programs include: a citizens police academy; community policing; and HEAT (Help End Auto Theft), which is a Texas-wide program where citizens obtain a decal for their car or truck that authorizes law enforcement officers to stop the vehicle and verify ownership, between 1 a.m. and 5 a.m., anywhere in Texas. "Are You OK" is a free service of a computer system monitored by police dispatchers to automatically check the welfare of the elderly homebound. At 170 officers strong, the police department includes special units, such as a bicycle patrol, dive team, K-9 unit, mounted patrol, and a marine unit. The island is divided into three zones, with each zone being divided into beats, where officers become familiar with the community and problems unique to their beat.

Fire: The Galveston fire department includes six fire stations and 115 personnel. Free blood pressure checks are available at the stations during the week.

Let the good times roll

Family fun: On dry land, outdoor sports enthusiasts can play tennis, golf, baseball, or softball, or picnic at one of 17 public parks. The Galveston Bay area hosts more sports fishermen than any other spot on the Texas coast, and more than 100 species of fish are caught here regularly. At 10.4 miles long, the seawall lining the Gulf of Mexico is the world's longest continuous sidewalk and attracts walkers, joggers, bicyclists, surfers, sunbathers, skaters, and sightseers year-round. Galveston's East Beach (also called R.A. Apffel Park) features Big Reef Nature Park. Seawolf Park was built on an immigration station site and offers a three-story pavilion with a view of Galveston Harbor, picnic sites, a playground area, and a fishing pier. The USS Cavalla, a World War II submarine, and the USS Stewart, a destroyer escort, are on display and open for tours. Moody Gardens, the 10-story glass Rainforest Pyramid, houses thousands of exotic plants, birds, butterflies, and fish, and offers an incredible tropical environment complete with waterfalls, cliffs, caverns, wetlands, and forests. Moody Gardens recently added a NASA Pyramid, Aquarium Pyramid, and ride films. See movies in the IMAX theater on a six-story screen. Docked at Moody Gardens, the Colonel, a 750-passenger, 19th-century-style sternwheeler, offers a unique view of the gardens and an enjoyable cruise.

Sports: This may be an island, but Texas teams are still a life blood for enthusiasts. You have to travel to see a game in person, but rooting for the home team is alive and well in Galveston.

Arts and entertainment: Galveston Island has more than 20 art galleries on the strand, pier 21, and in the postoffice street entertainment district. Summer band concerts are played on Tuesday nights. Or you can tour a restored 19th-century square rigger, *Elissa*, moored at the Texas Seaport Museum.

Annual events: Mardi Gras! Galveston, International Oleander Society, Feather-Fest, Annual Galveston Historic Homes Tour, Oktoberfest, Festival of Lights, Dickens on the Strand

Community life

Dickens on the Strand, a Victorian Christmas celebration, is a fund raiser for the local historical foundations. More than 4,000 residents volunteer to work during the two-day celebration, which attracts tens of thousands of people every year. Citizens get involved in clean-up programs and activities to keep Galveston beautiful. Even the glorious *Elissa* has over 200 dedicated volunteers helping to maintain the ship. The United Way of Galveston is a great place to register with the community.

The environment

Water quality, for both beach and bayside, is continuously monitored to protect the native marine life. As a consequence, shellfish and oysters are not harvested commercially. Air quality in Galveston is good, with ocean breezes clearing any pollution from the mainland, and recycling is active in the community.

In and around town

Roads and highways: I-45, highways 6, 3, 146, Galveston causeway, the San Luis Pass-Vacek bridge

Closest airports: Scholes International Airport is in Galveston. The William Hobby Airport is in Houston (37 miles), and the George Bush Intercontinental Airport is in Houston (78 miles).

Public transportation: Island Transit provides local bus service.

Average daily commute: 25 minutes

More Information

City of Galveston
823 Rosenberg
Galveston, TX 77553
409-797-3500
www.cityofgalveston.org

Galveston Independent School District
PO Box 660
Galveston, TX 77553
409-766.5100
www.gisd.org

Galveston Chamber of Commerce
519 25th Street
Galveston, TX 77550
409-763-5326
www.galvestonchamber.org

Reliant Energy
502 27th Street
Galveston, TX 77550
409-765-4033
www.reliantenergy.com

Southern Union Gas
402 33rd Street
Galveston, TX 77550
409-766-2801
www.southernunionco.com

BellSouth
1155 Peachtree Street NE
Atlanta, GA 30309-3610
615-557-6500
www.bellsouthcorp.com

42 ▶ Plano, Texas

Fabulous features

Plano is a "grand slam" of excellence for raising a family. With effective municipal leadership and services, top public safety programs, and being a corporate and residential hometown of choice, it's a home run! In 2004 *Money* magazine named Plano the top city in the western United States to live. Plano was ranked sixth by *Ladies' Home Journal* as one of America's "Ten Best Cities for Women" in 2001. The accolades continue with Plano being the fifth most "Kid Friendly" city with a population of more than 100,000 according to *Zero Population Growth*.

This small community has undergone a startling metamorphosis, yet kept its heart in place, with more than doubling its population in less than 10 years. The city has also enjoyed no less than four tax decreases. This "can do" city is out of the ballpark with spirit and effectiveness.

Compared to major metropolitan centers on the east and west coasts, Plano is an ideal place to call home. Check the players lineup: moderate housing costs, affordable property taxes, environmentally astute, and technologically progressive. It all makes this a World Series community.

Possible drawbacks: This is not *Dallas*, do not come expecting to buy a large cattle herd or oil mansion like you've seen on television. New housing developments are on economy lots with minimal yard care.

▶ Local Population: 243,500

▶ County: Collin

▶ Population of surrounding metropolitan area: 615,200

▶ Region: Northern Texas

▶ Closest metro area: Dallas, 20 miles

▶ Median home price: $191,000

▶ Median household income: $78,722

▶ Best reasons to live here: Award-winning schools, a booming economy, a pleasant year-round climate, affordable housing, and no state income tax.

301

Climate

Elevation 674'	Average temp. high/low (°F)	Average precipitation		Average no. days precipitation	Average humidity (%)
		rain (")	snow (")		
January	54/33	2.3	1.1	7	63
April	75/53	3.7	0	8	59
July	94/73	2.4	0	5	53
October	77/56	4.6	0	6	58
Number of days 32°F or below: 39			Number of days 90°F or warmer: 88		

Earning a living

Economic outlook: Plano is home to more than 6,000 businesses, including a multitude of global corporate headquarters, technology-related companies, and a large retail environment. Plano has a 4.4 percent unemployment rate. The economy is based on research, development, and manufacturing in the fields of computer technology and telecommunications. Government employment, insurance, real estate, and diverse mid-size manufacturing offer a variety of opportunities. With an educated, professional workforce (94 percent have more than 12 years of schooling, 53 percent have four or more years of higher education), and in prime location, business newcomers are drawn to Plano's fast-paced commercial development.

Where the jobs are: Legacy, a master-planned business, retail, and residential community consists of more than 36,000 individuals living and working for high-profile companies such as EDS, Frito-Lay, Dr Pepper/Seven Up, Countrywide Home Loans, Ericsson, Network Associates, Pepsico, Intuit, and AT&T Wireless. Quality childcare and educational programs are offered at two locations through a partnership with TLC Child Development Centers. These centers are convenient and provide secure Internet camera access, allowing parents to check in on their children at any time during the day.

Business opportunities: Plano's business development corridors are all conveniently located near major thoroughfares, such as US 75, Plano Parkway, and the Dallas North Tollway. Granite Properties developed a master planned Granite Park business center with over 50 companies located in the first two 10-story office towers, housing banking, daycare, and other quality services. The Research/Technology Crossroads have 500 acres fully developed for immediate construction.

Local real estate

Market overview: Plano also offers single-family and multi-family properties, townhomes, and urban living centers providing easy access to parks, recreation, and educational facilities.

Average rent for a two-bedroom apartment: $980 per month

Other areas to consider: Frisco is a great place to be, with major corporations headquartered here. Garland has the convenience of lightrail, and downtown sparkles during Christmas on the Square. Dallas is like a pair of dusty boots and a clean starched shirt, you can go from prairie to downtown skyscrapers in a short drive.

What things cost

ACCRA's national comparisons: Overall living costs are 5.4 percent below the national average. The biggest chunk is due to double digit housing and grocery items being 15.7 percent and 14.6 percent below respectfully. Healthcare is 11 percent above the national average. Utilities are 5.8 percent above average.

Utilities: Electricity: $108 per month; natural gas: $37 per month; phone: $25 per month

The tax ax

Sales tax: 8.25 percent

Property tax: $4.58 (est. property taxes paid per $1,000 of market value)

State income tax: There is no state income tax in Texas.

Making the grade

Public education overview: The Plano Independent School District is recognized for its special needs student curriculum, including gifted and talented, career education, special education, and bilingual programs. Plans are underway for the construction of a new high school. Setting a district record, 73 high school seniors achieved semifinalist standing in the 2003 National Merit Scholarship Qualifying Program. Plano exceeds state averages in the percentage of students taking college entrance exams, percentage above criterion score on college entrance tests, and percentage of students taking state recognized advanced courses. Plano's high school sports teams have won numerous state championship titles. Students continued to score higher than their peers across the nation on the American College Test in 2004.

Class size (student to teacher ratio): 23:1

Help for working parents: After school programs sponsored by the YMCA, and Boys and Girls Club are offered at many school locations.

Boys & Girls Club: There is one center available.

School year: From mid-August to the third week in May. Children must be 5 years old on or before September 1 to enter kindergarten.

Special education/programs for gifted students: Students with special needs are mainstreamed with support services whenever possible. Students who need very specialized attention may go to individual cluster sites. Gifted students are eligible for enrichment and honors programs.

Nearby colleges and universities: University of Dallas, University of North Texas, Southern Methodist University, Collin County Community College

Medical care

Hospitals/medical centers: In addition to excellent medical centers located in nearby Dallas, Plano offers a strong selection of diverse medical specialties. The Medical Center of Plano is a 427-bed, acute-care, medical and surgical hospital. Specialties include open-heart surgery, neonatal care, pediatric intensive care, neurological intensive care, and oncology. The Presbyterian Hospital of Plano is a 231-private-room facility offering programs and services designed for the entire family. Specialties include general medical and surgical services, critical care, and diagnostic facilities. The Baylor Health Care System has a hospital with private rooms, family lounges on each floor, and day surgery centers.

Specialized care: The Texas Back Institute, North Texas Regional Cancer Center, and Texas Heart Group offer specialized services. The Life Care Center of Plano is a 30-bed specialty hospital providing complete medical and rehabilitation services.

Crime and safety

Police: The Plano police department, with 323 officers, has maintained one of the lowest crime rates in the state of Texas for cities over 100,000 people. Citizen surveys continue to rank the quality of service provided by the department favorably. These survey results are due largely to the successful efforts of their crime prevention unit, using prevention strategies such as Crime Watch Programs, EXPLORERS, Cafeteria COPS, citizens parking patrol, citizens police academy, McGruff House, National Night Out, Neighborhood Crime Watch, Operation I.D., Resident Shield, Senior Citizen Police Academy, SMART shopping program, teddy bear program, and Youth Police Academy. The department recently won an award for their National Night Out events for the second year in a row.

Fire: The Plano fire department includes Plano fire-rescue, a full-time paid department staffed with firefighter/paramedics and firefighter/EMTs, operating paramedic engines, paramedic medical units, and paramedic ladder trucks. Staff is cross-trained and participate in the delivery of all services. The department has 10 fire stations with an 11th location currently in design. Each station is built with a minimum of two engine bays, and all stations are one-story with facilities for both male and female firefighters.

Let the good times roll

Family fun: Plano has expanded its park system to 3,658 acres. Six bike and hike trails cover 28 miles, plus four recreational centers, three public pools, three municipal golf courses, and a tennis center. The town also offers a complete summer recreation program for people of all ages through their award winning Parks and Recreation Department. Take a step back in time at Plano's Blackland Prairie Festival! This dynamic annual event gives a taste of Plano's historic beginnings. Downtown's cobbled streets fill with costumed performers, artists, food, and fun for all ages. Wondering small eyes will experience life as "Granny" did, reaching out to farm animals, quilts, soaps, and dipping candles. Nearby in Dallas you'll find the Dallas Zoo for animal adventures. If you're looking for amusement park fun, it's only an hour's drive to Arlington for Six Flags Over Texas. Sailing, water-skiing, and camping enthusiasts go to nearby Lake Lavon, Lake Lewisville, and Lake Ray Hubbard.

Sports: Pro sports teams include: the Dallas Cowboys (NFL), the Mavericks (NBA), Stars (NHL), and Sidekicks (soccer), the Texas Rangers (MLB), and the Dallas Burn (indoor soccer).

Arts and entertainment: Plano does not rely on nearby Dallas for culture. The ArtCentre is located downtown, and the Plano Repertory Theater is right behind it. The Cultural Arts Council of Plano includes Plano Repertory Theatre, Civic Chorus, Dance Consortium, Plano Dance Theatre, Plano Community Band, Connemara Conservancy, and the Younger Generation.

Annual events: Blackland Prairie Festival, Fourth of July Parade, the Friends of the Library Book Sale, State Fair of Texas, Plano Balloon Festival, Christmas in Old Downtown

Community life

Community spirit is centered on the town's two high school football teams and the friendly rivalry between East and West High Schools. Volunteering is also a major way of life in Plano. Companies encourage employees to become involved in charitable causes. The Volunteer Center of Plano has a list of organizations to help with the city's daily operations.

The environment

Keep Plano Beautiful is a city program to help individuals enhance their community through litter awareness and prevention, waste collection services, and community beautification. Programs such as the Great American Cleanup Awareness is definitely a major component of keeping Plano beautiful. In 2004 more than 2,800 volunteers participated in the Great American Cleanup, joining over 2 million people across the nation in the country's largest single clean-up effort.

In and around town

Roads and highways: State highways 5, 190, 121; US 75, I-635, and the Dallas North Tollway

Closest airports: Dallas/Fort Worth International Airport is 40 miutes away. Love Field in Dallas is 30 minutes away. Addison Municipal Airport is only 20 minutes away.

Public transportation: DART (Dallas Area Rapid Transit) has bus line and two lightrail train stations offering easy access to and from Plano.

Average daily commute: 30 minutes

More Information

City of Plano
1520 Avenue K
Plano, TX 75074
972-941-7000
www.planotx.org

Plano Independent School District
2700 West 15th Street
Plano, TX 75075
469-752-8100
www.pisd.edu

Plano Chamber of Commerce
1200 East 15th Street
Plano, TX 75074
972-424-7547
www.planocc.org

Green Mountain Energy Company
1255 West 15th Suite 100
Plano, TX 75075
866-301-3120
www.greenmountain.com

Direct Energy
909 Lake Carolyn Parkway #1100
Irving, TX 75039
888-305-3828
www.directenergy.com

Verizon
641 West Plano Parkway #30
Plano, TX 75075
972-516-1631
www.verizon.com

Provo, Utah

Utah

Salt Lake City

Provo

Fabulous features

Who say beauty and brains don't mix? Not anyone who's ever been to Provo, Utah! Situated at the foot of the majestic Wasatch Mountains, overlooking freshwater Utah Lake, Provo is at the epicenter of some of the earth's most varied landscapes with canyons, streams, and forests.

Provo is a booming business community that's out-producing some of the biggest cities in the United States. Rated 12th in the *Reader's Digest* article of the "Best Cities to Raise a Family" (1998), Provo was also in Sperling's "Best Places" ranked at the top spot for "Least Stressful" midsized city in the nation. Provo has consistently placed in the *Money* magazine Top 35. In 2004, Provo ranked in the top 20 of the safest metropolitan areas in the country by *Morgan Quitno* magazine.

From Los Angeles to Japan, journalists have tried to solve the mystery of what makes Provo run. It is simple: take a group of hard-working people, mingle them with intelligently managed businesses, throw in low living costs and taxes, a clean healthy environment (Utah has been identified as the second-healthiest state), and good schools. The puzzle is solved! When the quality of life is as high as the city (4,500 feet), you've got a winner! Beauty, brains, and power—what a combination!

Possible drawbacks: One thing newcomers find unnerving is constantly being asked if they were Mormon. The ground doesn't open up if you answer no, but it does take some getting used to.

▶ Local Population: 105,439

▶ County: Utah

▶ Population of surrounding metropolitan area: 410,768

▶ Region: Northern Utah

▶ Closest metro area: Salt Lake City, 44 miles

▶ Median home price: $186,545

▶ Median household income: $50,400

▶ Best reasons to live here: Fabulous mountain scenery, unbelievable recreation, wholesome family community, tremendous economic growth, affordable living, and beautiful neighborhoods.

Climate

Elevation 549'	Average temp. high/low (°F)	Average precipitation		Average no. days precipitation	Average humidity (%)
		rain (")	snow (")		
January	39/22	2.1	13.6	10	69
April	64/39	1.8	5	10	39
July	93/60	0.9	0	4	22
October	67/40	2.0	1.3	6	41
Number of days 32°F or below: 134			Number of days 90°F or warmer: 58		

Earning a living

Economic outlook: Brigham Young University, the country's largest private university, funnels a bright, young workforce to the area. Many are bilingual thanks to the Mormon church's practice of sending young people as missionaries around the world. Taxes are relatively low, and costs of doing business are reasonable, creating an incredible atmosphere for employers. Many high-tech companies are quickly carving a niche for themselves in the area. The 40-mile strip between Salt Lake City and Provo has been described in *The Economist* as "the world's second-biggest swathe of software and computer-engineering firms after California's Silicon Valley." Provo was ranked sixth in *Forbes* magazine's 2004 "Best Places for Business and Careers" survey and in 2002, *Cognetics* released a report called "Entrepreneurial Hot Spots" and the Salt Lake City/Provo area ranked third. The unemployment rate for Utah County in 2000 was 2.6 percent.

Where the jobs are: Brigham Young University, IHC Health Care Services, Novell, Inc., NuSkin Enterprises, Inc., Utah County Government, Provo Towne Centre Mall

Business opportunities: iProvo is providing a fiber optics infrastructure passing by each home and business, with an opportunity for residents and business owners to purchase enhanced services from private providers. Some bandwidth will be reserved for education and community purposes. iProvo is part of a public-private partnership where the essential infrastructure is owned by the public, but services are provided by private companies. In addition to high-tech success, the climate is right for small business development. Retail growth is expected to increase as more people relocate to this area. Boutiques, gift stores, and elegant gourmet restaurants are a few of the successful small business avenues.

Local real estate

Market overview: Provo is very heterogeneous. Less expensive homes share neighborhoods with luxury homes.

Average rent for a two-bedroom apartment: $700 per month

Other areas to consider: Orem, on the eastern shore of Utah Lake, is a high-tech community and home to the WordPerfect Corporation and the Osmond Studios. Cedar City, located on I-15, is surrounded by National Parks and a Shakespearean Festival every year. Salt Lake City is the largest community in Utah, nestled against a dramatic mountain backdrop. Here you can enjoy the big-city conveniences without all the headaches of cities on the coasts.

What things cost

ACCRA's national comparisons: Overall living costs are 2.7 percent below the national average. Healthcare is the main culprit at 16.9 percent above average. Housing is a respectable 7.4 percent below, with utilities a double digit 11.3 percent below average. Grocery items are 6 percent above the average with miscellaneous goods just about even.

Utilities: Electricity: $47 per month; natural gas: $56 per month; phone: $25 per month

The tax ax

Sales tax: 6 percent

Property tax: $9.90 (est. property taxes paid per $1,000 of market value)

State income tax: 2.3 to 7.0 percent

Making the grade

Public education overview: The Provo school district develops its own curriculum, and has a master plan of planning and implementation. The district is currently working with Brigham Young University's Department of Sociology to begin a five-year school dropout evaluation to help determine future needs. The majority of the professional staff has been there six to 19 years, and another 30 percent has been there 20 years or more. The Provo Early Education Program provides education and therapeutic programs for infants and toddlers under 3 years of age within the Provo School District who have developmental delays or who may develop delays because of an existing medical condition. The area also includes private elementary and secondary schools.

Class size (student to teacher ratio): 28:1

Help for working parents: Before- and after-school care programs are handled by outside agencies, including activities sponsored by churches.

Boys & Girls Club: There are currently eight centers available.

School year: Starts the first week of September and ends mid-June. Children must be 5 years old on or before September 1 to enter kindergarten.

Special education/programs for gifted students: Learning disabled students are in resource centers in neighborhood schools and mainstreamed when possible. The Individualized Education Program is used. The philosophy is that students benefit from a shared environment.

Nearby colleges and universities: Brigham Young University has a number of nationally ranked academic programs in business and communications. Utah Valley

State College has two campuses and offers two-year associate degrees. Stevens Henager College of Business, the University of Phoenix; the American Institute of Medical-Dental Technology, and Provo College are all within Provo or Salt Lake City.

Medical care

Hospitals/medical centers: The Utah Valley Regional Medical Center is a 330-bed facility and serves as a referral center to nearby hospitals. Operated by Intermountain Health Care, the hospital recently finished building new facilities for its behavioral medicine program, cardiology center, and speech and hearing center. The medical center provides cancer services, trauma centers, as well as a nationally recognized newborn intensive care unit. Life Flight services has added two additional helicopters to its fleet to ensure coverage anywhere in the region for round-the-clock service. The Primary Children's Medical Center is in Salt Lake City, just 45 minutes away.

Specialized care: Utah Valley Medical Center has a phone information line for parents to call regarding behavioral developmental concerns. Handicapped facilities and services include Kids on the Move.

Crime and safety

Police: The reason why the city of Provo's crime rate is consistently below the national average (okay, besides the great people), is a great police department. The Provo police department's commitment to community-oriented policing ensures a good quality of life atmosphere in the city. Programs include Neighborhood Watch and Mobile Watch. The department has an online report system to let them know of any questions or concerns.

Fire: The mountain rescue team is a joint fire and police team. The team is involved in eight hours of rigorous training each month with advanced life support. This joint team trains in winter survival, swift water rescue, caving, and high angle rescue. Provo fire and rescue has available a life safety trailer outfitted with a living room, kitchen, bathroom, and bedroom. The trailer has a built-in artificial smoke machine that demonstrates the need for an escape plan and smoke detectors in residential dwellings. It is an effective tool for teaching school children about the importance of fire and life safety.

Let the good times roll

Family fun: Why would you want to stay indoors? Provo has 18 city parks and one state park, and the east shore of Utah's largest natural freshwater lake, perfect for swimming, water-skiing, power boating, and ice skating in the winter. Also in winter there's snowmobiling and sledding. Speaking of snow, Utah boasts the "greatest snow on earth." Provo is an hour's drive from a number of major ski resorts: Brighton, Alta, Park West, Solitude, and Sundance, which has one of the state's most popular summer outdoor theaters. Take a ride on the Heber Valley Historic Railroad with their authentically restored coaches and working steam engine through the spectacular Provo Canyon. The Provo River has world class trout fishing and the High Uintas Mountain Range has hiking, fishing, and the most spectacular scenery in the country. Visit the Children's Museum of Utah in Salt Lake City. Downtown Provo, toted as the largest mall in the county, offers art walks, dining, and more. For indoor ice skating there's Peaks Ice Arena, where Provo hosted the 2002 Olympic women's ice hockey events.

Sports: Brigham Young University is known for its basketball, football, golf, and baseball teams. The Utah Jazz play NBA teams in the Delta Center in nearby Salt Lake City.

Arts and entertainment: The Sundance Film Festival, a program of Robert Redford's Sundance Institute, brings together more than 6,000 filmmakers every January. Closer to home is the Center Street Musical Theatre, Provo's new dinner theatre, located in the original "Firmage" building. Not only do they offer wonderful entertainment on the weekends, but offer dance, voice, and youth workshops as well.

Annual events: Sundance Film Festival, Jazz Festival, Freedom Festival

Community life

"Step-up Provo" wants a healthy community and encourages residents to break from their busy schedules and focus on walking or other forms of exercise. With the great scenery and clean air, walking is more of a joy than a chore in Provo.

The environment

Provo's water quality is good, but there is concern about the air quality. Geneva Steel contributes to the problem, as does a high concentration of cars. Additionally, Provo's valley location causes temperature inversions and poor air quality in winter. When this happens, outside activities can be canceled (three to four times a year) as it can pose risks to young children, the elderly, and those with respiratory problems.

In and around town

Roads and highways: I-15, US 50, 89, 91, 189

Closest airports: Salt Lake International Airport is 40 miles away. Provo City Municipal Airport is a general aviation airfield on the west edge of Provo where a new traffic control tower is expected in 2005.

Public transportation: The Utah Transit Authority provides daily mass transit service to both Provo/Orem and the Salt Lake/Ogden area.

Average daily commute: 20 minutes

More Information

City of Provo
351 West Center Street
Provo, UT 84601
801-852-6000
www.provo.org

Provo School District
280 East 940 North
Provo, UT 84604
801-374-4800
www.provo.edu

Provo Orem Chamber of Commerce
51 South University Avenue
Provo, UT 84601
801-379-2555
www.thechamber.org

Center Street Musical Theatre
177 West Center Street
Provo, UT 84601
801-764-0535
www.csmtc.com

Provo City Power
251 West 800 N Street
Provo, UT 84601
801-852-6000
www.provo.org

Vermont

Burlington

Montpelier

44 ▶ Burlington, Vermont

Fabulous features

Burlington is a magnet for university students, nuptial-seeking gay couples, and upper-class bobos, a term coined by David Brooks. Bobos favor $4 lattes, Volvos, Sierra Club memberships, and private schools for their children. You'll find aspiring bobos among University of Vermont students lining downtown Burlington's cobblestone streets. If you need to borrow a cup of sugar, your neighbor's door may already be open. Crime in this town is rare, and was one of many reasons the city was ranked sixth in the *Readers Digest* "Best Places to Raise Your Family" (1998).

Greater Burlington Vermont is a perfect blend of big city conveniences and small town charm. Crime and traffic are low and quality of life is high. Burlington and the schools are tightly linked to the community and offer excellent resources for pre-kindergarten through 12th grade students.

Life in Burlington is laid-back but lively. Burlington is a town filled with dreamers and free-thinkers. Award-winning schools and low crime are the icing on the cake. You can't help but have a warm feeling about the place!

Possible drawbacks: Frosty the Snowman spends a lot of time in the front yard. The 30-year average for annual snowfall is 81 inches.

▶ Local Population: 39,025

▶ County: Chittenden

▶ Population of surrounding metropolitan area: 149,301

▶ Region: Northwest Vermont

▶ Closest metro area: Boston, 215 miles

▶ Median home price: $136,000

▶ Median household income: $46,747

▶ Best reasons to live here: Quality education, community safety, recreation, diversity, economic growth, quality neighborhoods, affordable housing, and cultural opportunities.

Climate

Elevation 113'	Average temp. high/low (°F)	Average precipitation rain (")	snow (")	Average no. days precipitation	Average humidity (%)
January	27/8	2.2	19.3	15	64
April	53/33	2.9	4.2	12	52
July	81/60	3.9	0	12	53
October	57/39	3.2	0.2	12	60
Number of days 32°F or below: 163			Number of days 90°F or warmer: 5		

Earning a living

Economic outlook: Accolades add up for this area's economic outlook. In 2004, *Inc.* magazine ranked Burlington seventh in small cities in their "Top Cities for Doing Business in America" listing. The Community and Economic Development Office provides technical, financial, and relocation assistance to businesses, including targeted assistance to employers with livable wage jobs. Variety makes an excellent climate for starting small businesses, with career opportunities in healthcare, education, and services. The job market is very navigable.

Where the jobs are: Local industries include office and administrative support, construction, manufacturing, trade and transport, information/high-tech, education, and health services. Some of the major employers include International Business Machines Corporation, Fletcher Allen Health Care, Chittenden Bank, Verizon, IDX Corporation, Banknorth Group, and Ben and Jerry's Homemade, Inc.

Business opportunities: Burlington is in a positive position for growth. In order to continue on this path, Burlington relies upon its strengths in specialized technical services, niche consumer goods, educational services, and travel and tourism. Furthermore, the region's employment is expected to increase 79 percent by 2035, and population by 69 percent by 2035.

Local real estate

Market overview: A wide variety is available, including ranch-style, capes, Victorians, and split levels. Many are wood frame or wood sided, and few are brick.

Average rent for a two-bedroom apartment: $900 per month

Other areas to consider: Montpelier, the capital of Vermont, is an intimate, diverse community with a thriving downtown area. Hudson Falls had 15 minutes of fame as the setting of "The New Lassie Show" in 1997. The city of Plattsburgh sits on the northern edge of the country.

What things cost

ACCRA's national comparisons: Overall living costs are 17.6 percent above the national average. Housing is the major culprit at 34.8 percent above average. Utilities are next in line at 17.8 percent above. Healthcare runs 8.3 percent above and grocery items are running double digit at 10.3 percent above.

Utilities: Gas: $37.81 per month; electricity: $46.69 per month; water: $59.20 per month; phone: $24.24 per month

The tax ax

Sales tax: 6 percent

Property tax: 2.05 percent

State income tax: In 2003, the personal income tax was based on federal taxable income with five tax brackets.

Making the grade

Public education overview: The Burlington school district includes six elementary schools, two middle schools, a high school, and a technical center. The Champlain Elementary School initiated the curriculum for sustainability. The program, which has since moved to Barnes Elementary School, is a progressive, youth-oriented practice that emphasizes the importance of community by encouraging the consumption of locally grown foods and products. At Burlington High School students are required to complete 10 hours of community service for each year of high school.

Class size (student to teacher ratio): 12:1

Help for working parents: The Burlington after-school program services all nine public schools.

Boys & Girls Club: There are three centers currently available.

School year: First week of September to mid-June. Children must be 5 years old on or before September 1 to enter kindergarten.

Special education/programs for gifted students: Extensive special education programs are available, but the goal is to mainstream where possible. Accelerated programs are available at the high school level.

Nearby colleges and universities: University of Vermont, Champlain College, St. Michael's College

Medical care

Hospitals/medical centers: Flether Allen Health Care is a teaching hospital in alliance with the University of Vermont College of Medicine. The Medical Center Campus offers a pediatric intensive care unit and emergency services. Vermont Children's Specialty Center offers burn injury, cardiology, diabetes, neurosurgery, and more.

Specialized care: Ronald McDonald House, Vermont Regional Diabetes Center

Crime and safety

Police: The Burlington police has an award-winning community policing unit, as well as their crime prevention unit. This progressive and active department includes their public safety project, working with the community and economic development office. The department has a traffic safety coordinator who works in educating the public. The department has a 1:400 ratio of officers to population.

Fire: The Burlington fire department consists of 80 members. The department operates five engines, one tower ladder, two ambulances, and a command vehicle. There are five firestations in Burlington. The average response time is 2 minutes 40 seconds.

Let the good times roll

Family fun: With the natural scenic beauty, outdoor recreation is a must in any season. The Parks and Recreation Department maintains many programs for the community. Church Street Marketplace is an outdoor pedestrian mall with shops, restaurants, and special events. The Lake Champlain waterfront affords diverse opportunities, such as the Community Sailing Center, the 7.6 mile Burlington bike path, and the Burlington Community Boathouse.

Sports: Collegiate sports teams include University of Vermont Catamounts in hockey, basketball, baseball, and track. Some residents root for the Montreal professional teams and others seem to lean towards Boston or New York.

Arts and entertainment: The Firehouse Center for the Visual Arts provides several visual and performing arts programs. Memorial Auditorium hosts many different types of performance, events, and shows.

Annual events: First Night, Burlington Winter Festival, Magic Hat Mardi Gras, Discover Jazz Festival, Independence Day, Vermont Brewer's Festival, Latino Festival Parade, ArtHop, Halloween Parade

Community life

This community stays active, from clean-up projects downtown or on the waterfront, to matching volunteers with elderly or disabled adults. Residents wear their hearts on their sleeves and take care of the community.

The environment

Burlington boasts some of the best air quality in America. The community has many resources provided environmental services, including the Lake Champlain Basin Program, Burlington EcoInfo Project, and the Champ Quest, dedicated to finding and protecting the large reptiles presumed to be in Lake Champlain.

In and around town

Roads and highways: I-89, I-91, US 2

Closest airports: Burlington International Airport provides daily service.

Public transportation: Chittenden Count Transit Authority provides local bus service to the Burlington area.

Average daily commute: 14 minutes

More Information

City of Burlington
149 Church Street
Burlington, VT 05401
802-865-7272
www.ci.burlington.vt.us

Burlington School District
150 Colchester Avenue
Burlington, VT 05401
802-865-5332
www.bsdvt.org

Regional Chamber of Commerce
60 Main Street, Suite 100
Burlington, VT 05401
802-863-3489
www.vermont.org

Department of Public Works
645 Pine Street, Suite A
Burlington, VT 05401
802-863.4501
www.dpw.ci.burlington.vt.us

Chittendon County
Transportation Authority
15 Industrial Parkway
Burlington, VT 05402
802-864-CCTA
www.cctaride.org

Vermont Gas
85 Swift Street South
Burlington, VT 05402
802-863-4511
www.vermontgas.com

Burlington Telecom
200 Church Street
Burlington, VT 05401
802-865-7529
www.burlingtontelecom.com

Church Street Marketplace
2 Church Street, Suite 2
Burlington, VT 05401
80-863-1648
www.churchstreetmarketplace.com

Winooski Valley Park District
Ethan Allen Homestead
Burlington, VT 05401
802-863-5744
www.wvpd.org

Burlington Electric Department
585 Pine Street
Burlington, VT 05401-4891
802-658-0300
www.burlingtonelectric.com

45

Chesapeake, Virginia

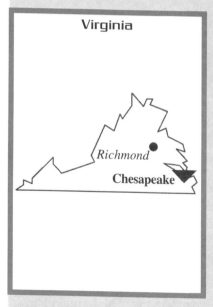

Virginia

Richmond

Chesapeake

Fabulous features

Chesapeake is one of those special cities where you could live from cradle to grave and not feel like you missed a thing. Situated in the heart of the dynamic Hampton Roads region, residents are a short drive away from the Atlantic Ocean and hundreds of cultural, historic, and "fun-omental" activities (Colonial Williamsburg, the Virginia Air and Space Center, and Busch Gardens are just a few.)

While the leisure suits you fine (a wilderness park has families camping, canoeing, and horseback riding), the opportunities for advancement will really dress up your life. Because of excellent transportation and its central location, Chesapeake, according to *The Wall Street Journal*, will experience some of the greatest job growth in the coming years. In fact, *Money* magazine has ranked Chesapeake as one of the best places to live in their "America's 50 Hottest Towns."

Regardless of nationality, everyone appreciates security (crime statistics rank Chesapeake as one of the safest cities in Virginia and one of the top in the nation). Whether you're 8 years old or 80, there is something to do in Chesapeake!

Possible drawbacks: Managing growth keeps city officials busy. The population is expect to reach 205,000 soon. Adequate water supply and roads are a concern, but long-term plans should soon catch up. Beware of high humidity in the summer.

- ▶ Local Population: 199,184
- ▶ County: None
- ▶ Population of surrounding metropolitan area: 2,000,000
- ▶ Region: Southeastern Virginia
- ▶ Closest metro area: Norfolk, 8 miles
- ▶ Median home price: $122,300
- ▶ Median household income: $50,743
- ▶ Best reasons to live here: It's a fast-growing coastal region, with affordable housing, good economic growth, progressive schools, great recreation and culture, and low crime.

Climate

Elevation 18'	Average temp. high/low (°F)	Average precipitation rain (")	snow (")	Average no. days precipitation	Average humidity (%)
January	48/32	4.2	3.0	11	59
April	67/48	3.5	0	10	51
July	87/71	5.4	0	11	59
October	69/52	3.7	0	7	59
Number of days 32°F or below: 54			Number of days 90°F or warmer: 30		

Earning a living

Economic outlook: Chesapeake has the second largest technology business center in the state. The fast-growing manufacturing sector includes plastics, machinery, and marine services, as they are the second busiest cargo marine port on the east coast. This area has been ranked in the Top 10 percent of metropolitan areas for technology employment, and a Top 10 city for small and home-based business. With more educated workers and higher annual research and development expenditures than Charlotte, more than 50 percent of the international firms doing business in Hampton Roads are located in Chesapeake. More than 25 new companies located to Chesapeake in 2003, while 64 existing businesses expanded their operations. The local workforce is augmented annually by 17,000 exiting military personnel, 40,000 military spouses, and more than 8,500 graduating college students.

Where the jobs are: Chesapeake General Hospital, QVC, Household International, LTD Management, Towers Perrin Administration Solutions, Cox Communications

Business opportunities: Chesapeake is a mix of industry, agriculture, and commercial activity. Home to more than 180 manufacturers, Chesapeake firms produce a wide range of products, including Sumitomo industrial gears and Mitsubishi copier components. Nearly 300 farms occupy 20 percent of the city's 229,640 acres and are among Virginia's leaders in soybean, corn, and wheat production.

Local real estate

Market overview: Most homes are ranch-styles or two-story models with brick or vinyl siding. Homes in the more rural areas come with acreage.

Average rent for a two-bedroom apartment: $750 per month

Other areas to consider: Emporia is a city of crossroads with a heavy travel industry slant. Williamsburg has an area transit system and is centrally located. Norfolk may be over 400 years old, but the city hosts the region's airport and has one of the busiest international ports on the East Coast.

What things cost

ACCRA's national comparisons: Overall livings costs are just 2.1 percent above the national average. Housing sits at 4.4 percent above, with utilities hitting 16.3 percent above the average. Healthcare rides at 3.6 percent below average and the cost of grocery items is 2.1 percent below the average.

Utilities: Electricity: $73 per month; water: $32 per month; natural gas: $75 per month; phone: $30 per month

The tax ax

Sales tax: 4.5 percent

Property tax: $13.40 (est. property taxes paid per $1,000 of market value)

State income tax: 2.0 to 5.75 percent

Making the grade

Public education overview: The Chesapeake public schools is an excellent school district, with a dropout rate of 1.93 percent, well below the national average. The district serves 28 primary or elementary schools, 10 middle schools, and six high schools. *Site Selection* magazine has awarded them the "Blue Ribbon School" award. Ironically, schools may be closed due to hurricanes, snow, ice, or even extreme heat. In 2003 the Grassfield Elementary School opened and the Great Bridge Middle School completed its renovations. A new high school in the Grassfield area is scheduled to open in September 2007.

Class size (student to teacher ratio): 20:1

Help for working parents: The district does not have a before- or after-school childcare program.

Boys & Girls Club: There are two centers currently available

School year: First week of September to mid-June. To enter kindergarten a child must be 5 years old on or before September 30.

Special education/programs for gifted students: The Center for the Academically Gifted, Chesapeake Center for Science and Technology, Chesapeake Alternative School

Nearby colleges and universities: The College of William and Mary, Virginia Wesleyan College, Norfolk State University, Hampton University, Old Dominican University, Tidewater Community College

Medical care

Hospitals/medical centers: There are nine general hospitals in the metro area, including Chesapeake General Hospital, which is a 310-bed facility offering cardiac care, geriatrics, obstetrics, pediatrics, and general emergency care. Mom's Mobile Unit offers free home visits to first-time mothers. The Riverside Regional Medical Center offers comprehensive healthcare, a drug overdose center, diabetes center, kidney dialysis service, and open-heart surgery. Sentara Norfolk General, a 569-bed facility, is the largest area hospital and the area's only level I trauma center and burn trauma unit.

Specialized care: Chesapeake General Hospital has a cancer treatment center.

Crime and safety

Police: The Emergency Dispatch Center is the public safety answering point for citizens and visitors needing assistance. The K-9 patrol unit is assigned to the special investigations section. Chesapeake's Explorer Post is a co-ed group of young adults between the ages of 14 and 20 interested in pursuing a career in the field of law enforcement. The underwater search and recovery team is comprised of twelve officers. With the large number of waterways in and around the city, the water patrol unit patrols the waterways to both enforce the boating laws and to give aid and assistance to boaters in distress.

Fire: The Chesapeake fire department has 15 stations. Many of the members are part of the tidewater regional technical rescue team, a specialized rescue organization serving southeastern Virginia. The department has provided emergency medical care since the first day the city existed and currently has a fleet of 10 units staffed by firefighter/ paramedics.

Let the good times roll

Family fun: Chesapeake has plenty of open spaces with 67 parks and play areas city-wide. There are three public and three commercial boat ramps, seven community centers, and six library locations, plus a bookmobile. The Northwest River Park is its "jewel in the crown." This 763-acre park features equestrian and camping facilities, nature trails, fishing, and paddle-boating. The park is open all year-round, and a leisure program for kids and adults offers more than 400 programs including ballet, karate, and dog obedience. The Intercoastal Waterway (running from Maine to Florida) passes through Chesapeake, and provides boating opportunities. Colonial Williamsburg and Busch Gardens are a one-hour drive.

Sports: Having no local professional teams close by, the fan base is split among a variety of teams. However, the local talent is excellent, and cheering is quite boisterous for the Hampton Roads Admirals (AHL), Norfolk Tides (AAA baseball), Hampton Roads Mariners (NSL), and Hampton Roads Piranhas (NWSL).

Arts and entertainment: Hampton Roads is Virginia's cultural hub, and it has everything you desire, including the Virginia Opera, the Virginia Stage Company, the Virginia Symphony, Chrysler Museum, and the Mariner's Museum.

Annual events: Paddle for the Border, Chesapeake Jubilee, Trailathon Fall Festival Weekend, Christmas Parade

Community life

This city has a strong sense of civic and community involvement. Attendance is very high at meetings for local government and community projects. "Paint Your Heart Out, Chesapeake" is a program sponsored by the Rotary Club, involving more than 750 volunteers who paint, repair, and beautify the homes of elderly residents.

The environment

Chesapeake's citizens have a chance to get involved at the grassroots level in helping keep the city clean and green. Last year, 7,813 volunteers got involved in projects and removed 153,568 pounds of debris from Chesapeake's waterways, streets, parks, and other public areas. More than 100 trees were planted at parks throughout Chesapeake during Arbor Day. In order to meet the increasing demands for water, the city has created an aquifer storage and recovery system that will store water underground.

In and around town

Roads and highways: US 58, 13, 168, 17, I-664, I-264, I-464, I-64

Closest airports: Williamsburg International Airport is 45 minutes north. Norfolk International Airport is 25 minutes north. The Regional Hampton Roads Airport is in northern Chesapeake and the regional Chesapeake Municipal Airport is in the central Chesapeake region.

Public transportation: Tidewater Regional Transit provides bus service to the Chesapeake area.

Average daily commute: 25 minutes

More Information

City of Chesapeake
306 Cedar Road
Chesapeake, VA 23322
757-382-6241
www.chesapeake.va.us

Chesapeake Public Schools
312 Cedar Road
Chesapeake, VA 23322
757-547-0165
www.cps.k12.va.us

Chesapeake Division
Hampton Chamber of Commerce
400 Volvo Parkway
Chesapeake, VA 23320
757-664-2591
www.hamptonroadschamber.com

46

Kent, Washington

Washington

Kent

Spokane

Olympia

Fabulous features

Surrounded by commercial giants (Boeing, Nintendo, and Microsoft), and incredible natural giants (Mt. Rainier, the Cascade Mountains, and the Olympic Peninsula), welcome home to the great community of Kent.

Centrally located between Seattle and Tacoma, Kent boasts award-winning parks, affordable real estate, and quality schools with a graduation rate of 96.7 percent. Kent was recently selected by *Sports Illustrated* magazine as Sportstown Washington because of its outstanding parks and recreation department, sports facilities, and volunteer involvement.

Kent's emphasis on public safety is commendable. Since 1997, the Kent police department has been awarded the "National Night Out Award for Outstanding Participation" from the National Association Town Watch organization. The Youth Board of Kent's police department garnered the "Director's Community Leadership Award" from the FBI in 2001, and in 2003 the Youth Board won the "Award of Excellence" from the King County Tobacco Free Council.

Possible drawbacks: Unless you're coming from New York or San Francisco, the high costs of living may scare you. Getting one of those high-paying jobs should help.

▶ Local Population: 84,560

▶ County: King

▶ Population of surrounding metropolitan area: 1,788,300

▶ Region: Northwest Washington

▶ Closest metro area: Seattle, 10 miles

▶ Median home price: $193,935

▶ Median household income: $47,057

▶ Best reasons to live here: It's central to Seattle and Tacoma, with a wide selection of homes, excellent schools, family-oriented community, and award winning parks.

Climate

Elevation 50'	Average temp. high/low (°F)	Average precipitation rain (")	snow (")	Average no. days precipitation	Average humidity (%)
January	47/35	5.3	6.8	20	81
April	61/42	2.8	0.1	15	57
July	77/55	0.9	0	5	50
October	61/44	3.3	0	14	66
Number of days 32°F or below: 32			Number of days 90°F or warmer: 3		

Earning a living

Economic outlook: Job growth in Kent continues to exceed regional and national levels. More than 14,000 jobs have been added in the city since 1997. Currently more than 64,000 people work in Kent. One program in place is the Kent Downtown Partnership, working between property owners, residents, the city of Kent and the chamber of commerce. A strong and thriving downtown is important to everyone. During the next 10 years, Kent will become a regional banking center, have the largest concentration of King County governmental services outside of Seattle, and become the focal point for international commerce.

Where the jobs are: Boeing, Kent School District, Muckleshoot Casino, city of Kent, Auburn Regional Medical Center, Mikron Industries

Business opportunities: Kent is one of the largest warehouse, distribution, and manufacturing centers on the west coast, due to its strategic location 10 minutes from SeaTac International Airport and halfway between the Ports of Seattle and Tacoma. With a growing population, a retail/office renaissance downtown, and a proposed $79 million hospital going up the community, the economy is growing. Green River Community College is one of the anchors for the Kent Station Project, a mixed-use town center project currently under construction.

Local real estate

Market overview: Most common are traditional two-story homes with two-car garages. Landscaping is usually green and plentiful.

Average rent for a two-bedroom apartment: $700 per month

Other areas to consider: On the shores of Lake Washington, Renton is more than a pretty face, it's home to Boeing. Issaquah, located in the foothills of the Cascades, is an intimate community, where beauty and brains come together. The Emerald City is also called Seattle. Tucked against the Puget Sound and surrounded by lush green hills, this thriving metropolis of Seahawk fans and Microsoft stock holders is a horse of a different color.

What things cost

ACCRA's national comparisons: Overall living costs are 22.7 percent above the national average in the Seattle area. Housing is 4.4 percent above the average with utilities running 16.3 percent above the average. Healthcare is 3.6 percent below and grocery items run about the same at 3.1 percent below.

Utilities: Gas: $70 per month; electric: $64 per month; water: $15 per month; phone: $60 per month

The tax ax

Sales tax: 8.8 percent

Property tax: $11.17 (est. property taxes paid per $1,000 of market value)

State income tax: There is no state income tax in Washington.

Making the grade

Public education overview: The Kent school district serves 28 elementary schools, six middle schools, four high schools, and one academy (grades two through 12). One of the many shining stars for the district has been the move to smaller learning communities by going to a two-year middle school and four-year high school system. The former Kent Junior High will reopen in 2005 as the Mill Creek Middle School, with remodeled facilities, new instructional programs, a renovated library, and enclosed walkways. The Big Blue Technology Bus is a free hands-on computer training and traveling technology center. With 150 software titles, the bus gives kids a chance to excel and succeed in a world full of computers.

Class size (student to teacher ratio): 23:1

Help for working parents: A free after-school program is held once a week at eight Kent elementary schools.

Boys & Girls Club: There are no centers available at this time.

School year: First week of September to mid-June. Children must be 5 years old on or before August 31 to enter kindergarten.

Special education/programs for gifted students: Children with learning disabilities are mainstreamed whenever possible. The district follows federal guidelines for its special education curriculum. The gifted and talented resources are varied depending on the age of the child and continue in both elementary and middle schools.

Nearby colleges and universities: Green River Community College

Medical care

Hospitals/medical centers: The Valley Medical Center (302 beds) serves as a regional center providing services in cardiology, oncology, high-risk obstetrics, orthopedics, neurology, and pediatrics. An additional resource is at Auburn General Hospital (129 beds) in Auburn.

Crime and safety

Police: The Kent police department has approximately 1.5 officers per 1,000 residents. Crime prevention programs include Block Watch and National Night Out, Crime Free Rental Housing Program, and personal safety training. The Safety Education Officer program is a new and exciting approach to educating young students on the issues of personal safety, drug abuse, anger-control, self-esteem, how to deal with threats, and threatening situations. The department has additional services such as their canine unit, marine patrol, and bicycle unit.

Fire: The Kent fire department received national accreditation this year. With seven stations, the department works on fire suppression, medical emergencies, and both natural and man-made disasters. The department provides educational classes to the community promoting safety for all ages.

Let the good times roll

Family fun: Kent is a family fun paradise surrounded by open spaces with beautiful Mt. Rainier only 45 minutes away. Practically the entire Cascade Range is National Forest land, open for back-country camping, hiking, and horseback riding. Kent has 68 parks with 1,349 acres of parkland and 26 miles of trails. Yes, it gets wet up here in the northwest, but that doesn't slow this community down! Hiking, biking, sports activities, and playgrounds keep the community moving. The Green River Natural Resource Area is perfect for a relaxing walk through nature. In 1999, 2000, 2001, 2002, and 2003, the Park Maintenance division received the National Softball Association Outstanding Park Award for the Russell Road softball park, which features five championship level softball fields. Take a swing at the Riverbed golf complex. Enjoy a cool afternoon skating at the Kent Valley Ice Centre. Or hope in the car for a short trip to the Six Flags Enchanted Parkway, or the Point Defiance Zoo.

Sports: Plenty of cheering goes on with almost all professional sports covered with the Seattle Seahawks (NFL), the Sonics (NBA) and the Mariners (MLB). Great baseball is also found at Cheney Stadium with the Tacoma Rainiers (minor league). The University of Washington Huskies are a top-rated PAC-10 college team.

Arts and entertainment: Not lacking for culture, you'll find the Centennial Center Gallery, Kent Arts Commission Gallery, City Art Collection, and Creative Artspace in Kent inspiring and beautiful places. Seattle is close by with ballet, opera, the symphony, and other performing arts. Meany Hall for the Performing Arts, located on the University of Washington campus, hosts many artists as well.

Annual events: Festival of the Valley, Kent Canterbury Arts Festival, Christmas Rush Fun Run and Walk, Holiday Bazaar

Community life

Volunteering comes with the community. Residents can use the Volunteer Match program and sign up to be available for various opportunities, or go right to the source and help out with the Seniors Activity Center, or the Volunteers in Police Service program.

The environment

Puget Sound Clean Air Agency ensures that people in King County have clean air. Recycling has been a big deal up here in the northwest for decades. These people are great at it. Carpooling is important and the Commute Trip Reduction Program tackles one of the top regional needs —*mobility*—creatively and with the efficient use of public resources. It's a collaborative partnership among major employers, the city of Kent, King County Metro, and the Washington State Department of Transportation. The goals of the program are to reduce air pollution, minimize the consumption of fossil fuels, and better utilize the existing transportation infrastructure through employer-based programs that decrease the number of commute trips made by single occupant vehicles.

In and around town

Roads and highways: I-5, I-405, route 167, highway 18

Closest airports: SeaTac International Airport is 12 minutes north of Kent.

Public transportation: The Metro Bus System serves Seattle and East King County. Free parking is provided for bus riders. Kent has two rail lines that run through town, providing passenger rail service along the coast.

Average daily commute: 35 minutes

More Information

City of Kent
220 Fourth Avenue South
Kent, WA 98030
253-856-5200
www.ci.kent.wa.us

Kent School District
12033 Southeast 256th Street
Kent, WA 98030
www.kent.k12.wa.s

Kent Chamber of Commerce
524 West Meeker Street, Suite 1
Kent, WA 98032
253-854-1770
www.kentchamber.com

City of Kent
220 Fourth Avenue South
Kent, WA 98032
253-856-5264
www.ci.kent.wa.us

47

Olympia, Washington

Washington

Kent

Spokane

Olympia

Fabulous features

The Olympia/Tumwater area takes a lot of flack for the amount of rainfall year-round, but local residents get the last laugh. Yes, bouts of gray skies and drizzles are interspersed with sun breaks, but it's all taken in stride. Despite the weather, this area is a wondrous place to raise a family.

With cultural events such as the Procession of the Species, and extensive recreation and services for children in these South Sound communities, new residents should be given an orientation session. Whether you're heading to Tumwater Falls or Timberland Libraries, rush hour traffic truly lasts only about an hour, twice a day.

As both a college community and the state capital, the unique mix of business and basics is like a good cup of coffee. People are educated and ambitious but not at the expense of settling for a lesser quality of life. This community loves its children.

Does the sun ever shine? Certainly! On average it's sunny about 40 percent of each month, with the summer season even better. Do the children care? Usually not. They're too busy having fun.

Possible drawbacks: If you want a dry, hot climate, turn the page. Mold, moss, and mildew are part of the area's challenge. The economy is undergoing change as the job market bounces back from tough times.

▶ Local Population: 43,040

▶ County: Thurston

▶ Population of surrounding metropolitan area: 218,500

▶ Region: Western Washington

▶ Closest metro area: Seattle, 60 miles

▶ Median home price: $143,500

▶ Median household income: $40,846

▶ Best reasons to live here: There is beautiful scenery, low crime rates, abundant recreation, great schools, and no state income tax, which makes Olympia a fabulous city.

Climate

Elevation 10'	Average temp. high/low (°F)	Average precipitation rain (")	snow (")	Average no. days precipitation	Average humidity (%)
January	45/32	7.5	6.8	20	81
April	58/37	3.6	0.1	15	57
July	76/50	1.8	0	5	50
October	61/39	4.2	0	14	67
Number of days 32°F or below: 89			Number of days 90°F or warmer: 6		

Earning a living

Economic outlook: The 2003 closing of the Olympia Brewery punched a hole in the local area's economy, displacing more than 400 workers into an all-ready tight job market. The economy in Olympia/Tumwater, and much of Thurston County, is at a crossroads, and everyone seems aware of it. The current unemployment rate is 5.6 percent. Government and education provides up to 42 percent of the jobs, but with government cutbacks over the last few years, these numbers may decrease. The active economic development groups in the area continue to attract private-sector growth.

Where the jobs are: Government remains the largest employer in the area, with offices both in Tumwater and Olympia, but the diversified economy is based on such industries as manufacturing, forestry, fishing, and construction, as well as retail and service industries.

Business opportunities: Tumwater Town Center is about to bloom. Residential, industrial, and commercial areas have been mapped out to provide the best of all worlds. Olympia's Downtown borders the state capital district and is a mixture of old world charm and activity.

Local real estate

Market overview: Tumwater has older neighborhoods and houses on the hills with lots of new developments popping up. Olympia has an east side, a west side, and downtown.

Average rent for a two-bedroom apartment: $900 per month

Closest metro area: Vancouver has no state tax, and across the Columbia River, Portland has no sales tax. Fort Lewis, one of the oldest Army stations, is just north of Olympia.

What things cost

ACCRA's national comparisons: Overall living costs are 2.2 percent above the national average. Utilities come in as the lowest cost factor at 13.8 percent below average. Housing runs at 5.5 percent below average and healthcare takes the biggest hit at 32.9 percent above average.

Utilities: Phone: $30 per month; electricity: $40 per month; natural gas: $30 per month; water: $20 per month

The tax ax

Sales tax: 8.25 percent

Property tax: $14.98 (est. property taxes paid per $1,000 of market value).

State income tax: There is no state income in Washington.

Making the grade

Public education overview: Whether your child is part of the Olympia School District (11 elementary schools, four middle schools, three high schools) or the Tumwater School District (six elementary schools, two middle schools, two high schools), quality education and community support are the number one priority around here. Standardized testing consists of the Washington Assessment of Student Learning. More than 85 pecent of Olympia high school students participate in school-sponsored co-curricular activities, including athletics, music, drama, and academic or vocational clubs. The dropout rate is a low 1.49 percent with the state average at 3.82 percent. Washington has a Guaranteed Education Tuition program where parents can pay into their child's account for college in the future.

Class size (student to teacher ratio): 18:1

Help for working parents: The Tumwater School District and the YMCA have joined together to provide before- and after-school care.

Boys & Girls Club: There is one center available in Tumwater.

School year: First week of September to the second week of June. Students need to be 5 years old on or before August 31 to start kindergarten.

Special education/programs for gifted students: The special services department provides quality services to students with a wide range of disabilities. Children are mainstreamed whenever possible.

Nearby colleges and universities: The Evergreen State College is a nationally known, innovative, four-year, liberal arts college. South Puget Sound Community College is a two-year public institution offering degree programs. St. Martin's University is a private, four-year, liberal arts college located in Lacey.

Medical care

Hospitals/medical centers: At Capital Medical Center, a 119-bed hospital, you'll find 24-hour emergency care, plus medical and surgical services, specially designed birthing suites, a same-day surgery center, physical therapy, and a diabetes wellness center. The physician's pavilion and acute-care unit complete an expansion of outpatient services. Providence St. Peter Hospital is the largest in the Sound area. The hospital is a 390-bed, nonprofit, regional teaching hospital offering a full spectrum of acute-care, specialty and outpatient services, medical rehabilitation, 24-hour emergency services and outpatient surgery. Providence was named one of the "100 Top Hospitals" in the nation for cardiology, orthopedics, and stroke care. In 2003 Providence opened its new 25,000 square foot emergency center with 39 treatment rooms, two trauma rooms, and crisis services for mental health.

Crime and safety

Police: In Olympia and Tumwater, citizens are active participants in community public safety efforts. The area's crime reports are so low, they fit on a half page of *The Olympian* newspaper once a week. Volunteer opportunities are numerous through community programs such as Neighborhood Speed Watch, and Harbor Patrol. Reserve Officers serve a vital function in Tumwater, donating countless labor hours in serving the community.

Fire: The fire departments are community active and supportive. The Black Lake Fire District's personnel regularly volunteers at the Black Lake Elementary schools, participating in annual events such as Family Fun Night for the children. Free blood pressure checks are available during certain hours at the Tumwater Fire District office.

Let the good times roll

Family fun: Not only is the incredible Puget Sound right there for water sports and enjoyment, but just a few minutes away is fresh-water Black Lake, one of the largest lakes in the South Sound. An abundance of parks such as Millersylvania State Park and Capitol Forest make relaxing an easy feat. Tumwater Falls is a breathtaking view, right in the middle of town. Tumwater Valley Municipal Golf Course includes an exercise facility and is home of the local Fourth of July fireworks spectacular. Chinook and Coho salmon are visible through September at Percival Landing. When conditions are right, the fish swim through Capitol Lake and up the Deschutes River. In nearby Tenino is Wolf Haven International, a 75-acre sanctuary for captive-born wolves offering tours and events.

Sports: Seattle holds the nearest professional sports with the Seahawks (NFL), Mariners (MLB), and the Sonics (NBA). The Tacoma Rainiers (minor league baseball) is great for family excitement. Local high school teams, Little League, and community recreation sports keeps the air ringing with the cheering sounds of fun.

Arts and entertainment: ArtsWalk shows off some of the local talent in partnership with the Olympia downtown business community. Enjoy Harlequin Productions, the Washington Center for the Performing Arts, and live entertainment at the Farmer's Market from April to December. Capital Playhouse offers both productions and classes for children and adults, or check out the Olympia Writers Workshop.

Annual events: ArtsWalk, Procession of the Species Parade, Wooden Boat Show, Swantown BoatSwap and Chowder Challenge, Capital Lake Fair, Sand in the City competition, Tumwater Falls Harvest Festival

Community life

The Olympia/Tumwater communities are a profusion of professionals, naturalists, children, artists, and art lovers. The Mixx96 radio station, broadcasting from downtown Olympia, keeps everyone informed of the constant variety of volunteering and support going on both on-air and on their Website. The station itself sponsors many community events such as the Little Red Schoolhouse collection and productions at the Harlequin Theater. From volunteering time at school to helping out with food drives, Thurston County residents care.

The environment

The NeighborWoods Program fosters a partnership between the city of Olympia and its citizens, planting and caring for street trees in residential neighborhoods. Through the program, the city gives free trees to residents, along with free training in the care of those trees, in exchange for planting and caring labor. Stream Team is an education-to-action program for people interested in protecting and enhancing the local streams, rivers, lakes, and Puget Sound. Twice a year, volunteers gather to clean-up downtown Olympia just before the ArtsWalk.

In and around town

Roads and highways: I-5, Highway 101

Closest airports: SeaTac International Airport is 60 miles away; and the Olympia Regional Airport provides convenient access to South Puget Sound for corporate jets, commuter-size planes, and light freight aircraft.

Public transportation: Intercity Transit provides local bus service.

Average daily commute: 25 minutes

More Information

City of Olympia
PO Box 1967
Olympia, WA 98507
360-753-8325
www.ci.olympia.wa.us

City of Tumwater
555 Israel Road
Tumwater, WA 98501
360-754-5855
www.ci.tumwater.wa.us

Olympia School District
1113 Legion Way SE
Olympia, WA 98501
360-596-6100
www.olympia.org

Tumwater School District
419 Linwood Avenue SW
Tumwater, WA 98501
360-709-7000
www.tumwater.k12.wa.us

Tumwater Chamber of Commerce
5304 Littlerock Road SW
Tumwater, WA 98512
360-357-5153
www.tumwaterchamber.com

48

Spokane, Washington

Washington

Spokane

Kent

Olympia

Fabulous features

New residents marvel that the pristine Spokane region was here all along. They compare the discovery to falling in love with the boy next door, the one with the gentle qualities and upstanding values, who was simply overshadowed by showier neighbors.

Boeing Aircraft moved here in 1990, and the Spokane Industrial Park (4.1 million square feet) is the largest in the northwest and is still growing. Downtown is booming, though the real growth is in technology. But what's more exciting about Spokane is its commitment to preserving ideals. Spokane is wooing corporations, but only those that will contribute to the quality of life. The city has worked hard to create a well-balanced school system, a safe community, and a place where families thrive. It's no wonder that Spokane ranked eighth in *Readers Digest* (1998) list of "Best Places to Raise a Family."

The Spokane River runs through downtown with spectacular falls on the western end and beautiful Riverfront Park is in the heart of the city.

Possible drawbacks: Looking for a place so far away that the in-laws will only write? Trips to Spokane by car take five hours through the mountains and commuter flights are costly. Isolation can be a nuisance. Air quality in the fall is not always favorable. Strong winds can cause mini-dust storms and air inversions can cause particles to linger. Those with allergies or asthma feel it. There's no state income tax, but some residents still bristle at the 8.1 percent sales tax.

▶ Local Population: 195,629

▶ County: Spokane

▶ Population of surrounding metropolitan area: 417,939

▶ Region: Eastern Washington

▶ Closest metro area: Seattle, 338 miles

▶ Median home price: $124,973

▶ Median household income: $41,326

▶ Best reasons to live here: Spoklane has a growing economy, affordable housing, no state income tax, minimal traffic, vast recreational activities, innovative schools and four pleasant seasons.

Climate

Elevation 2,000'	Average temp. high/low (°F)	Average precipitation		Average no. days precipitation	Average humidity (%)
		rain (")	snow (")		
January	33/22	1.8	15.4	14	79
April	58/35	1.3	0.6	9	44
July	83/54	0.8	0	5	28
October	59/36	1.1	0.4	8	49
Number of days 32°F or below: 141			Number of days 90°F or warmer: 21		

Earning a living

Economic outlook: Spokane, the largest city between Seattle and Minneapolis, is at the economic center of a dynamic and growing region. It serves as a distribution center for the entire region and connects the area's manufacturers to their markets. Even their events find a way to bolster the economy: Bloomsday's impact on the Spokane region is not limited to improved cardiovascular performance, but results in a significant economic impact as well. In 2004, a study prepared for the Lilac Bloomsday Association by Gonzaga University students showed an economic impact of over $9 million. The workforce is highly educated; and the cost of living, wage rates, turnover, and absenteeism rates are well below national averages.

Where the jobs are: The city of Spokane, Avista Corporation, Inland Northwest Health Services, Eastern Washington University, Billie Moreland and Associates, ILF Media Productions, Vivato, Steam Plant Square, INTEC, Connect Northwest, Downtown Spokane Partnership, Fernwell Building and Executive Suites

Business opportunities: Spokane is actively recruiting industries and manufacturers, as well as distribution and high-tech companies. All six academic institutions in the area join together on the Spokane Intercollegiate Research and Technology Institute, which develops commercial applications for research conducted in academic environments.

Local real estate

Market overview: Split-levels are popular, with ranch-styles, Cape Cods and larger three- and four-level homes available.

Average rent for a two-bedroom apartment: $700 per month

Other areas to consider: Coeur d'Alene is both naturally beautiful and economically handsome. Pullman is home to the Washington State Cougars.

What things cost

ACCRA's national comparisons: Overall living costs are 2.8 percent above the national average. Housing is at 4 percent below the average, with utilities in the double digits at 13.4 percent below. Healthcare costs are 34 percent above the average. Grocery items are 8 percent above average.

Utilities: Electricity: $37 per month; natural gas: $71 per month; phone: $22 per month

The tax ax

Sales tax: 8.35 percent

Property tax: $14.94 (est. property taxes paid per $1,000 of market value)

State income tax: There are no state taxes in Washington.

Making the grade

Public education overview: *Expansion Management* (2005) ranked Spokane second in the "Best Small" category for schools. Many of the projects paid for by the 2003 facilities and technology improvement bond will incorporate green building or sustainable design features. The new Lincoln Heights Elementary School, slated to begin construction in June of 2005, is one of five pilot projects in the state being designed to the green building standards set forth by Washington State. Green building features will also be used on the new Lidgerwood and Ridgeview elementary school projects, as well as the remodeling of Rogers and Shadle high schools and the Ferris high school athletic facility.

Class size (student to teacher ratio): 17:1

Help for working parents: Before- and after-school care is available and sponsored through the YMCA.

Boys & Girls Club: There is currently one center available in Spokane.

School year: Begins after Labor Day to mid-June. Students must be 5 years old on or before August 31 to enter kindergarten.

Special education/programs for gifted students: Special education students are mainstreamed to the greatest extent possible.

Nearby colleges and universities: Private colleges include Whitworth College and Gonzaga University. Eastern Washington University offers on-campus courses in Cheney, 15 miles from Spokane, as well as at their downtown Spokane center. Washington State University also has a branch campus in Spokane. Spokane Community College and Spokane Falls Community College, as well as several trade and technical schools, round out the educational offerings.

Medical care

Hospitals/medical centers: For the third consecutive year, five Spokane hospitals—Deaconess Medical Center, Holy Family Hospital, Sacred Heart Medical Center, St. Luke's Rehabilitation Institute, Valley Hospital and Medical Center, and Kootenai Medical Center in Idaho—were distinguished as being among the most technologically superior healthcare institutions in the United States. *Hospital and Health*

Networks, the journal of the American Hospital Association, surveyed more than 1,200 hospitals to name the "100 Most Wired" hospitals in 2004.

Specialized care: Shriners Children's Hospital specializes in treating children's diseases.

Crime and safety

Police: The Spokane police department has won national and even international awards for its leadership in community policing. They have ten "COPS Shops," each staffed entirely by neighborhood volunteers who maintain regular hours and support dozens of programs for the neighborhood. "Neighbor-to-neighbor" is the Block Watch motto. Spokane has over 1,000 McGruff houses. Operation SKID (Safe Kid Identification Disk) is a new community service program. "Cops and Kids" is a weekend event bringing police officers and young people together in an informal and relaxed setting.

Fire: The Spokane fire department has 14 stations. The department is the lead agency for the Children's Fire Safety House. This mobile, two-story, hands-on fire escape lab is equipped with synthetic smoke and offers a simulated residential setting for students to practice their fire escape plans. The Children's House is designed for third grade students and is brought to schools during the spring and fall.

Let the good times roll

Family fun: Named one of the Top 10 family-friendly cities (*Family Fun Magazine*, 2000), Spokane also seems to be the "golf capital of the Pacific Northwest" according to *Golf* magazine (August 2001). With more than 32 golf courses, it helps that Spokane has 260 days of sunshine during the year.

Sports: The Spokane Indians play a summer schedule of professional minor league baseball games at the Fairgrounds, and the Spokane Chiefs take over the arena ice in the winter months for hockey action. The region is also home to an excellent polo club with matches on most summer weekends. Spokane area colleges also field teams in a number of intercollegiate sports. For race fans, Playfair offers thoroughbred horse racing action during the summer and fall and simulcasting year-round.

Arts and entertainment: The Spokane Opera House plays host to the area's biggest cultural events, including Broadway shows on regional tour and the Spokane Symphony. The Metropolitan Performing Arts Center features ballets, concerts, and the Spokane Symphony. Plays can be seen at the Spokane Civic Theatre, the Coeur d'Alene Summer Theater, the Centre Theatre Group, the Spokane Children's Threatre, and the Spokane Interplayers Ensemble.

Annual events: Lilac Festival, Bloomsday Run, Hoopfest

Community life

Life in Spokane very much includes the great outdoors, so exchange your second TV for a good pair of cross-country skis. The annual May Bloomsday Run, for example, draws tens of thousands of adults and children. Resident participation is also evident in the arts. The Spokane Children's Theatre is always looking for local acting, directing, and writing talent.

The environment

A clean environment is Spokane's hallmark. Determination is strongest in protecting one of its greatest resources—natural wildlife—as it is estimated that one of every three Washingtonians hunt or fish. Spokane is also blessed with a never-ending supply of fresh water. Drinking water comes from the Spokane Aquifer, which is fed by the clean Lake Coeur d'Alene in Idaho. There is little concern for depleting the water supply source, and water quality is sampled every three months. Recycling is encouraged with weekly scheduled pickups. Spokane was named a Tree City USA in 2004 by the National Arbor Day Foundation to honor its commitment to its community forest. It was the first year Spokane has received this national recognition.

In and around town

Roads and highways: I-90; state highways 290, 10, 395, 195, 2

Closest airports: Spokane International Airport is seven miles west. Felts Field is five and a half miles northeast. Deer Park Airport is 24 miles north. Mead Airport is 10 miles northeast, and can accommodate private aircraft, charters, and helicopters.

Public transportation: Spokane Transit Authority operates more than 33 bus routes to all parts of the city. It also operates 11 park-and-ride lots in the city.

Average daily commute: 20 minutes

More Information

City of Spokane
808 West Spokane Falls Boulevard
Spokane, WA 99201
509-625-6250
www.spokanecity.org

Spokane School District
200 North Bernard Street
Spokane, WA 99201
509-354-5900
www.spokaneschools.org

Spokane Regional Chamber of Commerce
801 West Riverside, Suite 100
Spokane, WA 99201
509-624-1393
www.spokanechamber.org

49

Green Bay, Wisconsin

Wisconsin

Green Bay

Sheboygan

Madison

Fabulous features

Looking really good at 150 years old, Green Bay recently opened the new City Hall Welcome Center. Pride is the winning tradition of the Packers, and pride in the community defines the spirit of Green Bay. The natural beauty of the area and the warmth of its people are two of the most compelling reasons why people who come for a visit stay for a lifetime. The area offers almost every amenity of larger cities while maintaining a heritage that places great value on education, cleanliness, dedication to the family, and compassion for the less fortunate.

In 1998, *Readers Digest* named Green Bay one of the best places to raise a family. Green Bay's community spirit was also rewarded with the All American City award in 1999. Thriving residential communities and booming business growth earned Green Bay the *Inc.* magazine designation as the best medium-sized city to start a business.

Additional recognition as an excellent place to live includes being ranked as sixth best small city in the nation, according to the 2001 *Kid Friendly Cities Report* published by the organization Zero Population Growth. Green Bay is looking pretty good for her age!

Possible drawbacks: Winters can be tough, but residents work with the seasons, enjoying their seasonal festivals and making the most of the winter sports opportunities. This is small-town living at its finest, but if you are looking for a big-city environment, you might want to look elsewhere.

▸ Local Population: 103,750

▸ County: Brown

▸ Population of surrounding metropolitan area: 226,778

▸ Region: Northeast Wisconsin

▸ Closest metro area: Milwaukee, 95 miles

▸ Median home price: $96,400

▸ Median household income: $38,820

▸ Best reasons to live here: A sports and recreation paradise, with affordable housing, good schools, comprehensive family services, and a supportive community with small-town charm.

Climate

Elevation 594'	Average temp. high/low (°F)	Average precipitation rain (")	snow (")	Average no. days precipitation	Average humidity (%)
January	24/7	1.3	11.9	10	72
April	54/34	2.6	2.7	11	61
July	81/59	3.5	0	10	62
October	58/37	2.2	0.2	9	65
Number of days 32°F or below: 163			Number of days 90°F or warmer: 7		

Earning a living

Economic outlook: With one of the state's lowest unemployment rates, the Green Bay area offers opportunities in business, healthcare, industrial, manufacturing, and more. Green Bay's unemployment rate was 4.2 percent. Because of its proximity to Lake Michigan, the Port of Green Bay is a commercial shipping hub for points around the country and around the world. Three major railroads link Green Bay with the rest of the nation. Farming, the production of cheese, and some light manufacturing also help to maintain a stable workforce within the community and keep the unemployment level below the national level. Green Bay is the largest meat packing center east of the Mississippi, and one of the top convention centers in the Midwest.

Where the jobs are: Green Bay has three full-service hospitals and dozens of medical clinics, plus a strong manufacturing sector and a famous dairy industry. Major employers include: Georgia-Pacific Corporation, Humana, Green Bay Public Schools, and the Oneida Nation. Approximately 40 percent of the manufacturing segment is dominated by the paper industry. Packerland Packing is one of the largest beef packing companies in the country. Schneider National is the country's largest truckload carrier and logistics provider.

Business opportunities: A significant factor in creating new jobs and attaining a strong commercial and industrial tax base is the availability and affordability of land. The I-43 Business Center and the State Highway 54 Business Park are exceptional examples of the city's efforts to provide local businesses with expansion and relocation opportunities. The zoning accommodates a variety of uses and prices are below the market rate.

Local real estate

Market overview: Bayview, condos, townhouses, country side, or quiet residential, all can be found in Green Bay and surrounding communities.

Average rent for a two-bedroom apartment: $900 per month

Others areas to consider: Oshkosh has been ranked the fifth safest city in the United States. For peninsula living, try Sturgeon Bay, with a traditional downtown and marine industries. Milwaukee, home to Miller Brewing, means rooting for the Brewers

(MLB) at Miller Park during the spring and the Bucks (NBA) at the Bradley Center in the winter.

What things cost

ACCRA's national comparisons: Overall living costs are 3.3 percent below the national average. Grocery items are the lowest factor at 14.1 percent below the average. Housing breaks even and utilities come in at 4.8 percent below the average. Healthcare is 2.3 percent above average with transportation close at 2.4 percent below the national average.

Utilities: Electricity: $58 per month; natural gas: $81 per month; phone: $19 per month

The tax ax

Sales tax: 5.5 percent

Property tax: $4.27 (est. property taxes paid per $1,000 of market value)

State income tax: 4.6 to 6.75 percent

Making the grade

Public education overview: Green Bay students consistently achieve some of the highest scores in the country on SRA and ACT tests. The district has 25 elementary schools, four middle schools, four high schools, and two K-8 schools. The district offers academies with specialized themes in each of the four high schools: East High School has health services; Preble High School has integrated manufacturing; Southwest High School has international business; and West High School has computer and information technology. Wisconsin has one of the highest high school graduation rates and lowest dropout rates in the country.

Class size (student to teacher ratio): 16:1

Help for working parents: Over 100 licensed group centers and daycare homes provide peace of mind while you're at work. Bellin Hospital offers in-home care if your child is sick and you have to be at your job.

Boys & Girls Club: There are curently 10 centers available.

School year: Last week of August to mid-June. Children must be 5 years old on or before September 1 to enter kindergarten.

Special education/programs for gifted students: Green Bay has one of the finest special educational programs in the state.

Nearby colleges and universities: University of Wisconsin at Green Bay, St. Norbert College, Northeast Wisconsin Technical College, Bellin College of Nursing, Cardinal Stritch University, Concordia University, Green Bay Center, ITT Technical Institute, Lakeland College, Green Bay Center, Marian College, Silver Lake College

Medical care

Hospitals/medical centers: Green Bay is home to four regional medical centers, including two of the Top 100 hospitals in the country, and each facility is equipped to treat nearly every general or acute condition, including 24-hour emergency room care. St. Vincent Hospital/Prevea Clinic is the area's largest hospital, offering care in cancer, emergency, neuroscience, perinatal, pediatrics, and rehabilitation. Aurora BayCare Medical Center is the area's newest center, offering the latest in trauma, rehabilitation, neuro care, the Women's Center, the Vince Lombardi cancer center, orthopedic, and cardiac services.

Specialized care: Curative Rehabilitation Center, Unity Hospice, Aging Resource Center, Family Services, Crisis Center, Cerebral Palsy Center, Oneida Community Health Center

Crime and safety

Police: Green Bay police department's problem-oriented policing program was recognized in 1999 by the Police Executive Research Forum when it was awarded the Herman Goldstein Award of Excellence. Community officers have given training seminars for law enforcement agencies throughout the United States, as well as the United Kingdom and the Middle East. The department has the citizens police academy, police media academy, senior citizens academy, Latino teenage citizens police academy, and the Hmong teenage citizens police academy.

Fire: Just as the Fox River divides the city in half, it also divides the Green Bay fire department in half, both physically and organizationally. The department is divided into an east and west battalion. Seven fire stations are located throughout the city. These stations are staffed 24 hours a day by a minimum of 48 personnel, with seven engine companies, three ladder companies, three paramedic ambulances, and one tanker unit.

Let the good times roll

Family fun: Explore America's railroad heritage at one of this country's oldest and largest railroad museums, the National Railroad Museum. Heritage Hill State Historical Park brings history to life! You may get the chance to barter with the fur trader in La Baye (1672–1825), or march in a miliary drill at Fort Howard (1836). Watch the blacksmith pound iron in his shop in Small Town (1871) or perhaps make butter at the Belgian Farm (1905). The Bay Beach Amusement Park, NEW Zoo and Reforestation Camp, Bay Beach Wildlife Sanctuary, Tall Ship Tours, and Oneida Nation Pow Wow is fifteen minutes southeast of Green Bay.

Sports: The Packers have a fan club in every state of the country. The new Resch Center is across the street from the Packers renovated Lambeau Field. Don't forget the UW-Green Bay Athletics competing at NCAA Division I level, sponsoring five teams. Or younger yet, cheer on the Green Bay Strikers youth soccer.

Arts and entertainment: Museums, Neville Public Museum of Brown County, The Children's Museum of Green Bay, Bush Art Center, Lawton Gallery, White Pillars Museum, the Weidner Center for the Performing Arts, the Meyer Theatre, Green Bay Community Theatre, St. Norbert College Hall of Fine Arts, Frank's Dinner Theatre, UW-Wisconsin theaters, the Historic West Theater

Annual events: Bayfest, Celebrate Americafest, Celebrate DePerel, UW-Green Bay Jazz Fest, ArtStreet, DePere Fall Fest, Festival of Lights, farmer's market

Community life

The Rotary Club and other nonprofits contribute thousands of hours and dollars yearly to good works for the Green Bay community. The International Center at St. Norbert College in DePere reaches out to the business community with extensive programs in global ecology and community. Green Bay really cares about kids. It offers a wide variety of programs for recreation in each of its many parks.

The environment

Green Bay supports a clean tomorrow with an active recycling program, providing pick up for paper, glass, metal, plastic, appliances, and batteries, plus drop-off service for hazardous materials such as paint cans, used motor oil, and yard waste. Area schools and nonprofit organizations are also actively involved in regular clean-up programs. Because the area has a number of paper manufacturers, the city takes extra care to watch its air quality.

In and around town

Roads and highways: Wisconsin Highway 29, US 41, I-43

Closest airports: The Austin Straubel International Airport links Green Bay to Chicago, Milwaukee, Minneapolis, and Detroit with daily departures.

Public transportation: Green Bay Transit provides local bus service.

Average daily commute: 18 minutes

More Information

City Hall
100 North Jefferson Street
Green Bay, WI 54301
920-448-3005
www.ci.green-bay.wi.us

Green Bay Public School District
200 South Broadway
Green Bay, WI 54303
920-448-2000
www.greenbay.k12.wi.us

Green Bay Area Chamber of Commerce
400 South Washington Street
Green Bay, WI 54305
920-437-8704
www.titletown.org

Sheboygan, Wisconsin

Fabulous features

Sheboygan and Kenosha are the country's two best places to raise a family, according to an analysis in 1998 *Reader's Digest*. Sheboygan families take an active interest in children because multiple generations have put down deep roots in this town. Today a healthy economy and pleasant lifestyle keep young people in the area, and make a positive impact on the community where they grew up. After all, a great hometown is all about its people.

For the sports fan, Sheboygan County offers some of the best golfing in the nation, salmon and trout fishing on Lake Michigan, baseball, snowmobiling, ice fishing, and don't forget about races at North America's longest and finest natural road racing facility, Road America. For the artist, you will want to experience their performing art series ranging from symphony concerts to ballets, plays, and musicals.

The accolades pour over the city like melted cheese, including a rating from *Golf* magazine that included "The Bull At Pinehurst Farms," located in Sheboygan Falls and designed by Jack Nicklaus as one of the best golf courses. In 2004, *Morgan-Quitno* press ranked Sheboygan the seventh safest city in the nation.

Possible drawbacks: Tornado warnings are something to keep in mind. An average of 21 tornadoes touch down in the state of Wisconsin each year.

▶ Local Population: 50,792

▶ County: Sheboygan

▶ Population of surrounding metropolitan area: 112,646

▶ Region: Eastern Wisconsin

▶ Closest metro area: Milwaukee, 51 miles

▶ Median home price: $89,400

▶ Median household income: $40,066

▶ Best reasons to live here: Low crime rates, great neighborhoods, excellent schools, outdoor recreation, growing economy, and a friendly community.

Climate

Elevation 635'	Average temp. high/low (°F)	Average precipitation rain (")	snow (")	Average no. days precipitation	Average humidity (%)
January	29/13	1.8	14.6	11	71
April	53/36	3.0	2.4	11	61
July	81/61	3.2	0	10	63
October	59/43	2.5	0.2	9	65
Number of days 32°F or below: 146			Number of days 90°F or warmer: 9		

Earning a living

Economic outlook: The March 2004 issue of *Inc.* magazine ranked Green Bay the number one midsize city in America for the "Top Cities for Doing Business in America." Sheboygan boasts a diversified economy. The products of the area can be seen worldwide and include furniture, plumbing fixtures, stainless steel products, wood products, corrugated packaging, and the ever famous cheese and sausage. Out of 64,800 jobs, 25,400 are in manufacturing, 25,200 in services 7,600 in trade, with 6,000 in government. Sheboygan is a community built on industry and trade that has become known throughout the world and is rapidly becoming a top tourist destination.

Where the jobs are: Sheboygan Schools Education, J.L. French Aluminum, ACUITY Insurance, Aurora Health Care Healthcare, Lear Substrates Automotive, St. Nicholas Hospital Healthcare, Fresh Brands Food Services, Vollrath Co. Stainless Steel, Aurora Memorial Medical Healthcare, city of Sheboygan

Business opportunities: The locals swear their high quality of life, and a diversified economy and hard working labor force is nothing to sneeze at. Business opportunities in Sheboygan are only limited by your imagination.

Local real estate

Market overview: Houses are typically single-story with full basements, or two-story Victorian-styled.

Average rent for a two-bedroom apartment: $750 per month

Other areas to consider: Port Washington is on the shores of Lake Michigan, with history and tourism sharing the sidewalks. Family-friendly Plymouth is centrally located between Milwaukee and Green Bay, with an aquatic center and skateboard park. Milwaukee, home to Miller Brewing, means rooting for the Brewers at Miller Park during the spring and the Bucks at the Bradley Center in the winter.

What things cost

ACCRA's national comparisons: Overall living costs are 3.2 percent below the national average. Housing drops in at 10.3 percent below the average. Healthcare, though, takes a 21.9 percent above average leap. Utilities are 2.9 percent above average and grocery items are 4.7 percent below the average.

Utilities: Electricity: $59 per month; natural gas: $81 per month; phone: $19 per month

The tax ax

Sales tax: 5 percent

Property tax: $23.61 per $1,000 property tax

State income tax: Current information is not available.

Making the grade

Public education overview: *Expansion Management's* April 2005 report ranked Sheboygan School District second in the "Best Overall Metro School Districts" category (regardless of size of enrollment). The district is recognized as a leader in establishing innovative and successful academic programs. The district focuses on improving learning opportunities and raising expectations for student achievement.

Class size (student to teacher ratio): 16:1

Help for working parents: Before- and after-school care programs are available.

Boys & Girls Club: There is one center currently available.

School year: First week of September to mid-June. Children must be 5 years old on or before September 1 to enter kindergarten.

Special education/programs for gifted students: Several programs are available through the local schools.

Nearby colleges and universities: Lakeland College, Security Travel School

Medical care

Hospitals/medical centers: Aurora Sheboygan Memorial Medical Center offers more than 25 specialties, including obstetrics, pediatrics, orthopedics, surgical services, and emergency services. St. Nicholas Hospital is a Catholic, full-service facility, with specialties including cancer treatment, cardiac care, diabetes care, emergency services, maternity, and medical/surgical services.

Specialized care: No information is available at this time.

Crime and safety

Police: The Sheboygan police department embraces the philosophy of community policing, and strives to work with citizens to help make the city a safer place to live, work, and play. All officers are required by the state of Wisconsin to receive a minimum of 24 hours of training every year, and the department goes above and beyond, obtaining more than the state requirement, which translates into more effective officers for the community. The Sheboygan County law enforcement dive team was formed in 2000. It now consists of five officers from the Sheboygan police department, five deputies from the Sheboygan sheriff's department, and a dive team supervisor. Bicycle patrols during the daylight hours stay highly visible and concentrate on skateboard and bicycle violations, often times responding to general calls that occur in close proximity.

Fire: The Sheboygan fire department has 77 sworn members and three civilian members assigned to four stations strategically located throughout the city. Each station responds to single-alarm fires and emergency medical calls that are located in their respective districts.

Let the good times roll

Family fun: Blue Harbor Resort is a full-service, year-round, family destination resort designed to capture the nautical atmosphere and adventure of the Great Lakes, including a waterpark. A recreational community for all seasons, Sheboygan offers some of the best golfing in the nation, salmon and trout fishing on Lake Michigan, with baseball, snowmobiling, and ice fishing to round out the year.

Sports: Who else but the Green Bay Packers for a Wisconsin fan? Most parents are out cheering their kids on the community youth teams. Sport fishing and golfing will keep the weekends packed.

Arts and entertainment: The John Michael Kohler Arts Center is the place for exhibits and educational classes for artists, photographers, and others. The Stefanie H. Weill Center for the Performing Arts is home to the Sheboygan Symphony. The Sheboygan Theatre Company presents quality theatrical entertainment to the community and provides opportunities for area adults and youth who want to be involved in the theatrical arts.

Community life

When Sheboygan was selected by a *Reader's Digest* as "The Number One Place in the Nation to Raise a Family," the poll focused on family life, an absence of crime, low rates of drug and alcohol abuse, good public schools, first-rate healthcare, a clean environment, affordable cost of living, and strong economic growth. *Money* magazine looked at this same data when they talked to retirees who chose their new hometowns specifically for retirement. Sheboygan was ranked number one in the region and described as "a small town with everything: world-class golf courses, notable restaurants, even hot-stone massages." Indeed, Sheboygan is all of that and more.

The environment

Sheboygan County is located within an EPA ozone attainment zone. New manufacturing businesses or expanded facilities are required to meet certain emission reduction standards.

In and around town

Roads and highways: I-43; state highways 42, 32, 23, and 28

Closest airports: Sheboygan County Memorial Airport
Public transportation: Sheboygan Transit System
Average daily commute: 20 minutes

More Information

City of Sheboygan
828 Center Avenue
Sheboygan, WI 53081
http://ci.sheboygan.wi.us

Sheboygan Area School District
830 Virginia Avenue
Sheboygan, WI 53081
www.sheboygan.k12.wi.us

Sheboygan Chamber of Commerce
712 Riverfront Drive
Sheboygan, WI 53081
www.sheboygan.org

Alliant Energy
824 South 8th Street
Sheboygan, WI 53081
800-862-6222
www.alliantenergy.com

Wisconsin Public Service Corp.
933 South Wildwood Avenue
Sheboygan, WI 53081
920-451-3726
www.wisconsinpublicservice.com

Place	Local Population	Median Housing Costs	Reason to live here:
Albuquerque, NM	477,194	$141,000	Low taxes and living costs, pleasant year-round climate, ethnic/cultural diversity, excellent schools and universities, abundant recreation.
Austin, TX	680,899	$156,700	Phenomenal business growth, wonderful schools, exciting family recreation, affordable housing, beautiful lakes and hills, no state income tax, mild winters.
Bangor, ME	31,473	$105,500	Low crime, excellent schools, home town community, beautiful scenery, strong economy.
Bend, OR	59,779	$227,500	Scenic beauty on a grand scale, year-round recreation paradise, low crime, clean environment, friendly, small town atmosphere.
Billings, MT	89,847	$99,900	Incredible natural scenery, affordable housing, milder climate for Montana.
Bloomington, IN	69,987	$126,000	Friendly college town, affordable housing, sports, strong economy, great recreation, and all around good feeling for raising a family.

Place	Local Population	Median Housing Costs	Reason to live here:
Boise, ID	189,847	$120,700	Sparkling clean mountain town, great recreation, diversified business base, affordable housing, friendly people and low crime rate.
Bowling Green, KY	49,296	$111,000	Beautiful country, delightful year-round climate, low crime, range of housing options, good school system, abundant recreation.
Burlington, VT	39,025	$136,000	Quality education, community safety, recreation, diversity, economic growth, quality neighborhoods, affordable housing, and cultural opportunities.
Charleston, SC	96,650	$139,700	Charming Southern city, exciting history, great climate, affordable real estate, favorable economy, recreation and culture.
Chesapeake, VA	199,184	$122,300	Fast-growing coastal region, affordable housing, economic growth, progressive schools, recreation and culture, low crime, community spirit, beautiful historic area.
Chino, CA	72,054	$391,000	Centrally located, southern California climate for year-round recreation, affordable housing in great neighborhoods, and a growing economic climate.
Cincinnati, OH	331,285	$93,000	Lots of amenities, great schools, strong economy, riverfront views, friendly community, four definite seasons, low crime.
Colorado Springs, CO	373,328	$147,100	Stunning scenery; low overall cost of living; a thriving arts community; numerous schools, colleges and universities; a "hot spot" for economic growth.
Columbia, MO	84,531	$118,500	Award-winning schools, outstanding medical care, affordable housing, green space, booming job market, great college town.

Place	Local Population	Median Housing Costs	Reason to live here:
Coral Springs, FL	126,711	$267,795	One of the most successful planned communities, beautiful neighborhoods, award-winning parks, endless family recreation, great public schools.
Eden Prairie, MN	60,981	$325,000	Beautiful lake front city, outstanding health care and public schools, committed to family recreation and the arts, stable job market, and friendly people.
Fayetteville, AR	59,710	$130,150	Breathtaking Ozark Mountain country, delightful four seasons, affordable housing, strong employment possibilities, fabulous outdoor recreation, laid-back college town.
Fort Myers, FL	48,208	$99,300	Subtropical climate, "hot" job markets, affordable housing, good school system, gorgeous Gulf Coast beaches, no state income tax.
Fountain Hills, AZ	20,235	$217,200	Strong job possibilities, affordable housing, no state income tax, endless outdoor recreation, good schools, fabulous scenery.
Galveston, TX	57,247	$73,800	Coastal island with glorious scenery, semi-tropical climate, tremendous ethnic diversity, close-knit community, good schools, excellent medical care.
Green Bay, WI	103,750	$96,400	A sports and recreation paradise, affordable housing, good schools and family support services, and a supportive community with small town charm.
Greenville, SC	56,002	$118,100	Affordable living, low taxes, mountain views, pleasant climate, great education, growing cultural arena, environmentally sound.

Place	Local Population	Median Housing Costs	Reason to live here:
Henderson, NV	229,985	$156,000	Fast growing area, fabulous culture and recreation, dry desert climate, no state income tax, excellent medical care.
Hoover, AL	66,429	$203,327	Lush, green streetscapes, award-winning schools, dynamic business environment, low crime and pollution, natural beauty, culture, tremendous community spirit.
Indianapolis, IN	783,612	$98,200	Growing economy, good job prospects, affordable housing and living costs, outstanding medical care, exceptional higher education.
Iowa City, IA	63,816	$147,525	University town, excellent schools, friendly community, affordable housing, abundant outdoor recreation.
Jacksonville, FL	690,052	$95,860	Mild climate, reasonable cost of living, excellent housing prices, solid growing business economy and year-round outdoor activities.
Kent, WA	84,560	$193,935	Central to Seattle and Tacoma, wide selection of homes, excellent schools, family-oriented community, award winning parks and recreation.
Little Rock, AR	184,055	$102,500	Centrally located, strong job opportunities, low cost of living, award winning schools, great neighborhoods, and southern charm.
Loveland, CO	50,608	$155,900	Incredible scenery, excellent schools, growing economy, cultural amenities, tremendous sense of community.
Milwaukie, OR	20,490	$154,800	Clean environment, good schools, scenic beauty, abundant health care services, variety of cultural and visual arts, excellent transportation.

Place	Local Population	Median Housing Costs	Reason to live here:
Morristown, NJ	18,831	$224,400	Prosperous, fast-growing county, New England-style charm, wonderful parks, progressive schools and medical care, historic area.
Naperville, IL	128,358	$254,200	Quality education, lowest crime rate in the nation, best library in the country, beautiful scenery, and hometown atmosphere.
Nashville, TN	580,450	$113,300	Big-city living in a country setting, affordable housing, mild year-round climate, clean environment, great entertainment, excellent school system.
Olympia, WA	43,040	$143,500	No state income tax, beautiful scenery, low crime rates, abundant recreation, great schools, Olympia is the state capital.
Overland Park, KS	167,000	$220,722	Stable economy, low unemployment, superb public schools, affordable housing, and excellent health care.
Pismo Beach, CA	8,646	$313,100	Beautiful seaside scenery, excellent schools, dedicated community, clean environment, great year-round recreation.
Plano, TX	243,500	$191,000	Work-hard/play-hard attitude, award-winning schools, booming economy, pleasant year-round climate, affordable housing, no state income tax, ethnic diversity.
Portsmouth, NH	20,789	$168,000	A stable economy with strong technology base, a delightful downtown, cultural activities, and all the amenities of a cosmopolitan city in a small town package.
Providence, RI	174,000	$190,000	One of the East coast's best kept secrets, small-town feel, vast choices of housing and neighborhoods, capital city, good job growth.

Place	Local Population	Median Housing Costs	Reason to live here:
Provo, UT	105,439	$186,545	Fabulous mountain scenery, unbelievable recreation, wholesome family community, tremendous economic growth, affordable living, beautiful neighborhoods.
Raleigh, NC	276,093	$156,000	World-renowned research center, outstanding medical care, endless recreation, low unemployment, low crime, beautiful area, great climate.
Reno, NV	189,388	$179,300	Low taxes, great outdoor recreation, expanding job base, fabulous scenery, excellent public transportation.
Rochester, MN	95,000	$167,000	Abundant health care, clean environment and low crime rate. Rochester maintains a small-town friendliness with a "can-do" attitude.
Sacramento, CA	406,000	$129,500	One of California's most affordable big cities, stable economy, good job growth, broad range of recreational activities, vast choice of housing and neighborhoods.
Salem, OR	141,151	$131,100	Mild climate with four season attitudes, friendly neighborhoods, year-round recreation, state capital, and excellent schools.
Sheboygan, WI	50,792	$89,400	Low crime rates, great neighborhoods, excellent schools, outdoor recreation, growing economy, and friendly community.
Spokane, WA	195,629	$124,973	Growing economy, affordable housing, no state income tax, minimal traffic, vast recreational activities, innovative schools and four distinct, pleasant seasons.
Vista, CA	94,000	$487,000	Absolutely perfect climate, job and business growth, great schools, wonderful outdoor recreation, strong community spirit.

Kathleen Shaputis successfully juggles her career in writing, professional speaking, and teaching, while living in post-parental housing of adult children and grandchildren in Olympia, Washington. Kathleen worked in municipal government for 14 years and knows the importance of a balanced community and the effort it takes to run one. She is the author of three other books.